Black British Queer Plays and Practitioners

Black British Queer Plays and Practitioners: An Anthology of Afriquia Theatre

Basin
Boy with Beer
Sin Dykes
Bashment
Nine Lives
BURGERZ
The High Table
STARS

Edited by
MOJISOLA ADEBAYO
and
LYNETTE GODDARD

methuen | drama
LONDON • NEW YORK • OXFORD • NEW DELHI • SYDNEY

METHUEN DRAMA
Bloomsbury Publishing Plc
50 Bedford Square, London, WC1B 3DP, UK
1385 Broadway, New York, NY 10018, USA
29 Earlsfort Terrace, Dublin 2, Ireland

BLOOMSBURY, METHUEN DRAMA and the Methuen Drama logo are trademarks of
Bloomsbury Publishing Plc

First published in Great Britain 2023

Introduction and Commentary © Mojisola Adebayo and Lynette Goddard, 2023
Basin © Jacqueline Rudet, 1985
Boy with Beer © Paul Boakye, 1995
Sin Dykes © Valerie Mason-John, 1998
Bashment © Rikki Beadle-Blair, 2005
Nine Lives © Zodwa Nyoni, 2015
BURGERZ © Travis Alabanza, 2018
The High Table © Temi Wilkey, 2020
STARS © Mojisola Adebayo, 2018

The authors have asserted their right under the Copyright, Designs and Patents Act, 1988, to be
identified as authors of this work.

For legal purposes the Acknowledgements on p. ix constitute an extension
of this copyright page.

Cover design by Rebecca Heselton
Cover image: Rikki Beadle-Blair at the Liverpool Vogue Ball © fotocad

All rights reserved. No part of this publication may be reproduced or transmitted in any form or by
any means, electronic or mechanical, including photocopying, recording, or any information
storage or retrieval system, without prior permission in writing from the publishers.

Bloomsbury Publishing Plc does not have any control over, or responsibility for, any third-party
websites referred to or in this book. All internet addresses given in this book were correct at
the time of going to press. The author and publisher regret any inconvenience caused if
addresses have changed or sites have ceased to exist, but can accept no responsibility for
any such changes.

No rights in incidental music or songs contained in the work are hereby granted
and performance rights for any performance/presentation whatsoever must be obtained
from the respective copyright owners.

All rights whatsoever for these plays are strictly reserved. Application for performance, etc.
should be made before rehearsals begin to the respective playwrights' representatives
listed on page 423. No performance may be given unless a licence has been obtained.

A catalogue record for this book is available from the British Library.

A catalog record for this book is available from the Library of Congress.

ISBN: HB: 978-1-3502-3456-7
PB: 978-1-3502-3455-0
ePDF: 978-1-3502-3457-4
eBook: 978-1-3502-3458-1

Typeset by RefineCatch Limited, Bungay, Suffolk

To find out more about our authors and books visit www.bloomsbury.com
and sign up for our newsletters.

We dedicate this anthology to the memory of bell hooks (1952–2021), radical Black feminist scholar and activist who compelled us to 'challenge [the] imperialist, white supremacist, heteropatriarchy' and taught us the value of Black love.

Contents

Acknowledgements ix

Introduction and Survey of Afriquia Plays 1

Basin by Jacqueline Rudet 23

Boy with Beer with an introduction and afterword by Paul Boakye 69

A roundtable discussion on careers, audiences, collaboration and spaces 111

Sin Dykes by Valerie Mason-John 125

Roundtable discussion continued: On *Sin Dykes* and diaspora programming 167

Bashment by Rikki Beadle-Blair with an interview 171

On *Bashment* 251

Nine Lives by Zodwa Nyoni 253

BURGERZ by Travis Alabanza 273

On gender nonconformity 301

The High Table by Temi Wilkey 305

On *The High Table* 372

STARS by Mojisola Adebayo 375

On *STARS* 415

On Dreaming of Black Queer/Afriquia Futures 419

Performance Rights 423

Acknowledgements

We wish to express our enormous gratitude to all of the authors and contributors to the anthology and roundtable discussion: Travis Alabanza, Rikki Beadle-Blair, Paul Boakye, Topher Campbell, Valerie Mason-John, Tonderai Munyevu, Zodwa Nyoni, Jacqueline Rudet and Temi Wilkey. We also thank Dom O'Hanlon, Sam Nicholls and the production team for guiding us through the process.

Lynette wishes to thank the Department of Drama, Theatre, and Dance, Royal Holloway, University of London.

Mojisola wishes to extend her huge thanks to her PhD supervisors, the late Catherine Silverstone and also to Caoimhe McAvinchey, for championing her research. Thanks to the School of English and Drama, Queen Mary, University of London and the Institute of American and English Studies, University of Potsdam for the post-doctoral fellowship time afforded to work on this project. Last but not least, thank you to Nicole Wolf for her deep and enduring support.

Introduction and Survey of Afriquia Plays

Introduction

Black British Queer Plays and Practitioners: An Anthology of Afriquia Theatre celebrates the bold contribution of Black LGBTIQ+ voices to British theatre from 1985 to the present day.[1] We are writing in an incredibly exciting time, with the uplifting presence of Black queer performers, writers and theatre makers, from main stages to fringe venues. This anthology demonstrates our rich past and points to a future where the intersectional experiences of Blackness and queerness are no longer ignored or sidelined.

Afriquia is a new word that goes some way to expressing the oneness of being both Black and queer and the inherent Africanness of queerness or, rather, quia'ness.[2] As queer African theorist Stella Nyanzi argues, 'Thinking beyond the loaded and westernized frame of the LGBTI acronym, queer Africa must necessarily explore and articulate local nuances of being non-heteronormative and non-gender conforming.'[3] There are many historic, culturally specific, words for people who enjoy same-sex relationships, or who are not constrained within a gender binary, such as *adofuro* (Yoruba), *moffie* (South Africa), *zami* (Caribbean), *kuchu* (Swahili), *choza* (Shona) and *quaniis* (Somalia). These words demonstrate that queer sexualities existed before the European colonial sphere of influence, before the arrival of Christianity and Islam, thereby countering the pervasive and problematic myth that it is somehow not Black to be queer. Afriquia is a term that includes people from across the diaspora and the continent of Africa, beyond cultural specificity. Afriquia therefore reflects the breadth of experiences and identities represented by this book and we use the term Afriquia and Black queer interchangeably throughout.

Interwoven before, between and after the eight plays in this anthology are excerpts from an intergenerational roundtable discussion between just a few of the many Black queer theatre and performance practitioners who have made work in Britain since the 1980s, along with additional materials. Britain is just one small island in the Atlantic, but due to its long history as a colonizing and enslaving nation, together with the afterlives of mass-migration and globalization, the British (or Brit-*ish*) artists discussed in this book have roots that stretch to Barbados, Canada, Denmark, Dominica, Ghana, Jamaica, Nigeria, Panama, the Philippines, Sierra Leone, South Africa, Trinidad, the USA, Zimbabwe and beyond.[4]

1 We use the term Black to describe being a person of African descent, from the African diaspora or the African continent, including people of mixed-heritage. LGBTIQ+ = lesbian, gay, bisexual, trans, intersex, queer, plus a plethora of other terms including non-binary, androgynous, gender non-conforming, asexual, Afro-queer, Afriquia and so on. We sometimes use the term queer to summarize the collective LGBTIQ+ acronym and we acknowledge there are many more words to describe queerness, as we shall discuss. The I is placed before the Q in response to intersex activist Valentino Vecchietti's call for intersex identity to be more visible, and because it is too easy for the I to drop off the end of the acronym and be ignored.
2 A suggested pronunciation is with a West African inflection, enjoying an open 'a' sound.
3 Stella Nyanzi, 'Queering Queer Africa' in Zethu Matebeni (curator/editor), *Reclaiming Afrikan: Queer Perspectives on Sexual and Gender Identities* (Athlone: Modaji Books, 2014), 67.
4 See Afua Hirsch's *Brit(ish): On Race, Identity and Belonging* (London: Vintage, 2019).

There is a wealth of Black queer work to enjoy beyond this book that could not all be re-published here but that we do want to highlight. Therefore, Part One of this introduction is a short essay that presents an overview of Afriquia theatre through a survey of an inspirational archive of twenty-four plays that were produced and published in Britain since 1985. We briefly sketch each of the plays in this Afriquia archive, including the eight plays in this anthology. In Part Two we discuss the eight plays more closely and draw attention to significant recurring themes.

Part One

Histories, herstories, theirstories: A survey of Afriquia theatre in Britain

Although there has been a proliferation of Black queer theatre in Britain since the 1980s, the scarcity of critical material available to date indicates how much has been overlooked.[5] The late African theatre scholar Victor Ukaegbu attempted to sketch a brief overview but stated: 'black queer theatre is yet to define itself through its own materials.'[6] This introduction shines a spotlight on a wealth of stage plays, written by Black playwrights and first produced and published in Britain, which foreground Black queer lives and relationships expressed in a variety of dramatic forms.[7]

Although this survey focuses on published play texts, it is also important to highlight some of the ephemeral work of Black queer artists who have made significant contributions to the performance scene. Notable unpublished plays include: *Crystal Clear* by John-Lloyd Stevenson (Ovalhouse, 1994), *Wicked Games* by Paul Boakye (West Yorkshire Playhouse, 1997), Valerie Mason-John's pantomime *The Adventures of Snow Black and Rose Red* (Drill Hall, 2001), Jackie Kay's *Trumpet* (Drill Hall,

---

5 Notable exceptions include Lynette Goddard's *Staging Black Feminisms* (Basingstoke: Palgrave Macmillan), 2007, which charted the rise of Black lesbian theatre in Britain. For further research and inspiration visit the Rukus! Federation archive at London Metropolitan Archives, founded by Topher Campbell and Ajamu X. For more writing by Black British LGBTIQ+ authors see *Black and Gay in the UK: An Anthology* edited by John R. Gordon and Rikki Beadle-Blair (London: Team Angelica, 2014) and *Sista! An Anthology of Writing by and about Same Gender Loving Women of African/Caribbean descent with a UK Connection* (2018) edited by Phyll Opoku-Gyimah, Rikki Beadle-Blair and John R. Gordon (London: Team Angelica, 2018).

6 Victor Ukaegbu, 'Grey Silhouettes: Black Queer Theatre on the Post-war British Stage', in *Alternatives within the Mainstream 2: Queer Theatres in Post-war Britain*, ed. Dimple Godiwala (Cambridge: Cambridge Scholars Publishing, 2007), 329. See also Gabriele Griffin, 'Racing Sexualities', in *Contemporary Black and Asian Women Playwrights in Britain* (Cambridge: Cambridge University Press, 2003), 170–94.

7 This survey does not feature plays by Black LGBTIQ+ identified playwrights where Black queer experience is in the background or on the sidelines of the story, or where the characters or content is not identifiably Black. Such plays include Kofi Agyemang and Patricia Elcock's *Urban Afro Saxons* (2003), Rikki Beadle-Blair's *Gutted* (2014), Tristan Fynn-Aiduenu's *Sweet Like Chocolate Boy* (2017) and Travis Alabanza's *Overflow* (2020). White British writers' portrayals of Black queer experience are not included either, notably: *Cloud 9* by Caryl Churchill (1979), *This Island's Mine* by Phillip Osment (1988), *Beautiful Thing* by Jonathan Harvey (1993), *Perseverance Drive* by Robin Soans (2014), *Hopelessly Devoted* by Kate Tempest (2014) (now Kae Tempest). There has also been some Black queer presence on British Asian stages, such as the Black gay character Elvis in Gurpreet Kaur Bhatti's *Bezhti (Dishonour)* (2004).

2006), an adaptation of her novel of the same name, *Justin Fashanu in Extra Time* by Troy Fairclough (Rich Mix, 2010), *I Killed My Mother* by Ade Adeniji (Pinter Studio, 2013), *On Dis Ting* by Reuben Massiah (Ovalhouse, 2013), *Sunday* by Joy Gharoro-Akpojotor (Ovalhouse and Theatre Royal Stratford East, 2014), *OUT* by Rachael Young and Dwayne Anthony (Yard Theatre, 2017), *Brothas 2.0* by Topher Campbell (King's Head, 2017), *The Grey Area* by Lettie Precious (Royal Court, 2019) and *Nightclubbing* by Rachael Young (Edinburgh Festival, 2019). The Rukus! Federation commissioned new plays for *The Mangina Monologues* (2009) featuring as yet unpublished plays including *When Stars Fall* by Remi Weekes, *Sending Out an S.O.S.* by Christopher Rodriguez, *As It Happened* by Michael Bhim, *Batty Boy* by Dean Atta, *Ikebe (Backside)* by Deobia Operai and *Political Arse* by Topher Campbell. Mojisola Adebayo's *Asara and the Sea-Monstress*, the only published Afriquia play in the survey written specifically for children, had a rehearsed reading at Albany Theatre in 2013 but is yet to secure a producing company.

Black queer British history is incomplete without reference to the superb work of performance artist, actor and singer Le Gateau Chocolat, including *In Drag* (2013), *Black* (2014) and their queer play for children *Duck!* (2016) at various venues including Southbank Centre, Soho Theatre and Homotopia Festival. Stand-up comedians Stephen K. Amos and Gina Yashere have also done much to represent Black queer experience.[8] Lastly, we note the work of Black queer spoken-word artists and poets who include Dorothea Smartt, Dean Atta, Jay Bernard and Sonority. Club Nights such as Cocoa Butter Club – established by Sadie Sinner, Brownton Abbey – created by queer Black and brown people with disabilities, as well as Duckie! have also provided an important space for Black queer people to develop and perform spoken-word poetry, drag, stand-up comedy, dance, cabaret, music and more. The House of Suarez vogue balls of Liverpool, celebrating the art of vogueing with its roots in Black/Latinx/Trans culture, hosted by Rikki Beadle-Blair (featured on the cover of this book), has been an important space for vogue culture in Britain. This list is an indication of the breadth of Black queer live performance work and a culture that is burgeoning. The work of defining Black British queer theatre and performance, and developing the discourse around this radical work, is only just beginning.

Theatre Afriquiastory: A narrative of narratives

We will now survey the twenty-four plays in the archive asking: what might we discover about Britain in the late twentieth and early twenty-first centuries through reading, watching and studying these plays? What can be learnt by looking through a Black queer lens? Before embarking on a material analysis of these plays, we want to take a moment to speculate on why Black queer theatre may have emerged in mid-1980s Britain. By the 1980s, the children of Windrush Generation parents had grown up and were starting to tell our own stories of our experiences in Britain. These voices were informed and invigorated by resistance to the Conservative government led by Margaret Thatcher, culminating in a wave of uprisings (often referred to as riots) in urban areas

---

8   See *Batty Man*, a documentary written and presented by Stephen K. Amos, produced and directed by Paul Blake (Maroon Productions/Channel 4, 2003).

with high Black populations in the early 1980s, including Brixton, Handsworth, Tottenham and Toxteth, in protest against discriminatory police stop and search laws, the deaths of Black people in police custody, and racial discrimination in employment and education. Black political resistance saw the election of the first Black people to parliament in Britain in 1987, namely Diane Abbott, Paul Boateng and Bernie Grant, forming part of the Labour opposition. Black political activism was also paralleled in LGBTIQ+ communities who were fighting homophobic and transphobic discrimination and in the women's movement where the fight for gender equality continued. This Black, queer, feminist political climate may have emboldened Black authors to produce plays with queer and feminist inflections.

This was also a period of artistic uprising when the creative work of historically marginalized groups flourished. Black, lesbian and gay, and feminist theatre companies in London such as Black Theatre Co-operative, Double Edge Theatre, Munirah, Talawa, Temba, Theatre of Black Women, Umoja and Gay Sweatshop emerged as part of a wave of artistic activism against discrimination and the desire for self-representation on stage. These companies and all but one of the venues that staged the plays in this survey were subsidized by funding from Arts Council England (ACE), whose diversity and inclusion agenda since the 1980s has gone hand in hand with various acts of parliament seeking to address issues of (in)equality.[9]

Inclusive theatre programming has been even more important to ACE in London. Venues such as the Ovalhouse (now Brixton House) and Theatre Royal Stratford East (TRSE) are located in the increasingly multiracial London boroughs of Lambeth and Newham, where it makes sense in box-office terms to attract Black audiences.[10] Furthermore, the Black queer plays in this archive would not have been produced without the decision making of certain key white gay and lesbian artistic directors and heads of theatre programming. These include Philip Hedley and Kerry Michael (who is of Greek Cypriot heritage) (TRSE, 1979–2004 and 2004–17), Kate Crutchley (Ovalhouse, 1980–91), Nicholas Hytner (National Theatre, 2003–15), Ben Evans (Ovalhouse, 2004–10) and Dominic Cooke (Royal Court, 2007–13). For Black queer theatre to flourish we need solidarity from white LGBTIQ+ as well as straight people in positions of power.[11]

Our Afriquia theatre narrative of narratives begins in 1985, with Jacqueline Rudet's realist play *Basin* (Royal Court Theatre). The basin of the title refers to the bowl that Rudet says some young Caribbean women are given by their mothers to wash their vagina at night in case a man may want to 'relieve himself inside her'.[12] From the title onwards the play highlights that some Black girls and women experience sexual

---

9 The Equality Act 2010 merges nine pieces of legislation including the Equal Pay Act 1970, the Sex Discrimination Act 1975, the Race Relations Act 1976, the Disability Discrimination Act 1995, the Employment Equality (Religion or Belief) Regulations 2003, the Employment Equality (Sexual Orientation) Regulations 2003, the Employment Equality (Age) Regulations 2006, the Equality Act 2006, Part 2 and the Equality Act (Sexual Orientation) Regulations 2007.
10 ACE tends to use the term cultural diversity.
11 More recently, it is exciting to note that Lynette Linton, the (Black) artistic director of Bush Theatre since 2019, has programmed several Black lesbian and trans plays including Jackie Kay's *Chiaroscuro*, Temi Wilkey's *The High Table* and Travis Alabanza's *Overflow*.
12 Yvonne Brewster, ed., *Black Plays* (London: Methuen, 1987), 114.

subjugation, although in the two characters Mona and Susan we discover Black women having intimacy beyond men. These women are called 'zammies', a Caribbean word for same-sex love and intimate friendships between Black women that has its own resonance beyond the European word 'lesbian'. Although we witness the first of many scenarios in these plays where Christianity is used as a weapon that can damage relations between heterosexual and queer people, *Basin* is also hopeful in showing that it is possible for same-sex love to be accepted as an extension of Black women's sisterhood.

Like *Basin*, the cast of five Black women in Jackie Kay's *Chiaroscuro* (Theatre of Black Women at Soho Poly, 1986; revived at the Bush Theatre, 2019) affirms that Afriquia theatre is born from the Black women's movement. Jackie Kay is an out-lesbian who is better known as a prolific novelist and poet, and she has also contributed two plays to this archive. In its fluid and poetic form infused with music and movement, *Chiaroscuro* is a political play that resonates with Black feminist theatre forms such as the choreopoems of Ntozake Shange.[13] The title *Chiaroscuro* combines the Italian phrases for light (*chiaro*) and shade (*scuro*), which are evoked through an exploration of a range of Black women's experiences from Africa, Asia, the Caribbean and mixed heritages, as well as heterosexual, bisexual and homosexual. The women in this play highlight the importance of remembering and reclaiming our names, of self-defining through telling our own stories and of responding to and resisting histories of enslavement. Through the use of objects, Kay explores naming as something that is passed down, inherited and then redefined, showing gender identities as fluid and malleable. The play also explores the idea that some straight women find it difficult to accept lesbians and introduces perceptions of AIDS as 'God's vengeance' on gay people.[14] All four characters remain on stage throughout the performance, interweaving poetic monologues, dialogues and songs that emphasize both the parallels between them as Black women as well as showing their individual differences. The 2019 Bush Theatre revival reimagined the production as a contemporary spoken-word and music gig performance.

In Kay's *Twice Over* (Drill Hall, 1988), the diversity of lesbian experience is extended to elders and some young people who find the idea difficult. This is the first Black play to mention the word 'queer', although it is used in a pejorative sense from the mouth of a teenager, Evaki, who has discovered that her recently deceased grandmother had been in a long-term relationship with another woman.[15] As Evaki learns more about her grandmother's past, she rethinks her own stereotypical preconceptions about lesbians and encourages her young friends to think differently too. Kay's impetus for writing the play came after researching attitudes to lesbianism and discovering that young people overwhelmingly believed that all lesbians were young. As a Theatre-in-Education project, the play explicitly debates these stereotypical perceptions of lesbians, challenging ageist and homophobic prejudices. *Twice Over*

---

13 See Ntozake Shange's *for colored girls who have considered suicide / when the rainbow is enuf* (London: Methuen, 1974).
14 Jackie Kay, *Chiaroscuro* in *Lesbian Plays*, ed. Jill Davis (London: Methuen, 1986), 58–84.
15 Jackie Kay, *Twice Over* in *Gay Sweatshop: Four Plays and a Company*, ed. Phillip Osment (London: Methuen, 1989), 140.

was commissioned by Theatre Centre (a young people's theatre company based in London) but the play did not tour schools and was only later staged by Gay Sweatshop. Reading between the lines of playwright and director Phillip Osment's introduction, we can speculate that the law against the promotion of homosexuality by local authorities (including schools), known as Section 28, may have influenced Theatre Centre's decision not to stage the play in schools.[16]

Paul Boakye's realist play for two actors *Boy with Beer* (Man in the Moon Theatre, 1992) is the first to openly depict Black gay men in Britain. Through Karl, who is of Ghanaian heritage, and Donovan, of Jamaican heritage, Boakye explores the tensions that can arise between British African and Caribbean Black people of different class and educational backgrounds and indicates that the roots of this disparity go back to slavery. Boakye's portrayal of Donovan alludes to the notion that some men hide their sexualities, loathe their own homosexual desires and continue relationships with heterosexual women. We hear the word 'battyman', which also recurs throughout the plays in this narrative of narratives, a pejorative term for men who have anal sex with other men. In *Boy with Beer*, the question of top (penetrative)/bottom (receptive) sexual power relations between men who will only penetrate and men who want both (versatile) is raised and this is a recurring theme in plays about Black queer men. The question of fear and power in relation to anal sex between men and how this connects to slavery speaks to the complicated nature of homophobia in the African diaspora. Lastly, *Boy with Beer* teaches us that there was a virus called HIV (which we now know can lead to AIDS) and that it was at this time considered taboo. *Boy with Beer* offers a rare illustration of love and support between Black gay partners in a time of HIV/AIDS.

Boy with Beer is one of only two Afriquia plays from the 1990s. Staging new writing in this decade may have been inhibited by a wave of anti-gay panic that arose from the Conservative Government's homophobic Section 28 and their infamous tombstone campaign stigmatizing people living with HIV.[17] As gay men and African people have reportedly been affected by HIV more than many other groups, it is no wonder that few people stood up on stage to perform stories about Black gay life. This makes *Boy with Beer* all the more courageous and important. The play was undoubtedly a space of support and affirmation for Black, gay and HIV+ men sitting in the audience in the Man in the Moon Theatre in 1992.[18]

Looking back, the scarcity of Black queer plays in the 1990s demonstrates how difficult it is to get venues to stage these works and publishing houses to print them. Indeed, it is remarkable that twenty-four plays managed to be produced and published at all during the thirty-five years that this survey covers, and especially so considering the resistance we often face as Black LGBTIQ+ people and the dangers of making ourselves visible. This is why small politically motivated spaces, such as Ovalhouse

---

16 Osment, *Gay Sweatshop*, lxv.
17 Hateful attitudes almost received state validation through comments such as those by Manchester Chief Constable James Anderton who in 1986 described people living with AIDS as 'swirling in a cesspit of their own making'. Also see Paul Burston's 'The Stigma of HIV Still Remains' available at http://www.theguardian.com/commentisfree/2013/aug/15/stigma-hiv-nhs-ban-ended-fear (accessed 30 January 2022).
18 *Boy with Beer* is also one of the few in this history that has been revived, in a recent production at the King's Head Theatre in London (2017).

(now Brixton House) are so important to this history. It was also not easy for individual queer artists working in Black theatre companies to voice our experiences, especially at a time when so much of the focus in our communities was on pressing issues such as racism, criminal in/justice, unemployment and family break-down from the effects of migration. Black family life has tended to be at the forefront of Black plays, perhaps because Black heterosexual relationships are almost as contested as homosexual relationships, due to the legacies of slavery. As bell hooks says, love between men and women has been under siege since slavery where Black men and women were not allowed to marry.[19] Homosexuality, often misperceived as a threat to family, was evidently not high on the agenda of Black theatre companies.

Towards the end of the twentieth century, coinciding with a Labour government from 1997 to 2010, there was a relative proliferation of new Afriquia work in Britain. With the emergence of social media leading to more instant interactive socio-political debate, as well as the widely embraced Black feminist theory of intersectionality, this narrative of narratives becomes more complex. Afriquia theatre starts connecting with issues such as climate change, child abuse in foster homes, D/deaf and disabled culture, globalization, Islamophobia, sectarian conflict, refugees and asylum. Gender identities and sexual practices also start to diversify on stage.

Valerie Mason-John's *Sin Dykes* (Ovalhouse, 1998) shows more open sexual experimentation between women including sado-masochism (S&M) and the club scene. Stylistically, the play is realist in form, with humour threaded throughout and explorations of archetypal queer characters: a Brixton babe, a scene dyke, an afrekeke dyke, a bull dyke, a travelled Black dyke and an SM white dyke. Mason-John explores similar debates about Black lesbian identities that were raised in Kay's *Chiaroscuro* – showing how some ideas about race and gender have moved forward while others remain unresolved. In the ten-year period between Kay's *Twice Over* and *Sin Dykes*, the word queer has shifted from being used as a term of insult to being embraced as a reclaimed identity. In *Sin Dykes*, two Black lesbians have a conversation where Kat says to Trudy: 'One thing you've got to understand about some of these 1990s white girls is that they say it's alright to screw a man and call yourself a dyke. It's the phase at the moment, packing a dildo down their Calvin Klein's, picking up cute looking gay men. It's all the rage. They call it queer.' *Sin Dykes* spells a time of free and fluid queer sex and gender experimentation and interestingly it is the only play in this survey that makes no reference to homophobia or transphobia.

The age of sex and gender experimentation continues into the twenty-first century in DeObia Oparei's *Crazyblackmuthaf**in'self* (Royal Court, 2002) where sex meetings (hook-ups) are arranged online. Some gay men, such as the protagonist Femi, set up sexual encounters as a financial transaction. The sex sold by Black men, like Femi, to white men is often based on racial stereotypes reinforced by pornographic images of Black men as sexual savages, slaves and victims. The play implicitly traces these representations back to Shakespeare's *Othello* in which Femi plays the lead in a stereotypical street version entitled *Y'Othello*. Black sexual roles are further revealed as complex in *Crazyblackmuthaf**in'self* through representing gender play and trans experience.

---

19 bell hooks, *Salvation: Black People and Love* (London: Women's Press, 2001), 154.

In returning to an unnamed and misunderstood sexual love between two women in a small London flat under the critical eye of an unwanted guest, Doña Daley's 2004 realist play for three women *Blest Be the Tie* (National Theatre, 2004) parallels Rudet's *Basin*, through the portrayal of a long and intimate interracial 'friendship' between two older women. As with Rudet's play, we see that Black British experience is largely urban, informed by migration and too often financially constrained. We might speculate that prejudice and poverty sustain each other and that a consideration of economics is necessary in understanding animosity towards LGBTIQ+ people.[20] The difference in *Blest Be the Tie* is that Caribbean women such as Martha can make themselves a financial success and that Black pensioners like Eunice who came to Britain as economic migrants can end up in very humble circumstances.

Martha does not understand the bond between her sister Florence and her white English neighbour. *Blest Be the Tie* stops short of fully depicting their friendship as a lesbian relationship and a kiss between them is represented as the kind of platonic intimacy that is shared between friends. Yet, although the LGBTIQ+ content of the play is not made explicit, it is through the everyday domesticity of romantic love between two women that homophobia is challenged. Here same-sex love and interracial love is ordinary. It is the biological bond between two women who are blood relatives that is depicted as being uncomfortable and strange.

In 2005 this narrative of narratives takes a dramatic turn with Christopher Rodriguez's musical theatre play *High Heel Parrotfish!* at Theatre Royal Stratford East. This is the first play in the survey to fully focus on trans lives. Rodriguez explores how Black trans people and gay men in Trinidad are often victims of family and state transphobia and homophobia, which can lead to violence, violation of human rights and even murder. Yet the trans people resist the oppression that they face through drag performance, song, dance, loving each other and fighting back. This is the first play to show transphobic and homophobic hate in international contexts. It is clear through *High Heel Parrotfish!* as well as *Boy with Beer* and many other plays in this archive that connections to the diaspora are powerful and pertinent to Black Britons. Premiering in London, Rodriguez's play, set in Trinidad, raises questions about the relevance of the issues to the LGBTIQ+ community in Britain.

The questions posed by *High Heel Parrotfish!* are answered by the very next play to be produced at Theatre Royal Stratford East, Rikki Beadle-Blair's *Bashment* (2005), which introduces the audience to the bashment music scene where we see battles over more than just song lyrics. This realist play infused with music, exposes homophobia in the bashment scene, contempt for whiteness as associated with homosexuality and the association of Blackness with heterosexual prowess. The play expressly connects bashment music with gay bashing, and links homophobia in the Black community back to slavery. Yet the play is hopeful in exploring how homophobes can also be redeemed and make reparations.

---

20 When Mojisola Adebayo ran a leadership training course in Zimbabwe and raised the issue of LGBTIQ+ equality, much of the homophobia the young people expressed was based on the idea that not only is homosexuality a white condition, but that LGBTIQ+ people are privileged by their sexuality because they have more access to white people and to Western money. This false notion has been reinforced by various homophobic diatribes from African leaders and commentators.

Beadle-Blair returns to the subject of homophobia in the Theatre-in-Education play *FIT* (Queer up North tour, 2007–10). Homophobic language was so acute in this era that the word gay became an insult synonymous with anything negative in urban youth culture and the bullying of LGBTIQ+ school pupils was endemic. Beadle-Blair directly challenges homophobia through a fashion-conscious street-style play where a group of young dancers go on a bus journey to a competition that is also a journey into their identities, desires and prejudices. *FIT* toured three times to seventy-five secondary schools, reaching over twenty thousand pupils across Britain between September 2007 and February 2010, with an accompanying post-show discussion.[21]

Mojisola Adebayo's *Moj of the Antarctic: An African Odyssey* (Lyric Hammersmith, 2006) asks the audience to consider the connection between climate injustice today, the industrial revolution and the trans atlantic slave trade, melting Antarctic ice and melting identities, through Moj, a mid-nineteenth-century enslaved African-American woman who cross-dresses as a white man to escape from slavery. The fictional Moj is inspired by the real-life Ellen Craft, who in 1848 escaped from slavery by cross-dressing as a white man. The play draws from a wide range of historical texts proving that trans experience and Black same-sex relationships during slavery are very much part of Black history. Adebayo extends into fiction where, after losing her lover, May, Moj escapes and becomes a sailor bound for Antarctica. This one-woman choreo-poem, with multi-roling and singing also integrates images from Adebayo's own expedition to Antarctica with the queer visual artist Del LaGrace Volcano in 2005, thereby contributing Black/queer perspectives to snow-coated British Antarctic history.

In *Wig Out* (Royal Court Theatre, 2008), Tarell Alvin McCraney's flamboyant play with a large cast, African-American New York drag-queens create alternative families or dynasties, known as houses, away from both the straight and gay mainstream. During preparation for a Cinderella vogue ball (a high-stakes competition where one house challenges another through costume and performance), and in the midst of the glitter, Nina/Wilson is trying to develop a relationship with the straight-acting Eric. The seeming fixity of the top/bottom binary is an important subject, as it was in *Boy with Beer*. *Wig Out*, however, is written in poetic form juxtaposed with realist scenes, songs and monologues where each character describes the moment where they saw a matriarch take their wig out and how this affected their sense of self in terms of gender and sexual identity.

McCraney is African-American and *Wig Out* connects Britain to the African-American experience, in a look across the Atlantic that coincided with great interest in the election of Barack Obama as the 44th US President in 2008.[22] Adebayo's *Muhammad Ali and Me* (Ovalhouse, 2008) was running concurrently and also references Obama, through a clip of his voice.

Through the imaginary friendship between the protagonist Mojitola and her boxing hero, *Muhammad Ali and Me*, a multimedia play for three performers, parallels sexual abuse in British foster care and the racist state abuses in America in the 1970s. The semi-autobiographical story of the child Mojitola, growing up and coming out as a

---

21 Both *Bashment* and *FIT* were adapted for screen by Beadle-Blair.
22 In 2016, Tarrell Alvin McCraney won the Academy Award/Oscar for best adapted screenplay with *Moonlight*, a film adapted from his stage play depicting young Black gay men.

lesbian, is juxtaposed with the portrayal of Muhammad Ali, coming of age as a boxer and activist and 'coming out' as a Muslim. Vilification of Ali's conversion to Islam and his refusal to fight in the Vietnam War is subtextually connected to a contemporary era of Islamophobia in Britain, against a backdrop of further controversial wars in Asia. Like *Moj of the Antarctic*, this play has an African physical storytelling aesthetic through the role of the Griot. *Muhammad Ali and Me* highlights the intersectionality of Black experience and the importance of access and inclusion by integrating D/deaf culture through Jacqui Beckford's creatively incorporated interpretation of the whole show into British Sign Language in her role as the boxing ring referee.

Thug Ass (Soho Theatre, 2009) by Rikki Beadle-Blair is a short play first produced as part of the *Mangina Monologues*, directed and curated by Topher Campbell. Here, Black gay men took their cue from the feminist movement and Eve Ensler's *Vagina Monologues* (1996) to celebrate the anus and anal sex at a time when hatred against Black gay men is exemplified in the phrase 'battyman.'[23] The top and bottom binary is playfully overturned in the love affair between Thug Ass (real name Andre) and the effeminate Darnell.

In Tarell Alvin-McCraney's *Choir Boy* (Royal Court Theatre, 2012), we visit an institution of control in an American all-Black elite prep school called Charles R. Drew. The plot revolves around five competitive choir boys who are heavily invested in being Drew men. A high-achieving, intelligent, well-groomed feminine gay choir boy named Pharus is bullied and beaten. Pharus, however, is talented and privileged enough to rise above his adversity and sing solo. This image of social mobility and Black class privilege in the era of Obama is one that has only rarely been represented on British stages, indicating a difference between Black experience in British and American societies. Through this drama interspersed with a cappella singing, *Choir Boy* examines how Black LGBTIQ+ people do at times have straight and white allies, exemplified in Pharus's straight friend AJ.

The diasporic connections continue in Inua Ellams's *Black T-Shirt Collection* (Warwick Arts Centre and Fuel tour, 2012), where we are introduced to a time of increasing tension and conflict between Muslim and Christian communities in Nigeria. There was also rare brotherhood, literally through the foster brothers in the play, Muhammad and Matthew. Nigeria is a potentially dangerous place to be discovered to be gay (people engaged in same-sex relationships can face up to fourteen years in prison) and so the outing of Muhammad is the catalyst for their lengthy departure on overseas business, eventually settling in China. This play for two actors explores how the marketplace between Africa and China was growing at this time and the entrepreneurial brothers prosper. It is rare in this archive that we see Black people achieving a degree of economic success. However, Ellams seems to be questioning globalization and capitalism, as further layers of oppression are exposed through the exploited Chinese workers in the brothers' T-shirt factory.

The painful subject of the so-called corrective rape and murder of lesbians and trans men in South Africa is explored in *I Stand Corrected*, a theatre and dance collaboration between Mojisola Adebayo and choreographer and dancer Mamela Nyamza (Artscape,

---

23 Eve Ensler, *Vagina Monologues* (London: Virago, 2001).

Cape Town and Ovalhouse, London, 2012). Homophobic and transphobic violence are paralleled with the virulence of the anti-equal marriage debate in Britain in 2012, connected by a shared history of colonization. The fact that lesbians and gay men are not able to marry in a church in Britain, yet the post-apartheid South African constitution declares LGBTIQ+ people are equal citizens is critiqued by Charlie, a Black mixed-heritage British lesbian working in Cape Town. Charlie searches for her Black South African fiancée Zodwa, who has not shown up at the altar for their wedding in a Cape Town church where the audience are cast as guests. Meanwhile, Zodwa tries to understand what has happened to her 'corrected' body, through the medium of dance.

Nigeria connects to Zimbabwe in the diaspora through the autobiographical African storytelling performance *Zhe [noun] undefined* (Oxford Playhouse and tour, 2013), scripted by Chuck Mike (the director), Antonia Kemi Coker and Tonderai Munyevu. Through the real-life story of the performers, British-born Nigerian Antonia Kemi Coker and Zimbabwean Tonderai Munyevu, we are reminded that disproportionate numbers of Black children are taken into care by social services and some experience sexual abuse and racial discrimination. Munyevu's story highlights discrimination towards androgynous Black people in Britain, compared to being accepted in Zimbabwe: 'Most of my friends called me Choza . . . which means a boy that is really a girl . . . It was affectionate, a name that fit, a celebration of me.' When he comes to England and is bullied, he reflects: 'I never noticed that I walked differently or talked differently because in Zimbabwe people loved it.'[24] *Zhe* demonstrates acceptance of sex/gender differences as being part of Zimbabwean Shona culture. This is very important at a time of the intensification of religiously justified state sanctioned homophobia and transphobia and the application laws left by British colonisers in many countries such as Nigeria and Zimbabwe.

The consequences of state homophobia are highlighted in the monodrama *Nine Lives* (West Yorkshire Playhouse and tour, 2014) by Zodwa Nyoni, an intimate look at LGBTIQ+ asylum issues. *Nine Lives* explores questions of finding a safe place to call home for the protagonist, Ishmael, who has recently arrived in Britain after fleeing from persecution in Zimbabwe where it is a criminal offence to be lesbian or gay. Through his experiences of being in 'limbo' while waiting for his case to go through the bureaucratic asylum processes, the play exposes the urgent and current issue of LGBTIQ+ refugees seeking asylum and the precarity of Black queer citizenship. *Nine Lives* reveals the experiences of many asylum seekers arriving in the UK who are subjected to humiliating intimate interrogations at the border and in Home Office interviews, and experience xenophobia from British people, while living in poverty when expected to survive on inadequate welfare benefits. The solo form of the play accentuates Ishmael's loneliness and the anxieties he faces as a new arrival in Britain, where the challenges of navigating a complex and confusing system are heightened by fears of homophobic responses and loss of community if he reveals the real reasons for his asylum claim to other Africans in the support group. Asylum can be an extremely frightening and isolating situation, and love, fun and intimacy can be difficult to find when one is caught up in negotiating bureaucratic asylum processes. However, the play

---

24 Chuck Mike, Antonia Kemi Coker and Tonderai Munyevu, *Zhe: [Noun] undefined* (London: Oberon Books, 2013), 23 and 53.

is hopeful in showing how possibilities for friendship, solidarity and support exist, exemplified in Ishmael's friendship with single mother Bex and her child. Zimbabwean mbira music overlays each of the poetic interludes, situating a connection to the 'home' that Ishmael has left behind and creating a nostalgic feel.

There are many characters experiencing trauma and extreme challenge in most of the plays in this survey, so Rikki Beadle-Blair's romantic comedy *Summer in London* (Theatre Royal Stratford East, 2017) offers an alternative upbeat tone. A group of seven interracial young people flirt, play, date and give each other advice on romance at the end of a long hot summer in London, while not having a penny in their pockets and living in a park. Beadle-Blair highlights the problem of homelessness amongst LGBTIQ+ communities in London, albeit with a rainbow glow. What is radical about this play is that it makes his/her/theirstory by being the first play to be entirely cast with trans performers, and yet the word trans is not spoken once. Through the absence of reference to gender identity, the characters are allowed to just 'be', to behave as fun-loving young people looking for romantic love. *Summer in London* signals an era in Britain where trans people are taking space; trans voices are being heard more than ever before and the struggle for human rights is being strongly fought for in public life, from social media to the streets.

Trans lives on contested British streets steps centre stage in *BURGERZ* (Hackney Showroom and tour, 2018), an autobiographical 'monodrama' written and performed by Travis Alabanza. 'Monodrama' is in inverted commas because Alabanza involves the audience very directly in the action, prompted by their questions. *BURGERZ* is premised on a real incident where a white man threw a burger into Alabanza's face while shouting transphobic abuse and members of the public either looked on, looked away or otherwise said or did nothing to help. The play paints a picture of a society where expressions of anti-trans views are rife, and 41 per cent of trans people report having experienced violent attacks or threats in public.[25] However, Alabanza is radical in their approach by looking at transphobia as a problem that straight cisgender people need to address. In forging allyship, Alabanza invites a white cisgender male audience member to help them to make a burger, in an alternative cooking-show where gender identity is unpacked and audiences are asked to reflect on inactions in the face of discrimination and consider what it might mean to do something different, what it might mean to intervene, to help and protect when witnessing violence towards another person on the street.

Temi Wilkey's *The High Table* (Bush Theatre, 2020) is a drama and romantic comedy that not only portrays a Nigerian family living in London in 2020 but a Nigerian family that still thrives in the ancestral realm. The prospect of a lesbian wedding between Tara, a British Nigerian woman, and her girlfriend Leah is on the table. Eight years after *I Stand Corrected*, the possibility of LGBTIQ+ marriage in Britain is now a reality, but her parents need to be convinced and the ancestors need to give their blessing. Will they, won't they? is a question that runs through the play. The dangers of being openly gay in Nigeria are explored through the representation of Tara's Uncle Teju. As we see in Nyoni's *Nine Lives*, asylum is clearly an urgent and complicated topic in contemporary Britain, where the issue of immigration was

---

25 See Trans Key Stats: https://www.stonewall.org.uk/sites/default/files/trans_stats.pdf (accessed 19 January 2022).

undoubtedly a factor in the argument for the UK's exit from the European Union – Brexit. The damaging relationship between Christian colonial Britain and homophobic laws in Nigeria today is confronted again. *The High Table* is also another play that speaks to the unbroken link that so many Black Britons have to the wider diaspora and a desire for Black queer people to know our Afriquia his/her/theirstories, beyond European frames of reference.

The problem of European frames of reference are exemplified in the affronting question which sparks *Mugabe, My Dad and Me* (York Theatre Royal and touring 2019–present), described by the author and performer Tonderai Munyevu as a true story. 'Where are you from?', an elderly white man asks the barman and resting actor Munyevu in a London pub, before proceeding to dribble a diatribe of patronizing colonial tropes about the state of Zimbabwe. This sense of entitlement and prejudice is a moment that so many Black people still endure in Britain and Munyevu's aim is to engage the white people in the audience to reflect and change. Munyevu then reframes the performance as a bira for Zimbabwe, a traditional ritual for guidance, healing or celebration where the ancestors are called, through the music of the female mbira player who plays live. The desire for Black people in the diaspora to reconnect with traditional spiritualities is underlined once again through this play. Through gentle and often comical direct address, storytelling, jumping in time and playing several characters, an approach also employed in Munyevu, Coker and Mike's *Zhe*, Munyevu seeks to understand his relationship to Zimbabwe, the country formerly known as Rhodesia, that was colonized by Britain. In a collage of scenes, Munyevu sheds light on the rise and fall of President Robert Mugabe, racism, struggles for land rights, inflation, homophobia, how these issues connect to the struggles of Munyevu's own father and how it all informs who Munyevu is today, as a British-Zimbabwean Black gay man.

Lastly, Mojisola Adebayo's *STARS* (Tamasha Theatre Company at Institute of Contemporary Arts (ICA), 2023) portrays an elderly Black mixed-heritage science fiction lover who has repressed her sexuality during her sixty-year marriage but now her husband is dead. Inspired by Spexit, a (fictional) post-Brexit offer for migrants to be sent into space, the protagonist, Mrs, decides to go on a cosmic quest, in search of her own orgasm. Mrs' desire for an orgasmic odyssey is provoked by a series of encounters through which Adebayo brings those pushed to the edge of Brexit Britain – lonely and elderly Black mixed-heritage and working-class women, people on low incomes, council housing residents, migrant Muslim girl-children, survivors of gender-based violence (including FGM), lesbian travellers and intersex people – into the foreground and into the future, off the planet and into the imagination. In this Afrofuturist Afriquia play, framed by ancient African Dogon intersex mythology and astronomy and employing Adebayo's signature storytelling style, we see the possibility of creating a consensual magical queer-feminist reality, where we are not bound by sexual boundaries or gender binaries any longer. *STARS* embraces the word intersex and celebrates the too often forgotten I in LGBTIQ+ perhaps signifying a time when the struggle for intersex human rights are taken more seriously in Britain.[26] The all-important space of the club and the dance floor in the Afriquia story, mentioned and depicted in *Boy with*

---

26 Taking its cue from the disability rights slogan 'Nothing About Us Without Us', *STARS* was developed with advice and support from intersex activists Valentino Vecchietti and Del LaGrace Volcano.

Beer, *Sin Dykes*, *Bashment*, *Nine Lives* and *The High Table*, and discussed in the roundtable discussion, goes live in *STARS*, where a radio DJ (Mrs' son) spins tunes live all the way through the play which eventually transforms into a club night, celebrating the power of pleasure.

These plays are varied in style and form, serving to document Black queer lives in Britain from Afriquia perspectives by providing insights into the socio-political landscape of the times in which they were written. Homophobia and/or transphobia at the intersection of race is a thread that runs through almost every play. Yet there is also hope running through these Afriquia pages, in the love stories, friendships and moments of understanding and forgiveness, enabling audiences to empathize, celebrate and increase understanding of issues affecting Black LGBTIQ+ people in Britain and the world.

Part Two

Eight plays and some recurring themes in Afriquia theatre

Choosing the plays for this anthology was difficult as there is so much excellent work in this Afriquia archive. The eight plays have been selected for a variety of reasons. We have tried to choose plays from each decade since the 1980s. We have also attempted to represent work that focuses on stories from across the LGBTIQ+ spectrum, including a balance of work by women, men and trans and/or gender non-conforming writers. Although many of the plays have connections with various locations in the diaspora, we have focused on plays set in Britain. The eight plays are deliberately chosen for the range of identities and themes as well as to showcase different styles of writing. However, some issues recur across these plays and are indeed debated throughout the plays in the Afriquia theatre archive. Paying attention to these recurring issues shows the Afriquia messages threaded throughout this body of work.

Slave to religion

All of the plays in some way reference the interconnected effects of colonialism, and particularly interpretations of the Christian religion together with enslavement, as continuing to impact on Black LGBTIQ+ lives. From the first play in this anthology, Jacqueline Rudet's *Basin*, whereupon discovering that Mona and Susan are lovers, Michele shouts, 'It's an abomination against man and God!', to the last play, Mojisola Adebayo's *STARS*, where Mrs experiences a rather comical exorcism from 'the demon of lesbianism' at the hands of a white-led evangelical church, we see religion used as a justification for homophobia and transphobia. Makau Mutua has stated that in Africa, 'much of the revulsion of homosexuality can be traced to Christianity and Islam'. Mutua points to the paradox of Christianity and Islam being used to justify homophobia and the belief that homosexuality is, as Ishmael reads on Facebook in Zodwa Nyoni's *Nine Lives*, 'A disgusting import from the colonial days', when these two Abrahamic faiths originate in Asia and were widely disseminated by European and Arab colonizers. In a witty reference to the president of Zimbabwe, Matua writes, 'We have to wonder how consistent Mugabe is when he uses a foreign religion (Christianity) while speaking a foreign language (English) to claim that it is un-African to be gay.'[27] These plays reveal that homophobia and transphobia are often contradictory and interconnected with Christianity and colonialism that can also be traced through slavery.

Although it is almost impossible to prove that slavery contributed directly to homophobia and transphobia, Christian colonialism did not enable Black people to experience and enjoy freedom in their sexuality or their gender identities. Slavery did not allow any room for any existence outside of a heteronormative gender binary nor did it allow Black people to retain any African traditions or religions that celebrated what we might today consider to be queerness, such as women marrying women in Igbo culture and various other examples of *traditional* queerness, as brilliantly argued by Tara's ancestor Yetunde in Temi Wilkey's *The High Table*.[28] Slavery did not give people a sense of ownership over their own bodies and desires, it did not celebrate sexual pleasure for its own sake as sex was only valued for its reproductive purposes or as a tool of power for the repression of enslaved people. Slavery did not positively contribute to a feeling of love for one's own body and others, it did not instil confidence or champion individual identity or acceptance of difference in others, it did nothing that would enable a positive experience of homosexuality and trans identity to exist happily; in fact, it did everything opposite, everything to counter Black pleasures.

Journalist Decca Aitkenhead writing in *The Guardian* goes so far as to say that homophobia in Black communities today is the fault of white people through slavery.[29] Nowhere is this debate more hotly debated than in Rikki Beadle-Blair's *Bashment* where Kevan asks, 'They're allowed to feel what they like because they're still recovering from slavery, is that it? We're not slave-owners. We're not racists. But does that mean we have to be fucking punchbags just 'cause we're liberal white queers?' Though the play does not argue that slavery is an excuse for homophobic violence it does highlight the need for a greater understanding of the impact of slavery on Black sexualities and the potential dynamics in interracial relationships, as Valerie Mason-John also explores in *Sin Dykes*.

Trauma leaves scars that can be seen across the body of work in this anthology, which demonstrate that Afriquia theatre is a space not only to debate these issues but to begin the healing process. Post-colonial migration is also a site of trauma. As Ishmael, the protagonist of *Nine Lives*, who flees his home country of Zimbabwe due to homophobic laws left behind there by British colonizers, says, 'Oh, it is traumatic to be an immigrant.' Anti-homosexuality laws exist in over seventy countries, including thirty-three African countries (such as Ghana, Mauritius, Nigeria, Sierra Leone, Uganda, Zimbabwe) and eleven islands in the Caribbean (such as Barbados, Grenada, Guyana, Jamaica, Trinidad). In Nigeria, even knowing that someone is gay or lesbian and not reporting it leaves people vulnerable to punishment of up to ten years in prison, whereas in some countries homosexual activity is still punishable by death. Many of these legislations were put in place while these countries were under British rule and

---

27 Makau Mutua, 'Sexual Orientation and Human Rights: Putting Homophobia on Trial', in *African Sexualities: A Reader*, ed. Sylvia Tamale (Cape Town: Pambazuka Press, 2011), 452 and 460.
28 Yemisi Ilesanmi, *Freedom to Love for All: Homosexuality is not Un-African!* (London: Yemisi Ilesanmi, 2013), 28.
29 Decca Aitkenhead, 'Homophobia is Our Fault', available at http://www.theguardian.com/world/2005/jan/05/gayrights.comment (accessed 30 January 2022).

although things have since progressed in the UK, where same-sex marriage is now a legally sanctioned right, the stringent anti-gay and lesbian laws have been maintained in many African and Caribbean Commonwealth countries. Arguably, the UK has a responsibility to provide sanctuary for LGBTIQ+ asylum seekers.

Sin Dykes, by Valerie Mason-John, directly looks at the traumatic effect of slavery on same-sex relationships between Black and white people. Kat says to Trudy: 'Know your history, girl, white people have persecuted so many of our people. How can you hang with someone who reminds you of slavery?' Trudy replies: 'That was centuries ago.' Kat retorts: 'It's still happening now, look around you', and she points to the abuses of Black people by the police and within the mental health system. Yet *Sin Dykes* also illustrates the possibility of sexual liberation from the shackles of slavery through shackling ourselves to each other as Black women, in lesbian sex play, pleasure and power by consent. The distressing reality of slavery, however, was that most sex between white and Black people was not based on consent and this is another contributing factor in fears around sexuality in what theorist of post-traumatic slave syndrome Joy DeGruy terms 'slavery's children'.[30]

Battyphobia and betrayal

Rape was endemic in the slave trade. The rape of enslaved Black women is reflected in representations on screen and in literature, such as Toni Morrison's *Beloved* (1987). However, a fact that is seldom discussed is the anal rape of Black men over centuries of slavery.[31] The perceived link between the fear of homosexuality and the use of anal rape as a punishment meted out by white men on Black men in the Caribbean has been discussed by perhaps unlikely figures such as Jamaican clergyman John Hardy from the New Testament Church of God.[32] In *Boy with Beer* by Paul Boakye, Donovan uses the term 'slave' to describe 'Black guys who check for [have sex with] whites'.[33] Rape was used to 'tame' Black men and Black men were used to 'stud' Black women. The commercial value of Black men was measured on their perceived ability to breed. For enslaved Africans, this induced a fear of being penetrated on one side and a sense of self-worth through the act of penetrating on the other. This may be why there is a hateful fixation and fear of 'battymen', why homosexuality is so strongly associated with white men, why hyper-masculine machismo is still so deep in African diasporic cultures and this debate comes up in various ways through the plays.[34]

The term 'batty boy' is heard in *Bashment* and several of the plays in the archive. In *Boy with Beer*, Karl makes Donovan say 'I'm a big battiman' in his attempt to get Donovan to accept his own sexuality and break free of the macho power top/feminine

---

30 Joy DeGruy, *Post Traumatic Slave Syndrome: America's Legacy of Enduring Injury and Healing* (Portland, OR: Joy DeGruy Publications, 2005), 140.
31 Ibid., 76–80 and 84.
32 See Tony Grew, 'Slave owners responsible for Jamaican homophobia', available at http://www.pinknews.co.uk/2007/06/19/slave-owners-responsible-for-jamaican-homophobia/ (accessed 31 January 2022).
33 Boakye, *Boy with Beer*, 16.
34 See Michele Wallace, *Black Macho and the Myth of the Superwoman* (London: Verso, (1979) 1999).

bottom binary in which he is so invested. Karl asks Donovan, 'What makes you think the men you fuck are any less than other men?' The hatred of 'batty boys' evidenced in many of these plays is at its root a hatred for the internalized enslaved Black self. As the homophobic (and later redeemed) MC Eggy says in *Bashment*: 'There ain't one reason that n*ggas hate queers – there's every reason . . . Cause n*ggas are queers.' To be queer in these terms means to be abused, violated, enslaved, feminine and self-hating.

As we see in many of the plays in the archive, including *Basin* and *The High Table*, homosexuality is associated with white people and is therefore also seen by some as a betrayal of blackness. This is exemplified in *Bashment* during a conversation between Eggy and Venom in prison.

Eggy . . . every Black man is a brother.

Venom What about coppers? And queers?

Eggy They forfeit their Blackness.

Black queer people are perceived by some as betraying the race by engaging in homosexual acts and it is God who punishes this betrayal. In *Boy with Beer* we hear about having sex with white people as 'sleeping with the enemy', which is also a recurring conversation in *Sin Dykes* where Trudy struggles to go back to her white girlfriend, Gill. Trudy says to Gill, 'I don't trust your conditioning.' The question of whether white people can be trusted not to betray their Black lovers is exemplified here. We see the emotional cost of betrayal by a Black lover in *Nine Lives* and there is also the challenge to the Black family to not betray its own queer kin, such as Uncle Teju, in *The High Table*. Lastly, Travis Alabanza's *BURGERZ* offers a powerful challenge to audience members to actively forgo their own white, cisgender privilege and act when they witness transphobic and homophobic attacks.

Reach we reach

As we have seen, these plays do not shy away from brutal subject matter, yet many of them also recall the possibility of beautiful Black queer times, reclaiming our pre-colonial, pre-slavery African pasts and projecting into an Afrofuture. Paul Boakye reaches back to a time before Europeans stepped foot on African shores in *Boy with Beer* where the protagonist Karl's poetry is heard in voiceover:

> In days two thousand seasons past, our feet roamed freely through golden
> Ghana soil, our hearts flew up high with birds on a Ghana breeze. You loved me then.

> Of my tortured enslavement from *The Way* you must have heard the stories told.
> I bear some of the scars but time has changed me none. I love you now as then.
> Will we meet and love again? Or is our love for ever tainted by the historic chain of events since then?

> I have never lost hope completely. Don't you despair. This Black man is still in search of his African Prince.

Karl is reaching for his potential prince, Donovan. In *STARS*, Adebayo uses the Dogon creation stories of Mali and the intergalactic intersex figure of the Nommos, in particular, to frame a play that points to an Afrofuture free of sexual trauma through orgasmic space travel and collective club night pleasure for elders and young people alike. In *BURGERZ*, Travis Alabanza also recalls the God-like status that trans people had in cultures as diverse as Italy and the Philippines. Trans people are elevated and celebrated in this life-affirming play and cisgender straight people are called to address their inaction. No play is more categorical in its accusation of colonisation for the destruction of African same-sex loving traditions than *The High Table*, where ancient queer ancestors have important lessons for lesbians living on Earth today. All of the plays, in some way, name problems in Black queer experience and challenge audience members about the possible roots of homophobia and transphobia. Moreover, the plays not only reach back to an Afriquia past but also reach out to the diaspora of the present, reinforcing the relationship between Africa and the Caribbean for so many Black people in Britain.

Named love

As Ngũgĩ wa Thiong'o and other post-colonial theorists have shown, reclaiming language and self-naming is very important in a process of liberation and self-love for Black people and Black queer people, as can be seen in these plays.[35] Through stating our own names, our own terms, our own identities and naming our love in our own ways we challenge homophobia, transphobia and racism simultaneously.

In *Basin*, Mona and Susan name themselves 'zammies' and describe their love in Caribbean terms. They appeal to their communities to understand them through the vessel symbolizing female submission: 'If they want to know about zammies, tell them about their basin.' In *Nine Lives*, when Ishmael meets Bex on a park bench, he calls himself Sam and constructs a new identity, pretending to be a successful business student for fear of being discovered to be a gay asylum seeker. It is only when he is authentic with Bex that they can really form an allyship and be true friends. In *STARS*, Mrs' friend Maxi, the only self-identified intersex character in this anthology, in one of the few moments where a character comes out (in most of the other plays all of the characters are 'out' and coming out is not a big theme in this anthology), states their identity, claims the name intersex and plays with the name in an affirmation of the right to 'bodily integrity' and self-determination by playfully declaring 'too right I am intosex!' The final declaration of Mrs is a revelation of her own name, but she invites the audience to just call her Nommo, after the Dogon intersex deity.

More than any other kind of naming, though, it is love that is named through all of these plays. From romantic love in *Basin*, *Boy with Beer* and *Bashment*, to sexual love in *Sin Dykes*, family love through a lesbian wedding in *The High Table*, love between friends in *Nine Lives* and self-love in *BURGERZ* and *STARS*, love is the name of each play. As bell hooks has said, love is a verb.[36] Love is performative. It happens both in utterance and in action, exemplified in the 'I do' that Tara and Leah are striving to get

---

35 Ngũgĩ wa Thiong'o, *Decolonising the Mind: The Politics of Language in African Literature* (London: Heinemann Educational, 1986).
36 bell hooks, *All About Love: New Visions* (London: Women's Press, 2000), 4.

to in *The High Table*. Love is something that was denied to Black people through the slave trade. As hooks writes, 'In the racist mindset the enslaved African was incapable of deep feeling and fine emotions. Since love was considered to be a finer sentiment, black folks were seen as lacking the capacity to love.'[37] hooks says this dehumanization has led to a 'crisis of lovelessness'.[38] hooks goes on: 'To return to love, making it a central issue in our collective recovery and healing is not a move away from political action. Unless love is the force under-girding our efforts to transform society, we lose our way ... Love is profoundly political.'[39] These Afriquia plays provide new representations of loving possibilities for Black characters through profoundly political love stories that create spaces for reflection and healing. As Boakye writes in his notes accompanying *Boy with Beer*, it is 'a sign of health' when Black men love each other.

Audre Lorde describes homophobia as, 'Fear of feelings of love for members of one's own sex and therefore hatred of these feelings in others.'[40] Slavery produced a fear of losing love and a fear of love itself. In *Bashment* there is a gay bashing after a confession of love. It's not so much the sex that triggers the violence, it's love that the gang of men find so repulsive and the trigger (or perhaps excuse) is Orly's use of the 'N' word. The homophobia expressed by the Black men in *Bashment* is, more than any other fear, a fear of love. If homophobia is the fear of love in men it is also the fear of being unloved in Black women. In *Basin*, Mona says to Michele, 'Who will love us? White people? Black men? Who will love us if not other Black women?' Loving each other is for Black people part of our liberation, revolution and evolution from the past. As hooks states: 'To give ourselves to love, to love blackness, is to restore the true meaning of freedom, hope and possibility in all our lives.'[41] In *STARS*, Mrs remembers the words of her would-be lesbian lover from the launderette, Shahana, who, after some one-sided love making in the back of a converted delivery truck, tells Mrs she must 'love herself first.' The elderly Mrs is trying to do just this, catapulting the audience into a club night, celebrating pleasure and every kind of love that there is.

Happy endings

By way of conclusion, although the plays in this anthology all deal to a greater or lesser extent with the traumatic subject matter of homophobia and transphobia, its roots in slavery and colonisation and complicated feelings of betrayal, they also all create something profoundly beautiful out of the brutal. All of the plays articulate and express different forms of Black queer love and offer speculative happy endings. In live performance, the plays offer spaces of truth telling, listening, compassion, empathy, support, solidarity and an opportunity to understand ourselves through each other; or in returning to African terms, these plays generate *ubuntu*, that Southern African philosophy with no direct translation in the English language that broadly defines humanity as: I am who I am because you are who you are or, I am me through you and

---

37 hooks, *Salvation*, xix.
38 Ibid., 5.
39 Ibid., 16.
40 Baird, Vanessa. *Sex, Love and Homophobia* (London: Amnesty International, 2004), 46.
41 hooks, *Salvation*, xxix.

you are you through me. Whether in the basin we see ourselves reflected in *Basin*, the bed of *Boy with Beer*, the 'Stop' of S&M sex spoken in *Sin Dykes*, the reparative battle of *Bashment*, the camaraderie of the park bench in *Nine Lives*, the burger that refuses to be thrown in *BURGERZ*, the collective electric slide in *The High Table* and the rave, the club space that opens up in *STARS* and recurs in so many of these plays, there is an ancient and enduring ubuntu that is embraced; there is an Afriquia future of happy endings. This book is just a beginning.

Bibliography of published plays in the Afriquia theatre archive

Adebayo, Mojisola. *Moj of the Antarctic* in *Plays One*. London: Oberon Books, 2011.
Adebayo, Mojisola. *Muhammad Ali and Me* in *Plays One*. London: Oberon Books, 2011.
Adebayo, Mojisola. *I Stand Corrected* in *Plays Two*. London: Oberon Books, 2019.
Adebayo, Mojisola. *STARS* in *Plays Two*. London: Oberon Books, 2019.
Alabanza, Travis. *BURGERZ*. London: Oberon Books, 2018.
Beadle-Blair, Rikki. *Bashment*. London: Oberon Books, 2005.
Beadle-Blair, Rikki. *FIT: Screenplay, Stage Play and Teachers' Notes*. London: Oberon Books, 2010.
Beadle-Blair, Rikki. *Thug Ass* in *Black and Gay in the UK: An Anthology*. Edited by John R. Gordon and Rikki Beadle-Blair. London: Team Angelica, 2014.
Beadle-Blair, Rikki. *Summer in London*. London: Oberon Books, 2018.
Boakye, Paul. *Boy with Beer* in *Black Plays: Three*. Edited by Yvonne Brewster. London: Methuen, 1995.
Daley, Doña. *Blest Be the Tie*. London: Royal Court, 2004.
DeObia, Oparei. *Crazyblackmuthaf**in'self*. London: Royal Court, 2002.
Ellams, Inua. *Black T-Shirt Collection*. London: Oberon Books, 2012.
Kay, Jackie. *Chiaroscuro* in *Lesbian Plays*. Edited by Jill Davis, 58–84. London: Methuen, 1986.
Kay, Jackie. *Twice Over* in *Gay Sweatshop: Four Plays and a Company*. Edited by Phillip Osment. London: Methuen, 1989.
Mason-John, Valerie. *Sin Dykes* in *Brown Girl in the Ring*. London: Get a Grip, 1999.
McCraney, Tarell Alvin. *Wig Out*. London: Faber and Faber, 2008.
McCraney, Tarell Alvin. *Choir Boy*. London: Faber and Faber, 2012.
Mike, Chuck, Antonia Kemi Coker and Tonderai Munyevu. *Zhe: [Noun] undefined*. London: Oberon Books, 2013.
Munyevu, Tonderai. *Mugabe, My Dad and Me*. London: Methuen Drama, 2020.
Nyoni, Zodwa. *Nine Lives*. London: Methuen Drama, 2015.
Rodriguez, Christopher. *High Heel Parrotfish!* London: Oberon Books, 2005.
Rudet, Jacqueline. *Basin* in *Black Plays*. Edited by Yvonne Brewster. London: Methuen Drama, 1987.
Wilkey, Temi. *The High Table*. London: Methuen Drama, 2020.

The Eight Plays

Basin

Jacqueline Rudet

Basin was first performed at the Royal Court Theatre Upstairs on 29 October 1985, with the following cast:

Mona   Dona Croll
Susan   Beverley Hills
Michele Susan Harper-Browne

Directed by Paulette Randall
Designed by Vanessa Clegg

Author's preface

Basin took three years to write. It was my first attempt at putting pen to paper but the second play I finished. Between starting and finishing it I wrote *Money to Live*. *Basin* was previously called *With Friends Like You* and, along with some friends, I directed a production which we performed at assorted small venues.

Soon after, I became rather disillusioned with my writing, seeing its inadequacies but not knowing how to rectify them, so I went on holiday to Dominica to visit relatives I hadn't seen in a long while. I returned to England with a love for Black women. While out there, I'd suddenly realized how strong, how loving yet how abused and unappreciated Black women are. I realized I had lost my love of Black women through the general pressures and distractions of domestic life. Through a play, I wanted to show that all Black women had much in common. This led me to much thought about the word 'zammie'.

Zammie was a word I'd forgotten about. It was a word my mother would use to describe a very close friend, but it had connotations of being more than friend and, in a strange way, it was a rude word that only grown-ups could use, as if 'zammie' meant lover. In *With Friends Like You*, I was writing a play about a friendship between two women but I hadn't been able to find a way or a word to describe that friendship.

The two zammies in *Basin* become lovers but zammie is not lesbian in patois. The word refers more to the universality of friendship between Black women; no matter what nationality, no matter what class, all Black women have very important things in common. They're the last in line; there's no one below them to oppress. Whether they like it or not, every Black woman is the zammie of every other Black woman. It's almost an obligatory thing. As one of the girls in *Basin* says, 'Who will love us?'

The basin symbolized the one article that all Black women possess. Mothers always teach their daughters about cleanliness. If not dressed in smart, new clothes, at least clean. An important matter of pride. As a girl grows up, it's less a matter of pride, more a case of a woman making herself smell fresh, just in case her husband wants to relieve himself inside her.

Jacqueline Rudet

Characters

Mona
Susan
Michele

Act One

Scene One

Mona's *flat. She is clearing up after the previous night's party. She sings to herself.*

Mona
    Honey, pepper, leaf green limes,
    Pagan fruit whose names are rhymes,
    Mangoes, breadfruit, ginger root,
    Granadillas, bamboo shoots,
    Sugar cane, cola nuts,
    Citrons, airy coconuts,
    Fish, tobacco, native hats,
    Gold bananas, woven mats,
    Plantains, wild thyme, pallid leeks
    Pigeons with their scarlet beaks,
    Saffron, yams,
    Baskets, ruby guava jams,
    Fustles, goat skins, cinnamon, allspice,
    Oh, island in the sun,
    Gave to me by my father's hand,
    La, la, la, la . . .

She hears a knock at the door.

Coming!

She goes to open the door. **Susan** *kisses her and comes in.*

Susan   Mona, I've been knocking and knocking. Were you asleep?

Mona   Sorry, I was miles away. Back home, in fact. Thinking about all the good times. So you decided to come. Don't you think you're a little late?

Susan   Looks like you had a good time here!

Mona   Well, if you'd come, you'd have enjoyed yourself too.

Susan   What happened?

Mona   It was great! I mean! Pat and her new man business! The boy is so dry! He spent the whole night in the corner giving everybody cut eye! He's a joke. I don't know what she sees in him. I said, 'Pat, what do you see in this boy? He must have one big wood!' You could see Pat was shame. First, she kept making excuses that he wasn't feeling well, then she couldn't take it anymore, just walked out and left him! It was really funny.

Everybody enjoyed themselves. And listen to this, nah! Herbert brought this box full of whisky. I don't know where he got it from because every minute him just a peep through the window to see if bull a come. So Michael plays this trick on him. He rushes in and says, 'Bull outside! Someone a thief a box of whisky from the off-licence!' Girl, I never see Herbert move so fast! When Herbert found out, him so vexed him fit to burst!

Susan I would've liked to see that. Good! I can't stand him. And how was your Michael?

Mona The boy makes me sick. The guy love woman! I'm serving drinks and the guy's got some piss an' tail gal in the corner a wind-up in front of me in my own fucking house! I'm fed up with the guy. All he wants me for is jook, jook, jook.

Susan I thought all you wanted was jook, jook, jook!

Mona Michael's just taking the piss.

Susan I've told you that too many times.

Mona Never mind about me. Look at you! You look well miserable!

Susan *tries to speak, but can't.*

Mona Come on, start at the beginning. I'll listen, no matter how boring.

Susan Thank you!

Mona Only joking! (*Pause.*) Come on!

Susan Well . . . You remember when I was at drama school?

Mona Back that far!

Susan Are you interested?

Mona All ears! Come on!

Susan (*pause*) I was the only Black student. I felt really proud of myself. I was the only one of my friends to get somewhere and achieve something. I was being kept back and not being given the chance to prove myself, but I knew I had the talent, so I just kept on going.

Mona This isn't what's on your mind!

Susan I'm getting to it. (*Pause.*) One month, I missed my period . . .

Mona What's this got to do with drama school?

Susan I'm jumping. Sorry. While I was at drama school, one month, I missed my period, took a test, found it was positive, but I felt so stupid, I couldn't bring myself to tell you. Anyway, I had an abortion, of course.

Pause.

Mona Are we getting to it?

Susan We're getting there.

Mona This is all stuff to set the mood is it?

Susan I'm building up to it.

Mona   Is this why you didn't come to the party?

Susan   I would've liked to have come, but I had so much on my mind.

Mona   I organized the party so everyone could cast aside the troubles in their life and have a good time. Everyone said, 'Where's Susan?' I said, 'She's probably down Handsworth earning some pocket money.'

Susan   I was at home. I got to the top of your road and turned back.

Mona   There's this really cheap psychiatrist I can recommend.

Susan   I got to the top of your road and just turned back. I couldn't face it.

Mona   Face what?

Susan   Everyone.

Mona   Our friends?

Susan   The noise, the smoke, the chat-up lines, Michael . . .

Mona   You wouldn't have seen him anyway! He was tucked away in that corner getting all slippery with this little girl. I don't even know who invited her!

Susan   That's what I couldn't have stood! Michael: fucking around with another woman right under your nose!

Mona   What's new?

Susan   I would've said something.

Mona   We used to go out to parties. I'd go and get some drinks, or go to the toilet, and when I'd get back, where would he be? Pressing some girl up against a wall, supposedly dancing! Michael's a big slag, he always has been.

Susan   I've never understood this about you. You can't tell me you love him!

Mona   You've never been in love, have you? Michael was my first real man. He's been the only man in my life since I was nineteen. A man like that becomes part of your life. You don't 'go out' with him, it's not a 'love affair', he's just there. It's pathetic, I know, but I can't imagine life without him.

Susan   I can't bear the way he treats you.

Mona   And that's why you didn't come to the party?

Susan   You never rang me last night. You can't have been that bothered what had happened to me!

Mona   So you need an invitation and then a call on the night to check you're coming? What's eating you, woman?

A knock on the door. **Mona** *opens the door.* **Michele** *walks in.*

Mona   Ah, now we come to the interesting part of the story!

Michele   What story? Hi, Sue, where were you?

Mona Now we come to the *very* interesting part of the story!

Michele *helps* **Mona** *clean up.*

Michele What story?

Mona Michele finds herself in the unenviable position of being in the same room as four of her ex-boyfriends.

Susan Michele, you're good!

Michele Where were you?

Susan I didn't feel like it.

Michele You missed one party!

Mona What does Michele do?

Susan Dunno.

Mona She ignores all her ex-boyfriends and takes up with someone man!

Susan Michele, you're good!

Michele They're ex-boyfriends. Ex. You know, in the past.

Susan So, who's the new one?

Michele A guy called Steven. I don't know where he came from. Heaven, I'm sure!

Mona Of course, Michele's looking so good, all of her man dem a eye-up her backside. So Michele's getting it on with number five while numbers one to four try their best all night long to get a dance.

Susan Michele, you're a star!

Mona Could it be charisma?

Michele Leave it out!

Mona Could it be the perfume she uses?

Susan What perfume do you use?

Michele Who'll make the tea?

Mona She's just a regular girl really. See? She drinks tea like the rest of us.

Susan Want a cup, Mona?

Mona No thanks.

Susan *goes into the kitchen.*

Michele Mona?

Mona Yes.

Michele Have you still got that nice red dress?

Mona   You want to borrow it?

Michele   Could I?

Mona   Whatever you want.

Michele   And do you still have those nice red shoes?

Mona   Take them too.

Michele   Thanks, Mona. I'm going out tonight but all my stuff needs mending or dry cleaning.

Mona   Aren't you tired?

Michele   Yeah, but I feel like going out (*Beat.*) Mona, you did see that Steven boy, didn't you? Don't you think he's nice?

Mona   He bores me.

Michele   I could really check f'him!

Susan *enters and puts two cups of tea on the table.*

Mona   You're always talking about man and going out.

Michele   What should I talk about?

Mona   I tell you, you love man. Man fever, you have. It'll be a real problem in time to come.

Michele   How could it?

Mona   You rely too much on men. You think all a man thinks about is you? He's got lots of things on his mind; other women for a start!

Michele   What can I do? I seem to get on better with guys. Girls really irritate me; they look at me and see where they can fault me.

Have you ever been to a party where women are just looking you up and down, checking you out to see which parts of them are more expensive than you. I've never been able to get into girls and what they talk about. All these girls at my school, all they ever talked about was marriage, kids and having big houses. I never wanted that. I always dreamt of having a little place of my own and doing what I wanted.

Susan   Your wish came true.

Michele   I'm working on it.

Susan   Sounds like you're overdoing it!

Michele   We all like being complimented, don't we? Where else am I going to get praise? If you stick with a guy too long, the compliments dry up, so do the presents, so does the passion. That's why I keep checking new men. When you first get a guy, he takes real good care of you; takes you out, buys you things, tells you how good you look, and the loving is sweet! I like that.

Susan You can't live on that.

Michele I live on it. Believe me, I live on it.

Mona Like I said, you rely too much on men. You've never been alone for two minutes. You don't even know who you are and what you're capable of.

Michele Don't give me a hard time. All I came here to do was borrow the dress and some shoes.

Mona The way you bring my things back sometimes, I might as well throw them away!

Michele That's not true. I'll have the dress back, washed and ironed, by tomorrow night.

Mona . . . I'm going out with Marcus tonight . . . and I've got to have money. Could you lend us a fiver?

Mona You think I print money?

Michele As soon as I get my cheque I'll pay you back.

Mona By Friday. No later.

Michele Mona . . . (*Long pause.*) . . . you know that whisky?

Mona Yes.

Michele What did you do with it? Have you got any left?

Mona Yes, lots, take a bottle.

Michele You're an angel. (*To* **Susan**.) So, where were you? Having a little party of your own, were you?

Susan I just didn't feel like it.

Michele (*to* **Mona**) If you can't find the red dress, I'll take the black one.

Mona (*wearily*) Take whatever you want, Michele.

Michele Have you got Steve's number?

Mona (*looking in her bag for her address book*) What, are you going to go from Marcus to Steve tonight? Michele your poom-poom must be well hot! (*She finds her address book and shows* **Michele** *the number.*) You want Michael too? Michael's probably got some for you if you want it!

Michele (*copying the number on a piece of paper*) Thanks. No, I'm not going to Steve tonight. Tomorrow.

Mona Go on, have another pickney! That's what you want, innit? You can't breed pickney like dog!

Michele Everyone's allowed one mistake. I'm all equipped now, anyway, so it won't happen again. (*Beat.*) He's so nice though! How can I resist?

Mona There are so many pretty boys, Michele.

Michele I like pretty boys. Girl, I could eat him!

Mona (*to* **Michele**) Have you got any weed?

Susan (*to* **Mona**) You smoke too much weed.

Michele No, she doesn't.

Susan I wasn't talking to you!

Michele There's nothing wrong with a smoke every now and then.

Susan I don't like people who smoke a lot of weed. Everything's too cool with them. They haven't got a job, that's cool. They haven't paid the rent, that's cool. They just got pregnant, that's cool. Everyt'ing cool!

Mona Have you?

Michele Not with me.

Mona I've got some, but just enough for one. I don't like not having any. Sometimes, you just fancy a spliff.

Susan *looks at her disapprovingly.* **Mona** *shrugs her shoulders.*

Mona I don't know why you two bicker at each other.

Susan We don't bicker.

Michele No, you just dig at me.

Susan I dig at you only when I have a reason. It just so happens that I find your manners a little lacking these days.

Michele What have manners got to do with it?

Mona Are you sure all this doesn't date back to Roland?

Susan That was years back! I got over that years ago!

Mona Are you sure?

Susan Roland and I fell out, we split up, Michele was his next woman. I was glad to get rid of him.

Mona That's not what you said at the time.

Susan I was caught up in the heat of the moment.

Mona You accused Michele of one set of crimes!

Susan Mona, stop shit-stirring! I wasn't going to fall out with a friend over a man, a good friend at that.

Mona So what is it between you two?

Michele It's nothing.

Susan It's not nothing, Michele. I don't like to see you abuse Mona.

Michele Times are bad for me right now. I'm supporting myself. What I need to find is a rich man.

Susan You won't find a rich man. You don't move in those circles.

Michele I feel bad but I just haven't got any money. I'm feeding my baby rubbish. Things'll get better. I'll pay Mona back.

Susan Things will get better?

Michele (*irritated; to* **Mona**) Can I just take those things and go?

Mona Go look in the bedroom, you'll find them.

Michele And where's the whisky?

Mona (*pointing*) Over there in the corner.

Michele Mona . . . (*Long pause.*) . . . I know what Susan was just saying . . . but I haven't got any food in the flat. My dole comes on Friday. Is there anything left over from the party?

Mona There's a tin of cheese biscuits on top of the fridge. I didn't even open them.

Michele Are you sure that's all right?

Mona You just sit there. I'll get it all together for you.

She goes into the kitchen, then the bedroom, collecting things for **Michele** *in some plastic bags. Uncomfortable silence between* **Susan** *and* **Michele**.

Susan It's getting a bit bad these days, isn't it?

Michele What?

Susan The way people treat each other.

Michele *shrugs her shoulders, not understanding.*

Susan The world is run by those who get the breaks. Some people are born into the breaks, others just strike lucky. Those who get the breaks – there's not many of them – they rule our lives; we; the mass; the majority. There's no such thing as an oppressed minority, most of us are part of the oppressed majority. What do we do, we minions, what do we do? We squabble amongst ourselves. They find that very funny.

Michele Who?

Susan Those in power; those who get the breaks. They laugh at us. As long as we run around in circles, they'll be all right.

Michele, *not really understanding, looks blankly at* **Susan**, *not sure what to say.*

Susan I'm talking about us, Michele. We help you. You're meant to help us at some stage of the day.

Michele I'm having it bad right now.

Susan You're always having it bad!

Michele It's not my fault, is it?

Susan Whose fault is it? It takes two to make a baby. What, are you going to blame him for the pregnancy? Who spends all the money that comes into your hands? Someone else? No, you. It's your fault. You let men into your life. Try and give your fanny a rest and you might be able to save some money for yourself, and spend some time with your child.

Michele All right, I feel bad. Happy?

Susan *looks mildly remorseful.*

Michele Happy?

Susan I'm sorry. You seem to upset me whenever I see you. You keep saying, 'Things will get better', but it's not 'things' that need to get better. It's you!

Mona *comes back in with several plastic bags, which she gives to* **Michele***, who gets up and makes for the door.*

Michele (*to* **Mona**) So, when am I going to see you again?

Mona When you want something.

Michele Don't say that!

Mona Michele, it doesn't really matter.

Michele (*to* **Susan**) I'll see you, madam.

Susan Girls, just don't work it too hard tonight!

Michele You jealous?

She opens the door.

See you both.

She exits. **Mona** *pulls a tobacco tin out from underneath a cushion, throws it to* **Susan***, who rolls a spliff for her.*

Susan Just this once.

Mona Share it with me. Stay over?

Susan You want me to stay?

Mona It'll be good for you to relax and have a laugh. (*Beat.*) It used to be different when we were young. We were all living with our parents, money was something they had. We had nothing to give, nothing that could be borrowed.

Susan It's like a blind spot with Michele. You've lent her more fivers than you can remember. She's forgotten about them all, that's for sure.

Mona Maybe it gets to the point – that point where you can't feed your shrieking infant – when you don't really care what you're doing, you don't really care what you've become.

Susan You can't say 'no', though. She needs all the support she can get.

Mona You never did tell me what was bugging you.

Susan It's not really distressing me. It's something that's rather pleasing me, actually. I'm not unhappy at all. I feel great.

Mona Tell me about that.

Susan (*pause*) There's someone I like.

Mona You must definitely tell me about that! Yes-I! News for me! Come on, tell me, who is it?

Susan Well . . .

Mona Having a quiet one on the sly, eh? Now tell your Auntie Mona.

Susan What would you do if you liked someone but you weren't sure how they felt?

Mona I'd tell them.

Susan But what if it was someone you'd known a long time?

Mona I'd tell them.

Susan Mona, I'm really confused. I know little girls go through phases but I'm really not sure about some of the phases I'm going through!

Mona There's nothing the matter with you. Everyone gets confused. That shows how normal you are. If you're caught up in some dilemma, you're at peak fitness. Whatever's going on in your head, it's not going to shock me, is it?

Susan *finishes rolling the spliff and lights it. She takes a few puffs and passes it on to* **Mona**.

Mona Come on, girl. Before this makes us into a pair of idiots. What's your problem?

Pause.

Susan I was walking down the road the other day, and I could see this young guy walking towards me. I could feel him looking at me and, as he got closer, I watched his eyes. He was obviously into tits 'cause he was staring at my chest. Then he moved down to my lower half; a few seconds on my crotch, a few seconds on my legs. Something seemed to please his eyes 'cause he then moved up to my face, seeing if I was good-looking. Not that that matters. Haven't you heard guys say that they don't need to look at the mantelpiece to stoke the fire?

Systematically, this guy checked me out. If he'd looked in my eyes, he wouldn't have seen something he liked, but my head didn't interest him. First he wanted to see if my implements for fucking were all in order. I really hate that, you know.

It's true, there are more female politicians, more businesswomen, more women in influential jobs, but that still hasn't improved men's outlook on women. I'm still, first and foremost, a fuck. I really can't stand that.

What I'm struggling to say is that I think I'm growing tired of that lovable, household pet know as the boyfriend.

She kneels before **Mona**, *opening her arms, asking to be held.* **Mona** *hugs her.* **Susan** *pulls back and tries to kiss* **Mona**. **Mona** *is shocked and stands up.*

Mona   Susan!

Susan (*embarrassed*)   I'm sorry.

Mona   You're fed up with boys and you want women instead?

Susan   Not really . . . I just . . . I just feel something for you. It's not really that I'm turned off men, it's not really that I'm turned on by women, it's just . . . well . . . you're really special. You're so patient with Michele, you're so patient with me, you're so patient with Michael . . .

Mona   I don't know about that.

Susan   . . . and that's the reason I didn't come to the party; I couldn't bear to see you in public with Michael. I couldn't bear to see him treat you with such disdain in public. He's disgusting. I don't know why you care for him. I don't know how you ever did. You're too maternal; I can't bear to see Michele and Michael take and take and give nothing in return.

You're really special . . .

Mona (*embarrassed*)   Cut it out!

Susan   Mona, seriously, you're just the best friend I'll ever have. I think you're really great . . . and I just happen to fancy you as well.

Mona *passes the spliff to* **Susan**.

Mona   This is getting well out of order . . .

Susan   . . . stop and think about it . . .

Mona   . . . this is the spliff talking . . .

Susan   . . . when was the last time you felt loved?

Mona   Maybe there is something wrong with you!

Susan   There's nothing wrong with me!

Mona   This is one of the phases that little girls go through. Come on, girl, pass it, nah!

Playfully, **Susan** *moves away.*

Susan   Come and get it then.

Mona   Come on, pass it, before I give you two kick!

Susan *moves behind a chair.*

Susan If you want it, come and get it.

Mona *comes towards* **Susan** *and tries to retrieve the spliff.* **Susan** *dodges out of her way.*

Mona Look, I'm not joking, Susan, pass it!

She tries to make a grab at the spliff and burns her hand.

Ouch! Stupid!

Susan Who tell you to put your hand on burning weed? (*Pause.*) Are you all right, Mona?

Mona No, I'm not all right. Look what you've done! I'm scarred! Why can't you behave yourself? What's got into you today?

Susan *tries to look at* **Mona**'s *hand but* **Mona** *moves away.*

Mona Don't bother. I'm fed up with your foolishness.

Mona *exits.* **Susan** *raises her eyes to the ceiling, feeling regret, but picks up the tobacco tin and follows* **Mona** *out.*

Blackout.

Scene Two

Mona's *flat. The morning after. She walks from the kitchen, dressed in dressing gown and slippers, carrying a bowl of cornflakes and a cup of tea. She sits down and starts eating.* **Susan** *wanders in wearing similar attire.*

Susan (*cheerily*)   Good morning!

No reply from **Mona**. **Susan** *goes into the kitchen – to put the kettle on – then comes back out again.*

Susan Tea?

Mona I've got some, thank you.

Susan Sleep well?

Mona Yes, thank you.

Susan Feeling talkative? Feeling revived and refreshed, are we?

Mona *gets up, gets out her carpet cleaner and starts aimlessly pushing it up and down the floor.*

Susan What's wrong, Mona? Are we still friends? Don't you feel well? I feel wonderful. I feel really happy. Don't you feel any kind of happiness? I knew this is how it would be, you know? I feel really different, don't you? Mona, please say something! Please! What's wrong?

Mona *continues hoovering.*

Mona Look, it may be important to you but I don't intend to discuss last night.

Susan But I really want to talk about it!

Mona I know you do!

Susan It's important to me, Mona, don't dismiss it.

Mona I said I don't intend to discuss it!

Susan Come on, Mona . . .

Mona Don't 'Come on, Mona' me! It's a bit of a shock to the system, you know. I've got a boyfriend, you know. It's a bit of a shock.

Susan Can't we talk?

Mona Stop it! In fact, I'm seeing Michael later on.

Susan How can you!

Mona He's my boyfriend and while I'm going out with him you'd better relax.

Susan Last night meant nothing to you, did it?

Mona You're right. I'm too maternal. I'm too soft. I make sacrifices for everyone. You wanted me, I complied.

Susan How can you say that!

Mona People act funny when they're charged. I just let you do what you wanted.

Susan That's really considerate of you. So, now you're off to Michael so he can do what he wants. You could run a little business, you know. Make people pay, Mona. Tell them they can do what they want, all they have to do is stick a coin in the slot!

Mona Why don't you get hysterical! Why don't you insult me!

Susan I just can't bear to see Michael use you. He doesn't need you, I do!

Mona We go a long way back, you know. Michael and me talk. I like him – strange as it may seem – I like him. He was the first person that ever talked to me. He taught me a lot, he still does.

Susan He just calls you when he want a jook!

Mona Don't stop there, Susan, get really unpleasant!

Susan Come on, Mona, admit it, you enjoyed last night. Don't let it bother you.

Mona Get dressed and piss off, nah!

Susan Don't be like that.

Mona I don't want to talk!

Pause.

Susan What are you doing tonight?

Mona I'll probably end up staying at Michael's, won't I?

Susan OK. (*Pause.*) I'll see you tomorrow?

Mona Don't start all that again. We made love. I don't know why. I don't know what's come over you. Maybe you were just upset.

Susan Upset? I was happy! I'm really happy! When we were back home, didn't we sleep together? As kids, didn't we kiss? Didn't we touch? Have you erased it from your memory?

Mona Susan, we were kids. We didn't know what we were doing.

Susan Didn't we?

Mona Did you?

Susan I did. You didn't know what you were doing? You didn't love me?

Mona Susan, we were kids. This is now.

Susan But you love me, don't you?

Mona Of course I do.

Susan In love?

Mona In love? (*Dawning on her.*) Well, yes, I suppose I am. (*Pause.*) But we're talking being 'lovers'!

Susan Not that much difference.

Mona Of course not.

Susan I'll come back here around tea-time. I'm auditioning for this small touring production today. This left-wing group are dragging some radical piece all over Britain. They obviously feel they should have a Black person in the group, so I'm going along to keep the side up.

Mona You don't look happy at the prospect of work.

Susan It'll carry me miles away from you.

Mona Don't worry about me. I'll be here when you get back.

Blackout.

Scene Three

Mona's flat. The morning after.

Mona Now that I think about it, who was always there for me? Susan. Where was Michael when I needed him? It doesn't bear thinking about!

What about when I couldn't find a job? Was I depressed! What miserable company I must've been! She was here, though. She stayed, she listened.

Who came up with the suggestion? She did. 'If you can't find a job,' she said, 'create yourself one.' So, I did. I started holding exercise classes at the local school. A few newspaper ads and I was away! She not only picked me up, she helped me find a way.

Maybe we've always been lovers? I'd never made love to her before, but maybe we've always been lovers? I always turn to her when I need comfort. I always turn to her when I need help. Maybe we've always been lovers.

The doorbell rings. **Mona** *opens the door,* **Susan** *stands there.* **Mona** *puts her arms around* **Susan**. *The two hold each other for a while.*

Susan   What a welcome!

Mona *pulls away and goes over to the sofa. Silence.*

Susan (*with sarcasm*)   No, no, I won't be rushed. I know you're anxious to hear how the audition went but I won't be rushed.

Silence.

No, no, you'll have to control yourself. Let me make myself some tea first, then I'll tell you.

She goes into the kitchen to put the kettle on, comes back out, sits down next to **Mona** *and waits expectantly.*

Mona   OK, what happened?

Susan (*calmly*)   I got in. Starting Thursday, I'll be doing two weeks' rehearsals and a three-week tour with the Network Theatre Group.

Mona (*kissing her*)   Well, congratulations.

Susan   Does that mean I can go out and buy some vino?

Mona   Oh, yes, definitely!

Susan   Yes-I!

She goes back into the kitchen to make her tea.

Mona   What are this group about?

Susan   They're some political group but they don't seem too heavy.

Mona   What's the play about?

Susan   Unemployment, the dole, depressed school-leavers, you know the stuff.

She comes back in with her tea.

The people in the group seem rather nice. (*Beat.*) You look a bit down, girl.

Pause.

Don't tell me: another eventful night with Michael. He hasn't done the decent thing and killed himself, has he?

Mona *is not amused.*

Susan If he's gone: good! Come on, Mona, what could be wrong? If he's gone: good! If he's gone, then it's a blessing!

Mona (*pause*)   He's gone.

Susan Praise the lord! You're free!

Mona (*pause*)   When I went to see Michael yesterday, I immediately felt there was something wrong. I knew he'd been with somebody because there was a stale smell of fuck in the air and the room felt different. I got the feeling I was intruding on something. I didn't want to say anything just in case I was wrong, but I felt really isolated as if I was in an affair that Michael had left long ago. Michael's body was there but Michael was not there.

Susan Mona, he was a poor specimen. You can do much better than him.

Mona Anyway, we spend the night together, but when I wake up Michael's gone and all that's left is a letter. Something about the relationship losing momentum and how he wants to end it because he doesn't think we've got any future.

Susan Fairly standard.

Mona So, that's it.

Susan Good!

Mona I don't really care.

Susan A really poor specimen. You could easily find better.

Mona Maybe.

Susan You idolized him.

Mona I know.

Susan He saw that and took advantage of you.

Mona True.

Susan It was no basis for a relationship.

Mona (*pause*)   Have you ever been in love, you know, like it is in those Mills & Boon books? Have you ever been really, pathetically sloppy?

Susan Me? No, man!

Mona You must have!

Susan I can't really say I've felt that 'head over heels' feeling.

Mona It's nice.

Susan Is it?

Mona You'll feel it one day.

Susan I can't believe I'll feel that way about a man.

Mona Remember what your mother taught you: you're not a woman unless you have a man to look after. Unless you have the love of a man, you're not a real woman.

Susan It doesn't make sense to me at all. Don't you remember when we first came here? We were – what? – eleven or twelve? Boys were the last thing on our mind! We wanted to be film stars, didn't we? We didn't want those little boys trailing round after us anymore.

We'd just spent the first twelve years of our lives splashing around in a river. Then what did we do? We fell for those same lines. We fell for that same sweet-talk and climbed right back into the river!

Back home, we made these plans, didn't we? We were going to become rich, fly home, drive into town in our big cars and take care of our grandparents. Look at us! When did we last go home? When did we last send them money?

Things like Michael have been nothing but distraction. Distraction and destruction. He's kept you apart from your family, apart from your career and apart from me.

Women don't need men, I'm telling you. A man rapes a woman, so what? The judge is a man too! They think they can do whatever they want with a woman! Little girls as well! Sometimes I think the greatest mistake we women make is the breeding of more men!

Mona (*giggling*) Well, you know what I was thinking about last night? While Michael was doing his stuff, you know what I was thinking about? The time I lost my virginity.

While Michael was doing his thing, I suddenly realized I didn't feel any different. He was no different to that first guy and I knew nothing more about sex.

When I was about fifteen, I used to know this guy. It was innocent. A peck on the cheek, holding hands on the way home. Then, all of a sudden, he put this proposition to me which was more like blackmail! He said that unless I went to bed with him, he wouldn't go out with me again.

Susan So?

Mona So I did! But for what? For nothing! It wasn't much cop!

Susan I was so young – when I lost mine – that I can't really remember much about it. I was only about eight or nine.

Mona How old?!

Susan They don't care how old you are in the West Indies! If you can say 'hello' you're no longer a child! I remember I didn't bleed and, at first, I thought he hadn't done it, but he had. Nobody knew. I didn't tell anyone.

Mona No pain?

Susan Nothing. Nothing at all. I was numb all the way through.

Mona Who was he?

Susan I can't remember. It's part of the way of life over there, isn't it? It happens and everyone turns a blind eye.

Do you know what really hurts? The fact that I wasn't given a choice how I should experience my first fuck. Caribbean girls don't have the chance to enjoy childhood, we're capatulted into womanhood from an early age! How can I help but feel a special warmth towards other Black women. You see, not only do I love you but I know how it is to be how you are. Sorry if I embarrass you but I love you. You're beautiful. Everything you do has beauty in it. You radiate! I know you haven't had it easy but still you've become strong and wise and independent. You inspire confidence. I love you because you listen to everything I say, and you're always truthful. The love I feel for you is one I could never feel for a man.

Long pause.

Mona (*dumbly*) OK.

Susan OK what?

Mona OK, I hear what you're saying. What do you want me to say?

Susan (*smiles*) No, there's nothing I want you to say. I just wanted to let it all come out . . .

Mona That's cool.

Susan . . . and to propose myself as an alternative to Michael.

Mona That's not so cool.

Susan You're so reserved, though. You've never been one for expressing emotions. I remember when we were kids, I remember telling you that you were my best friend, but you never told me I was yours.

Mona Of course you were my best friend. You still are. Of course I love you. I always have and always will, but now we're talkin' somethin' else! You want to settle down and have a family with me?

Susan Why not? A few kids, an estate car, family holidays.

Mona (*shaking her head*) Back home, it's different. Two girls can walk along the street, arm in arm, and no one will bat an eyelid. You know that. We were intimate, yes. We loved each other, yes. But you didn't have to ask me to be your lover. It was the natural thing to do.

Susan My point precisely!

Mona Things haven't changed, and yet you're talking to me about some kind of marriage.

Susan I'm grown-up. I want to live with you.

Mona Michael's been part of me for a long time. It's going to take time to get that out of my system. (*Pause.*) I'm sure I can get over it.

Overjoyed, **Susan** *hugs and kisses* **Mona**.

Susan Getting over a love affair is a traumatic time. You can come to me and cry on my shoulder.

Mona And you'll start telling me about mortgages, insurance schemes, bulk-buying and home-improvement!

Susan There's nothing wrong with being house-proud!

Pause.

Mona Funny. I was remembering all the good times we had as kids. The fun we used to have at school. Those early morning smells: granny cooking bakes, the woman selling milk outside.

Susan And the silly things we used to do!

Mona Going to the most dangerous places just to pick fruit!

Susan What was it called?

Mona Washcase (*pronounced 'Wash-kassay'*).

Susan The things I used to believe! Remember that time at Washcase I gashed my knee and my grandmother told me that if I let any boy see my knee something terrible would happen?

Mona Mine told me that if I looked too long in the mirror, the devil's face would appear!

Susan I liked the rainy season best. It was like having a shower in the open. We just ran around in the street, didn't we?

Mona At seven o'clock, we used to gather around and listen to our grandparents telling stories or singing.

Susan All the women would sit outside in the yard cooking, talking, putting out, washing, feeding children and cursing the old drunk that hung around hoping to cadge a meal. *Mal cochon*! *Mal chien*! But he'd get his meal eventually.

Mona My mother threw my father out once, after a drunken fight. But she took him back after a few days, only to discover that she had a few more step-sons and step-daughters.

Susan Our mothers vowed to themselves that the men their daughters set up with would be different, but they never were.

Mona It was for the woman to hold the family together. The men drifted in and out like irritating mosquitoes, and no matter how much the women swatted them, they still seemed to be there.

Susan That's why Caribbean girls are instilled with a special sense of responsibility, a special type of strength. Men breed, men earn money, but where can a woman look for support and friendship?

Mona My auntie brought up seven children by herself. She didn't even get his income. All on her own. Not a man in sight. She didn't need one, though.

Susan After they got what they wanted, the men left like thieves in the night.

Blackout.

Scene Four

Mona's *flat. Evening.* **Mona** *exercises to a bouncy tune. A knock at the door.* **Mona** *stops her cassette machine to answer the door.* **Michele** *follows her into the room.* **Mona** *continues doing a few more bends and stretches.*

Michele Wish I was as firm as you!

Mona I bet parts of you are very fit!

Michele Do you think I should exercise?

Mona You probably don't need to. I'm sure all your limbs get stretched fairly regularly.

Michele Well, it's a lot cheaper than aerobics classes.

Mona *picks up a towel and dries herself.* **Michele** *paces about uneasily.*

Mona And to what do I owe the pleasure?

Michele Well . . . I need a couple of favours, don't I?

Mona Are Susan and I your only friends?

Michele Well . . .

Mona You know why? 'Cause you're a real pain in the perineum!

Michele I don't want much.

Mona Whatever you want, Michele.

Michele You know that nice, blue, patterned dress you've got?

Mona What about the last dress you took?

Michele Have I still got that?

Mona Somewhere!

Michele (*thinks*) Oh, yes, I know why I haven't brought it back. I haven't had time to wash it. Look, I'll bring both dresses back at the same time.

Mona Going anywhere nice?

Michele Just out.

Mona Do you think if I had a baby I'd get asked out as much as you do?

Michele I'm not going out with anyone, I'm just going out. If I had to stay in with my baby every night – as well as every day – I'd go loopy! I might even turn into a baby-batterer!

Mona A very convincing argument. So, you're going out with anyone but you are going out? (*Thinks.*) Gosh, isn't this fun? (*Thinks.*) I've got it! You're not going *out* with someone – you're going *to* someone!

Michele Sort of. (*Pause.*) And there's something else.

Mona Oh, yes, I forgot; a *couple* of favours.

Michele Will you or Sue come over and babysit?

Mona Well, I don't know.

Michele Maybe I could bring him over?

Mona How do you know Susan and I haven't planned a little candlelit dinner together?

Michele (*smiling*) Candelit dinner! Come on, is it OK?

Mona How do you know Susan and I don't want the evening to ourselves?

Michele Look, if you want to get charged or drunk at my place, it's cool.

Mona Susan's got a job on a touring production, she'll need time for the show. I probably won't see her until the end of the production.

Michele Mona, I don't see what the problem is. You can both babysit together.

Mona Maybe we'd like to spend tonight alone?

Michele You can both babysit together! What do you mean you'd like to spend the evening 'alone'? You will be alone! You're not going to want to get into bed before midnight, are you?

Mona We might.

Michele *stares at* **Mona**.

Michele 'We'? (*Smiling.*) Don't wind me up!

Mona Michele, I am not winding you up.

Michele I think you're serious!

Mona I am serious.

Michele (*pause*) You and Susan?

Mona Me and Susan.

Michele *stares at* **Mona** *again.*

Michele Stop fooling around, Mona. I know you don't want to babysit, but I promise he won't make a sound. Put him to bed and you can do what you want!

Mona (*sighs*) Battered into submission! Bring him over later.

Michele, *relieved, kisses* **Mona**.

Michele I don't know what I'd do without you. (*Pause.*) You weren't serious were you, Mona? About you and Susan?

Mona What if I was, Michele? Does that mean you'll stop borrowing my clothes?

Michele Mona, tell me straight.

Mona Yes, I'm serious.

Michele Oh, come on, Mona. Truthfully?

Mona (*exasperated*) Michele, what do you want to do? Inspect the sheets?

Michele (*rambling*) But . . . Mona . . . but . . .

Mona You're shocked?

Michele Nah, man, you can't have!

Mona What's so shocking about two women making love?

Michele Mona, you haven't!

Mona Oh, this is priceless! The liberated woman is going to tell me I can't sleep with another woman!

Michele Mona . . .

Michele *pulls repulsed faces.*

Michele Another woman?

Mona Michele, take the dress and piss off! There's no way I'm going to listen to your thoughts on morality. You drag your fanny from bed to bed and you're going to tell me I'm perverse! Go away!

Michele (*pause*) Your mother would be heartbroken!

Mona We don't intend taking my mother to bed with us!

Michele She'll find out! Michael will find out! What's going to happen to him?

Mona He'll be OK.

Michele Does he know?

Mona He'll find out soon enough!

Michele That's no way to treat him!

Mona Isn't it? Didn't I tell you? Michael's left me. Gone. I have been left.

He wrote me this heartfelt note in which he thanked me for opening my legs – without complaint – twice a week for the last five years. Twice on my birthday! The note continued: he didn't think my pussy would hold an endless fascination for him, and he was moving on to crotches new. I think it's time for a little romance in my life. Susan says she loves me. It's a long time since I heard someone say that. Susan told me she loved me. I liked the sound of that.

Michele (*stunned*)   It's sick!

Mona   Michele, take the dress and go away!

Michele   Forget about tonight!

Enter **Susan**.

Mona   Cutting yourself off from us, are you? Think we'll infect you and your child, do you?

Michele   I don't think it's right, that's all. I don't know how you can say all these things! I know you're not a lesbian.

Mona   How do you know?

Michele   Because I know you. I've known you from time, so I know you're not. Look, I can tell one.

Mona   How? Describe a lesbian to me.

Michele   I just know. You see enough of them down Moseley! Hair-cropped looking like man in trousers, braces, big boots, badges there . . .

Susan (*to* **Mona**)   Michele's shocked! You haven't had girlfriends, Michele? I thought you'd done it all!

Michele (*to* **Mona**)   Look, I can tell a lesbian from a heterosexual! And I know you're not a lesbian. (*To* **Susan**.) I don't know about you!

Mona   Stop giving it names. This person says she loves me. We all need someone to love us.

Michele   But I went to school with you. I've been out with you.

Mona   That doesn't say anything!

Michele   'Course it does!

Mona   What?

Michele   It says you weren't born that way. You have to be born a lesbian. It's a biological thing. You don't suddenly wake up and you're a lesbian.

Susan (*to* **Mona**)   Has she got a degree in biology that I don't know about?

Michele (*to* **Susan**)   Look, I'm not listening to you! You've obviously got a hormone deficiency!

Susan   So, you mean the way you carry on is OK? Having all those men, apart from not helping your child, is very unhealthy. Disease, Michele, promiscuity carries disease.

Michele I'm not talking to you! I know you don't like me!

Mona Cut it out, you two. Michele, look, you'll just have to get used to it.

Michele No, man! No way! It's not normal! It's an abomination against man and God!

Susan Michele, if you think we're such sinners, just go! You need never see us again.

Michele, *still trying to save* **Mona**, *takes her aside.*

Michele (*to* **Susan**) You keep out of it! (*To* **Mona**.) Do you know what lesbians do? Do you know what people think of lesbians?

Susan What now!

Michele (*to* **Mona**) It's dirty! You can't make love to another woman! It's not natural!

Susan There's more to it than that, but you're so bloody small-minded, you can't see it!

Michele Yeah? I can see – just as plain as day – that you've poisoned Mona with this lesbian crap. Just because you're incapable of loving a man, that doesn't give you the right to mess up other people's lives. I blame you for this. You're sick! It's your fault you fucking, filthy, dyke bitch!

Susan *walks over and slaps* **Michele**'s *face.* **Michele** *grabs her hair and the two begin to fight, rolling around on the ground.* **Mona** *dives in to separate them.*

Mona Now just hold on there, girl! Michele, if you haven't understood what we've been saying, then you never will. So, just take your backside and go!

Michele If that's the way you feel about it, Mona, I'll go, but you'll never see me again, that's for sure!

She exits, slamming the door. A few seconds' pause while calm is restored.

Mona She wants us to babysit for her tonight. She'll be back.

Blackout.

Scene Five

Mona's *flat. The morning before* **Susan** *leaves for her tour.* **Mona** *and* **Susan** *share a breakfast of tea and toast.*

Mona You're eating too fast.

Susan I'm going to be late.

Mona You really will be late if you throw up. Slow down, nah!

Susan I'm sure I've forgotten something.

Mona Everybody always does. There's no point worrying. Everybody forgets something when they pack.

Susan So what have I forgotten?

Mona Have you remembered a pen and some stationery?

Susan What for?

Mona What for! To write to me!

Susan I'll write.

Mona I bet you forget.

Susan Three weeks, Mona! It's only three weeks! I bet you're glad to be rid of me!

Mona On the contrary! I've got used to it and I think I like having you around.

Susan Have I passed the audition?

Mona I like your cooking.

Susan Is that all?

Mona I like having you around. It's been . . . interesting. (*Pause.*) Michael and I tried living together, remember?

Susan I remember how bad-tempered you were.

Mona It was hell, wasn't it? He expected me to clean up behind him, iron his shirts, be a wife. That took the romance out of things! Living with you is different, though. I feel secure. What have we done? Nothing. We just sat around, watched telly, got charged, but I really enjoy myself. You make me feel at home. I know it is my home, but I've never felt so at home. It feels right.

Susan *stares at* **Mona**, *half-moved, half-stunned.*

Mona What's wrong with you?

Susan I think I'm going to cry.

Mona Don't take the piss!

Susan I'm not! That was . . . really . . . touching. You . . . like me?

Mona Of course I bloody like you! I think I'm used to it. We're lovers. If they don't like it, they can lump it.

Susan You don't have to say 'lovers'. There's a Dominican word for it: 'zammie'. Tell people we're zammies.

I couldn't just take up with any woman tomorrow. She'd have to be someone who understands what I've been through. Someone who I'd known for a long time. It would have to be spiritual.

I can't hate Michele. She's the same as me. I'm not going to criticize any Black woman. I know where she's coming from. We all share a spiritual bond. You and I have just taken it one step on.

She looks at her watch.

Look at the time! I knew I should've eaten fast!

Mona   Zammies.

Susan   Tell them we're zammies.

Mona   That's a word I haven't heard for a long time. I remember Mummy used to use that word when she was talking about an old friend of hers. Zammies! Yes-I!

Susan *gets up and begins packing things into bags.*

Susan   If they want to know about zammies, tell them about their basin. All Black women know about their basin.

Some don't have hot water, some need the hot water to wash their kids, some don't have time to take a bath! We all know about boiling a pan of water and using a basin to wash ourself.

My mother gave me my own basin when I was about four. I think it was probably the first thing I possessed. Just before we went to bed, my mother would tell us, 'Go wash your kookalook!' That was when I first became conscious of being a woman and what it meant to be feminine. That was when I first began to think about my mother, and her mother.

Mona   At the end of another, long, unrewarding day, they'd wash themselves in preparation for the evening's ritual. No matter how tired they felt, they had to wash themselves in case their husbands wanted to make love.

Susan   Zammies. It's spiritual. Don't tell them about love, they'll never equate two women with love. Just tell them about their basin if they can't understand what's happened to us.

She has gathered together a suitcase and some holdalls, and has put on her coat.

Now I have to go.

Mona *gets up and hugs* **Susan**.

Mona   You're really something! You will call me, won't you?

Susan   Three weeks will pass in no time. (*Pause.*) I feel really good. I'm working, and my love life has finally come together. (*Pause.*) I hope. (*Pause.*) Thanks.

Mona   You're thanking me?

Susan   I'm grateful. Thanks.

Mona *kisses her.*

Susan   My pleasure.

They embrace again. Blackout.

Act Two

Scene One

Mona's *flat. Some days later.* **Mona** *reads a letter from* **Susan**.

Mona (*reading aloud*) 'My dearest Mona, I miss you very much and wish you were with me sharing the many wonderful moments we experience. Wherever we go, people are hospitable. Wherever we perform, audiences are generous. Because we're not playing in cities, we don't spend much time on boring motorways. Riding around the backroads of an area has proved fascinating. Performing in small village halls has meant winding our way through beautiful country roads. This is my kind of touring. Instead of stopping at service stations and eating greasy food, we stop in scenic pubs and share fresh food and conversation with the locals.'

Well, I'm glad you're having fun!

(*Reading aloud.*) 'The members of the company have proved stimulating companions.'

I wonder which part of you they're stimulating?

(*Reading aloud.*) 'After every performance we have long interrogations into the faults of the night's show. I've learnt so much.'

How fulfilling!

(*Reading aloud.*) 'I've made numerous friends on this tour and when I come home I'll invite them over so you can meet them.'

I don't want to meet any of your fucking friends.

You don't need me.

She paces about, her body full of tension.

What does she take me for? Does she think I'll sit in here waiting for her to finish screwing the entire company?

She stops suddenly, taking stock of herself.

Oh God! What am I saying?

The doorbell rings. She goes to answer it. **Michele** *stands at the door.*

Michele (*cheerfully*)   Hi!

Mona   What are you doing here?

Michele *stands uncomfortably in the doorway trying to get in.*

Michele   Are you going to let me come in or what?

Mona   Girl, what are you doing on my doorstep?

Pause.

Michele I've brought your dress and shoes back.

Mona *finally lets* **Michele** *in. The two women walk into the room.*

Michele The dress has been dry cleaned.

Mona *looks at the dress in disbelief. (The dress hangs from a hanger, covered in a clear, plastic cover.)*

Mona Is it my birthday?

Michele So, Mon', how are you?

Mona All right. (*Pause.*) No that's a lie.

Michele What's wrong?

Mona You don't want to know.

Michele I do.

Mona You don't.

Michele What? Is it something to do with you and Susan?

Mona I wouldn't want to shock you.

Michele So what's wrong?

Mona I miss her.

Michele (*embarrassed*) Oh.

Mona I shocked you, anyway.

Michele So? You miss her.

Mona She's been gone ten days and only this morning I get a letter.

Michele Ten days? So what? What's the matter, woman? Ten days? I thought she'd left you!

Mona (*thinks*) Yeah . . . ten days . . . so what? You don't want to listen to me. I get irrational when I fall in love.

Michele You're serious about this thing you and Sue are having aren't you? Got anything to drink?

Mona In the kitchen.

Michele May I?

Mona Of course.

Michele *lays the dress over the sofa and goes into the kitchen.*

Michele So, how are you otherwise?

Mona (*thinks*) I'm wound-up. I'm irrational.

Michele *re-enters with a glass of orange juice.*

Michele You're what?

Mona Irrational.

Michele Why?

Mona You wouldn't know about it. It's all related to love. You're lucky, you don't suffer from such complaints, you just fuck.

I haven't seen you in a while. I wonder why?

Michele (*pause*) That whole thing about you and Susan . . . it came as a bit of a surprise. I want to apologize for all that noise I made. It was just a bit of a shock to my system, telling me about it so directly.

Mona You came here just to tell me that? You haven't come to borrow anything? You don't want me to do you a favour? What happened to you, woman?

Michele I don't always come round when I want something.

Mona But you do! Maybe we're not the only ones who have changed?

Michele I just came here to bring the dress back, apologize and find out how you are. I haven't seen you for a while.

Mona Yeah but I know what you've been doing! You've got a lot to answer for. I was appalled by your outburst last week and now I discover that the whole district knows about my business.

Michele Mona, honest . . . I only . . . well, what did you expect me to do?

Mona Michele, if you told one person, that's all it takes. If you say to someone, 'Now, you promise not to tell anyone else', that person will run straight to someone else. You see, you shouldn't have told that first person.

Michele (*remorseful*) Mona, I'm sorry . . . girl. I've known you for so long . . . and now you tell me you're getting into women . . .

Mona Be sensible, Michele. I'm someone who's been honest, you probably know lots of people who're afraid to be honest. Think about it: there are probably cousins of yours that are gay but do you think they'd tell you! 'Course they wouldn't! Look at the fuss you're making!

Michele It's just . . . I've known you for so long . . .

Mona I don't like your attitude. I thought we were friends. You never have anything nice to say about people. Everybody's now talking about Susan and I. Not that I mind but you should have more respect for your friends.

I don't want an argument with you. We can't spend our whole lives fighting with one another. Tell me, what made you so uncaring? How come you hate so much? You make it so hard for people to understand you, you make it so hard for people to like you, no wonder you have so few friends!

Maybe you've forgotten what good friends Susan and I have been to you. We all understood each other, and that was special, and that's why I can't believe you can't understand Susan and I.

Michele, we're all in the same boat. We all have so much in common. Black women have so much in common, so why are we arguing? Who will love us? White people? Black men? Who will love us if not other Black women?

I'm the one who's always making an effort. I'm tired of caring for people, selfish people. You should make the best of a friendship like this.

Michele I don't want to be your enemy. I do care about you and Susan. It's taken me a long time to understand how you and Susan had become lovers. I'd known you for so long. I had no idea you had those tendencies. Me? I like the love of man. I'd do anything for the love of a man!

Maybe you think I'm loose. You tell me I think about men too much. What am I supposed to do? I mean, what am I on this earth for? I don't know. To breed? Well, I've done that. I've done my bit. Now I want to enjoy myself. I'll be old soon. I'll be dead soon after that. I want to enjoy myself. You can understand that?

That's what I now realize. You're happy. You want to enjoy yourself, and you've found out how. You've told me how men will hurt me but, well, it's a physical thing. Men make me feel good.

Maybe I'm like my mother? No matter what my father did to her, she stuck with him. Sometimes the man would come home, fight with my mother and that used to hurt me so much because neither of us could control him.

Mona Why didn't your mother leave?

Michele She said she had nowhere to go. She said that my father was the only man she knew. Whenever they had problems, my mother used to say to me that we had to stick together because, back home, families stuck together. Back home, she'd been taught that blood was thicker than water.

Daddy was so possessive, so violent. He used to love us in a very primitive way. That's why I left. I couldn't bear to hear her cry anymore. The only way I could've left home and got a flat was to get myself pregnant. That's why I'm now imprisoned in my home.

Mona That's why you should treat other Black women as zammies. So many of them are imprisoned in their homes by their children. So many of them have to fight with their husbands at night.

Michele Zammies? What are they?

Mona It comes from '*ami*'; French for friend. Only in Dominica, it's more than friendship. It's not only comfort, it's not only companionship, it's not only physical.

Zammies are friends, spiritual friends; zammies know about each other without knowing each other. Zammies are not necessarily lovers.

Black women know things that only Black women know. They have so much in common. Susan and I won't preach to you about men, but you must consider us your zammies.

Michele I know what you're saying.

Mona Have you got a basin?

Michele I used to have. Why did you ask that?

Mona I just wondered.

Michele *gets up and makes to leave.*

Michele Listen, I have to go. See? I didn't come to borrow anything or to ask any favours!

She kisses **Mona**.

Michele I'll call you in a few days.

Mona See ya.

Exit **Michele**.

Mona *thinks for a second then begins looking around to see where she discarded* **Susan**'s *letter. She finds it and begins to straighten it out. The phone rings.* **Mona** *looks at the phone.*

Mona It can't be!

She picks the phone up.

Hello?

On the other side of the stage, **Susan** *talks into a pay phone.*

Susan Hello, darling.

Mona It can't be!

Susan It's me, Susan.

Mona I know who it is. After ten days I finally get a letter and a phone call. Wow! All in the same day! What, did you forget your own number?

Susan Don't give me a hard time, we've been really busy.

Mona What, interrogating each other? Having scholarly discussions after supper?

Susan Mona, what's wrong?

Mona What could be wrong? You've been away for ten days, not a word from you, I've been worried . . .

Susan Ah, isn't that nice.

Mona . . . then, this morning, a letter arrives. No, 'letter' would be dignifying the garbled note I received. Now, lo and behold it's the first phone call.

Susan Mona, I've been busy.

Mona I'm sure. Basking in the stimulating company and making friends? Have you made some nice friends?

Susan I do believe you're jealous.

Mona Me? You carry on! You can pass out your pussy amongst the cast. Don't worry about me.

Susan What are you saying? What do you think I'm doing out here?

Mona I don't know.

Susan You think I'm screwing around!

Mona You say you've been busy.

Susan Woman, you're jealous! I don't believe it! Well, kiss me granny neck-back!

Mona Don't be silly, Susan. I haven't heard from you in ten days, you should have called . . .

Susan But I suppose if you're jealous, that must mean you've fallen for me too. That's nice to know.

Mona I'm not jealous, I was just worried. I thought maybe something had happened. I thought they wouldn't know my number . . .

Susan You've fallen for me too!

Mona Come now, Susan . . .

Susan So you care about me!

Mona Course I bloody care! Come on, you'd be worried too.

Susan And what's all this about me having all these affairs?

Mona Keep me in contact, will you please? If you don't know how to use a phone box, ask a grown-up to help you.

Susan What's all this flak for?

Mona Just call me, please.

Susan Do you miss me?

Mona No way! I've had the entire West Indian cricket team keep me company all week!

Susan Mona, please!

Mona Oh sorry, I don't want to distress you. I wouldn't want to affect tonight's performance.

Susan Darling, I have to go. I'm phoning from a petrol station.

Mona Go, go, don't worry about me.

Susan I'll be home in a few days.

Mona Now there's something to look forward to!

Susan I love you.

Mona Do you?

Susan Yes, and I really miss you.

Mona Then call me.

Susan I will and I'll be home soon. Bye, Mona.

Mona Bye, Princess.

She puts the phone down and looks down at her feet, disgusted at herself. She stalks around the room.

I mean, who needs Michael? Susan causes me just as much distress, what do I need Michael for?

Zammies, huh? If we're so zammie-zammie, how come you don't call me? You said you understood me. If you did you'd call me.

Yeah, we're zammies, but I'm in love with you as well. That'll cause me the problems it always does.

Blackout.

Scene Two

*Mona's flat. A Saturday afternoon. **Mona** is curled up on the sofa with a book. The doorbell rings. She gets up to open the door. **Michele** stands in the doorway, beaming, a bottle of wine in her hand.*

Michele You haven't got any plans for this afternoon, have you?

*She embraces **Mona**, hands her the wine and comes into the room.*

Mona Look at you! Look at the smile on your face!

Michele I feel good.

Mona Really?

Michele Here all alone?

Mona Just me.

Michele Good, that means we can sit down, drink this bottle of wine, chat and get merry.

Mona What's the matter with you?

Michele I got a job.

Mona *embraces* **Michele**.

Mona That's great! Congratulations. Doing what?

Michele General duties in that bingo hall on the high street.

Mona You in a bingo hall? That's a joke!

*Silence. Stony glare from **Michele**.*

Mona Really good news!

Michele It's a start. It'll be boring and dirty, I'm sure, but I took your advice, I got a job. Now I won't have to keep borrowing so often.

Mona It never bothered me. Look, we're friend and what are friends for?

Michele Nah, you can't keep borrowing and scrounging all your life. Besides, I was getting lazy. You know, laying in until midday, watching TV all day. My big arse was really beginning to spread out.

I was getting lazy and I was running out of people to go to. I went into my mother's to have some supper and she hardly had enough for two, let alone four! That was it! I thought, my God, my mother's run out, she's got nothing left to give me. That really hurt: my poor mother going without. I think it's about time I gave a little back to my old mum.

Mona That's really good. I'm glad you're getting yourself together.

Michele I met this really nice girl at the bingo hall. I thought the place was going to be full of stuffy, white people but there's this Black girl there, just a few years older than me. A really nice girl called Thelma. We got on right from the word go. Chat, chat, chat. We talked for hours!

She told me about this friend of hers. This is a really sad story. Thelma's just found out that this friend of hers is having an affair with her man. Thelma said she'd known the girl since they were in primary school, since they were in skirts and socks. One day, the girl breaks down in front of Thelma and tells her she's in love with Thelma's man. Thelma says to her, 'How does my man feel about this?' The girl says, 'I think he loves me too.' Thelma says 'You can keep him!'

Mona Damn right!

Michele Is she?

Mona If my man's in love with another woman, what use is he to me? I'd get over him. What's the point of staying with someone if their mind is on someone else? The girl's smart! Fuck him! She's better off without him.

Michele You really wouldn't worry if it was happening to you?

Mona No, not at all.

Michele It wouldn't matter if the man you were in love with was having an affair with a friend of yours?

Mona Good luck to them!

Michele *goes into the kitchen and brings out a corkscrew and two glasses. She pulls the cork out of the bottle and pours the wine as the next lines are being said.*

Mona So, you'll be all right, you've got this girl to talk to?

Michele Yeah, she's nice.

Mona And the money's OK?

Michele It's not bad.

Mona How many hours?

Michele As many as I want.

Mona And the baby?

Michele Mum says she'll take care of him.

Mona That's great.

Michele *takes a sip of her wine and sits back almost looking as if the conversation has come to a complete end. Rather mystified,* **Mona** *reclines as well.*

Michele Mona . . .

Pause.

Mona What's wrong?

Michele I know about the letter.

Mona What letter?

Michele The letter from Michael.

Mona His letter to me?

Michele Yes. I know why he wrote it.

Mona Did I tell you about that?

Michele No, Michael did.

Mona Oh, that's nice. Why is Michael telling everyone about my business?

Michele I know what he wrote in the letter . . . and I know why he wrote it . . . and I know that he wrote a pack of lies.

Mona You know more than me. Please, go on.

Michele (*pause*) This is really hard for me.

Mona Don't worry about me, child. Michael's someone who I used to care for, you're not going to hurt anyone's feelings.

Michele Are you sure?

Mona Believe me. We haven't been broken up long but, in that short time, not only have I found someone who loves me but I've realized how little Michael cared. Just tell me, Michele.

Michele He gave you all this crap about how it wouldn't work, how you weren't suited, how we wasn't ready to settle down . . .

Mona That was the gist of it. Well, what's the subtext?

Michele . . . he's in love with me.

Long pause.

Mona Like I said, I'm better off without him.

Michele Mona, I'm really sorry . . .

Mona What are you apologizing for? You don't feel sorry, I'm sure he doesn't feel sorry . . .

Michele . . . I would've told you sooner . . .

Mona You don't have to explain or excuse yourself, I truly mean what I say: what good is Michael to me if it's you he wants?

Michele . . . there was nothing I could do about it . . .

Mona I don't blame anyone. I'm really not that bothered . . .

Michele . . . it sort of happened . . .

Mona . . . everything's fine . . .

Michele . . . I feel really bad . . .

Mona Why? Everything's fine, Michele.

Michele . . . I hope it won't spoil our friendship . . .

Mona MICHELE, EVERYTHING'S FINE!

Long pause.

How long has this been going on?

Michele A few months.

Mona He always fancied you. He knew about your infamous appetite, of course, and he always wondered what it was like making love to a really horny woman. You know, someone who was really into trying everything!

I guess I never really satisfied him. He wanted me to suck him off but I could never really do that, it didn't really turn me on. I guess you must be doing the job properly.

I just feel that there are certain things you should know about him and, because you're a friend, certain things I ought to warn you about.

Michele Like what?

Mona Oh nothing drastic. It's not that he's got some disease he hasn't told you about. Nothing serious. Just some things you might be interested to know.

She picks up the wine bottle and fills up their glasses. With **Michele** *on the edge of her seat,* **Mona** *uses a few moments to further increase* **Michele***'s discomfort, then she begins.*

Mona Michael's breath has a smell all of its own, doesn't it? I think it's because he puts so much salt and pepper on his food. Have you noticed that?

Michele Yes. Why are you telling me about Michael's breath?

Mona Plus the fact that everything is washed down with Lucozade. Salt, pepper and Lucozade. The combination makes for a very distinctive odour. Does it still smell like that?

Michele I don't really know. He seems to drink a lot of Lucozade.

Mona Does he bite your breasts?

Michele *looks slightly embarrassed.*

Mona Does he?

Michele Mona!

Mona I used to like that. I like the way he bites, it's a harmless kind of bite. Does he still bite like that?

Michele *is silent.*

Mona Does he?

Michele (*embarrassed*)   Sort of.

Mona He'd always make sure I was undressed first. As if he was scared that, having undressed himself, I'd run away! Crazy guy! Is he still like that?

Michele Why are you asking me all of this?

Mona So, most times, he'd undress me first, make sure I was there, in bed, waiting, and then he'd undress himself. Does he still do that?

Michele Sometimes. Why are you asking me all of this?

Mona His impulsiveness excited me, and he became excited for no reason at all; that made things unpredictable. I liked that. Just out of the blue, he'd want to make love, in unlikely places too! We did it in a car once, out in some dark car park. Is he still like that?

Michele I don't know yet.

Mona Is he still so impulsive?

Michele He seems to be.

Mona That's what I loved about him: we did it anywhere. He was such a slag but I suppose that's what I loved about him.

Michele Is there a reason why you're asking all these questions? Why are you acting like this?

Mona There are just a few things I think you ought to know about him . . . and I'm reminiscing.

You know, it's funny, Michael was ony the second boy I'd been to bed with. The first time it'd been just a rushed and embarrassed fiasco which was more enjoyable for him than me, but Michael helped me enjoy making love. Michael was more experienced. I like the way he's able to keep going. Does he still retain his stamina, Michele?

Michele *now looks embarrassed, hurt and close to tears.*

Mona Does he? Michele? Can he still pump and pump and pump until you're sore?

Silence.

Can he, Michele?

Michele Stop it, Mona.

Mona Can he still fuck for so long, Michele?

Michele (*angrily*)   Yes, yes, yes! Mona, stop it!

Mona What's the matter? I'm not embarrassing you, am I? Has he taken you to Blackpool yet?

64   Basin

Michele *looks up slightly shocked.*

Mona   Have you spent the dirty weekend in the hotel in Blackpool? Have you, Michele?

Michele   Yes, yes.

Mona   We did that trip quite a few times. We stayed in the same little hotel, we took the same long walk along the promenade, we spent the same amount of time riding on the big dipper and the big wheel. Did you do that, Michele?

Silence.

Have you done all the things that I did?

Michele (*suppressing tears*)   OK, Mona, that's enough . . .

Mona   Have you done the same things? Of course you have. Michael's still the same person. He's still the same. He's doing the same things and going to the same places.

Michele (*softly sobbing*)   Mona, please . . .

Mona   Ah, but Michele – and here's his *pièce de résistance* – has he told you about this plot of land he's inherited in Dominica? Has he told you about hat?

Silence. **Michele** *cries to herself.* **Mona** *fills up both glasses with wine.*

Mona   Has he told you that, in a few years time, you'll go back to Dominica and build a beautiful house on his plot of land? Has he told you that? Has he?

Michele (*crying – angry*)   Yes!

Mona   Well, that is one of the many lies Michael will tell you. I met his aunt when she was in Lnodon recently and I asked her about Michael's so-called inheritance. When his grandparents die, he'll inherit a broken-down shack, and that's it! That's your dream home!

He tells lies, Michele. He always did and he always will because he'll never change. Michele, that boy will make love to you in the same way he did me, he'll take you to the same places he took me, and he'll probably love you for as long as he loved me, at which point, he'll climb in bed with another girl.

Michele, you're just another month in his calendar.

Michele, *weak from sobbing, collapses into* **Mona***'s arms.*

Blackout.

Scene Three

Michele *asleep on* **Mona***'s couch.* **Mona** *enters, crosses to the kitchen, puts the kettle on, comes back out, tickles* **Michele***'s feet.* **Michele** *wakes up suddenly.*

Mona   Morning!

Michele   Mona!

Mona Look at you! Didn't you sleep well? You couldn't fall asleep, could you? You were tossing and turning and then you came out here!

Michele I snore. I didn't want to disturb you.

She gets up.

I'll make some tea.

Mona I've already put the kettle on.

Michele *stops dead in her tracks.*

Mona Don't lie, Michele. You shouldn't be afraid of sleeping with me just because Susan and I have become lovers.

Michele It's not that . . .

Mona How many times we've slept together! What did you think, I was going to molest you?

Michele *looks ashamed.*

Michele Kettle's boiling!

She goes into the kitchen.

Mona No milk, no sugar.

She folds up the blankets that were covering **Michele**. **Michele** *re-enters with two cups of tea.*

Michele I'm going for a wash. Can I borrow some underwear?

Mona Oh, we're back to borrowing are we?

Michele *looks guilty.*

Mona Only joking, Michele.

Pause.

Michele About last night. You made me realize a lot of things. I know Michael has his faults, I know men do, but I couldn't feel for a woman the way I feel for a man.

Mona I wasn't trying to convert you!

Michele I know, I still love and respect you and Susan, but you mustn't condemn me for loving Michael. Sometimes people find themselves unable to resist things that are bad for them.

Mona I know how you feel, girl. Believe me. I loved him once, didn't I?

Michele Thank you for understanding. Even if I'd tried to stop myself falling for Michael, how long could I have stopped myself? How could I have stopped Michael falling for me? You know how he is!

Mona I know what you love about him. I know precisely what you love about him. I won't condemn you for loving Michael.

Michele I know how he is but I've grown used to men and their ways. I've accepted affection where it's been given. If someone wants to love me, I'm happy. Some people go through life waiting for a love that doesn't exist! There's no such thing as everlasting love, so I just get love where I can. I think Michael loves me, I don't know how long he'll love me for but I'm happy!

Mona Sometimes you love someone and it's hard to explain to other people what you love about that person, but you just can't help yourself.

I'm not much better. Look what I've fallen in love with! It doesn't matter what sex you fall in love with. It's all too much hurt and worry.

Keys in the front door. **Susan** *bursts in.* **Mona** *and* **Susan** *embrace.* **Michele** *looks slightly embarrassed, and puts her shoes on.*

Susan What, Michele, can't you say, 'Hello, Susan, did you have a nice time?'

Michele Hello, Susan. Did you have a nice time?

Susan Yes, thank you.

Michele *gathers up her bag and makes to leave.*

Michele I have to pick up Tony from my mum's.

Susan What's the hurry, Michele?

Michele I'm sure you've got lots to talk about.

Susan Don't you want to hear about it?

Michele Must go, really. See you, Mona, Susan.

She exits.

Susan She looks so embarrassed.

Mona *and* **Susan** *hug again.*

Mona So you decided to come home!

Susan What was I going to do?

Mona I thought you might have decided to shack up with somebody else!

Susan Like who? What are you talking about?

Mona One letter, one phone call. A bit low on your priority list, aren't I?

Susan I don't believe this! Mona, it was really hectic! I'm sorry I didn't phone more often, I was just really caught up in things.

Mona Make friends, did you?

Susan Of course I did ! (*Smiles.*) Come on, Mona, you're not giving me the whole suspicion-of-adultery routine.

Mona Haven't you got an innocent face? I'm almost inclined to believe you, but I don't.

Susan (*half angry/shocked*)   I don't believe what I'm hearing! This is really taking me back to my youth. I used to give this whole number to my boyfriends. I used to do this whole offended and mistreated act.

I didn't know you were the jealous type.

Mona It doesn't really matter what you've done. You've had fun. I've had fun.

Susan You've actually gone to the extent of sleeping with someone just to spite me? I like your idea of a steady relationship. You're so childish. You think I've spent the entire tour fornicating my way down the credits in the programme? This is ridiculous!

Mona, is it always gonna be like this? I thought you understood what I meant by being 'zammies'!

Mona You got me into this, you know. I was a peaceful, law-abiding heterosexual. True, I was co-habiting with a skunk, but at least he was male!

Susan Maybe I should be flattered? Maybe I am. Mona, tell me, did you really fuck around?

Mona 'Course I fucked around! What, did you expect me to wait in for your call? I went out, met someone, had a few drinks, back to their place. You know how it is. I enjoyed it, but it was nothing serious.

Susan Oh yeah?

Mona All right, then, you know that's a lie.

Yes, I am the jealous type. Just slightly. It's taken me a long time to realize but, yes, I am – and I always was – in love with you.

Susan What!

Mona You heard!

Susan Girl, you're mad. Truly mad. So you feel for me, do you?

Mona No big deal.

Susan *smiles. The two embrace.*

Mona You'll never guess what?

Susan What?

Mona Michele's been having an affair with Michael for the last few months!

Susan You lie!

Mona She thinks they're in love!

Susan Nah!

Mona That's what she came to tell me last night. Where's me present?

Susan Finish the story first.

Mona Anyway . . .

Conversation continues and trails off, swamped by music. Lights fade.

Boy with Beer

Paul Boakye

Boy with Beer was first presented by House of Boache Productions, in association with This is Now Theatre Company, at the Man in the Moon Theatre, London, from 14 January to 1 February 1992, with the following cast:

Karl   Clive Wedderburn
Donovan   Tunde Oba

Directed by Steven Luckie
Designed by John Lynch
Lighting by Nicola Stammers
Sound by Jimmy Mackness
Produced by Paul Boakye and Steven Luckie

The action takes place in a London flat on two levels.

Introduction by Paul Boakye

Back in the early eighties when I was learning to read for pleasure because the lives of Black people were not reflected on British TV, I would recite '*The Politics of Rich Painters*' and other similar poetry to any and everybody who cared to listen. A few years later, when I first started to write, no wonder my thoughts were filled with the language and imagery of Amiri Baraka and the 'agitprop' tones of the Black Power Movement. To my family, friends and colleagues in our part of multiracial London, I was generally considered a very angry young man. 'Too Black, too outspoken, too political, offensive.' It didn't help that I couldn't relate to any concept of 'Black Power' lacking an economic base, nor that I was in a 'mixed-race' relationship at the time, both of which only served to propel my anger at the world and fuel a sense of self-loathing. Amiri Baraka had introduced me to the possibility of writing 'Black', and at the same time writing anything I wanted to (even that which other Black people may not understand or embrace). Blackness was not formulaic, but was it universal? In hindsight, however, I know now that I was writing from a restrictive position of opposition to the world and myself.

James Baldwin's *Giovanni's Room* was the first book I read by a Black author. It may well have been a subconscious inspiration for the play *Boy with Beer*, but at the time, I found the whole novel sombre and very depressing. Yet, that didn't prevent me seeking out other available titles by Baldwin within a ten-mile radius of my local library. I already knew the works of Shakespeare, Dickens and even Mark Twain; now I was hungry to see the contemporary world through the eyes of others who looked more like me. Jimmy served this purpose to a certain extent, but I could not warm to his sentimentality or the overtly religious sermonizing of his novels, that is until I read *Just Above My Head*. That book opened a lot in me because it was so full of love and passions. That's when I started thinking. Up until that point, I was used to reading and writing so much about people who despise us that my priorities had become a bit jaded. *Just Above My Head* was like walking into a Black community and opening the door to a whole other world where wild things happen, but there is still so much devotion. Before then, my heart had been filled with anger and pain at the 'motion of history' as Baraka puts it, but now my characters could live.

When I wrote *Boy with Beer* in 1991, I didn't know what I was doing. My best friend Derek St Louis had just died suddenly of an AIDS-related illness, and I knew that I wanted to commemorate his life, but beyond that I had only some vague idea of taking the concept of self-love to its conclusion. With some plays, you know exactly what you want to say, and with others, it's a case of opening up your mind to allow what comes to come from beyond your own direct experience or knowledge. This is the essential difference between *Wicked Games* and *Boy with Beer*. The former came out of a real trip to Ghana, and the latter just evolved. I remember sitting down to draft the first scenes between Karl and Donovan after coming back from the theatre with Black filmmaker and director Topher Campbell. He had invited me to see a gay play by a white writer, and at the end of the production, he turned to me and said, 'That was crap. You could write better than that!' I thought, 'Bloody cheek!' I went home immediately, sat down and wrote the first act. I fell asleep at the computer, woke up later, looked at what I'd written and thought, 'What the hell is this?' It wasn't until I showed it to a group of friends, triggering a massive discussion, that I realized what I had done. 'But can you write another thirty or forty pages,' they kept on asking. 'This is not the end?' Never one to miss a challenge, I thought I'd give it a go.

I had always been attracted to the works of Toni Morrison; I just couldn't read her novels. I would get through thirty or so pages, but just don't ask me what it was all about! I must have struggled with *The Bluest Eye* for years before I finally gave up and decided to read something completely different. Dad had always talked about Ghana, and I naturally turned to Ayi Kwei Armah's *The Healers* and *2000 Seasons* when Dad died in 1984. I had never heard of Jungian psychology, so when I finished these two books, I thought that I had discovered the term 'collective consciousness'. I found out later that Jung's great achievement was to explain how the unconscious could be accessed through mythology and archetypes, and Armah had certainly accessed my unconscious with his vision of reciprocity and unity. I kept thinking as I read, 'I know this . . . I know this. This is so familiar.' Thereafter, reading Toni Morrison was a breeze, I started with *Beloved*, and everything fell into place. In fact, I now craved elements of the wild and magical in all fiction, and I just had to write for public consumption.

No prizes for guessing that writing for film and television was my first choice (many people say they can detect this from my writing style), but since this area of the industry was already sewn-up, theatre seemed a more realistic option. Yet most theatre professionals will tell you that 'Black people don't go to the theatre in England', and even as I write this, our one Black theatre company, Talawa, doesn't own a building, has to rely on co-productions and apologizes for only accepting material from Black writers.

> I'm ashamed to observe that we lost many opportunities for what is called colour-blind casting. We even staged plays about young Londoners and one about the merchant Navy with a cast of twenty and managed to have no Black actors in them. That wasn't even realistic for British life at the time, let alone progressive for out theatre policy. Such narrowness of mind was the result of a middle-aged director like myself and all the White guest directors we employed at the time casting principally from actors they know, and from their minds running along 'conventional', meaning White, lines. (Philip Hedley, Artistic Director of Theatre Royal Stratford East in his essay 'A Theatre Director's Journey to the Obvious.')

Theatre Royal Stratford East was among the first places I sent the finished *Boy with Beer* script, but the various rejection letters spoke of 'pornographic', 'lewd' and 'unworkable', so I decided to produce it myself. Many prominent theatre directors were among the first-row audience, and the play has been produced several times since (although a screenplay continues to languish in a drawer somewhere).

I started to write because the lives of Black people were not being portrayed on British stage and screen. Although there have been some improvements lately with the inclusion of Black characters in mainstream television programming, it is still rare to see Black life at the centre of serious drama in England. In this respect, I owe a debt of gratitude to the Internet in its ability to bypass traditional borders and barriers in bringing the work of Black writers and artists to the attention of wider audiences.

Paul Boakye
London, June 2001

Characters

Karl
Donovan

Act One

A kitchen-dining room. **Karl** *frantically prepares dinner for two. He sets the table, lights an incense stick and puts on 'Loving Pauper' by Gregory Isaacs. The doorbell rings. He panics and runs to the door.*

Karl Donovan? Hi! Come in.

Donovan This place is hard to find.

Karl Come in. It's not numbered properly.

Donovan Went right past it at first.

Karl It says thirty-five upstairs. People don't notice there's a thirty-five-A down here. Pass your coat. Ta. Go in. Grab a seat.

Donovan So that's what you look like.

Karl And that's what you look like. (*Silence.*) What's in the bag?

Donovan I got some beer on the way.

Karl Cheers. Do you want one-a-these now?

Donovan Might as well. (*Silence.*) What's that smell? Have you cooked? You haven't cooked, have you? I couldn't eat a thing.

Karl No problem.

Karl, *clearly disappointed, removes cutlery from the table.*

Did you have a nice Christmas?

Donovan Christmas is boring, man.

Karl Let's hope the New Year gets better.

Donovan I'm looking forward to summer this year, though, man.

People are bubbling in the summer.

Silence. **Donovan** *coughs.*

Karl What do you do? You said you were phoning from work. What do you do?

Donovan I wasn't phoning from work. I was phoning from round some girl's.

Karl No. The first time. You said you were phoning from work.

Donovan Oh, then.

Karl What do you do?

Donovan I drive.

Karl Mini cabs?

Donovan I drive a van for this building firm.

Karl Right.

Donovan So you live here on your own, do you?

Karl Yeah. What about you?

Donovan I live with a friend. Not too far from here.

Karl What sort of friend?

Donovan A good friend.

Karl How good is good? I mean, do you . . .

Donovan What, sex? Sometimes. Depends on the mood. Nothing much these days, cos she's going through a bad patch.

Karl So you're living with a woman?

Donovan I'm with her, yeah, cos she's going through a bad patch.

Karl Well, that's a shame.

Donovan I been there a year. She kind-a-needs me, y'know.

Karl We all need someone.

Donovan That's it, ennit. But it's petering out now our relationship, petering out. There's always a weak one, ain't there. You just gotta hold them up. That's what I'm doing. She's very good-looking. That's what all my mates say, anyway.

Karl They're the ones you got to watch.

Donovan You'd like her.

Karl You should have invited her round, Donovan.

Donovan I can ring her if you want.

Karl *gives him a 'you're very funny' look.* **Donovan** *walks around the room – like a burglar casing the joint.*

Donovan This is a nice place you got here.

Karl It's not bad. (*Opens a beer.*) Do you want this in the can or a glass?

Donovan You could have some raves here, man.

Karl Raves?

Donovan Yeah, you could have some wicked parties here.

Karl I'm thinking of having a party.

Donovan Do you do hardcore?

Karl The porno or the music?

Donovan Parties, man, parties.

Karl Not lately.

Donovan They still have 'em, you know. Contortions, Rumours, and all them. Don't you go to none-a-them?

Karl Never heard of them.

Donovan They still have 'em, man. Sussex, Surrey, Aldershot . . . them kind-a-places.

Karl They move about?

Donovan Every time.

Karl Sounds like too much hard work to me.

Donovan Madness, ennit. There's this place up in Dalston. Reggae place called Scandals. Doesn't open 'til seven in the morning. What you do is you go out to other places first. Get home for about five. Get a couple hours sleep. Get up, have a shower, something to eat, and get down there before the queues start up. That's a nice place Scandals. But you get tired, though, man. (*Coughs. Takes a swig.*) That club last night . . . I was buzzing, you know, in that club last night.

Karl Me too.

Donovan I got this chest infection, right, so I don't smoke. That Bluenote Club, man, it was hot and sweaty and full-up-a-ganja smoke. It was giving me a buzz but it was getting in my eyes. I couldn't breathe. The club never had no air-conditioning. They should do something about that.

Karl How many clubs have air-conditioning?

Donovan Some have holes in the roof.

Karl I'll take your word for it.

Silence. **Donovan** *drinks and watches old reruns of Dame Edna on the television.*

Donovan She's good ain't she. What's her name again? Possum?

Karl You're into Dame Edna?

Donovan I wanna see this later. Saw it last week. She's good, man. She's a man, ain't she?

Karl Probably.

Donovan In twenty minutes. OK. I wanna watch that. (*Drinks*) What did my friend say to you last night?

Karl He asked if the guy I was with was my boyfriend, as he put it. I said, 'No, he's a friend.' He said that his friend liked me and his friend wanted to know if he could talk to me. I told him I talk to anyone.

Donovan He's out of order, man.

Karl Why, wasn't he following your instructions?

Donovan I never said nothing to him.

Karl I thought you two were a regular double act.

Donovan Naw, man. Sometimes. Sometimes when I'm shy.

Karl You, shy?

Donovan Yeah, man.

Karl You don't seem shy to me.

Donovan And sometimes we mess about – chat people up for fun.

Karl For fun?

Donovan Yeah, you know, flirting.

Karl So you're a big flirt, are you?

Donovan Yeah.

Karl Do you flirt at your parties? Your hardcore parties?

Donovan I flirt with everyone, man. It's packed, ennit. You have to flirt with them jus' to get 'em out've your way. Hardcore's brilliant. You're just dancing there. Everybody doing their own thing. Moving their arms about like this. Wild, man, wild. The girls are just tripping and wriggling their arms in-front-a-your face like inviting you for a fuck. Then there's the boys. I love white boys at hardcore, man. They'll do anything for you. Share their joints . . . their Es . . . their girls . . . even give you a lift right back to your own front door. Man, I mean, them white boys are so fucking good – I just love 'em. Step on a Black guy's toe, you could be dead within seconds, step on a white geezer's foot, he'll want to buy you a drink.

Karl *laughs.*

Donovan No, serious! The other night, right, I was pushing through this crowd. Where was I? – can't remember – anyway, I was pushing through this crowd. Spilt beer all down this white guy's shirt. I mean, all the beer, all over him. The guy turned round, smiled, 'Don't worry about a thing, mate, naw it's auright. It's wet enuff in 'ere as it is.' Big grin across his face like this. Brushed it off. Just carried on dancing. I couldn't believe it. I wouldn't-a-done that, would you? I would-a-brushed it off, but I wouldn't-a-smiled about it. I would-a-said, 'That's auright, mate, just make fucking sure you don't do it again auright, cunt?!'

Karl *looks at him disapprovingly.*

Donovan Well? What would you-a-done? Tell me something about yourself. I'm well and truly tired, man, but I'm a good listener.

He sits back in his chair, balancing on the two back legs.

Come on then?

Karl I'm twenty-seven. I smoke a lot. I take photographs and I live here.

Donovan Did you tell me about you took photographs last night?

Karl We didn't get that deep.

Donovan I can't remember what I said to you, you know. I'm so fucking tired as well. I feel like shit crawling. I was fresh before I got here.

He yawns, sits down on a piece of paper, pulls it from under him and reads it.

What's this, is this a love letter?

Karl No, give it here, that's private.

Donovan No, wait a minute, man, what's this?

(*Reading.*) 'We are not a people of yesterday. Ask when first a Brother's lips kissed a Brother's mouth.' What's this? 'We are not a people of the destroyer's world, our roots return to Anoa.'

Karl So you can read.

Donovan I ain't an idiot, you know.

(*Reading.*) 'There by the banks of the sacred Pra we met. Before Ghana became just a distant memory. Before the desert became desert.'

Wait, wait a minute, man!

(*Reading.*) 'In that fabulous Black time when Poets among us still sang songs of praise to the spirit of Brotherhood holding our people together.'

Karl You're taking the piss.

Donovan No, I'm not. Let me finish.

(*Reading.*) 'Under the shade of a young Nim tree we slept, while the Prophet Densua pictured a time: The destroyer's would come; nail our soul to humiliation and hurl our benevolent ways into defeat and obscurity; where now in dream or awake, I think of you.'

What's this? You don't write poetry, do you?

Karl What do you think?

He snatches the poem. **Donovan** *laughs and swigs beer.*

Donovan Naw, man, you should try writing songs. Then you could chat a thing or two about Africa.

Karl And you know all about Africa?

Donovan Did I say that? I didn't say that, did I? I know a thing or two about Rastas, but I didn't say I know anything about Africa, did I? Are you African?

Karl Ghanaian.

Donovan What?

Karl I was born in Ghana, West Africa. I came here nine years ago to study.

Donovan I thought you was African.

Karl Is that a problem?

Donovan No, man, no, why?

Karl Only Africans and West Indians . . .

Donovan Ain't s'ppose to get on. I know, that's what people say.

Karl Doesn't mean it has to be that way.

Donovan (*flinches. Changes the subject*) There's a party tonight.

Karl Oh, yeah?

Donovan There was a guy last night giving out invitations. Didn't he give you one?

Karl All I've got is this.

Donovan It was on a small piece of white paper.

Karl Unless it's in my coat pocket. Look, are you staying or going?

Donovan I'm s'ppose to page my friend. I'm so tired, though, man. I wanna relax a bit. Aaaaahhhhhh. Had two hours sleep last night. Woke up at five this morning. Driving some stuff up town. You get really worked up with the roads so full.

Silence, **Donovan** *suddenly laughs out loud.*

You was doing some really weird dancing last night in that club.

Karl Stoned outta my head and enjoying the music.

Donovan You was doing some really weird weird dancing, man. Your legs look like the Rubber Band Man's. (*Giggles.*) Bending down, you were. Way, way, down as well. You was dancing right in-front-a-me.

Karl I didn't see you.

Donovan I was watching you. I said to myself . . . Aaah . . . yeah, man . . . that's nice! Then all of a sudden, you just grab your drink and went. I thought – he'll come back.

Karl I didn't notice you.

Donovan I was right behind you.

Karl I didn't see you until you said hello.

Donovan That guy you were with?

Karl Mark?

Donovan He was clinging.

Mark's my good mate. I like Mark a lot. He has his faults. Don't we all. He's white . . . yeah . . . but he's a better friend to me than many Black guys have been.

Donovan (*takes a swig*) So what's happenin'?

Karl What do you mean?

Donovan What's happenin' now?

Karl Nothing, by the looks of it.

Donovan Are you fit?

Karl (*on edge*) What kind of question is that?

Donovan Are you fit?

Karl Fit enough.

Donovan How fit are you?

Karl Right now? About as fit as I need to be.

Donovan D'you reckon?

Karl Have you got something in mind?

Donovan I like to be blunt about these things.

Karl Go ahead.

Donovan Are you gonna give it to me tonight?

Karl Is that what you want?

Donovan Yeah.

Karl Are you going somewhere special in a hurry? You've bought all this beer. We've got all night. What's the hurry?

Donovan I didn't mean right-right now.

Karl But you'd like to hit the sack soon?

Donovan No, no, not at all now.

Karl Have another beer. Wait for Dame Edna.

Donovan Might as well.

Karl Nothing better to do.

Donovan *goes to the fridge and takes another beer. He crosses to the window and looks out at the rain.*

Donovan You remind me of that singer.

Karl What singer?

Donovan Cockroach.

Karl Roachford.

Donovan (*laughing*) I said Cockroach, didn't I?

Karl Similar.

Donovan Roachford.

Karl I'm sexier than he is, though.

Donovan You're what?

Karl Sexier than he is.

Donovan How do you work that one out?

Karl I don't think he's sexy. He tries to be. But he could learn a thing or two from Seal.

Donovan You think Seal's sexy?

Karl Linford Christie is sexy.

Donovan Would you admit to another Black man that you thought he was sexy?

Karl Why not?

Donovan No, man! (*Laughs.*) You go out with a lot of white guys, don't you?

Karl I have white friends.

Donovan And your boyfriend now – he's white?

Karl No. I've slept with white men, if that's what you want to know. But I want relationships with Black men.

Donovan Yeah?

Karl Yeah.

Donovan I don't check for white people at all.

Karl Your girlfriend is Black?

Donovan Susan? Your colour.

Karl That's good.

Donovan She's a little joker Susan is. She makes me laugh.

Karl That's nice to hear.

Donovan She ain't too well right now.

Karl What's wrong with her?

Donovan Just woman problems, I s'ppose. I dunno. I mean, she's fit an' everything. It's jus' if it ain't one thing with her it's the other.

Karl So does she know about you?

Donovan No way, man. You joking! You couldn't tell a girl that you go with men. Unless the girl was a lesbian.

Karl Some couples work it out.

Donovan Some white couples work it out.

Karl But not you and your Susan?

Donovan   I don't see how the relationship could work.

Karl   So you lie to Susan instead?

Donovan   I tell her what she needs to know. What else you gonna do? You ain't exactly gonna go up to her, 'Excuse me, babes, but I fuck men – hope you don't mind.'

Karl   Is that what you do?

Donovan   All the time.

Karl   There's a problem.

Donovan   What's that?

Karl   I want to make love to you too.

Donovan (*shakes his head*)   Uh-huh, man! Not possible!

Karl   That's a big problem then.

Donovan   That's why two bulls can't get laid.

Karl   Sorry?

Donovan   Why two men can't get it together.

Karl   So what are the men you fuck?

Donovan   Don't get me wrong . . .

Karl   No! I think I know exactly where you're coming from. Don't get me wrong! I enjoy a good fuck and I give as good as I get. What makes you think that the men you fuck are any less than other men? And what would you know about it anyway?

Donovan   I didn't mean it like that. I don't know why I said it. Do you think I'm out of order? I'm out of order, 'en I? I know I am. So what are you saying?

Karl   I'm saying I don't sleep with men who have a problem turning over.

Donovan   So what are you saying?

Karl   I want your arse too.

Donovan   What – in the same night?

Karl   No big deal!

Donovan   We'll see how it goes.

Karl   We'll see how it goes before you fall asleep.

Donovan   Who's gonna fall asleep? (*Swigs.*) Do you take poppers?

Karl   I don't have any.

Donovan   Good thing a brought some then.

Karl   You've got a bottle with you?

Donovan In my jacket pocket.

Karl Whatever turns you on.

Donovan Drink some more wine.

He pours **Karl** *a glass of red wine.*

Donovan Red wine is good for you, anyway. Lots of iron.

Karl Red is my favourite.

Donovan I've never developed a taste for red wine. Can't stand the stuff really. Champagne is nice, though. You can get dead pissed on Champagne. No headaches, no hangovers, no nothing. I used to work in this off-licence in Peckham. Me and the landlady used to get pissed all the time on Champagne. Then she'd tempt me round the back with a fiver in her bra. I was only a kid, but she'd get me to give her one on the cold stone floor. Sometimes, if I was really good at it, she'd give me a tenner.

Karl (*teasing him*) Are you any good at it then?

Donovan I think I am.

Karl There's a big difference . . .

Donovan What – thinking?

Karl Between being good at it and thinking you're good at it. They're not always the same thing.

Donovan There's only one way to find out. Try it!

Karl (*flirting*) Is that a challenge or a boast?

Donovan There's only one way to find out.

Karl The bed's upstairs.

Donovan What kind of bed is it? Is it a comfortable bed?

Karl There's only one way to find out.

Donovan Maybe I should go up and test the bed. Bounce on it a bit. What do you think?

Karl *leads the way to the bedroom. Hanging from the walls are several black and white photographs of Black men in various stages of undress.*

Donovan This is a nice bed. This is a nice room, man. Don't tell me, you're into wood. Are you a yuppie?

Karl Are you stupid?

Donovan Don't call me stupid! (*Testing bed.*) This is a nice bed. Let's have a look at your pictures. Is this your boyfriend?

Karl Was.

Donovan (*looking at photos*) He's nice. He looks very . . . hmmm . . . This is nice.

Karl That guy has got a beautiful arse.

Donovan I'm gonna have forty winks. Do you mind?

Karl I thought you wanted to watch Dame Edna?

Donovan That's in twenty minutes, man. I'll just rest for twenty minutes. Wake me up. Is there a TV up here?

Karl The television's downstairs.

Donovan I'm tired, you know.

Karl Take your clothes off.

Donovan If I take my clothes off, I'll only want to make love to you. You take yours off.

Karl If I take my clothes off, I'll only want to make love to you.

Donovan You're being silly. You're being very silly now.

Karl I think we both are.

He removes **Donovan**'s *shoes.*

Karl Shall I turn the television off downstairs and bring everything up?

Donovan Might as well.

Karl Well, don't sound too eager. You might ruin your street cred!

Donovan I'm tired.

Karl You must have known that before you got here.

Donovan I know.

Karl (*annoyed*) I'm going downstairs to roll another joint. I forget you don't smoke.

Donovan Look in my jacket pocket, bring the poppers up, will you.

He closes his eyes and begins to snore. **Karl** *enters and sits on the bed to roll a joint. He leans forward and kisses* **Donovan** *hard on the mouth.*

Donovan What's happenin'?

Karl You were about to take your clothes off.

Donovan *jumps up, undresses and gets back into bed in his underpants. He fumbles under the covers, removes his underpants and throws them out onto the floor.*

Karl Progress! How much more of that can you handle in one night?

Donovan *sucks his teeth.* **Karl** *removes condoms from a bowl and throws a few at* **Donovan**, *who fumbles under the cover again as* **Karl** *strips and gets into bed naked.*

Donovan Lights off! Lights off! Hit the lights, man!

Karl *turns out the light. Silence.*

Karl Well?

Donovan *jumps on top of* **Karl** *and starts gyrating like a mad dog on heat.*

Karl Easy! Easy! Wait a minute! Isn't you ever heard of foreplay? Huh! Auright . . . auright . . . Huh!

Donovan (*moaning and groaning*) I'm gonna cum!

Karl What?

Donovan I'm gonna cum!

Karl Don't cum now!

Donovan I wanna cum.

Karl Don't cum! Save it!

Donovan I have to!

Karl You'll fall asleep.

Donovan I won't!

Karl You will.

Donovan I'll cum again.

Karl How long?

Donovan Half an hour.

Karl I don't believe that!

Donovan How long do you think?

Karl Two . . . three hours . . . if you wake up at all.

Donovan Uh! Let me cum. I'm gonna cum. I can cum again!

Karl *switches on the light and sits on the edge of the bed.*

Donovan What you doing?

Karl Let's go back downstairs.

Donovan What you doing, man? What you let me out for? Turn over.

Karl I ain't your woman.

Donovan Let me go back in.

Karl Let go of my arm.

Donovan You can't do this to me, no, man, please.

Karl What's the rush? Got some pussy to see to uptown? Why hurry? We've got all night.

Donovan I couldn't be bothered now.

Karl You couldn't be bothered?

Donovan I couldn't be bothered.

Karl Just as well then. (*Rising.*) Let's get up.

Donovan (*grabs **Karl**'s shoulder*) What's that? Is that bone? (*Giggles.*) I could break every bone in your body if I wan'ed. (*Giggles.*) Why are you so skinny?

Karl Who's skinny?

Donovan That's bone, man. Never mind! I thought I was skinny. Have you got AIDS?

Karl Why? Have you?

Donovan Serious. Do you always use a condom?

Karl I always use a condom.

Donovan And this bloke last night, you gave it to him, yeah?

Karl What are you getting at?

Donovan You sleep with a lot of white guys, don't you?

Karl We've had this conversation.

Donovan Tell me the truth. You sleep with a lot of white men?

Karl None of your business! And if I do, it's probably because I keep meeting jerks like you. Big, dumb, vulnerable Black men with no sense of love for themselves let alone anybody else.

Donovan You think I'm out of order, don't you?

Karl I think you're childish, selfish, emotionally immature, sexually retarded and confused.

Donovan Ah, ah, ah, ah . . .

Karl And if, on top of that, you're trying to say that AIDS is a white man's disease, then you're even more stupid than I thought.

Donovan Don't call me stupid.

Karl White man-made disease or not, Black people are dying of AIDS all over the fucking place – so don't talk crap!

Donovan Have you got AIDS?

Karl If you're so afraid of AIDS, use a condom like the rest of us, or don't have sex. It obviously wouldn't be a great loss to the world.

Donovan I'm out of order, en I?

Karl I know enough Black men living with HIV and AIDS. None to my knowledge have ever slept with white men.

Donovan Yeah? How old are they?

Karl   None of your damn business!

Donovan   I'd betta go now, you know. What time is it? Shit! I've forgotten the number. I was s'ppose to page my friend, but I've forgotten the number. I'd betta get up. Can I use your phone?

He gets out of bed, grabs a nearby towel and wraps it around his waist. He dials a telephone number.

Do you think I'm out of order?

Karl (*making bed*)   Don't worry about it.

Donovan   No, man, I just couldn't be bothered now.

Karl   Because you didn't cum or because you think I've got AIDS?

Donovan   I feel all funny now. (*Hangs up phone.*) I'll just go to the bathroom. Wash my hands. Make sure I have a bath when I get home. Where's the bathroom? Is there one up here?

Karl   Straight ahead.

Donovan   Nice.

He exits smelling his hands. We hear running water as **Donovan** *washes his hands in the bathroom. There is a loud crash as he drops the soap.*

Shit!

Karl   What's that?

Donovan   I dropped the Simple soap.

Karl *makes the bed and dresses as* **Donovan** *enters smelling his hands.*

Karl   Clean now?

Donovan   Safe!

He dresses in silence. **Karl** *leads the way downstairs where they sit as before.*

Donovan   I s'ppose I'd betta finish my drink.

Karl   Take the rest with you.

Donovan   No, no, man. You have them. I nicked them, anyway.

Karl   It wouldn't surprise me.

Donovan   I used to go to school near here. I know all this area really well.

Karl   What school was that?

Donovan   Why?

Karl   Just asking.

Donovan   I went to Dick Shepherd's.

Karl   I know Dick Shepherd's.

Donovan Not really. I went to Forest Hill Boys. Do you know it?

Karl I've heard of it.

Donovan What do you think of it?

Karl It's a school like any other school.

Donovan Useless bunch-a-bastards, en they? I left when I was fifteen.

Karl Did you leave or were you asked not to come back?

Donovan (*laughing*) No, man. Nothing like that. The teachers didn't like us. We used to mess about. Enjoy ourselves. You know how kids are.

Karl *looks at him.*

Donovan No, not really. I was expelled when I was fifteen. Hitting a teacher. Busting his nose. That was two years ago. I'm seventeen now.

Karl *looks at him hard, disbelieving.*

Donovan Don't look it do I? It's cos I'm tired. Sometimes I look a sweet and innocent seventeen. Girls are always coming up to me in clubs and saying . . . 'How old are you? You're really cute aren't you?' Why? How old do I look to you?

Karl Twenty-one.

Donovan I am twenty-one. I look it, don't I?

Karl Twenty-one isn't a bad age. Some people think I'm an old man.

Donovan You?

Karl In my shirt and tie, I'm a mature thirty-five.

Donovan And I'm immature, right?

Karl You'd better watch yourself. You might be getting a bit drunk.

Donovan Are my eyes red?

Karl Red as blood.

Donovan Shit!

Karl I think you should go.

Donovan I used to have really clear eyes once. But that's before I started enjoying myself. I was fifteen at the time. (*Long deep swig.*) My parents spent the night with this Black minister. We're Pentecostals, and his son, a right rude bwoy, but very good-looking – shared my bedroom. Separate beds, of course. The son was twenty-one. In the night, he strip back his top sheet and lay in white Y-fronts wanking away right at me. I pretended to sleep but watched it all. He took fifteen minutes to cum. Squirting cream towards me in my bed. Next morning I found him wanking off all over my jeans and he stained the front pure white. He never seem to mind whether I saw him or not, and the room was light enough for me to see him in. He never said a word about it next day at church and I never mentioned it either. But it was very sexy to watch, believe me. (*Swigs.*) About a week later, my mate Sticks who was sixteen spent the night by me on the put-you-up-bed. I thought I'd try the same on him. Just after he said 'goodnight' I pulled back my quilt and face towards him in his bed. I could see him watching, but he never said a word, breathing heavy, making me think he was asleep.

In the silence, **Donovan** *coughs.*

Karl   Is that it?

Donovan   I know it might sound funny to you, me telling it like this, but it turned me on something rotten that I did it whenever I stayed, or friends stayed, overnight.

Karl   Same room of course.

Donovan   Try it sometime. See what enjoyment you get, or give, to the one who's watching.

Karl   I think you should go.

Donovan   What? What for? I don't know why I told you, you know.

Karl   I like it. I do. It's a good story. Pity you couldn't muster up some of that imagination upstairs.

Donovan   I just couldn't be bothered, man. I couldn't be bothered.

Karl   Hey, my brother, no problem. But what are you still doing sitting here?

Donovan   I don't know, you know. You ask a lot-a-questions.

Karl *looks up at him.*

Donovan   Where's my poppers?

Karl   Left-hand pocket.

Donovan   Oh, yeah! Look . . . what's your name again?

Karl   What's my name?

Donovan   I've got your number, haven't I? It's on that piece of paper. Shall I give you a call?

Karl   If you want.

Donovan   See you around, then.

Karl   See you around.

Donovan (*off*)   You forgot to lock the security gate. You'll lock it now, though.

Karl   Don't worry!

Donovan (*off*)   Ouch! It's cold out here.

Karl *enters and sits as before.*

Dim lights to darkness.

Act Two

The kitchen-dining room. One month later. **Karl** *is sorting his washing when the doorbell rings. He goes to the front door:*

Karl Who is it?

Donovan (*off*) Me.

Karl Who's me?

Donovan (*off*) Me-me.

Karl There are many mes. Who is it?

Donovan (*off*) Me.

Karl Michael? . . .

Donovan (*off*) Don't you know?

Karl Look, Michael . . .

Donovan (*off*) Why do you keep saying Michael, is he one of your men?

Karl Look, whoever it is, if you're knocking on my door to talk sensibly to me, then let's talk, OK. If not . . .

Donovan (*off*) It's Donovan.

Karl Who?

Donovan (*off*) Donovan from the garage.

Karl What garage?

Donovan (*off*) It's raining out here, man. Can I come in?

Karl *opens the door.* **Donovan** *enters.*

Donovan What's up?

Karl You alright?

Donovan I ain't too bad, y'nuh. What's been happening with you?

Karl Nothing much.

Donovan I was just passing.

Karl Come in, if you're coming.

Donovan I saw your lights on, so I . . .

Karl Come in.

Donovan Cheers, man.

Karl Hey, wait a minute. What've you done to your hand?

Donovan I had a fight jus' now with this bloke outside the toilets.

Karl Stay there. Don't come in yet. I'll get you something to wrap on it. Don't drip the blood on my carpet.

He grabs a towel, runs to the door.

Does it hurt?

Donovan Yeah, I can't move my thumb.

They enter. **Donovan** *has the towel wrapped around his hand.*

Karl Wait there a minute.

He exits. **Donovan** *looks around.* **Karl** *returns with a first-aid kit, disinfectant, cotton wool, plasters and bandages. He attends to the wound.*

Karl So you cut up your hand?

Donovan (*sucks his teeth*) I'm there pissing, fucking idiot comes into the loo staring at my dick. I turn round to him, 'What's the matter with you, mate, seen something you like?' 'Fucking battyman!' he says. I goes, 'Fuck off, cunt! Me nuh want yuh. Me fuck bigger man dan yuh a'ready!'

Karl That was brave.

Donovan I step outside, now the pussy pulls a knife. You shoulda seen him as well, skinny little pop-eyed runt. I nearly killed him.

Karl You should be careful who you're trying to pick up.

Donovon I wasn't pickin' nobody up, man, I was havin' a piss.

Karl Those toilets are dangerous.

Donovan Like I said, I wen' in there to have a piss, OK.

Karl How's that?

Donovan Auright.

Karl You might need some stitches.

Donovan It's just a cut.

Karl You should get it seen to anyway. You don't want it to get infected.

Donovan Don't worry about it.

Karl *returns the first-aid kit. Pause.*

Donovan Hey, so what – you guys couldn't stop an' chat the other day when I saw you?

Karl We were in a hurry.

Donovan Oh, yeah?

Karl Didn't think you wanted to.

Donovan   Didn't I say hello to you? I said I was gonna check you, didn't I? Where was you going?

Karl   I was with an American friend. I was taking him out to dinner.

Donovan   What was his name?

Karl   Wendell.

Donovan   Sounds like a girl.

Karl   He definitely ain't that.

Donovan   Yeah – so did he enjoy himself ole Wendell?

Karl   Yes, he did.

Donovan   You showed him a good time?

Karl   We enjoyed ourselves.

Donovan   So he's gone now?

Karl   That's right.

Silence.

Donovan   So what you been up to then, Karl, man?

Karl   Not much.

Donovan   You know I ain't working far from here now.

Karl   Where's that?

Donovan   Up in Stockwell Park there. That same garage where you saw me.

Karl   That's a change from the van driving.

Donovan   I'm a good mechanic, man. Thought I'd learn a trade. Well, Susan's idea really.

Karl   Makes sense.

Donovan   I'm glad you only live round the corner here, though. You know sometimes you don't wanna go home. You never know, our friendship could blossom.

Karl *laughs.*

Donovan   What's the matt'r now?

Karl   Sorry.

Donovan   No, man, what's funny?

Karl   You make me laugh.

Donovan   That's what people say. I was always the joker at school . . . the kid who'd make all the other kids laugh an' get everyone in detention.

Karl A disruptive element.

Donovan A born comedian.

He walks around. **Karl** *watches him.*

Donovan So, Karl, man, looks like you fixing up the place. Bought some new statues and things. That's nice, man. That's real nice, man. This wood or stone?

Karl Wood.

Donovan I should-a-known, ennit, cos you're into wood. Looks stone to me, though, man. Guy who carved this sure knows his stuff. You never bought these here, though; these must-a-come straight from outta Africa.

Karl I went home for a while.

Donovan That's perceptive of me, ennit?

Karl *smiles*.

Donovan What you laughing at?

Karl Just smiling.

Donovan It ain't a word you'd expek me to use, is it? Perceptive. I like to surprise people. Like this bloke comes up to me, 'Hey, guy, how you feel? With my hands,' I says. 'How about you?' I tell you, he creased up. Ha, ha, ha.

Karl *laughs too*.

Donovan I did, too, cos I surprised myself.

Karl (*mock Texan*) You should-a-been on the stage, kid.

Donovan Or under it.

Karl Don't put yourself down.

Donovan So what was Africa like, man? What's the people like out there?

Karl Poor and clean.

Donovan Yeah? What part was you in, Guyana?

Karl Ghana.

Donovan That's what I mean, man. Ghana.

Karl Yeah, travelled right through the country this time. From Paga up north to the beautiful Lake Bosomtwe and south down into the dungeons at Cape Coast.

Donovan Dungeons?

Karl Where the ancestors were kept as slaves.

Donovan What, they still have 'em?

Karl Filled with the moans and the crying of ghosts and the scratches they made on the walls with their fingers. The survivors were herded through a dark, narrow tunnel to the sea and the waiting ship to another hell.

Donovan Jamaica.

Karl Made me sick to the stomach after all these years. But that's me all over, when I don't know a thing, I always like to put myself in situations that will end my ignorance, and standing in that dungeon on the fossilized shit of my ancestors, suddenly I could feel all your pain, and I understood . . .

Donovan What?

Karl Why you are the way you are. I don't just mean you, Donovan, I mean, West Indians. And Africans. The lot of us. Because we Africans lost out too. We lost over forty million of our people.

Donovan You joking?

Karl Half of those bones at the bottom of the sea.

Donovan So what the Jews got to moan about, man?

Karl You tell me. I couldn't see it before looking with eyes only. Now it's made me want to try harder to connect.

Donovan Did you take any pictures?

Karl Too pissed off to get them developed. I just want to get on the plane and go back.

Donovan I'm gonna have to set foot in Africa one day. I just know one day I gotta be there. I was listening to this bredda in Hyde Park one time, chatting about all the things that unite us.

Karl If only we could learn to love each other.

Donovan That's the key, ennit, man. (*Sucks his teeth.*) Chuh! You wouldn't mind, would you, Karl, if I jus' put these clothes in to wash with yours? My jeans got all blood on 'em.

Karl Will they dry in time?

Donovan You got a dryer, ain't you? Do you mind?

Karl Go ahead.

Donovan *undresses.* **Karl** *looks away for fear of revealing his physical attraction, of which* **Donovan** *is aware, but plays it cool.*

Donovan Tell you the truth, Karl, man, I been having a bit-a-trouble at home. Susan, y'nuh, the missus. Don't know what's the matter with her, man. Must be something. Maybe it's me. I dunno. Don't wanna bother you or nothin' with my shit, anyway, y'nuh. Ain't been back there since last Sunday. Jus' need a space to think, man. I mean, seen as though you can't sleep as well. I was wonderin'; don't wanna keep you up or nothin' . . .

Karl You wouldn't be keeping me up.

Donovan You sure?

Karl Sometimes, I need to get away myself. The sofa turns into a bed.

Donovan Cheers, man.

Karl I'm doing it again.

Donovan What's that?

Karl Nothing.

Donovan Where do you want these?

Karl Just drop them there.

Donovan Do you mind if I take a shower?

Karl (*points up*) You know where it is.

Donovan You're a mate, you know that.

He sits next to **Karl**. **Karl** *gets jumpy, gets up, busies himself with washing and tries to fill the uncomfortable silence.*

Karl People are funny.

Donovan I know, I was just thinking that.

Karl A guy used to come here. I liked him, nothing like that, met him in the street. We got on well. I took him as a brother. He came here about six weeks ago. We sat down one night – drank a few beers, smoked a few joints and chatted. We used up all my weed so he said he'd see me the following day with a draw. But when I woke up the next morning, I couldn't find my wallet. I knew I had when he was here but now it wasn't anywhere. I saw him for the first time yesterday. 'Oh, hello, Karl!' he says. I said 'Hello!' He says, 'How are you?' I said, 'I'm fine. Couldn't be better!' Even though I'm sick as a dog for being back in this bloody country. And I expect he was waiting for us to chat. I just walked on. I mean, no quarrel, no argument, nothing, to just steal from the hand of friendship like that. How low down we are. Is it wrong to do good?

Donovan People ain't used to it.

Karl But if you don't try, how can you ever progress?

Donovan They don't appreciate it, Karl, man. You should know that by now.

Karl That's the trouble with the Blacks in this country. At least in Ghana, we band together. We may still die for the little we want to eat but at least we have heart. My biggest regret is coming to this country. Because now I might never be able to live in Ghana again, and that scares me.

Donovan Don't worry, man. You'll go back when the time comes. You got any beers?

Karl None at all.

Donovan (*sucks his teeth*) I was gonna bring a couple as well. Off-licences shut now, ennit.

Karl What's the time?

Donovan Ten past twelve.

Karl I hate this fucking place – can't even sleep and can't get a fucking drink when you want one.

Donovan What's that up there?

Karl Cheap American vodka.

Donovan Vodka?

Karl Try it. The American brought it.

Donovan What, not that Demetri? You wanna kill me? You can drive a car on that stuff. You should-a-told that American to take that shit back with him.

Karl I'll have to feed that one to the real winos.

Donovan The wino children would love you. You don't drive, do you?

Karl Love to be driven.

Donovan You got a bike?

Karl Me, no, why?

Donovan I was gonna nip round this Indian offie I know . . . stays open all hours. You should get you'self a mountain bike, man. A bit a pumping does you good.

Karl Here bicycle riding is a form of sport. Back home bicycle riding is a sign of poverty.

Donovan It's jus a different way a seeing things. You miss home, don't you?

Karl Missing home now would be like saying I miss hunger. When I can make something good there, then I'll miss home.

Donovan You've done alright for you'self, though. This place and everything. That's a nice pin you're wearing.

Karl It's a badge.

Donovan Bob Marley, ennit?

Karl Peter Tosh.

Donovan Red, green and gold.

Karl The colours of my heart.

Donovan It's nice, man.

Karl This guy came up to me in the airport at Accra, 'Oh, my brother, you have returned!', and pinned it on there.

Donovan Fancy going all the way to Africa and coming back with a Peter Tosh badge.

Karl We Ghanaians love our reggae.

Donovan How do you know it's not bad luck or something?

Karl It's been there ever since and I'm fine.

Donovan That's nice, though, man. That was a nice thing to do.

Karl Some round here would kill you for less.

Donovan Can I have it?

Karl No.

Donovan Can I wear it for a while?

Karl It was given to me.

Donovan I'll give it back to you.

Karl I don't give away things that are given to me.

Donovan I know, it's not good manners, man, but . . . Thank you.

Karl Don't lose it.

Donovan It's all the way from Africa.

Karl The shower you want is upstairs. I'm going to bed.

Donovan You gone already?

Karl Knock me up if anything exciting happens.

They laugh.

Donovan You know, you look familiar.

Karl You look familiar, too.

Donovan Must-a-seen you before in one-a-my other life.

Karl Good night.

Donovan See you in the morning.

Exit **Donovan**. **Karl** *puts clothes in the washing machine.*

Dim lights to darkness.

Act Three

One month later. We hear the shower running. Maybe a radio plays the news. **Karl** *is writing at the table when the lights come up. More paper balls are scattered at his feet:*

Karl I can tell a lie from a mile. After a while, you get to know the steely-eyed confidence of a liar. When the person you're going out with, you say to them . . . 'Are you seeing so and so? Are you sleeping with them? Tell me. I won't be upset. I just want to know.' When they look you in the face and say 'No! Never!' And you know the truth. Because when you knocked to call for your best friend to go swimming – she was obviously too busy. So you looked through the letterbox and you saw your lover's coat hanging on the back of your best friend's door. You get to know a liar when you see one.

Donovan *enters dressing to go out. He has a shirt in his hand.* **Karl** *screws up the piece of paper and throws it at the bin.*

Karl Where's the broom?

Donovan Leave the cleaning. I'll do it tomorrow.

Karl Tomorrow? What's happening tomorrow?

Donovan I was gonna do . . .

Karl You were going to do what?

Donovan I was gonna do some spring cleaning.

Karl Spring cleaning? What kind of spring cleaning?

Donovan Oh, gawd!

Karl I never see you touch broom in here before.

Donovan For fuck sake, man!

Karl Don't expect me to do everything round here.

Donovan I can look after myself.

He goes to the fridge and takes a beer.

Karl Those are my beers. Not yours.

Donovan *replaces the beer angrily.*

Donovan What are you playing my music for? Who said you could play my music?

He turns the music off. **Karl** *turns it back on.*

Karl This is the one CD of yours I play.

Donovan You locked your music up somewhere.

Karl I locked my music away because my music was going missing.

Donovan Well, it's nothing to do with me or my friends.

Karl I left the ones you like down here so that you could play them.

Donovan Just be careful with my things.

Karl Tell your girlfriends not to keep ringing this number. You brought your woman into this house.

Donovan Who told you that?

Karl You brought your woman into this house, drinking my drinks, eating my food.

Donovan Who told you that?

Karl Nobody needed to tell me that. The whole place stinks of fish every time.

Donovan Ahh, naaaw, man, that's nasty. Where'd you get that from?

Karl You brought your woman into my house, and you have the nerve to watch dirty videos with her in my bed.

Donovan Naw, naw, man. It wasn't nothing like that.

Karl The videos were all over the place.

Donovan Look, I gotta go out now, man. My friends are coming to get me any minute now.

Karl Did you hear what I said?

Donovan What?

Karl I don't want your girlfriends ringing this house.

Donovan Safe! Are you watching telly later?

Karl I'm watching the telly!

Donovan I was wondering if . . .

Karl You don't come and tell me that you want to use the dining room.

Donovan Did I say that?

Karl You were going to say that.

Donovan Forget it, man. Just forget it!

Karl I'm taking the television up to the bedroom.

Donovan It's your telly, ennit.

Karl You don't come and tell me at ten minutes to ten that you want to use the dining room.

Donovan For fuck sake, man. Just cos I'm going out.

Karl Ask me if I care.

Donovan I was gonna ask you, as well, if you wanned to come.

Karl *looks at him. Silence.*

Karl We never go anywhere. We never do anything.

Donovan So why bother then, man?

Karl Why did I bother?

Donovan Yeah?

Karl Because . . . because I care.

Donovan We go out.

Karl We don't exist, except maybe within these four walls, and that's a bad dream.

Donovan I'm off now.

Karl When are you moving out?

Donovan When?

Karl Date and time? I'm not about to spend another month in this flat with you. I'm going away for a few days, and when I come back, I'm putting the flat on the market.

Donovan I been doing my homework on tenants' rights – it ain't as easy as that.

Karl Speak to my solicitor.

Donovan I'm speaking to you.

Karl Well, I don't want to hear it.

Donovan But, Karl, me and you are friends. Just cos I went off with a girl? Sex with a girl is for having babies. She don't mean nothing, man. She's just a girl.

Karl And when you have these kids now – what do you do with them? Fuck them off? Leave them to steal and rot and die shooting each other? What kind of love is that?

Donovan You and me are friends, man. You can't put me out. You know how things stay already

Karl Any sperm bank can father a child, Donovan. It takes a man to show commitment and love. It takes a man to take responsibility for his own. You'll never know.

Donovan Cos I'm not a man, is that it? This says I'm a man!

Karl Why – was she a good fuck?

Donovan That's for me to know and for you to find out, ennit. It can't a been a bad one cos she's pregnant.

Karl What? (*Pause.*) Donovan, you may turn women on with your boyish charm and straight teeth smile, but you can't deliver. You could never deliver. Nice body and everything. But you use people.

Donovan What?

Karl You lie. You manipulate.

Donovan *chuckles.*

Karl Stay there and laugh.

Donovan *smiles broadly.*

Karl You're so stupid!

Donovan (*pushing* **Karl**) Don't call me stupid!

Karl Excuse me!

Donovan Don't call me stupid!

Karl Excuse me, please.

Donovan Or else what?

Karl Get out of my fucking face!

Donovan Come on then, mister big shot big mouth photographer. You think you know it all. What's all this crap?

Karl Put my work down.

Donovan It's crap!

Karl It's my crap. Put it down.

Donovan *very casually throws the photographs to the floor.*

Donovan Sorry about that.

Karl *bends to pick up the photographs and* **Donovan** *pushes him.*

Karl Touch me once more, Donovan.

Donovan What are you gonna do?

Karl Once more.

Donovan *shoves* **Karl**, **Karl** *punches* **Donovan**, *and they begin to fight.* **Donovan** *has strength but* **Karl**'s *agility gives him the upper hand. He has* **Donovan** *in an arm-lock, twisting his hand high behind his back.* **Donovan** *screams.*

Karl You were saying?

Donovan Auright, man, auright! Let me go. You win!

Karl Trying to make me look like a fool.

Donovan I ain't. You win!

Karl Damn right, you ain't! On your knees.

Donovan What?

Karl You heard me.

Donovan   No, Karl, man, my new trousers.

Karl   I won't tell you again.

Donovan   OK! OK!

Karl   You wanna play games? Lick my shoes.

Donovan   No, man, you mad?

Karl   Lick it!

Donovan   You joking? You joking?

Karl   You think I'm joking?

He yanks **Donovan**'s *arm.* **Donovan** *screams.*

Karl   Found something you like, at last – a real man for you. Lick it, I said!

Donovan *licks the shoe.*

Karl   I wanna hear you say, 'I'm a big Black battyman and I love big Black men.' I wanna hear you say it.

Donovan   No, man, naw . . .

The doorbell rings.

Donovan   That's my friends them. Come on, Karl, let me up, man.

Karl   I wanna hear you say it.

He yanks **Donovan**'s *arm again,* **Donovan** *screams.*

Donovan   What's the matter with you, man? You gonna let everybody know what we're doing?

Karl *yanks* **Donovan**'s *arm again.*

Donovan (*shouts*)   I'm a big Black Battyman and I love big battymen!

The doorbell rings again.

Karl   Louder!

Donovan   I'm a big Black battyman and I love big Black men!

Karl *releases* **Donovan**'s *arm.*

Karl   That should teach you.

Donovan   You nearly broke my arm off.

The doorbell rings again for a long time.

Donovan   Don't answer it!

Karl   It's my door; I'll answer it if I want.

Donovan   I'm not in.

Karl   Oh, fuck off!

Donovan That's them going now anyway.

Karl (*picking up photographs*)   Ask me if I care.

Donovan Yow!

Karl *looks at him.*

Donovan Undress me. Come on, man. It's a turn-on. I've never been undressed before.

Karl I forget, everything with you is a first. Ain't you going out?

Donovan No, man, I'll catch 'em up later. What you saying?

Karl Say 'Hello!' to Susan for me. Or whatever it is you call your woman. If you change your mind, you know where to find me. I won't be running away.

Exit **Donovan**. **Karl** *turns to the audience.*

Karl 'In days 2000 seasons past, our feet roamed freely through golden Ghana soil, our hearts flew up high with birds on a Ghana breeze. You loved me then. Of my tortured enslavement from THE WAY, you must have heard the stories told. I bear some scars but time has changed me none. I love you now as then. Will we meet and love again? Or is our love forever tainted by the historic chain of events since then? I have never lost hope completely. Don't you despair. This Black man still in search of his African Prince.'

He goes upstairs to make the bed. He undresses and gets into bed turning the lights off. Long pause. Silence. In the dim moonlight, **Donovan** *appears in the doorway. He sits on the bed with bowed head, then climbs into bed fully dressed.* **Karl** *wakes.*

Karl Donovan? Are you sleeping? I was thinking, you know, about the things we said . . . and just the way the whole relationship is going. And I think we should . . . I'm like . . . I really want things to work out. It's just . . . maybe . . . Donovan, are you asleep? What time is it?

No answer. **Karl** *turns on the light, pulls back the covers,* **Donovan** *is curled up in bed crying.*

Karl Donovan, what's the matter? Dee, babes, please.

Donovan Don't touch me!

Karl Donovan – what's this? What's going on?

Donovan Just leave me alone.

Pause. **Donovan** *starts to whimper.*

Karl Hey, hey – it's alright. It's alright to cry. Tell me what's wrong.

Donovan It's nothing.

Karl Donovan, please.

Donovan I went to see Susan. She's in hospital.

Karl Susan? Is she OK?

Donovan She ain't having the baby alright!

Karl Oh, Donovan, I'm sorry.

Donovan The doctors just kept going on at me. Talking, talking, talking. Sat me down and did all kinds-a-test.

Karl Tests? What tests?

Donovan All these big words they kept coming out with. I didn't know anything.

Karl What, was it a miscarriage?

Donovan I didn't know what the fuck they were going on about. They jus' stuck this needle in me and took out my blood.

Karl What? What for? What's it got to do with the baby?

Donovan She's aborting my kid all right! She's got AIDS. Jus' leave me!

Karl AIDS?

Donovan *starts to cry.*

Karl You're all right. You're all right.

Donovan When AIDS first come out, man, I said, 'Boy, I ain't going swimming again.'

Karl Didn't you and Susan use condoms?

Donovan She look good, man. She look nice. How was I s'ppose to know?

Karl We always use condoms.

Donovan I'm dying. I feel I'm dying. I've got AIDS, haven't I? It's in my blood. I know I have. Susan gave it to me.

Karl Dee, your nose is bleeding.

Donovan Oh, my God, my nose, it's coming out my nose!

Karl Donovan, are you HIV-positive?

Donovan I'm going, man, I'm going.

Karl What are you talking about?

Donovan I'm dirt, man. I'm filth! You don't want nothing to do with me. I'm no good.

Karl You're a beautiful Black man. I'll have to keep telling you that because you don't believe me. Do you think I'd let a little thing like this stop us from being together? You don't know me, Dee. I want this relationship.

Donovan I'm no good.

Karl I need you. It's not all gloom, is it? We don't know if you're HIV-positive, do we? You've just got to hang on to the goodness and brilliance, yeah? You've got beautiful eyes, do you know that?

Donovan *shakes his head.*

Karl I like big eyes.

Donovan *shakes his head again.*

Karl I'll call you deer eyes.

Donovan You're being soppy again now.

Karl I'll call you Bambi.

Donovan You're being really soppy again now.

Karl I'll be as soppy as I like with you.

Donovan You're being really . . .

Karl Stay there.

He exits to return with a picture of **Donovan**.

Karl Look at this picture of you. You look so good when you hold up your head to smile. You should hold your head up to smile more often.

Donovan You remind me of this Rasta bloke.

Karl You've got a thing about Rastas.

Donovan One day I was with my dad in this pub in Battersea, just after Bob Marley died, and my dad turns round to this Rasta bloke and says, 'Now that your god is dead, who you gonna pray to?' And coolly, you know, this Rasta bloke turns to my dad and says, 'We been worshipping him in the flesh. Now we got to worship him in the spirit.' Nobody said another word. He just come over with it cool like. It was the coolness of it. You remind me of him.

Karl *helps* **Donovan** *up; they hug and hold each other tight.* **Karl** *slowly removes* **Donovan**'*s shirt and the belt of his trousers, and then his own clothes. They kiss and hold each other in bed; make love until daybreak;* **Karl** *riding* **Donovan**, **Donovan** *riding* **Karl**; *then they fall asleep in each other's arms.*

Next morning, **Donovan** *wakes first and leaves the room, then* **Karl** *wakes.*

Karl Donovan? Donovan? Dee, are you down there? (*Gets out of bed, puts on boxer shorts and exits. Off.*) Donovan, are you there?

Donovan *enters in dressing-gown and sets the table.* **Karl** *runs in carrying today's newspaper.*

Karl Dee. There you are. I thought you'd left me. I thought you'd decided to call it a day and gone back to Susan.

Donovan No. I'm here.

Karl Hi!

Donovan Hi!

Karl My mouth taste like the bottom of a sewer, so I won't.

Donovan   So's mine.

They kiss passionately.

I'm doing us some breakfast.

Karl   Good, I'm starving. (*Smiles and looks out the window towards the audience.*) Hello, little birdie-wordie.

Donovan   Where? Oh, yeah. His head's all ruffled. Looks like he's growing locks.

Karl (*broad patois*)   Wha'appen, Star?

They laugh.

Donovan   Those birds are really funny. They sit around all day with their mouth wide open waiting for insects to drop in.

Karl   That's not gonna get them far. Where's this food – I'm starving.

Donovan   It's coming up.

Karl   No bacon for me. Did I tell you I stop eating pork? A lotta people never touch pork.

Donovan   Unclean meat, man.

Karl   There're some burgers in the freezer.

Donovan   I'll have to start fattening you up.

Karl   I burn up a lot of energy.

Donovan   I know you do!

Karl   It's about time you did some cooking 'round here. You can cook!

Donovan   I like cooking. Fresh, wholesome stuff. I did this course as a chef once. Then I got bored, man. They wouldn't let me cook anything nice where I was working.

Karl   I used to hate cauliflower and things like that.

Donovan   My mum boils vegetables to mush. Her carrots dissolve on the plate. Serious, man. Her mushy peas turn liquid green, and everything swimming around in grease and beef Oxo cube.

Karl   You shouldn't boil too much of the goodness out.

Donovan   Tell her for me, nuh.

Karl   Your mum sounds nice.

Donovan   She is. We should go up there and see her, you know. She's on her own now. What you smiling at?

Karl   You.

Donovan   What?

Karl The way you were that night we met.

Donovan Out of order, man. Nothing going on up here. I was at that club again the other night.

Karl The Bluenote.

Donovan Yeah.

Karl Haven't been back since. I hear they weren't letting Black people in.

Donovan They were letting people in – they close the club three hours early. There was this slave on the door.

Karl Slave?

Donovan That's what we call Black guys who only check for whites.

Karl Right!

Donovan I don't hate white people, you know.

Karl I prefer my own myself.

Donovan That's what it is, ennit? We've got white in our blood anyway.

Karl No, *we* haven't!

Donovan I didn't mean it like that. I mean me and my family.

Karl Oh.

Donovan You're funny, you are. You get all worked up sometimes. Sometimes I think your heart's too big for your body.

Karl I let my feelings show.

Donovan You should see yourself sometimes, man. Bang out of order!

Karl I'm sorry.

Donovan Naw, man, it's awright! You know where you are, don't you.

Karl You don't give much away yourself.

Donovan I'm like that, though, you know. You say it's cos I don't give. I used to give all the time to people. You ask my mum. But the more I give, the more people want to take. Take, take, take, that's all people do. And then I don't wanna give, cos I don't wanna feel, and I don't wanna feel cos I don't wanna get hurt. Candy hurt me. Candy my . . . we were gonna get married, man. It's so stupid. D'you know she slept with my brother. My big ole fat ugly brother. If he was the last man in the world, I'd rather shag a sheep. She slept with him to hurt me. I s'ppose she'd say she wasn't getting enough. Trevor hurt me. Trevor was the first man I met. Trevor is pathetic! That's one of your words, ennit? Do you know he'll swear to God he screwed me. I overheard him on the phone one night showing off to his friend. I said, 'Trevor, you've never screwed me!' He said, 'Yes, I have!' I said, 'When? Where was I?' D'you know what I mean? He's so stupid! I met Nathan right after Trevor. Nathan was quite nice at first. Then he started to want to treat me like a woman. I wasn't having none-a-that! I met Susan in Safeways. I thought, 'I ain't having any luck with men.' Susan was really good in bed. 'You don't think I'm a slag, do you, Donovan? I'm not a slag, you know. I'm just really really attracted to you!' Susan didn't hurt me. I hurt Susan. She need love, you know. I didn't mean to hurt her. I wanted to have a son. That's what it was. It was mainly to have a kid. How could I love Susan when all the time I was attracted to men? That'll only breed anger and suspicion, ennit? And anyway, here I am now with you – another man – and feeling good about it for the first time in my life. I ain't making no promises to you, Karl. But just to be with you, you know. Talking to another Black man. Someone who can listen without passing judgement. You make me feel so good.

Karl I love you.

Donovan You an' me then?

Karl You and me. Where's this food?

Donovan It's coming up, man.

Karl We should get some sleep later.

Donovan I feel like going for a walk, you know, man, but I'm tired too. We didn't get much sleep last night.

Karl We didn't use any condoms last night either.

Donovan I know. How do you feel?

Karl I feel fine. How do you feel? I mean, now?

Donovan You make me feel good, man.

Karl We should go to the clinic and get tested. Every three months, or do they say, we should check again.

Donovan So we can know, if anything.

Karl If anything.

Donovan Yeah.

Karl We'll see how it goes. One day at a time. Shall we go up or eat down here?

Donovan I love you, you know.

Karl *smiles, surprised.*

Donovan I liked you from time, man. It's just me, ennit? Call it progress, if you wanna.

Karl *laughs.* **Donovan** *laughs too.*

Dim lights to blackness.

The end.

Afterword

Boy with Beer is a love story that tells of the relationship between two Black men. Though certain of that, however, some theatregoers have been inclined to assume the obvious: that the theme is the conflicts/contradictions involved in being both Black and gay. Confronted by racism in society, and heterosexism in their own communities, Black gay men do face formidable challenges, but, in fact, the theme is much broader than that and concerns itself with issues of Black self-love and the power dynamics at the heart of human relationships.

As a play about power, prejudice and the pressures of machismo, about an odd love affair and an extraordinary 'rite of passage', the struggle of strength in *Boy with Beer* is not just a conflict of men, or of male same-sex relationships, but is a conflict at the centre of any Black love. Particularly in the diaspora where Black men and women have had to be strong, Black love is almost automatically a competitive dance of strength between strong individuals who must find some level on which to communicate and operate as equals. So often what we find in our heterosexual community, for example, is the Black man who needs a weaker partner, who is not going to confront him on the level of an equal, going for a spouse of another race, where perhaps the women have been taught to be meeker, more subservient, through their history.

As a story about two Black men from different backgrounds, *Boy with Beer* also throws into relief some aspects of the love – hate relationship between Africans and Afro-Caribbeans, and between the working class and the upwardly mobile professional class living in Britain today. It investigates some of the social, emotional, political and historical baggage that Black people carry as individuals and collectively. Because Karl is more emotionally and mentally developed than Donovan, we follow his attempts to raise Donovan's consciousness, and how he has to resolve himself in order to share love and understanding with the younger man.

Bar the threat of HIV infection, the ending is ostensibly upbeat – 'and they lived happily ever after'. However, we know in our heart of hearts that there is still more work to be done; for 'Mr Right', our ideal mental construct, does not exist except in our own mind's eye, and we must open our hearts to allow him to emerge in the best approximation that destiny has to offer. In this instance, history has conspired to make Black men hate themselves. Yet despite this, Black gay men love each other, can protect, comfort and care for each other in a society that despises 'Blackness', and a Black community that condemns their love. If there is a purity in a love that is as essential as the loving of oneself, then when Black men love each other in an environment that negate them, it is not a sign of sickness – it is a sign of health.

Then, on the other hand, and these are crucial questions for the reader and audience, can Donovan really love Karl and put him at risk of HIV infection? Does Karl really love himself when he forgoes the use of condoms? Is this simply a slice of real life? Or is there some deeper spiritual significance, a reunion of souls after 'two thousand seasons past', and a quest for unconditional love that transcends the physical here and now? Is it better for a brother to be prepared to die for a brother or to shoot him in the back with a gun?

Perhaps these musings are purely subjective and find no common ground at all with your own thoughts on the subject. Yet if *Boy with Beer* is nothing more than a simple tale of 'Black gay love' and a call for respect, understanding and dialogue, then I believe it benefits every Black man or woman who sees or reads it, some of whom I hope may see themselves reflected in the characters.

Very special thanks to Topher Campbell, for seeing potential where others saw none; Steven Luckie, for commissioning this extended version of *Boy with Beer* and his dedication to bringing it to the public; and to Tunde Oba and Clive Wedderburn, whom I happen to think are two very special actors. My love, respect and gratitude also go out to Patric McCoy, my Chicago buddy, and to Amon James of Washington, DC, without whom this afterword would not have been written.

Boy with Beer is dedicated to my friendship with Dave Duncan.

Paul Boakye
New York, 1994

A roundtable discussion on careers, audiences, collaboration and spaces

With Afriquia playwrights and performance practitioners: Mojisola Adebayo, Travis Alabanza, Rikki Beadle-Blair, Topher Campbell, Lynette Goddard, Valerie Mason-John, Tonderai Munyevu and Temi Wilkey (2 March 2021)

On careers

Rikki Beadle-Blair   I make films, theatre, music, and we publish books as well. I have a company called Team Angelica, a very welcoming collective of people making films and plays and other stuff. I've been a writer since I was three when my mum taught me to read, and I immediately wanted to become a writer. I went to a hippie school where we could wear what we wanted, turn up when we like, go home when we like. I made art all the time for my friends to act in and that's essentially what I do now – I just have a lot wider range of friends. So, I've written a lot of plays, about forty, and for television, films and radio.

Temi Wilkey   I am an actor, a playwright and a screenwriter. I have been acting for seven years. I was in a play with Travis in 2017. I wrote *The High Table*, which is my first play, which debuted at The Bush Theatre in 2020. I also write for screen. I've been writing on the Netflix series *Sex Education*.

Tonderai Munyevu   I'm an actor, a writer and a director. As soon as I graduated from drama school, I was very lucky enough to come into your orbit, Mojisola, and Chuck Mike's and Antonia Kemi Coker's, people who really encouraged me to tell stories. We created *Zhe* basically because we felt ashamed, and we were trying to be less ashamed. I remember Mojisola came to one of our readings. And you were like, 'It's full of shame. You need to celebrate.' I live by that today and I hope that the work from this point starts to be a bit more celebratory. Once I had gone through *Zhe* and experienced all of these concerns around how I present myself and who I am in the world, I realized that there were other stories that I hadn't even thought about because I was so busy addressing my sexuality, my gender and my position in the world. And I remember thinking, 'Oh my God, Robert Mugabe is dead and what does that mean to me?' So, I wrote *Mugabe, My Dad and Me*.

Travis Alabanza   I often credit my first foray into calling myself a writer and having that confidence because Rikki Beadle-Blair published me in *Black and Gay in the UK*. I definitely didn't call myself a writer before that and probably not really that long after that. But now I do. So, I'm a writer and a performer. I started mainly writing poems and performing in clubs and hosting club nights and cabaret performances across East London and I hosted a night at the Royal Vauxhall Tavern. Then I acted with Temi in Chris Goode's adaptation of Derek Jarman's *Jubilee*.

BURGERZ was my first theatre show as a writer. I made it because I was tired of only talking about harassment, but I knew I hadn't created a show yet that for me matched the scale of the amount of harassment I was receiving for being visibly gender non-conforming in London. All of the other little performances I was doing – ten minutes here, fifteen minutes there – didn't feel like they captured the gravitas of what I wanted to talk about: the specifics of harassment. So, I made *BURGERZ*.

Topher Campbell   I'm an Afroqueer artist, a filmmaker, theatre maker, performer, cultural critic and archivist. I've been around since the mid-1990s, making work, since I made my first film. I trained as a theatre director in a regional theatre directors' training scheme at a time when there were just no Black, young directors doing that. It was a pathway to fame and fortune: Sam Mendes, Stephen Daldry and those sorts of men all did the same thing. But I discovered that I was also Black and queer in a very strange environment, which at that time was even more elitist than it is now in British theatre; and it was very much centred around writing, and I was here as a director. I found myself being given new writing by mainly Black and brown people. I was very much interested in creating spaces for Black and brown artists including people like Paul Boakye who wrote *Boy with Beer*. Then I went up to Leeds [West Yorkshire Playhouse] to be the associate director there in the late-1990s. I created a whole season of work by queer playwrights, and Black and brown playwrights like Maya Chowdry and Paul Boakye. I directed Paul Boakye's piece called *Wicked Games*, a very unknown piece of work, which is a story about a bisexual man called Kofi, who comes to the realization of his roots. Then I worked with my creative husband and collaborator Ajamu X, a fine art photographer, to create various different things including Rukus! Federation, which created a space again for writers with a project called *Mangina Monologues*, and that platformed a few writers that we know of today. Then I did a piece called *Brothas 2.0* for the King's Head. Now I also make films or essay films and very personal work. So, really, it's the intersection between the different creative disciplines that has given me a really good insight into the way things have gone.

Valerie Mason-John   I've always been queer and I've always been a writer. I started off as a journalist, working as an international correspondent. I worked for *The Voice*, I wrote for *The Morning Star*, and also *The Guardian*. My first two poems were actually installations in a housing association in Leeds. I co-wrote and edited the first two books to document African and Asian lesbians in Britain. I think really, in a way, that I have been a documentary writer, even my plays are documenting certain periods of time. Even here in Vancouver, I co-edited the first African-descent anthology of poetry. *Sin Dykes* was very much documenting a particular time in history. I started off with the title 'Scene Dykes' because I was writing about the scene and then it became *Sin Dykes*.

Mojisola Adebayo   Like lots of us, I'm something of a theatre all-rounder. My connection with this book is a play called *STARS*, which has been developed, like so many of us here, through the support of Rikki Beadle-Blair. *STARS* is my way of trying to address sexual trauma, FGM [female genital mutilation], also known as traditional harmful practices, and also non-consensual surgeries on intersex children. But I'm trying to deal with a lot of very traumatic material through a very fantastical and hopefully very uplifting story about a very old woman who goes into space in search of her own orgasm. I'm always trying to make work that addresses probably some of the most brutal, toughest kind of material, and stories that are very on the edge, voices that are very suppressed or not listened to, and trying to bring those voices in and trying to deal with very tough material in a way that is hopefully elevating in some respects. I call myself an Afriquia artist.

Lynette Goddard   I used to be a stage manager working mainly for Black theatre companies, including Black Mime Theatre, Black Theatre Co-operative, and at the Tricycle Theatre on a production of August Wilson's *The Piano Lesson*. I discovered feminist theatre at university, but we didn't learn very much about Black women's theatre. I'd come from an industry where I'd been working mainly with Black women, including Joan Ann Maynard, Paulette Randall and Denise Wong. So, I questioned why their history is not well documented and I set myself the task of documenting the history of Black British women's theatre since the 1980s. I'm interested in how Black playwrights engage with issues that we face as Black people in the world, how the playwrights who critique those issues create the terms of dialogue and debate and bring perspectives that contest what we see in the mainstream media.

On audiences

Rikki   I've been a member in the audience of everybody else and every single person struck me with their almost shocking ability to be vulnerable. I've seen the film *Fetish* where Topher is actually physically naked in public. Of course, if you see him standing up, he is this tall, strong-looking person; and he knows that he is that, and so much more than that; and he knows that, in a way, his tall Black man thing makes him one of the most vulnerable people in our society. But it's not easy to give that up. It's not easy to let on that that's happening, because we're taught that's not what big tall Black men do. The same with Travis's piece *BURGERZ*; what stunned me the most about that piece was how vulnerable it was; I mean it was about being attacked, about having a burger thrown in your face. Each of these people has been attacked so obviously, but they were willing to be so vulnerable in their writing and in their performances. That's the thing that leaps out at me and how inspiring that is because that's where our power lies – in that courage. The way you dress up sometimes when you perform, Valerie. It's like you make yourself into a kind of target, like opinionata; it's like you don't hide; you put yourself right out there and you just confront the audience. That's what I feel everybody here has in common, that each time I've seen the work I've been struck by my shock at the vulnerability.

Valerie   I wanted to say something about what you said about audiences, Rikki, about how Black people laugh at something and white people are really surprised because I was really aware of that with *Brown Girl in the Ring*, a piece where I claimed to be the Queen of England. I had one hour to prove to the audience that I was the Queen of England. The Black people would just laugh and get it and the white people would be there in shock and horror; and then the Black people would be laughing at the white people in the audience and I'm having to keep it together. It's so fascinating that years after people would come up to me say, 'Are you really related to the royal family, are you really?'

I've had one experience of actually being in the audience and watching one of my plays and that was at the pantomime *The Adventures of Snow Black and Rose Red*. That was really quite amazing to be in the audience and hear children responding to it. There was a queerness in it; it was about who's going to marry the prince or the princess and the cross-dressing and bringing in Anansi and Kali juxtaposed to each other. Because it was pantomime, the play was written for the audience to take part and for me it was just so uplifting to feel that.

Topher   For me, especially in the nineties and into the noughties, seeing Black writers and Black queer writers coming through was really exciting, because there was a sort of cultural movement happening in some sort of way. When I first went to see *Sin Dykes*, it was one of those moments where I really thought the world was going to change. What I love about that period of my own life was the sense of being, that this Black queer world was the world I inhabited; and it felt like it was everything. I remember coming to your club nights at The Fridge, Valerie, and it was anarchic; it was brilliant. It didn't feel like we were in a subculture or underground. That nineties period of making work was exciting because it was new, nobody was doing this, nowhere else. And it was British, it wasn't just from North America. As a theatre maker that was really exciting for me.

Now, in terms of audiences, as a theatre maker who's also a producer, it was also a really contested space because the kinds of conversations I was trying to have as a director in the theatre, or as a programmer, were really difficult conversations, where people in power would say 'this stuff is just not worth investing in'; I'm not talking about the Ovalhouse or Theatre Royal Stratford East, who were hugely supportive of Black queer work, I'm talking about the majority of other theatres. I was directing plays all over the country from 1995 onwards and there was just no interest. They would say: 'There's no audience, we don't have the audience.' There's also that conversation to be had around the ways in which people saw the possibility of this having an impact on audiences. So, it's beautiful to hear the curation Rikki that you had when you did *Bashment*, it's really beautiful to hear that curated, that kind of consciousness around what it is to have an audience, and Valerie too – that's fantastic.

It's interesting to see the new generation coming through and you've got a body of work, Valerie and Rikki. And work that is talking about masculinity and Black masculinities in spaces that were not permitted for certain kinds of Black masculinities to come into being; and a lot of the work that I wanted to promote – whether it be Paul Boakye's work, or Kofi Agyemang's work, or my own work – were Black queers who were working within a place which is not about positive imagery, which is not necessarily about easily digestible ideas of Black masculinity, which were not necessarily about victimhood. That was something that didn't find very much space in the wider society. So, I think there's a real powerful subversion in the kinds of audiences that the work that everyone here generates and attracts. I remember seeing Travis's work at the Free Word Centre in Farringdon and noticing the difference that happens when the work is in front of white audiences and what that does to the work. Seeing that twenty-five-year shift between saying, as I think we said at the Rukus! Exhibition many years ago, that there was a pioneering generation; filmmaker Campbell X talked about the first aging generation of Black queers coming into maturity in the noughties and over the last ten years.

Tonderai In terms of *Zhe*, we did it because it was our life stories. One of the reasons why we found it really difficult to be celebratory was that it was our lives; it was Antonia Kemi Coker's life and my life and we were in the midst of it as we were creating it. I remember, I just couldn't find the metaphors, or any sort of distance. There's one scene in *Zhe* that I went home and wrote and that was a scene about my father, because I had enough distance from my father's death to be able to write a little bit about him. The rest was very much in the moment and as we opened, as we were going onto the stage, we were like, 'We can't do it, there's no way we're going to get up on that stage and tell these stories about our lives.' Then we got on stage and there was an energy in the audience that I don't think I've experienced ever again, which I can only describe as kind of like a belly, like I could feel everyone's belly all the time. We had lots of experiences of people crying in the audience or people just being on a journey that involved a lot of laughter to begin with and then just tears streaming through. That was hard to manage. Eight years later, I think, 'God, what else could we have done to be more joyful and to present people with a sense of celebration?' There was a song that we did in there, which was supposed to be the celebratory moment of the play. Yet it was all about why are people getting killed across the world for being gay?

What was extraordinary was that the types of people that we didn't think would understand the story absolutely 100% understood that story. We were concerned about our mothers, our sisters, our aunties and every one of those understood that story. In Hull, there was a rugby team that came in and they all loved the story. So, it was a very healing process to understand what story means. I can definitely say that everywhere we performed it, in Zimbabwe, in America, in the UK and in London, and the response was always the same. The feeling of how life passes through people. Rikki, you're right to say it's the vulnerability, I can't believe how vulnerable I was with that. I would never perform *Zhe* again; I can't believe I did it. I think audiences were surprising in their ability to relate with us as human beings.

Travis Audience played a huge role in *BURGERZ* and it was never an option for *BURGERZ* not to be an audience-participation work, because it was about public scrutiny and about being watched all the time. We were about to be watched on stage and so there was no option but to heighten that. In the 2019 *BURGERZ* tour, I made sure that when we were in different locations that we'd reach out to local schools, because I saw a disparity between certain audience members I wanted to see at the work and not; so we wanted to make sure that we got all the types of audiences that I felt the show could hold. We had a group of students in Edinburgh, in the middle of Traverse Theatre, which was a predominantly white older crowd. I'd invited some school kids, and they were predominantly Black. There's a moment in the show where I undo my boilersuit and show a fifties-style dress and they started to laugh and snigger in that way that I'm really used to with young people when they see someone gender non-conforming in public. I'm on stage, I've invited them into my place, I welcome that; but I know it, you know, as a performer you know it, you're like, 'OK, over there, there's people that are laughing at you and not in the way that you're intending to, what are you going to do?' Fast forward to the end of the show where I re-create the moment with the burger and this happened to be a show where the lady that was asked whether she would throw the burger at me actually said yes. I watched these same students that had started the show sniggering at me stand up and stick up for me and say, 'No you don't get to do that.' That experience will always stay with me; I had to have a really deep cry after that show, because it reminded me so much of the kids I grew up with and the kids I grew around. I remember watching how the audience judged them for laughing at me and me really deliberately not acknowledging them laughing at me because I didn't want to give the audience permission to scold them for their natural response. And then I watched how those same white women didn't say anything, didn't interject, and the school children did. That's the moment I'm thinking about the audience, and why then choose audience for that work so that those moments could happen in real time in front of us.

Topher In terms of audiences, that was really interesting being in Brazil when I was showing *Fetish* in São Paulo and in Rio de Janeiro, because I had this idea, like you, Travis, the way I was so in the work that I didn't have any sense of anything other than being in the work; I wasn't really thinking about audiences, I was just thinking about what I wanted to say. I was in São Paulo and I was speaking to some friends, activists and artists there, who are part of a collective that's run by the first trans politician in São Paulo, and they introduced me to this place called Casa Sharma, House of Flames. Casa Sharma was run by this gender non-conforming person who presents masculine and they showed me where the screening room was and it was the garden of Casa Sharma; I'm like, 'Oh my God, I don't know about this'; and fifteen trans women came to see that piece of work, and there were tears everywhere. Because they saw in that work something of their own vulnerability and of their own story. And I think the film connected to the idea of what it is to be on the street and exposed. Even now listening to Travis has just reminded me of that emotional moment. I literally felt, 'Oh my days this is really overwhelming.' So, although it wasn't theatre, it was performance, but the idea of audiences was expanded in my own mind, because I had a very particular set of ideas about what this is about and who should see it. And the other side of it is that the online audience is new today. There's an online audience now, and an online audience is a very vocal audience. I'm sure you as artists, you've all experienced this as well, to get these incredible, sometimes essays back on your Instagram, and that is a really emboldening and really empowering space, because a lot of the time we work in isolation.

Mojisola I'm really moved by listening to Topher and Travis talk about those experiences of audience as a performer. One recollection that I have is of performing *I Stand Corrected* with my collaborator Mamela Nyamza. *I Stand Corrected* is a response to so-called corrective rape or hate rape of trans men and lesbians in South Africa. There was a first performance in Soweto and Mamela and I were very nervous about responses. The responses to other performances had been really positive. But in this particular performance, we knew that there was a very big audience of elders and older South African women, bringing grandchildren and children in the front row. And there's a moment towards the end of the performance when Mamela and I kiss and we kiss for a very long time. And so we were really nervous; we thought we'd just about get away with it, but will we get away with this moment? And I suppose that thing that I think Topher was saying about one's own presumptions coming to your audience, 'Are we OK here?' And we are not just performers, we're also Black lesbian women, for real; and so we kissed. And this is the first time two Black lesbians have ever kissed on stage in Soweto and in London and in Singapore and wherever we performed it; so we kiss, and we are really conscious of these elders in the front row. Then after a while in the silence, one of these elder women calls: 'Ah, stop now!' And it was a beautiful moment, it was almost like your granny saying, 'All right we've seen enough.' But they were not telling us off. They were like, 'OK', yeah, you know. I didn't realize as an artist how much I needed a grandmother to tell me I was OK and that it was just a kiss. So, in her kind of almost telling us off it was almost affirming. 'Yes, you're just young people kissing.' The feeling of not realizing as an artist how much I needed the audience to affirm my right to just be.

And another wonderful memory was *Sin Dykes*, the first queer performance I ever saw, in the heat of the Ovalhouse Theatre Upstairs, hot with lesbians, Black lesbians, lesbians in mixed relationships, sweat pouring. It was a rehearsed reading, and I sat next to Lynette Goddard who I'd met at a lesbian wedding that was on the stage of the Ovalhouse; a wedding, actually, on the stage, a real wedding. And I sat there and I felt like, 'Wow, I can do anything, I can be anyone because of these artists; if this writer and these artists are doing this, I can do anything, I can be anyone, I'm in a community, I'm in a culture.'

On collaboration

Mojisola Rikki highlighted that the audience are always part of the story. So, they are our collaborators in some way.

Valerie I love collaboration because when you collaborate with other people you get out of your own head; because when you're in your own head you can only see it from one perspective. So even with *Sin Dykes*, you have your director, you've got your characters and people are bringing their perspectives to it, and it makes your piece bigger and better.

Rikki I don't actually collaborate with my actors in an improvisational way. I love doing it as an actor myself, but as a writer it's not useful because they can't improvise my style of writing. So, it's a bit like I assemble a group of models that I'm going to make a collection for. And then I think, 'Oh I see you as a Greek goddess, I see you as . . . So, my actors really super-inspire me. They choose the names of their characters usually and sometimes they leave me with problems because I don't censor it; so, they might choose some really strange name that doesn't go with the theme of the play. And then I find a way that person would have acquired that name anyway. Otherwise, I'm just writing they're tall or they like playing football, or something that might affect it. That's not how I collaborate with them; they inspire me enormously, and it would be a different play if I'd written it for someone else.

My main collaboration is with the writers that I support and mentor, of which there are quite a few, including Lynette Linton and Tom Wright. They write the play, I don't write any of it, but I go through the play with them in detail, we play all the characters together. We read the whole thing together, and that takes days if not months, and we go over it and over it until they're happy with it. I'm encouraging them to cut and add and change and I'm asking lots of questions. That kind of collaboration is very exciting. I particularly work with writers who've never written anything before. I'm very passionate about them writing the plays that I can't write but that I desperately want to see. I'm very prolific, but obviously you get to a point where you think, 'OK, if I live a hundred years more, I'm not going to be able to write all the plays and represent all the people I want to.' So, the way I've done that is to be a grandparent to as many different writers as I possibly can and encourage them to get started and get finished. That's a big part of my working life is to encourage the proliferation of our voices. I'm always shocked when a young actor, performer or writer says to me: 'I didn't know anybody else who was your age who I could talk to' and that would encourage me; because I know that there's Topher and I know there's other people around; you must have had this a few times yourself, Topher, you realize: 'Oh my God. There's just me.' And then, because you're so busy being you that you don't understand that you're doing something that very few people are doing. But that shouldn't be the same thing when I leave this earth, I shouldn't be the only one doing what I'm doing.

Topher As Rikki said, ever since I got into a position where I could, I enabled; it's as simple as that. Even from my early twenties I'd be fighting for that person and that person to be and especially if they were Black and if they were Black and queer all the better. My entry into the industry was as a theatre director. I was somebody who was about building teams, and I was somebody who was about collaborating. But in the way that I think about collaboration, Ajamu has definitely been an artistic collaborator, 100%, probably the most important, and a mentor and somebody who will forever be so; and then in terms of making work Paul Boakye, has been an amazing collaborator. Then, in the Red Room, theatre and film company, which I was artistic director of, I created a platform of collaboration called The Platforms, which included collaborations with artists like Shabnam Shabazi and Dean Atta, and with Gay Africa. Then also as a filmmaker. You can't make a film without collaboration, there's just no way. Even if you want to call it the mainstream side of things, even with television and film in that space I've also collaborated, including the last film I did with the BBC earlier this year.

But the enabling that Rikki's talking about is part of the politics. Rukus! was part of that politics, allowing space, or encouraging space, or fighting for space for voices that are marginalized or not heard or nobody else is interested in. There are people like Gbolahan Obisesan who's taken over Brixton House – I was mentoring him in the Red Room – Roy Alexander Weise, Zoe Lafferty. There's a generation of directors who are coming through, and some writers too. I think the collaboration creatively and artistically is bound up with collaboration politically and strategically for me. I'm still interested in new voices. So, the next film I'm making I want to collaborate with an all-Black and queer crew; it's intrinsic to the work, the work is enriched by it. The work is it. It's not really about a choice, it's also about making a new world. It's also about making the world into a space which I can feel safe in as well.

On theatre venues, nightclubs and alternative performance spaces

Mojisola Rikki and Topher, you talked about ways in which you create space, and carve out space that perhaps isn't there and the idea of mentoring and developing supporting artists being a form of collaboration as well. It's really inspiring how you've created spaces for many of us here. I wondered about other people's thoughts about the different kinds of spaces and also particularly in the ways in which particular spaces inform the kind of work that might happen, and queer form. So, in terms of physical space, we'll be thinking a lot about the Drill Hall, in terms of historical spaces, the Ovalhouse, Theatre Royal Stratford East, Hackney Showroom, The Yard, the Bush Theatre. We're not just interested in physical spaces but the kinds of spaces that are created and how those spaces affect form, or whether they do, or even restrict form?

Temi The thing I find interesting about *BURGERZ* is that it started at Hackney Showroom, and then the calibre of the work meant that it pushed it beyond a space that was young and queer and ended up in spaces like the Traverse Theatre, Edinburgh, which is a really white and older audience, and the Southbank Centre, which will have a queer season every once in a while but isn't literally known for that. It's really interesting how that show, especially because it's so much about the audience and so influenced by who's in the audience, how that affects the work, but then also how fundamentally queer the work is, the fact that it breaks out of certain spaces and re-creates space in a really amazing way.

Travis It's funny I was thinking about space too, because the last place *BURGERZ* was before Covid was São Paulo, with some of the people in spaces that Topher mentioned. So, I was also thinking about there and how good they are at hosting performance. But actually, I was thinking about the Cocoa Butter Club as a space where I wouldn't have been able to create *BURGERZ* without. I found it really hard recently, as I've started being referenced in the theatre world, to remind myself that I can reference my collaborations and my inspirations and my spaces outside of that. Because if I'm honest, I haven't yet built many authentic connections that would be classed as Theatre with a capital T. But when I think of the spaces that homed me as a performer and where I got to see what I count as, like, theatrical work that became canon for me was when I first saw Le Gateau Chocolat when I first moved to London and I saw their show *I ♥ Chocolate*. And I was, like, 'this is theatre'. And then when I saw Sadie Sinner, the first time she took over an East London club with the Cocoa

Butter Club, and I saw all of these Black performers that were doing roller skating, or hula hooping, or fire breathing, or monologues, or a monologue mixed with fire breathing, mixed with hula hooping and some projection, all this stuff that now that I'm more working in theatre, maybe would never be proposed as formally correct, whatever that means, because it maybe didn't have a clear arc or a clear space of conflict or whatever.

But I saw these people who were like me in the sense that they didn't have any formal training, they didn't have any time to dramaturg the work, or did not really even know the word, I didn't know what dramaturg meant at that time, but we're seeing bold theatrical work at the Cocoa Butter Club, and we're seeing what happens when you present direct address to an audience. I learned from Lasana Shabazz how to turn an audience on its head. I learned from Lasana Shabazz at the Cocoa Butter Club, after seeing them perform numerous times, what happens when you go too far, and how you'll know when you go too far. What happens when no one wants the mirror or it's the wrong mirror that you're turning back. I learnt what happens when you get it right, I learnt how people can feel uncomfortable in the first five minutes, but then if you win them back at the end of the fifteen, they'll forget about the first five. So, when I think of spaces, I think about the Cocoa Butter Club, hands down. I think the work that Sadie Sinner has done to nurture Black performers and give us our sense of dramaturgy, not in this formal sit-down sense, but in the sense of, 'OK I booked you this month, and now you'll come back in three months but you can't do the same thing you did last time.' Hats off to her. Cocoa Butter Club, I miss it so dearly.

Valerie Thank you for talking about the nightclub because for me space was in the shebeens and that's where I was inspired to perform. Because in the shebeens you had the toasters and the toasting [rapping or talking over a reggae beat], and I always wanted to be a toaster. You would hear what was happening on the street. That to me was space. I ran a nightclub; so to me nightclubs have been a real great place to play and experiment. Looking at the space of *Sin Dykes* is really interesting because I think that actually, although I framed it as a play of the 1990s, it was a bit of ahead of its time. Because I think that if that had been done later, it would have got much more leverage, because it was still very much in your face and still really controversial. There was a Black play at the Royal Court [*Basin*], which was kind of straight that had just touched on these politics but just no way in the same way, and people were likening *Sin Dykes* to that. Sometimes with space we can produce stuff, and the society isn't ready for it. But that doesn't stop you. I mean that shouldn't stop us from performing because, in a way, it's like, is our space niche? And if we are a niche space, how can we mainstream the space? Because we're very important to our communities, a really important part of our communities. So, how can we really mainstream our work and have the mainstream space and not just the niche space?

Lynette Also, how can we have the mainstream spaces without the kind of compromises on the work? That's one of the challenges that comes with moving into those mainstream spaces is that they'll dramaturg the work or they'll do things that change what you want to do.

Mojisola Sometimes they dramaturg the queerness out of it or cast the queerness out of it. You are conflicted because you still want to be recognized in that mainstream space.

Topher Sometimes you want both things to be happening and sometimes you're fighting yourself against both because part of the politics is you want visibility, you want the culture to move forward. The spaces that allow that to happen are the spaces with a lot of energy, a lot of focus and those are the well-funded spaces. But those spaces are corporatized and they have different kinds of bottom lines about what they think is respectable for their spaces and for their audiences. So, when you go into these spaces and you have a conversation with the management, the cultural gatekeepers, and for us, for me, it's life or death, I need to breathe my stuff into these spaces. So that's why when I think about spaces in terms of the work I've been doing, especially in film, it's about the streets. Valerie was talking about the clubs, that was a space I grew up in, as a queer boy. I definitely grew up in the clubs, that's where I found out who I was. I performed my own masculinity as I saw other masculinities performed, I went to the lesbian clubs and saw that masculinity is performed there too.

But in terms of the film work, the first thing I did was created on the streets of Brixton, on the frontline, where the uprisings were happening in the eighties. Similarly, I did a piece in the City of London. Now, the last piece, *Fetish*, was on the City of New York streets. On the notion of taking over spaces, this kind of notion of queering spaces and making those spaces have different perspectives and intersectional kind of emotional experiences is part of what being queer and Black is. Also, in terms of my work, site specifically creating theatre in building-based theatres, doing work in estates, doing work in office blocks, doing work in cars, and making those spaces performative in heightening them, freeing and queering spaces in which you feel sometimes very unsafe, very vulnerable, very invisible or very stereotyped in. So, I think that's something that I was very interested in. In terms of theatre, in terms of film, but also site-specific theatre. And that's why I love the stuff that's going on in Brazil, Travis. Because a lot of their stuff is around spectacle – collective or demonstration performance spectacle – that's just so beautiful to me.

Mojisola Wonderful. I'm so glad that we're talking about club spaces, queering spaces and streets in a book about theatre. When we start talking about space, the next thing we start thinking about is funding and that's when I feel like my energy goes down, because so much of my experience is actually closed doors or 'you can come in but it has to be through *this* frame'. So, I love the fact that we're talking about other kinds of spaces. I remember in a live roundtable discussion after *Muhammad Ali and Me* at Albany Theatre in Deptford and Rikki was there, and you just boldly said: 'We are the National Theatre.' I was talking about wanting to get *into* the National Theatre, but you were like, 'We are the nation, whatever the nation is', I'm paraphrasing you Rikki; and I just I got really excited.

When one looks at who were some of the artistic directors of some of the spaces where our published plays did go on, there were a lot of white gay men and lesbians in solidarity with us. There was Philip Hedley at Theatre Royal Stratford East, Kate

Crutchley and later Ben Evans at the Ovalhouse Theatre, Dominic Cooke at the Royal Court Theatre and there are the people in solidarity like Lynette Linton is at the Bush Theatre now. But those solidarities of heterosexual, cisgendered people are very limited, because when they leave, like Ben Evans left the Ovalhouse Theatre, I found myself banging on the door saying, 'Hey, I sold out two seasons in this theatre, you can't shut me out', 'This is where the first Pride march began in London'. I kept banging on the door and they eventually let me in and *I Stand Corrected* sold out the venue.

Rikki It's a problem because, of course, the more you fight to get into the space, the more you empower the space. So, it's a real dance between the hallowed spaces and that desire, as we naturally have, to get to that audience and into those spaces. And at the same time, there's a balance between acknowledging the power of those spaces, without forgetting about our own power. Because the spaces will come and go, but the work you make is eternal. All of the theatres that Shakespeare had his plays put on in are no longer, but Shakespeare is still here. The art is powerful, and having that faith in ourselves is a real daily battle that I spend a lot of time in and a lot of time encouraging other people to be alert to. And it is so many different things, it is nurturing people to be allies and to be supporters and to be family, and investing in other people as well as investing in ourselves so that we can get somewhere; otherwise it doesn't work. So, getting the whole balance is the hardest thing. Because otherwise, we can use the lack of access to the space to not create any work at all. I've done panels with young Black creatives and they're all, like, 'I sent my play to the National and they don't read them', and these young people haven't even put on a play in a pub yet! They expect to go straight to the top and stay there, all of which destroys you if you do anyway; if you get that immediate speed, it destroys you.

Valerie I think so what if they go for the top and they haven't had anything on in a pub? Why should we just go to the places where we've been ghettoized?

Rikki You're right, but you do have to do the work. If you send your play to the National Theatre and then just sit around wondering why no one's putting your plays on, you're never going to get a play on. Even someone who is a solid ally like Lynette Linton, who has done an amazing thing and she virtually in the same season put on two Black lesbian plays at the Bush Theatre [Jackie Kay's *Chiaroscuro* and Temi Wilkey's *The High Table* at Bush Theatre]. But she can only put on four or five plays a year. I'd love to have a play on at the National Theatre obviously, but it's not the most important thing; my audiences don't go to the National Theatre, they don't like going to the National Theatre. Some of the up and coming actors I work with love going to the National Theatre, but a lot of them don't. I hate going there. I don't mean to disparage anybody being ambitious, I encourage that one hundred per cent, but be realistic. Years ago, I had a sudden revelation that my desire, which hasn't dimmed, was to get an Oscar and a Tony and a Grammy and to get an Olivier and to get a BAFTA. But I realized that my ambitions for all of those things were not ambitions, they were me trying to be like other people and do what other people had done and walk in other people's footsteps and not lead the way, and make my own prizes and make my own value judgements and my own universe of success. I realized that wanting an Oscar was the least ambitious I could be because it's so obvious.

Valerie   Just coming back to this thing of space, there's a part of me that the rest of my life really is to be about the uplift of Black people. And for me, it's about leaving a legacy. As you say Rikki, a lot of your audience won't go to the National Theatre, but a lot of your audience will switch on television, or switch on Netflix; so how do we leave that legacy? Just as we're talking, I'm even more convinced that we need a queer *Small Axe*, because watching *Lovers Rock* is fine, but we need a queer *Small Axe*. We here, us here, should put together a queer *Small Axe*.[1]

Rikki   *Queer Axe*.

Valerie   Exactly! Let's put it together.

Tonderai   I totally agree with what you're saying. And to go back to that question of space, one of the things that happened in the first Covid-19 lockdown around Black Lives Matter was really interesting because I realized how much the approval of white people was so essential to who I was as a creative; I wanted so much to be part of the Royal Court writers' programme, or to be a Bruntwood Prize winner, or whatever the tests were that were supposed to make me.

Rikki   Impressive at cocktail parties?

Tonderai   Exactly. What I want to do is make people laugh, and make people think, and to actually, above all, have fun, and to heal myself and other people in the process. I am writing a play, which I'm really super-excited about, but the question for me as a writer within this piece is: As Black people what are we saying about our experiences today in 2021? And are we presenting those experiences to white people to do what with? Or are we really looking at ourselves? And the thing that excites me most about that is that if we are looking at ourselves, then I have an eighteen-year-old nephew, I'm looking at what is it that I need to give him, what sustains him? What is the healing? I'm interested in the village hall, I'm interested in Brixton Community Base, I'm interested in the space that says Sunday night at 5 p.m., £5, come in, come in, and let's have a laugh about being Black in a way that is spiritually healing. Because we can't keep crying about this, we can't keep complaining to white people that we need their help.

Rikki   I've worked in those big spaces in LA, I've done films for the BBC, I've had a series on Channel Four, all of that stuff. And it affords a certain thing, you know, you get certain things out of it; but you have to be so careful, because it's very devouring, and it's very distracting, and it's very disempowering in many ways if you let it be. It's really important that while achieving all of that, we venerate our own

---

1   *Small Axe* is a five-part television series directed by Steve McQueen, portraying stories from Black life and experiences in Britain in the 1970s and 1980s.

spaces. Seeing you, Valerie, being the Queen of England, I've never forgotten that; and that was a small space, and it wasn't diminished because of the size of the space – if anything it was a greater influence to me and a more powerful moment. And so we can operate, we can venture out into the great unknown and colonize, you know, in return. But we should never forget who we are and where we came from and that we have lands within ourselves.

Sin Dykes

Valerie Mason-John

A hard-hitting comedy which puts the sting in the story of Black and white relationships.

Dedicated to the late Jenny White, writer, artist and journalist, who believed in this play and encouraged me to stage it. The spirit of you permeates *Sin Dykes* – thank you.

The story of one woman's exploration of sexuality, as she comes face to face with the issues of relationships between Black and white, SM in mixed relationships and SM in relationships between Black women.

Set in the late 1990s, in London, dykes are out of the closet. Black dykes openly do SM, dykes openly sleep with gay men. There is dialogue, debate and outrage, but nobody is listening anymore.

Sin Dykes was first presented in January 1998 at the Ovalhouse Theatre, London. The production was directed by Paul Everitt and produced by Jennifer Dean. Flick Ansell was Stage Manager and Lighting Designer; Tina Paulson was Sound Designer; and Tamasin Rhymes was Theatre Designer. Jo Fraser-Odin was Language Consultant and Jane Campbell was SM Consultant.

The play received no public funding and staging was made possible only through sponsorship from the community, including: Sabine Baur, Jennifer Dean, Jenny White, *DIVA* magazine, *QX Magazine*, Cyberdog Paradiso, Prowler Soho, Sh!, FIST, Target Distribution and Ovalhouse.

The cast was as follows:

Trudy	Suzann McLean
Gill	Kathryn Drake
Kat	Jo Fraser-Odin
BD	Gailen Manuel
Clio	Queenie
Trace	Paola Cavallin

The character of Trace was renamed Pietro for this production.

Characters

Trudy, *a Brixton babe, African-Caribbean, aged twenty-five; non-specific Black British accent; femme.*

Gill, *a scene dyke, white European, aged thirty-two; non-specific English accent; butch/femme on the streets, butch between the sheets.*

Kat, *an Afrekeke dyke, African-Caribbean, aged thirty-three; Jamaican accent (patois); femme.*

BD, *a bull dyke lesbian, white English colonial, aged forty; English accent, with a trace of South African twang; bull dagger dyke, closet SM queen.*

Clio, *a travelled Black dyke, aged twenty-eight; Black Cockney ('Essex girl') accent; dominatrix, whether top or bottom, always in charge.*

Trace, *an SM white dyke, who sleeps with gay men, and enjoys the role of the slave; as a slave she is submissive but butch and adores her mistress; when not in role of slave is laddish and cocky; when in slave role speaks only with her body.*

Place: London; Trudy's bedroom; Diva's Bar; Gill's bedsit.
Time: Late 1990s.

Production notes

Set and props: The set for the first scene is a drinking bar, with a few tables and chairs. In the original production the bar was designed to be easily convertible into a double bed for use in the other scenes.

Stage action: Includes some physical theatre and mime, as indicated in the text.

Patois: Phrases used mainly in Kat's dialogue, often as oaths or terms of abuse, are glossed below:

'bloodclart' or 'clart' = sanitary towel

'rasclart' = toilet paper

'ratied' [pronounced to rhyme with 'parteyed'] = backside

'under manners' = under her thumb

Clio's Cockney accent: Clio drops her hs throughout her dialogue, as in 'ave' for 'have' and 'be-ave' for 'behave'. This should sound natural, not 'stage' Cockney.

Dialogue: The / [back slash] signifies an overlap in dialogue. This indicates the point at which the following character's line should come in while the first character is still speaking.

Music: Popular club music accessible to both Black and white women.

Scene One

Diva's Bar. Night.

On stage there is a bar with tables and chairs (see production note). The audience enter into a clubby atmosphere and are frisked by **BD**, *the owner of the bar.*

Music is playing. Disco lights flashing.

Other members of the cast – **Clio**, **Kat**, **Gill**, **Trace** *and* **Trudy** *– can be seen on stage dancing to the music.*

Once the audience settle, stage lights slowly raise.

The tune 'Dance Hall Queen' (Bonza Mix) begins to play.

Clio *begins to flirt with the dancers. She subtly goes up to each character in turn and dances with her. However, when she finally reaches* **Trudy**, *the energy is different, their eyes meet, they connect and move closer together rhythmically.*

Clio *and* **Trudy** *dance in a sensual manner.* **Kat**, **Gill** *and* **Trace** *are frozen in position, watching with jealousy.*

BD *makes her entrance from the auditorium, marching into her bar.* **Clio** *and* **Trudy** *continue dancing to dimmed music.*

BD Music off.

Music is turned down, but not completely off. **Trace** *turns to* **Kat**.

Trace Who's rattled her cage?

BD It's like a bloody shabeam in here. Lights on.

Kat Oh come on, BD, you got to admit it's better than any peep show / you visit

BD Two minutes.

Gill Can't you cope with the competition?

Kat Give us a squeeze, what happened to a bit of / fun?

BD Exactly. I'm the boss around here. Last orders.

Trace I'm leaving.

Gill Is that a revelation? You've been leaving ever since you arrived.

Trace Well the scenery is nothing to die for.

Gill If you don't like the furniture you know / what you can do.

BD I said last orders.

Disco lights stop flashing and lights go to sudden blackout.

Scene Two

Trudy's *bedroom. Morning after the club night. The loud sound of a radio alarm clock rings out.*

Lights come up on **Trudy** *and* **Clio** *entwined with each other.* **Clio**'s *hand appears and tugs at* **Trudy**'s *shoulder.*

Clio   Ere, where the ell do you think you're going?

Trudy   Some of us do work / you know.

Clio   Excuse me.

Trudy *snuggles back up to* **Clio**.

Trudy   What do you mean, 'Excuse me'?

Clio   Oh great, you bring me ome for a shag, get stoned on your own dope / and pass out.

Trudy   Alright, alright, you've made your point, I'm embarrassed enough as it is.

They cuddle, begin to kiss. **Clio** *pushes* **Trudy** *affectionately away.*

Clio   You're gorgeous you know, the way you looked at me in Diva's last night just sent me electric. I've been masturbating all night. Look, feel your / sheets.

Trudy   Please! Stop! I can't be late for work again, BD will sack me.

Clio   Fuck BD.

Trudy   In her dreams.

They giggle and cuddle again, and hump a little. The radio alarm rings out again.

Trudy   I must get up for work. What time is it?

Clio   It's sex time.

They playfully wrestle with each other.

Clio   Ain't you into submission?

Trudy   Right that's it. I'm getting up.

Clio   Don't I turn you on? Or is it just my fantasy?

Trudy   You know you do, I've been watching you for months.

Clio   Ave you now?

Trudy   Yeah, I remember the first time you walked into the bar, with your girlfriend.

Clio   Girlfriend! More like ex.

Trudy   Let me finish, huh. I remember thinking I've never seen two Black women flaunt their sexuality so publicly. You were kissing and groping . . .

Clio   Give us a break, sistah, she's an ex.

Trudy   I know, but the point I'm making is that I've only ever seen two white women, or one Black woman with a white woman, be so passionate in public.

Clio   Where ave you been anging, oney?

Trudy   I give up.

Clio   No don't, you're turning me on.

Trudy   Really! Do you feel the same way I do?

Clio   That depends.

Trudy   Last night I was so turned on. Your bum in those chaps looked so cute.

Clio   Be-ave.

Trudy   I am. (*Giggles.*)

Clio   So you're not Ms Naive after all.

Trudy   No, yes, no, what I'm trying to say is I've only seen white gals in chaps, and their buttocks are usually flat as pancakes.

Clio *grabs her, they begin to play. All of a sudden* **Trudy** *jumps out of bed looking terrified. She's dressed in baby doll night wear.*

Trudy   Shit, what the hell is that? (*Points.*)

Clio   A labia piercing.

Trudy   A what?

Clio   A piercing.

Trudy   Are you serious?

Clio   No. Me cunt just appens to ave a Tampax dangling from it.

Trudy   Right that's it, I'm taking a shower.

She exits leaving **Clio** *in bed.*

Clio   What's the problem, don't you like diamantes?

Trudy   No! I just like you.

Clio   Like! Is that all? I thought you ad the ots for me all summer.

The sound of a shower begins. As **Clio** *speaks the shower gets louder and louder.* **Clio**'s *speech is also very physical and humorous; she produces some of the things she speaks about and plays with them.*

Clio   Hey, Trudy, I don't scratch or bite, you know. God knows what you'll tell the gals at work tonight. Just to fill you in. I fist, I pack and whip, safe sex of course. Dental dams, gloves and condoms. If you come back to bed, I'll andcuff yer to the bedposts. Tie you up and make love to you. All with your consent, your permission and your undying love of course. Sold out of course, I know that's what you're thinking. Black girls are vanilla dykes. Well, this one is made of äagen-Dazs, mate, chocolate chick cookie to be precise. Oh well, better wear a dog collar next time I go cruising, obviously ankies in back pockets are too confusing for Brixton babes.

Sound of shower abruptly stops.

Trudy (*shouts from back stage*)   Right, that's it, out now, I'm off to work.

Clio   Oh come on, babe, where's your sense of umour?

Trudy   I hate to remind you, but I consented to sleep only. Put your clothes on and leave.

Clio   It ain't appening, is it?

Blackout. **Clio** *exits with bed.*

Scene Three

Diva's Bar. Sunday evening.

Lights up. **BD** *and* **Trudy** *in mid-confrontation,* **Gill** *and* **Kat** *in the background*

BD   Late again.

Trudy   Give us a break, it's only 8.15 –

BD   It isn't fair, Trudy, you're always late, and with no suitable excuse. Cleaning up the mess from the night before / is all part of the job.

Trudy   All right, all right, all right.

BD   One last chance Trudy, and then you're out. There are plenty more cute girlies who can pull a pint just as good as you, and don't mind breaking a nail or two.

BD *exits and* **Trudy** *walks up to the bar, where* **Gill** *and* **Kat** *have been avidly watching the confrontation.* **Gill** *and* **Kat** *giggle.*

Kat   So what did Madam BD have to say?

Trudy   Oh the usual.

Kat   Shush, she's in her office.

Gill   Oh come on, I'm more interested in your bit of homework last night.

Kat   Give the girl a squeeze, she hasn't even taken her coat off. She'll tell us all in good time, Gill.

Gill   I'm not jealous.

Kat   Who mentioned jealous? I wasn't thinking of any such thing. Surely you're over the break-up by now.

Gill   Is jealousy supposed to be one of those emotions I should pretend not to have?

Kat You know what I mean.

Gill No I don't.

Trudy Hey, do I get to say anything, before you two kill each other?

Gill and **Kat** *turn to* **Trudy** *and speak together.*

Gill So come on spill the beans.

Kat So come on spill the beans.

Trudy I fell asleep.

Kat Bitch, some 1990s dyke.

Gill Didn't I teach you anything?

Trudy I couldn't cope with all her piercings.

Kat You need educating, African sistahs loveup their jewellery.

Gill Not that type / of jewellery.

Trudy Shush, BD's on the warpath, speak to you later. (*Scowls at* **Gill**.)

BD *enters.*

BD What do you call this? A WI meeting.

Trudy Actually it's a witches' circle.

BD Button it, Trudy, you're already in trouble. I want some action in here tonight. You all looked like you had just risen from the morgue yesterday. Smiles, polite manner and no flirting. Gill, you're glass collecting / this shift. And I want breakages down. At the rate it's going, they'll be more staff than glasses.

Gill Again!

Kat That's out of order, we've been stuck behind the bar all week, BD.

BD You heard me, now think your self lucky, with all those nymphs you've been able to entertain.

Kat (*sucks teeth*) This place is full of funeral and diesel dykes.

BD Exactly. Just your type, I would have thought, Kat.

Kat, **Gill** *and* **Trudy** *look off stage and laugh.*

Kat Are you for real? Sorry, BD, I'm married.

Trudy Married, since when?

BD Get to work. If it's quiet you can swap around but I want everything to run like clockwork tonight. Well, what are you all staring at? Get this place sparkling before the punters arrive. And Trudy, I'll see you back here after hours.

BD *exits. The others giggle and mimic* **BD** *'s bulldaggerish swagger.*

Gill You better watch out, I think she's leaking after you.

Trudy Well, that makes two of you, doesn't it?

Gill OK, smart arse, one day you'll fall flat on your face, and then we'll see who's smiling.

Kat You two, keep your domestics at home.

Gill You're a fine one to talk.

Trudy Yeah, since when have you and Alfia been married?

Kat Later.

Trudy, **Gill** *and* **Kat** *begin to do some work: polishing glasses, wiping down bar, etc. They look off stage and begin commenting about the punters.*

Gill Check those fingernails out.

Trudy Where?

Kat Fancy having those inside you.

Gill *laughs, spreads her hand out and chases* **Kat** *and* **Trudy**, *both screaming.*

Gill Freddy Krueger, here I come.

They all crack up laughing, and begin to get the bar ready.

Trudy Who's that?

Kat Me nah no.

Trudy She's a bit of alright.

Kat Hands off, it's my turn to wind and grind tonight, daughter [*pronounced 'darter'*].

Trudy I thought you weren't into white gal dem?

Gill She's pre-menstrual.

Kat *sucks her teeth, and takes a look off stage.*

Kat She ah definitely fit.

Trudy Fancy taking her home for the night?

Gill You can use my bedsit if you like.

Kat Girl, you too damn fresh, and talking of taking punters home, when are you going to give us the gory details?

Another punter **Trace** *enters. Mutual hostility and eyeballing between her and* **Gill**.

Trace Half a pint of lager?

Kat Hi, Trace, how's it going?

Trace Young, free and single.

Kat Cruising tonight?

Trace Am I that obvious?

Gill Yes.

Trace *ignores* **Gill** *and turns to* **Kat**. **Gill** *walks off and collects some glasses.*

Trace What's the clientele like?

Kat Gaby and her posse are here.

Trace No thanks, I'll keep well away from that crowd.

Kat Can't you take the pressure?

Trace You know the score.

Kat Take a wander, you never know what you might find. Can't talk now, catch you later.

Trace Yeah and tell Gill to get off my case. (*Walks off.*)

Gill *brings some glasses up to the bar.*

Gill Kat, your date for the night is the cutest ever feline faggot.

Kat Are you for real?

Trudy You're joking.

Gill Take a look, they say the best-looking dykes are gay boys. Larry would like a Beck's.

Kat *and* **Trudy** *look off stage,* **Kat** *reaches for the Beck's and slams the bottle on the bar.*

Gill I take it you won't be needing my keys.

Kat I've always preferred my own.

Gill Oh sorry, darling, two pints.

Trudy *pours the pints and* **Gill** *leaves with the tray.*

Trudy Look who's just walked through the door.

Kat Who?

Trudy Billy and Claire, they've just gone into the pool room. Didn't take them long to make up after last week's drama.

Kat Me nah boddah with those two you know. Me have no time for people who wash their dirty linen in public.

Trudy You can be so hard sometimes.

Gill *walks back up to the bar.*

Gill It's quiet now, I've come for the second instalment.

Kat Yes, man, me forget to ratied.

Trudy Well, no thanks to you.

Gill I don't believe it, what have I got to do with your one-night stand?

Trudy I got stoned on that grass I scored of you last night. It knocked me out before the count of ten.

Kat You better watch out she doesn't lace your drink, next time you pull a woman.

Gill Ha ha, you're so funny. Come on, Trudy, is that the reason? The grass isn't that strong.

Trudy Well / she wouldn't let / me out of the bed every time I went to get up she enticed me back.

Gill I knew it [*at first /*].

Kat Listen [*at second /*].

Kat Eh, is that it? Nah boddah tell me you just jump braps in and out of bed siddam so, and nuttin a go-on.

Trudy That's it.

Gill What about the piercings?

Kat Me warn you, the woman weird, with her bottom hanging out of those leather trousers.

Trudy You call yourselves friends?

BD *enters and beckons towards the bar.*

BD Gill!

Gill I better go, looks like there's trouble at the door. (*Exits with* **BD**.)

Kat Me di think say tonight would a quiet, but me corn toe already a burn me.

Trudy Sunday normally is.

Kat I want to be home early.

Trudy That reminds me – Since you're married, how is the Mrs?

Kat Fine, things sweet right now. Not much sex though. We're in that phase of eating tea together while watching *Brookie*, going to the market on Saturdays, and visiting the rellies on Sunday.

Trudy It sounds a wee bit patriarchal.

Kat That's marriage, but it's good for me.

Trudy Yeah like a hole in the head.

Kat I know you're surprised, but I'm enjoying just relaxing, and getting into my college work. It's good for me. Keeps me out of trouble.

Trudy Sounds like you're ageing rapidly.

Kat No, just enjoying being under manners, she's got me well sussed. It happens to the best of us. And you no say every dog have him day, and dis is mine.

Trudy Speak for yourself, Kat. Anyway how are you coping, for money?

Kat Don't ask. As you know, a month after beginning my social work course Alfia was made redundant. It's been a nightmare.

Trudy What about the mortgage?

Kat I'm grafting, a bit of this and that, you know how it goes so.

Trudy Shush, BD's on the prowl again, we better stop talking.

Kat We should be stock taking.

Trudy and **Kat** *begin to check the stock.* **Trudy** *exits behind bar, and re-enters with a crate of beer. She puts it on the bar and looks off stage, catching sight of something. She stops and watches intently, and suddenly turns to* **Kat**.

Trudy Hey, is that your friend Trace?

Kat Where?

Trudy Look over there. She's smooching with that woman, I mean that guy you fancied earlier.

Kat (*sucks teeth*) Joke's over. Didn't take Trace long.

Trudy What do you mean? I thought she was a dyke.

Kat She is. She's most probably packing for the night.

Trudy Packing?

Kat Of course, that's why you and Gill split / up.

Trudy That's not true. We split up . . . Why the hell should I defend myself? . . . Is 'packing' something else I'm missing out on?

Kat You're such a babe, when I really take you under my wing and show you one or two tings, you'll never look at a white girl again.

Trudy Kat.

Kat Trudy, you got no excuse to check white gal, now you know where the Black women's scene is.

Trudy Look, Gill might have her faults, but so have you and I. I'll go out with who I fancy.

Kat One thing you've got to understand about some of these 1990s white girls is that they say it's alright to screw a man and call yourself a dyke. It's the phase at the moment, packing a dildo down their Calvin Kleins, and picking up cute-looking gay men. It's all the rage. They call it queer.

Scene Three

Trudy You're so informed, have you tried it?

Kat I'm a one-woman-only, me dear.

Trudy Since when has that stopped you?

Kat Girl, you're feisty bad you know. (*Sucks teeth.*)

Trudy Anything else I need to know?

Kat Why don't you join your white friends dem, and book up on one of those genderbending courses. They'll teach you to strap you breasts down, don a tash, and how to bulge in the right places.

Trudy Oh you're so funny, you make me cringe.

Kat *picks up duster from the bar rolls it up and hands it to* **Trudy**.

Kat Here, stuff these down your pants.

Trudy Too big for my knickers, sistren.

They crack up laughing, but are interrupted by **BD** *who enters looking flustered. She pours herself a drink at the bar.* **Clio** *appears on a dog collar, with* **Trace** *holding the lead. She stands at the doorway and stares at* **Trudy**. **Trace** *leads* **Clio** *who walks proudly and gracefully, clicking her metal-tipped heels on the floor. They freeze.*

Kat But stop, what the ras a go-on?

BD None of your ethnic talk, girls. You might alienate the customers.

Kat *sucks her teeth and throws a look at* **Trudy**.

Trudy You know that's definitely out of order, BD.

BD Sorry, darlings, just a little joke.

Kat Any more jokes like that, you can flush down the loo with the rest of your shit.

BD Sorry, sweetie pie. I'll make it up to you later.

Kat No thanks, keep it.

BD *takes her drink and sits at a table. Lights go up on* **Clio** *and her white slave* **Trace**.

Kat Trudy to rasclart, is that una gal wey [*the girl who*] you pick up last night?

Trudy You know it is.

Kat But wait, but what she a tink she a do?

Trudy Why don't you ask her?

Kat Me talk to dat? Forget it. Tell me something. So what you do last night? You never no say she into bondage. No wonder you never wan talk bout it.

Trudy You never know who you may end up in bed with. You nearly end up in bed with a man / tonight.

Kat This is serious, gal. She's into / SM.

Trudy You're such a hypocrite, Kat. Gill's a self-defined SM dyke. You smoke her dope, smile and rub up against her.

Kat But this different.

Gill *enters and takes* **Clio** *to a table.* **Clio** *continues to stand.* **BD** *catches her attention. They smile.* **BD** *pulls a black and white hanky from her bra and blows her nose.* **Gill** *notices while bringing some glasses up to the bar.*

Gill Guess what, girls? I told you BD's into black tops.

Trudy Not now, Gill, later.

Gill What's going on? Black girls only, is it?

Trudy Gill, is that necessary?

Gill It's been tense out there.

Trudy It's tense in here too.

Gill *leaves bar and continues to collect bottles.*

Kat So what you're saying, Trudy?

Trudy Look, I told you what happened last night.

Kat Me no say you have to start dating Black women but you can forget that one, she's a coconut. Sistahs like her are tearing our Black community apart.

Trudy If you've got a problem, tell her.

Gill *brings* **Clio** *to the bar with the white woman still holding the leash.* **Gill** *tries to act cool as if everything is normal.* **Clio** *notices* **Kat**'s *reaction to her. Playfully she tries to interact,* **Kat** *sucks her teeth.*

Clio Alright, sweet art?

Kat Me nah serve.

Clio I'll come dressed all Afrekeke for you next time, dready.

Kat Black women like you are renk.

Clio They crucified your Lord on the cross, natty.

Kat You too damn fresh.

Clio Pulpit's crumbling, darling.

Kat *sucks her teeth, steps back and observes.* **Clio** *turns to* **Trudy**, *smiles and becomes seductive.*

Clio Hi, babe, meet me slave. She's brought me along as a gift for you.

Trudy 'Not tonight Josephine'. What did you say you were drinking?

Clio   I didn't. Don't you play?

Trudy   I work too hard. Remember? Now, what would you like to drink?

Clio   Um . . . I'll ave a 'Sloe Comfortable Screw', an 'Inbetween the Sheets' for you and a 'Bloody Mary' for my slave.

Trudy   Sorry, we don't do cocktails. Lager, spirits or wine.

Clio   I prefer clittails myself, ow about you?

Trudy   Choclate fudge with a crunch.

Clio   Impressive! Oh well, it will ave to be just two glasses of water, and anything your crunch desires.

Trudy   That will be two pounds exactly. Thank you.

Clio   Ave you got time for a break?

Kat   Yeah, Trudie has got all the time it takes for you to remove that dog collar. Are you off your box or what?

Trudy   Kat, leave it out. Give me five minutes.

Clio   My girl doesn't seem to like my dress sense.

Trudy   No, and neither do I, and Kat is a friend.

Gill *comes up to the bar and joins* **Kat**.

Gill   Can I be of any help?

Trudy   Yes, distract Kat.

Clio *and* **Trudy** *sit at a table.* **Gill** *and* **Kat** *finish off the stock check.* **Clio** *notices* **Gill**.

Clio   Who's that?

Trudy   I thought you wanted to speak to me.

Clio   I do, I came to say sorry.

Trudy   I can see you took great lengths to apologize.

Clio   You can whip me for being a bad girl if you want.

Trudy   It's not my style.

Clio   Ow about a play date?

Trudy   What's a play date?

Clio   Oh you know, dressing up, strawberries and cream.

BD *gets up from her table.*

Trudy   I've got to get back to work. She's the boss.

140   Sin Dykes

Clio   Ere, take my card. Give me a call next week. Take a night off work for a change.

BD *saunters up to the table where* **Trudy** *is sitting.*

BD   Excuse me please, you seem to be upsetting the clientele. This is a vanilla club, no chains allowed.

Trudy   That's not true. And the bar is empty.

BD   Exactly. I'm the boss, no leather.

BD *continues to assert her power.* **Trudy** *walks back to the bar.* **Clio** *stands, beckons to* **Trace** *who pulls a black hanky from* **Clio**'s *left back pocket and presents it to* **Clio**. *She whips* **BD** *with it.*

Clio   Like a bit of bondage, do we?

Clio *beckons* **Trace** *again and she pulls a grey hanky from her back left pocket and presents it to* **Clio**. *She slaps* **BD** *around the face.* **BD** *smiles.*

Clio   Or would you prefer some eavy SM whipping?

BD   When are you visiting my Trudy again?

Clio   That depends when you give er the night off from this dump.

BD   That could be arranged.

Clio *laughs, beckons to* **Trace** *who pulls an orange hanky from her right pocket and polishes* **Clio**'s *boots.* **Trace** *gets carried away and raises her backside for a slap.* **Clio** *slaps her and beckons* **Trace** *for the hanky.* **Clio** *turns her back on* **BD** *and throws the hanky over her shoulder.*

Clio   Not tonight, I'm just looking.

Trace *picks the black and grey hankies from the floor, and they exit,* **Trace** *leading* **Clio** *off.* **Gill** *rings the bell.*

Gill   Last orders.

BD *goes to her office while the others clean up for the night.*

Kat   Trudy, will you cover for me? I'm going to be late next shift.

Gill   You're not going awol, are you?

Kat (*sucks her teeth*)   Trudy, do you mind swapping?

Trudy   As long as you don't mind scrubbing the cellars tonight. I'll just finish of drying these glasses.

Gill   BD gave you that for being late.

Trudy   Yep, but looks like Kat's volunteering.

Gill   Right I'm off. (**Kat** *and* **Trudy** *ignore her.*) What's up with you two?

Trudy Don't worry, we'll get over it. I'll ring you when I get home.

Gill *exits.*

Kat Me never get over how you love up white and weird women so.

Trudy *stops drying the glasses and flings tea towel down.*

Trudy What's wrong with white women?

Kat What's wrong with Black women?

Trudy Nothing.

Kat So why you never boddah date them?

Trudy Why do you have to keep on giving me a hard time about who I sleep with?

Kat It's not so much who you fuck, it's who you choose to have relationships with.

Trudy Why?

Kat *sits on bar facing the audience,* **Trudy** *leans on the bar facing the audience.*

Kat Because I can't understand how you can have relationships with the enemy. Know your history, girl. White people have persecuted so many of our people. How can you hang with someone who reminds you of slavery?

Trudy That was centuries ago.

Kat It's still happening now, look around you. I've got four brothers and all of them have done time. Three behind bars, and the fourth is in a psychiatric unit.

Trudy They must have done something.

She finishes polishing the glasses.

Kat Something, yes me dear, Alvin tried to protect his friend from being beaten by the police, Hugh got fed up of being told 'Sorry, the job is gone' when he arrived for interview, and lashed out. When Bradley left school, he realized him and thousands of other Black men weren't going to be Pele, so he became a pimp and drug dealer, and the youngest cracked up on his eighteenth birthday and was sectioned. So yes, me dear, oona right, them a do something, them a react against this racist system.

Trudy But not all white people are racist?

Kat Of course they are, this society breeds them. Them can't help it, oona call it white privilege.

Trudy You're friends with Gill.

Kat That different. Me nah boddah with pork. I don't want to wake up every morning to a face which reminds me of those kids at school, who asked, 'Wogga matter? Are you all white? Ah nigger mind, go black home, eat your coon flakes and you'll be all white in the morning.'

Trudy *laughs and* **Kat** *scowls.*

Trudy Oh come on, Kat, you've got to laugh, it's so awful it seems unreal. I suppose you've got a point, but it's not my experience, and I don't go out with women like that. So tell me, who should I go out with, since Clio doesn't fit the bill?

Kat If them have something to give you, take it but don't stay. Find yourself a nice Nubian queen. Them plenty out there, so fine and sweet.

Trudy I love women, and I refuse to be trapped by my colour. I won't compromise myself for anybody. Take me or leave me.

Kat You better leave, me have business to attend to. Nah boddah tink say me finish with you yet, we still have tings to talk bout.

Trudy Just remember to give my apologies to BD.

She puts out her hand to touch **Kat**. **Kat** *slaps it.*

Kat Later.

Kat *sucks her teeth,* **Trudy** *exits switching the lights off.*

Kat *hides behind bar in blackout and pretends to be* **Trudy**.

BD *enters bar, switches a dim light on and walks to the bar. She runs her finger along the bar checking for dust and sensually picks up a glass on the bar.*

BD Glasses, glasses on the bar, who's the sexiest one by far?

Kat Madame BD is of course.

BD Is that you, Trudy? Oh my honey suckle, you've finally decided to play with me. What kept you, my petal? No need to scrub floors anymore, come and sit behind the bar. (*Lights become brighter.*) No, don't come any closer, I'll tell you the rules. You'll be safe in my hands, it's a simple routine. (*Lights fade and a spot appears on a table.*)

BD *walks to the table and sits with legs straddled. As she speaks she takes her trousers and jeans off, revealing sexy suspenders.*

They're wrapped in white lace, with nipple clamps and knickers to match. Oh silly me, they're in the cupboard, in one of the old ice buckets.

(*Done in sync with the dialogue.*) I can't believe my Trudy has finally come to me. (*Excited gasp.*) It's like Christmas. I bought you some suspenders today so you could wear them for me. I wanted to surprise you. Have you found them?

This afternoon I imagined you wearing the knickers over the suspenders so I could pull them down, leaving your stockinged ebony legs straddled apart. I placed my head between your feet, and you bent over, gently squeezing my breasts, and I waited for you to drip all over my face. Are you ready for me? Have you fastened the collar to your neck. How silly of me! I nearly forgot, shall I help you?

Kat (*in* **Trudy**'s *voice*) No, I'm OK.

BD That's good, because I don't want to spoil our fun. Ooooh, I've waited so long for you. Just one more thing and then we'll both be ready to play. In the drawer are my favourite toys, handcuffs and a whip for you. You get to whip me if you handcuff one of your arms to the cupboard. Will you play, Trudy? No, don't answer, just throw the keys back. (**Kat** *throws the keys onto the bar floor from behind the bar.*) Now there's a good girl. Are you dressed for me? I can't hear you, sweetie pie, I know you're out there. (**BD** *gets up from her chair and puts her black lacey cloak on. She begins to walk towards the bar.*) I'm coming, Trudy, oooh I'm coming, I can't hear your whip, Trudy, crack the whip. (**BD** *reaches the bar and peers over she recoils.*) Kat!

Lights come up on bar with 'Kat!' **Kat** *remains hidden from the audience.*

Kat   What's the matter, I thought all blacks look the same?

BD   Kat! It's not Tuesday. Where's my Trudy?

Kat   We swapped shifts, she sends her apologies.

BD   Where's my Trudy?

Kat   Trudy's never going to come. I need the extra cash, and you've had some fun, what more can a woman ask for?

BD   You're still dressed! You've only locked yourself to the cupboard. You've spoilt my game, it will never be the same. Broken the rules, naughty girls don't get paid.

Kat   Cha give me my money.

BD   Money, what money? You haven't earnt it.

Kat   Give me my bloodclart money.

She throws the underwear at **BD**'*s feet with her free hand.* **BD** *picks them up and sniffs them.*

BD   Trudy's underwear, poor little things.

Kat   Me want me money.

BD *walks towards her chair and catches sight of the key. Picks up key and smiles.*

BD   Money or key, Kat? Naughty girls get punished.

Kat *takes hold of the handcuff and tries to pull it off.*

Kat   Give me my money.

BD *throws a roll of notes on the floor, and walks back into the office, slamming the door.* **Kat** *tries pulling at the handcuffs again but nothing happens. She curses out aloud. She pulls at the dangling handcuff again. The lights slowly fade to a blackout.*

The sound of a handcuff falling to the floor immediately follows the blackout.

Kat   Lord have mercy.

Trace *and* **Clio** *enter.* **Trace** *is dressed in her laddish clothing. She switches the light on.*

Clio   Smells of sex in ere. Look, over ere, some one's lost an andcuff.

Trace Looks like you're late, mate, BD's already been served by one of her staff. If we wait she may come up for seconds, depends on her mood.

Clio So what are my chances of providing a service for BD and getting Trudy the night off?

Trace BD no problem. As for Trudy, she's a strange fish.

Clio What do you reckon, Trace?

Trace Not sure, Clio, I know she's still into Gill even though they don't do sex.

Clio I want er.

Trace What's got into my mistress? She's just a babe.

Clio I've been wet day and night since I met er, they call it chemistry, mate.

Trace My guess is you frightened the hell out of her earlier.

Clio You're my slave, it was your job to seduce er.

Trace Mine, why me?

Clio I ad Kat to deal with, the wretch kept on trying to distract my attention. Look, I need you to find out if she fancies me. I'm going crazy inside.

Trace Is it just a fuck you want, coz I know for a fact Trudy definitely isn't a one-night stand girl. She's far too respectable / for that.

Clio Shut the trap up.

Trace She's the marrying kind.

Clio Great, that explains it.

Trace What?

Clio Nobody ever goes to bed with Clio without doing sex.

Trace *laughs and pats* **Clio** *on her back.*

Trace Oh, so she's one of those virginal girls, opens up your heart, fucks you in the head, gets you addicted, and hooks you into her neurotic drama of 'Not tonight, I don't know you well enough'. Next, I'll be taking my mistress to therapy.

Clio Sounds like you've got a broken art

Trace No, just a hole in the head from babes like Trudy.

Clio So I like the girl, she's kinda special, fresh, not contaminated by all that feminist and Afrocentric crap.

Trace Looks like BD's in recovery, you're out of luck Clio.

Clio Trace, sort it!

They exit turning the lights out.

Scene Four

Gill's *bedsit. The next day.*

Gill *is in bed nestled under the duvet. Telephone by bedside dresser rings. She stirs. It rings again. An arm appears from beneath duvet and grabs receiver, pulls it under the covers.*

Gill (*speaking from under duvet*) Hello . . . (*Slams receiver down. Sound of another phone ringing, similar bell. Sits up in bed, looks around room, and suddenly grabs jacket from a chair beside bed. Pulls a mobile out.*) Of course you've bloody woken me up . . . What time is it? . . . You're joking, ring me later.

Snaps mobile shut and switches it off, puts it back on chair, and snuggles under duvet. Sound of first phone again, she ignores it. Goes to grab the mobile, and stops midway, realizing it's telephone set.

Picks up receiver and lies back down. Pauses in following should be long enough to allow **Gill** *to be seen reacting variously to the other person.*

Gill Wrong number, ring 999 . . . I don't care how urgent it is . . . No you can't come round . . . I'm not a bloody locksmith . . . What type of key . . . Handcuffs! (*Sits up in bed.*) What like the pigs use? . . . Am I supposed to laugh? . . . Actually I gave them back with the uniform, sorry . . . No! . . . That's your problem, I'm wrecked, I need my sleep . . . I'll look, but that's all I'm doing. Hold on.

Puts receiver down and bends over bed, pulls a small trunk from beneath bed. Opens it and rummages around. Closes the trunk and pushes it back under bed, and picks receiver up.

Gill You're in luck . . . No promises it will fit . . . Don't push your luck . . . No! . . . Tomorrow . . . Five hours . . . Three . . . One and a half, I need to chill.

Hangs up, leaving the phone off the hook. Aggressively throws herself under duvet. Doorbell rings.

Gill (*shouts from beneath her duvet*) I'm out.

Trudy *lets herself in. She carries a bag.* **Gill** *pulls the duvet off her face.*

Trudy Are you alright?

Gill Oh just a bad dream.

Trudy *moves the clothes and phone off the chair and sits down. She looks around the room.*

Trudy You're not going to stay in bed all day?

Gill Oh not now, I'm sleeping.

Trudy No peace for the wicked.

Gill Look, entertain yourself.

Trudy How comes you're in bed alone?

Gill (*sits up in bed*)   Oh you know how it is. I was up the Rub Club last night, dropped an E, and spent half the night fisting in the toilets. I ran out of KY and rubber gloves. And then Suzanne came along and propositioned me.

Trudy Sometimes you're so boring. Obviously the E still hasn't worn off. Why don't you admit you're losing your charm?

Gill Now I might be on E, but I'm not stupid. You didn't come all the way over here to give me a hard time. You normally ring me to do that. And if you did, you know where the front door is.

Trudy I've brought you breakfast.

Gill What's the celebration?

Trudy Six months of separation.

Gill You're strange, it's all those self-empowering workshops you go to.

Trudy Well, it's an achievement to break up. Not everyone manages it. Most of us hang on in there to the bitter end, almost destroying each other.

Gill Trudy, I can't cope with deep and meaningfuls so early in the morning. Pass me the skins.

Trudy It's two o'clock in the afternoon.

Gill Who cares what the time is! Pass me the skins, and I'll build a big fat joint to go with brekky. You know where everything is?

Trudy I've brought everything including paper plates and cups.

She unfolds a paper tablecloth and puts it on the bed, unwraps fresh bagels, salmon and cream cheese. **Gill** *looks for her dope, searching her clothes while talking.*

Gill I know we've been working at friendship for six months, but what's this in aid of? (*Gives up looking and takes half a joint from the ashtray on her dresser and passes it to* **Trudy**.) Here, you light up.

Trudy No thanks. You got me into that shit. I'm trying to stop. I came round for an honest chat / you're the only person I feel safe speaking to.

Gill I knew it –

Trudy Kat is up on her high horse, screaming Black girls don't do SM, and my other mates refuse to talk about it.

Gill I knew you had something else up your sleeve. Shit, where are the matches?

She gives up looking and puts joint back in the ashtray. **Trudy** *passes her a bagel and takes one herself. They both take a bite.*

Trudy Please, Gill, I'm serious. I've decided to play.

Gill You what! (*Puts her bagel down on dresser.*)

Trudy Play – I want to explore and experiment with sex.

Gill Great! What made you change your mind? This is worth celebrating. Where is the Champagne?

Trudy I knew you would support me.

Gill Does that mean we're back together again? Separation was definitely worth the angst.

Trudy *puts her bagel down on the bed.*

Trudy Gill . . . I want to play with Clio.

Gill Oh, oh, I see, it's just that I thought maybe we would perhaps . . .

Note: actors should play the following sequence up to [add page no.] as an intimate and physical scene, through contact and use of voice/tone.

Trudy It's over between us as lovers. I've moved on.

Gill Well, I can see that. But are you sure? I mean, do you understand what you may be letting yourself in for?

Trudy Not you too. I thought you would be the last person to be unsympathetic.

Gill I'm sorry, it's just that . . .

Trudy Just what?

Gill Well, you know . . . I mean, you couldn't even cope with the thought of me using a dildo, or even using a dildo to penetrate me. Anytime I mentioned whips, or scarfs, we argued. Sex toys cost me my relationship with you.

Trudy It's different.

Gill How is it different?

Trudy We're both Black.

Gill What's that got to do with it?

Trudy I don't believe I'm going through the same shit with you six months later. I thought you understood the issues it brings up for me around race and power.

Gill No! I don't understand, and I resent you assuming that I'm racist just because I'm white. As far as I'm concerned people like that hurt and offend others. Whenever the issue of SM comes up, why do we always end up down the same black hole?

Trudy *gets up from the chair and points at* **Gill**.

Trudy 'Down the same black hole'! Did you hear what you just said? Down the same black hole you were happy to put your tongue down six months ago. You see, Gill, you've just hurt me. Your choice of language offends me.

Gill Here we go again. Can't fuck with you in case my sexual preferences make you feel like a slave. Can't speak to you in case I offend you.

Trudy It's hard being close friends with a Black woman, isn't it?

Gill No it's just hard being friends with you.

Trudy When are you going to recognize I'm Black and you're white?

Gill When are you going to forget it?

Trudy When I can trust you.

Gill Oh so you don't trust me now?

Trudy *sits down in a tense manner.*

Trudy I don't trust your conditioning. I don't trust what thoughts you may have in your head if we played together. I don't trust that you wouldn't get carried away while acting out a fantasy.

Gill What the hell do you mean?

Trudy Calm down.

Gill Calm down! You've got some bloody cheek, you come waltzing into my space to let me know you've got a new girlfriend, and now you want me to listen to this crap.

Trudy I'm sorry.

Gill Don't bother, why don't you leave and find some other white woman to guilt trip?

Trudy How can I make you understand, Gill. So many of Black/white relationships in this society are based on the fact that Black people have very little power. How do I know that when I give up my power to you in the bed you're not thinking nigger, slave, mugger? And if you are, how do I know you won't play those thoughts out on my body?

Gill But, Trudy, I could never think like that.

Trudy It's a risk I'm not prepared to take. What risks do you take, Gill?

Gill I haven't thought about it.

Trudy Typical, you don't have to.

Gill So you've made your point, but . . .

Trudy Gill, listen to me for a change. I know what you think.

Gill Listen, how many times do I have to listen to the same tape?

Trudy I'm scared of all that bondage stuff, but when we spoke about it it did excite me. I'm not sure why, but every time I thought of you and I experimenting, I could hear my Black sisters screaming, 'Remember slavery'.

Gill What's this got to do with me, Trudy?

Trudy White people have got the power. They had the power and tortured my ancestor, in the same way people use bondage in sex. / Shit I don't even have to go back centuries.

Gill Trudy, this is me, Gill, the woman you made love with every day for a year. Ate off the same plate, shared our lives and intimate secrets.

Trudy Exactly. When I fantasize about you handcuffing my hands, all I can think of is the police beating Michael White, gagging Joy Gardner to death and shooting Cherry Groce. The images, flashbacks and memories are endless.

Gill How's all this stuff related to me, Trudy? I love you.

Trudy *breaks down in tears. Begins to unwind.*

Trudy That day.

Gill What day?

Trudy I was fourteen, protesting against the Nazis marching in Southend, and the police picked on the only Black person on the demo, arrested for not giving them my banner. They handcuffed me, slung me in the van, frisked me and drove me to the station. Two women stripped me, forced me to bend over and touch my toes, and shoved their hands up my genitals.

Gill Shit, why didn't you tell me?

Trudy They said it was a routine check. To make sure I had no dangerous weapons up there. (*Laughs to highlight how unbelievable it all seems.*)

Gill Trudy, I know I was a copper. I don't think of the police beating up all the queers when I'm having sex, far from it. Look, I understand your anger.

Trudy How dare you, no you don't understand, that's your problem.

Gill But I do, I gave up my job for you.

Trudy You left because you couldn't cope with your colleagues bragging about how many poofs they had savagely beaten up, every night they went off duty. You couldn't cope pretending to be straight, you couldn't cope with how the force treated women when they reported rape, and when you started dating me, that was it, the overt racism was all too much.

Gill God, it seems an age since I worked there, but you're right, they're things I choose to forget.

Trudy You have the luxury, the choice to forget. You've only started thinking about race, since I've been in your life. You can't understand the best you can do is sympathize. You can never know what it's like to be a Black person.

Gill I suppose you're right.

Trudy How could I let you tie me up? How could I let you whip me? How could I? Those same whips were used to keep my ancestors at work on the plantations. My mother's and father's backs peeling raw, blood oozing, a tree trunk of slashes that can never be the same. I am the scar, my thoughts are still in pain.

Gill I'm on fucking Ecstasy, not a bloody guilt trip.

Trudy Kat has a point.

Gill Maybe she has, but when are you going to stop being a mouthpiece for her, and tell me what you really think?

Trudy How can I go out with somebody who triggers of all these memories? And to introduce whips, chains and handcuffs is all to scary to explore with a white woman. Especially my first time. I need to be able to trust, feel safe. Maybe I can feel safe with Clio.

Gill But she was in a dog collar, and with a white woman, Trace, holding Clio on a leash.

Trudy Clio obviously isn't a novice. And in any case she had all the power. The white woman was her slave.

Gill I don't know what else to say.

Trudy You don't have to say anything. It's the first time you've heard me, and not got all defensive. I appreciate that, thank you.

She moves the bagels to the end of the bed, takes hold of **Gill** *and they hug.* **Gill** *pulls away and looks into her eyes.*

Gill What does this all mean? Can you never love a white woman?

Trudy Gill, I love you. I wouldn't be here sharing my pain with you.

Gill I love you too, but I'm confused – can you ever have a sexual relationship with a white woman?

Trudy I love women, all women, and I don't want to be caged by my legacy, but where I am at now in my healing, I want to explore with Black women, but you know me, since I've been a lesbian I can't stop looking at women.

Gill I have a lot to think about. The irony is, that just as I've begun to question my sexual practices, you seem to be adopting them.

Trudy No, I'm in a similar place as you. I'm just questioning and exploring my sexuality. You can't avoid it on the scene.

Gill Where's that healthy breakfast? I'm beginning to feel a bit rough. Where did I put that joint?

Trudy There is something else.

Gill Oh no, not more d and ms [*i.e. 'deep and meaningfuls'*], I can't cope first thing in the morning.

Trudy It's the afternoon for God sake. Some of us do get up to hear the morning chorus.

Gill Yeah, I've heard yours, thank you very much. Now get a life.

Trudy I'm trying to. Champagne.

She pulls a bottle and two plastic glasses from her bag which is lying on the floor beside the chair. She shakes the bottle and loosens the cork.

Gill Don't you dare.

Trudy What's it worth?

Gill That depends.

Trudy I want to borrow your equipment.

Gill What?

Trudy You heard.

She passes **Gill** *a glass, places part of sheet over cork and slowly pulls cork making sure nothing spills. She takes a bow and pours each of them a drink and puts bottle on dresser.*

Trudy Cheers, to my sexual liberation.

Gill *ignores the cheers, takes a sip and puts her glass down.*

Gill You don't even know her. Look, don't be coerced into anything you don't want to do.

Trudy I'm a big girl now.

Gill Big or not, you don't even know what to do.

Trudy What makes you think that?

Gill Go on, enlighten me

Trudy Well, you know BD / likes to.

Gill BD, BD, not you too. That says it all. I've just listened to you harp out all that emotional stuff, and you have the audacity to mention BD. What an insult. At least I'm working on my racism / she's the biggest racist going.

Trudy Calm down, and it's not emotional, it's my reality. Just listen for a moment.

Gill (*in patois*) Kat will cuss your clart.

Trudy Cha so you tink you're Black now?

Gill No, just wanted you to hear me too. I'm all ears for this one. Where's that joint?

Trudy Shouldn't think you'd need it.

Gill Cut the crap. Get on with it.

Trudy BD's one of those white colonials.

Gill As if I didn't know.

Trudy Don't make it hard for me.

Gill Hard for you? What about me? She's one of those women you were talking about earlier, the ones with / fucked-up fantasies.

Trudy Let me finish. She escaped the country because of politics.

Gill Is that supposed to make me feel better? She is so racist it's unreal.

Trudy That's an understatement. She's one of those white women riddled with guilt, about what her ancestors / have done to Africa.

Gill Ancestors! More like grandfathers, fathers and brothers. Cut the sob story, and give me the bare bones.

BD and Clio enter. Spotlight comes up creating a surreal cameo affect. Clio walks around BD menacingly three times, with her rubber whip flexed over her shoulder. BD drops to her knees.

Trudy Remember last year when all the bar staff used to complain that BD was favouring me, and pointed out it was obvious because I was the only Black woman working there, that she was either scared of me, or being / tokenistic?

Gill Out and out racist more like it. Yeah, I wondered how you felt about losing your special entitlements.

Trudy One night she hauled me into her office and broke down crying. Blabbering how sorry she was that things in South Africa hadn't seemed to have changed. She asked me to whip her as much as my ancestors had been beaten by her people?

Gill And . . .

Trudy I told her it would take me more than a lifetime. And she said, 'Perfect.'

Clio whips BD several times. BD gets turned on. Clio pokes the handle of her whip in BD's back. BD stands, and Clio guides her off stage.

Trudy and Gill crack up laughing.

Gill Perfect! I can just imagine her. What a closet SM queen. She sounds well fucked.

Trudy Aren't we all?

Gill Some more than others, obviously. Trudy, did you whip her?

Trudy Nope, I was waiting for that. Who do you take me for anyway?

Gill I'm beginning to seriously wonder. But let's not get off the point, Trudy – what did you do?

Trudy Nothing. She used to send me all this kinky fetish underwear, and letters with money. I didn't know who to tell or what to do, so I just kept it.

Gill Everything?

Trudy Of course, her family is rich from diamonds.

Gill That's politically incorrect.

Trudy Well, you didn't complain about the Champagne dinners and presents.

Gill You swine, you never told me

Trudy You never asked.

Gill Those underwear you gave me in the past, were they from BD?

Trudy She's got good taste, hasn't she?

Gill I don't believe you. You harp on to me about buying goods from South Africa, even though Nelson Mandela is free. Yet it's OK for you to take diamond money.

Trudy Oh, so working for the police is any better?

Gill We all make mistakes.

Trudy You can say that again. So have I passed the test?

Gill Maybe.

Trudy So where is the equipment?

Gill Hold on, hold on, I don't remember saying yes. In fact I don't even remember you asking. What's it worth?

Trudy Sorry, ideologically unsound, remember?

Gill You can do better than that. On your knees?

Trudy Are you sure?

Gill What day did you say you were playing?

Trudy I didn't.

Gill When are you going to start learning?

Trudy Not from you, that's for sure. I'm just here for the gear.

Gill Who's a clever girl? Anyway, what did you want?

Note: The following part of this scene, up to and including the dildo sequence, uses physical theatre and mime, and should last between ten and fifteen minutes.

Gill *pulls a small case from underneath her bed, picks it up and opens it.*

Gill Have you made your mind up? You're not having the whole lot.

Trudy *begins to look uncomfortable.*

Trudy Oh you know, the usual, a harness, strap – and whip. Oh, I don't know, you're the sexpert.

Gill *rummages through case.*

Gill I suppose I better give you the smallest of what I've got. (*Pulls out a large black dildo.* **Trudy** *almost jumps out of her skin.*)

Trudy That's the smallest?

Gill Well you can have this one if you want. (*Pulls out a two-foot pink double-ended dildo.*)

Trudy I'm not having that white thing dangling between my legs. You've gotta be joking.

Gill Hope you're not being racist.

Trudy Look, forget it, I can't go through with it.

Gill Oh come on, I'm only teasing. But this one really is the smallest I've got. (*Takes hold of the black dildo again and throws it at* **Trudy**.) Here, catch. (**Trudy** *tries to catch it but drops it in embarrassment.* **Gill** *gets up and picks up dildo. Laughs.*) You really are a vanilla girl, if you get my drift.

Trudy Forget it. I'm going home.

Gill Come over here. It's OK. All it is is a bit of dyed moulded rubber. Go on, touch it?

Trudy *puts her hand out, and then pulls it away.*

Trudy It's so ugly.

Gill This is Kat's favourite.

Trudy The cow. Kat uses a dildo! – she's never let on to me. You give me a hard time, but Kat can obviously help herself.

Gill For a price. You'd be surprised to know what else your mentor gets up to.

Trudy I'm not interested. In fact I've had enough, I'm leaving.

Gill *grabs* **Trudy**, *and puts her hand over her eyes.*

Gill Trust me. Close your eyes, relax and count up to a hundred. (*Straps a waist-and-leg harness and dildo onto* **Trudy** *over her trousers. Spins her around gently.*) You can open your eyes now.

Trudy *nervously opens her eyes, looks straight ahead in fear.* **Gill** *pushes her towards the mirror.*

Gill Go on look into the mirror.

Trudy *looks front stage, into an imaginary mirror, and looks petrified. She looks down at the dildo very slowly and freezes. This and the rest of dildo sequence is acted out in mime technique.*

Gill Go on, move your hips a bit. Get comfortable, familiar. Get in touch with its power. Let the energy pulsate through your body.

While **Gill** *talks,* **Trudy** *begins to move her head and hand awkwardly towards the dildo.* **Gill** *rummages in her case, finds a condom and throws it towards* **Trudy**.

Catch. **Trudy***, taken off guard, drops it and bends to discover what it is.*

Gill (*while* **Trudy** *is bending*)   Always wear one of these. Go on, you'll have to put it on yourself.

Trudy *gingerly opens the condom wrapper. She tries not to look at what she is doing.*

Gill   You're not an expert at this. You're going to have to look at what you're doing.

Trudy *looks down and diligently puts the condom on. As she rolls the condom down the dildo, she slowly becomes turned on. Engrossed with putting the condom on, her hips begin to gyrate.* **Gill** *snuggles up behind her and grabs her hands.*

Trudy   How do I look?

Gill   Dare I say?

Trudy   Oh go on, I trust your opinion.

Gill   Horny.

They burst out laughing. As they calm down they begin to gently move, falling into rhythm. They both appear to be turned on in a subtle manner. **Gill** *begins to grope at* **Trudy** *who responds. Just as they are about to kiss, the sound of the doorbell ringing frantically.*

Instantly **Trudy** *pulls her knees together and tries to hide the dildo with her hands. She freezes with terror.* **Gill** *stands upright and turns to the door.*

Gill   Shit, the key! That's Kat, wait here. (*Exits and answers door.*)

Gill *re-enters with* **Kat***,* **Trudy** *still frozen.*

Kat   Ya alright, sistah?

Trudy   Yeh.

Kat   You don't look it. You look like you're all knotted up in that coconut's dog lead. Can I give you a hand?

She beckons towards **Trudy** *with her left hand, and then quickly grabs the handcuff with her right hand, pushing it up her sleeve. She throws a glance at* **Gill**.

Trudy   No, no, I'm alright. I just need the bathroom. (*Stands upright and bares all to* **Kat**.)

Kat   Bloodclart.

Trudy *exits, rushing past* **Kat** *and* **Gill**.

Kat   You sell-out. So, we're into SM, are we?

Gill   You're a fine one to talk. What the hell has SM got to do with dildos?

Trudy *re-enters, without harness and strap-on.*

Trudy Speaking of dildos, a little dicky-bird tells me I was wearing your favourite one.

Kat (*turns to* **Gill**) What have you two been gossiping about?

Gill Me, gossip? As if... My lips are sealed.

Trudy What else have you got tucked away in the closet that you're trying to protect me from, Kat?

Kat When are you going to learn that there are some things you don't discuss and do in front of white gals?

Gill Great, but you fuck them.

Trudy What's that supposed to mean?

Kat Nothing.

Trudy You're such a hypocrite.

Kat Hush ya mout.

Trudy No I bloody won't. You give me a hard time about sleeping with white women, but it's alright for you to screw white girls, as long as nobody knows.

Gill Oh so, I'm a secret am I?

Trudy Go on, worm your way out of this one.

Kat So I slept with Gill, one night. What's the big deal?

Trudy I suppose you were drunk? You're the sell-out.

Gill Look, if you girls don't mind continuing your fight outside, I've got a date tonight.

Kat Key.

Gill In the trunk.

Kat *tries to move slowly around the room so that she can look into the trunk while keeping an ear on the conversation.*

Trudy Who with?

Gill Never you mind.

Trudy You kept that under wraps.

Gill You never gave me a chance. I've been listening to you all day. You've got what you need. Now leave, I need some space.

Kat What's that all about? (*Sits on the bed, still trying to move closer to the trunk.*)

Trudy I'm having a scene with Clio.

Kat Ratied, who ya tink you are, a Miss Whiplash?

Trudy Yes.

Kat She a serious to bloodclart.

Trudy I'm fed up of your advice.

Kat I thought you was a feminist?

Trudy I was christened a womanist and Zami when I met you.

Kat (*sucks teeth*) Same difference. Zamis don't do SM.

Trudy So what is Clio?

Kat Well, she aint a Zami, that's for sure. Zamis are cultural women, who love women sexually and spiritually.

Gill Anyone for a joint, bagels, Champagne?

Trudy and **Kat** *both scowl at her.*

Gill Well, if you two are going to be miserable, I'll take the champers with me. (*Takes bottle and tries to put cork in. The others ignore her and continue their argument.*)

Trudy Clio is Black / isn't she?

Kat Black women don't / do SM.

Trudy Says who?

Kat It's common knowledge.

Trudy Just like lesbianism is a white disease.

Kat It's not in our genes. Clio must be one of those confused Americans.

Trudy Wrong! She's an Essex girl.

Gill Look you two, if you don't mind, finish your conversation somewhere else. (*They both ignore* **Gill**'s *request.*)

Kat How can you hang out with that woman? You saw her last night. She was acting out white master/Black slave scenarios.

Trudy The white woman was her slave.

Kat That's supposed to make it better? Next you'll be in a Hitler uniform brandishing swastikas, telling me it's alright, coz Black people didn't kill Jews.

Trudy That is not true! What do you take me for? All I want to do is play. Explore pleasure, desire, fun. And if strapping a dildo on, wearing fetish gear, or playing with Clio is SM, so be it.

Kat I'd rather you fucked with white women, than hang out with that bounty.

Trudy That's great, isn't it? You'd rather I fuck a Black man than go out with white women, and fuck white women than go out with a Black SM dyke. Anything else I need to know?

Gill A girl can't even get peace in her own home.

Kat I'm scared for you, Trudy. I don't want you to get corrupted. This SM is a total fuck-up. It's not for Black girls.

Trudy How can you say that?

Kat Things are changing / admittedly but –

Trudy The only thing I can see what's changed is, years ago when you were my age, dykes seemed to frightened to talk about sex.

Kat Maybe we were but we had politics.

Gill Politics . . . More like the fucking Gestapo.

Trudy So have I.

Kat Promise me one thing. Please don't parade your sexual activities in public.

Trudy What, do it behind closed doors like you? (**Kat** *sucks teeth.*) Collude with the myth, pretend I don't like being overpowered, restrained, tied up?

Kat (*sucks teeth*) Girl, you too damn English.

Gill Trudy, you've got my keys, lock up, I've had enough. This is worse than a fucking acid trip.

Kat Gill, the key!

Gill They're in the trunk.

She exits.

Trudy Key, what key? Don't say you've got keys to Gill's flat as well?

Kat No, just me need a key.

Trudy For what?

Kat Nothing, man, it alright. (*Moves toward the trunk and stretches to enter it.*)

Trudy (*pointing to* **Kat**) Handcuff! (**Kat** *sits upright and grabs hold of her wrist.*)

Kat Yeah, man, I can explain.

Trudy I'm sure you can. Next you'll be telling me that your Mrs has to keep you on a dog lead because she can't trust you.

Kat It's not like that, honest.

Trudy Oh, so you got arrested, and escaped from police custody.

Kat Gill, me a kill your pussyclart.

Trudy Leave Gill out of this.

Kat Give me a squeeze.

Trudy A squeeze! I can't take no more.

Kat   Me sorry, me know what oona must be thinking.

Trudy   Cut the patois, I've had it up to here with you and your sermons.

Kat   What's your problem?

Trudy   My problem! How fucking dare you, you've got more front than Brigitte Bardot.

Kat   Oprah Winfrey, to be exact.

Trudy   Is that supposed to be politically aware? (*Looks at her watch.*) Shit, is that the time? I'm covering for you tonight. If I had known it was because of this, I would have said no.

Kat   I'm going for an interview.

Trudy   Can't you take the pace?

Kat   I'm just fed up of having to work my butt off in the bar and earning extra cash teasing BD. Come on, Trudy, you know the score. You wasn't interested in BD's offer so I jumped in while the fire was hot. It was either that or live on the streets.

Trudy   Some of us have politics.

Kat   Yes, me dear, you nah see it.

Trudy   I'm serious, Kat, I need to think. I respected you and your opinions, but now I just don't know who to listen to anymore.

Trudy *and* **Kat** *exit.*

Blackout.

Scene Five

Diva's Bar.

Disco lights are flashing, trance music is pumping.

Clio *enters with* **BD** *and her slave* **Trace** *in dog collars.* **Clio** *walks as if she is riding in a chariot, with her slaves in dog collars pulling her along.* **Trudy** *enters the bar and does a double take. She switches the light on.*

Trudy   What the hell is going on here? Not you too?

Clio   I've found meself another slave.

Trudy   A what?

Clio   Isn't she a good girl? She's done all the cleaning for yer.

Trudy   Including the toilets?

Clio   Everything. What else would you like er to do? This is your night off.

Trudy Nothing.

Clio Watch me. Turn, you son of a bitch. (**BD** *is on all fours. She turns to face* **Clio** *with head towards the floor.*) Lick my boots. (**Trace** *prepares the boot, caressing it with her face.* **Clio** *yanks her by the collar to bid her stop.* **BD** *seductively licks both boots.* **Clio** *pulls* **BD**'s *head up and spits in her face.* **Trace** *is jealous.*) You've left a mark. (**Trace** *pushes* **BD** *out of the way and licks the boot.*) Good girl.

Trudy Stop ! Let them go, it's horrible. (**BD**, **Trace** *and* **Clio** *stop.*)

Clio What do you think, BD?

BD Wonderful, absolutely wonderful.

Clio Why don't you join us? BD would love yer too.

Trudy No / no –

Clio It's fine, I know everything. BD and I ave ad a long talk, setting out the ground rules.

Trudy I'm not interested, in fact I'm handing in my notice as of now.

Clio Easy, easy, babe, I've just earnt you a night off work.

Trudy I can't take anymore, lesbians are screwed-up like everybody else.

Clio *pulls the leash, and cracks a whip on the floor.*

Clio Time's up, BD. Trudy and I ave got things to talk about.

BD *exits on all fours.* **Trace** *takes hold of the leash and leads her off.* **Clio** *drops whip to the floor and tries to embrace* **Trudy** *who pulls back.*

Trudy There's nothing to talk about, I've had enough.

Clio Oh come on, babe, I've just earnt you a night of from that motherfucker, don't bottle out now.

Trudy That was repulsive, it's no different when the roles are reversed either.

Clio It's just a game, I'm only giving BD what she wants. It's the only kind of sex she knows.

Trudy You call that sex?

Clio Well, there's sex and sex, babe. I own Trace, she's my slave. But it's you I wanna make love to.

Trudy Clio, I just don't know, I need time to think, you and Trace are such a contradiction. I can't cope with it all. Maybe I'll meet with you in the bar, for half an hour when Kat shows up.

Clio It's a date.

Trudy Half an hour, and then I'm going to have the evening all to myself.

Clio Be-ave. (*Begins to exit.*)

Scene Five

Trudy (*picks up whip and throws it at* **Clio***'s feet*)   You've forgotten omething.

Clio   Why thank you, mam. (*Takes a bow.*)

Trudy   You're impossible.

Clio *exits.* **Trudy** *walks to the bar and begins setting up for the night.* **Trace** *enters.*

Trudy   Hi, Trace, what are you doing back here?

Trace   I thought I'd grab a drink.

Trudy   Sorry, we're closed.

Trace   Not even a little one?

Trudy   Just this once, don't make it a habit. (*Gives her a drink and continues to stock check.*)

Trace   Are you OK?

Trudy   No I'm not, I feel as if I'm going mad. I thought I was a lesbian until I began working here. Are you dating Clio?

Trace   Believe me, Trudy, all I do is serve my mistress. I belong to everyone and no one.

Trudy   Did you go home with that gay guy last night?

Trace   Why?

Gill *enters and walks up to the bar.*

Trudy   I thought you were a dyke?

Gill   Yeah, so did I.

Trace   I am, I just happen to get a thrill showing those faggots who really did invent penetration.

Gill (*sarcastic*)   Oh, you're so cool.

Trace   Right, I suppose it's time for me to go. Tell Kat I'll pop by tomorrow.

Trudy   Seeyah.

Trace *exits.*

Trudy   You don't have to be so nasty.

Gill   She just gives me the creeps.

Trudy   Each to their own.

Gill   Did Kat find the key?

Trudy   I'm not interested.

Gill   Hasn't she explained?

Trudy You heard.

Gill Oh come on it's not as bad as you think.

Trudy Has she asked you to try and butter me up?

Gill No, but I know for a fact Kat may be hypocritical at times, but she's not into bondage, that's for sure. She's got politics –

Trudy Oh, and I haven't?

Gill I know how you must feel?

Trudy Tell me, because I don't.

Gill Betrayed, but chill out a bit, and when you're ready give her a chance, she believes in you.

Kat *enters looking smug.*

Trudy I believed in her once.

Kat Got the job, girls.

Gill Doing what?

Kat Working nights in a refuge hostel. The money is brilliant.

BD *walks of her office, having changed out of bondage gear.*

BD So what's the celebration?

Kat It's my last night in this hole.

BD Well, right now you're still an employee of mine, let's see some action. Kat, Gill, everything needs cleaning tonight. I've got the inspectors in tomorrow morning. We're opening an hour later.

Gill What about Trudy?

BD She's on a date tonight. (**Trudy** *joins others at the bar. To* **Trudy**.) Go on then, what are you waiting for? It's your night off.

Kat Date?

Gill Who with?

Trudy Nobody, I'm just having a quick drink with Clio.

BD Enough chat, I want to see your beautiful teeth sparkling on the glasses.

Kat *sucks teeth and mutters.* **BD** *exits into office.* **Trudy** *pours two glasses of water and sits at the table.* **Gill** *takes a coin from her back pocket and flips it. She catches it and puts both clenched fists out in front of* **Kat**. *Coin is concealed in left hand.*

Gill Tails waitress, heads bar dyke.

Kat *taps the left fist.* **Gill** *seductively opens her fist and tails appears.* **Gill** *smiles.*

Gill I've always wanted to see you in a mini.

Kat Cha, me stay right here.

Gill Spoil sport.

Clio *walks in, dressed in club-style trousers, T-shirt and baseball cap, and a studded dog collar round her neck. She has a full-size leather mistress whip. She saunters up to* **Trudy**'s *table and sits down. They both look apprehensive of each other.*

Kat Me can't stand that woman.

Gill What has she done to you?

Kat She's into sado-masochism and that stinks.

Gill What's wrong with consensual sex?

Kat What's consensual about being tied up, pierced, being whipped?

Gill Oh come on, stretch your imagination, would you let me tie you up?

Kat No what oona take me for?

Gill Precisely, if you want it you get it.

Kat Me nah care, what's consensual about her?

Gill You mean Clio? She's a work of art, she's stunning.

Kat You might score good weed, but that's as far as it goes. SM is violence, end of story.

Gill New story, if violence happens in an SM relationship that's abuse. Your last relationship was violent, you and Kya used to knock the shit out of each other. When you confided in me you realized you didn't have to stay with each other. If I was into violence, I would have said, great, stay, enjoy the party. You know how concerned I was. I couldn't even get advice from friends, through fear of being called racist. Instead I laid awake every night wondering if you would be alive the next time we met.

Kat That's different. You'll never convince me that SM is not violence. I've seen it all in here, whip marks, knife slashes, piercings.

Trudy *walks up to the bar.*

Trudy You two look intense. Hey, Clio says BD's cleaned the place from top to bottom.

Kat And how would she know that?

Trudy She's got a name, why don't you ask her?

Kat Cha she's got attitude to rasclart.

Trudy And you haven't?

Kat Let's talk.

Trudy Not now, I'm on holiday.

Gill We better check the cellar is clean.

Kat I'll ring.

Trudy I've got an answering machine. Two Beck's, please.

Kat I'm sorry, Ms Ting, we're busy cleaning.

Gill and **Kat** *exit.* **Trudy** *takes two Beck's from the bar and sits back down with* **Clio**. *She raises her hand and seductively runs it along* **Clio**'s *collar. The rest of the scene to the end of the play should have a sense of unreality, aided by use of lighting to denote a private space.*

Trudy I absolutely adore this.

Clio Really, it's a relic from my Ell's Angel days.

Trudy You a Hell's Angel? I've heard it all now.

Clio Why are you so surprised? I still wear most of the same clothes as I did then.

Trudy I've always wanted to be a punk with pink and green hair.

Clio What's stopping you?

Trudy They're out of fashion now, silly.

Clio Why don't you come ome with me?

Trudy I'm scared.

Clio You can trust me.

Trudy How can I? I don't even know you. I thought I could trust Kat.

Clio It doesn't matter, as long as you can trust yourself, the magic word is 'Stop'.

Trudy How do I know you will stop? How can I trust you? You come gatecrashing into my workplace, shocking the living daylights out of everybody.

Clio That's coz I'm Black.

Trudy It was because you were on a dog lead.

Clio I'm sorry, I just wanted to surprise you.

Trudy Well, you managed that.

Clio I thought you andled me very well. I can't stop thinking about you.

Trudy I said, I'm scared Clio.

Clio Why?

Trudy You, BD and your slave, it gives me the creeps, but part of you excites me. I've never felt so charged before.

Clio Can you name it? What are you feeling?

Trudy All I know is that the same thing which turns me on is the same thing which scares me. You push my boundaries, press my buttons, and I just hate feeling out of control.

Clio But you can always be in control if we talk about sex first. Talk about what we will do and what we won't. That is the exciting thing about sex, talking, exploring fantasies. Acting out what we feel comfortable with.

Trudy I can't, Black girls don't do your type of sex.

Clio Be-ave. What am I? A snowflake in disguise? Sounds like your girlfriends ave given yer a right grilling.

Trudy You are different.

Clio The only difference is that I don't pretend. I sleep with who I want to. I ave great difficulty pretending I'm not on eat just because the woman is the wrong colour, or size. And I've ad my fair share of Black girls who ave taught me a thing or two.

Trudy I didn't mean to say that. I know it's a stupid comment.

Clio Come on, let's play a little. Ead fucking gives me chronic migraine.

Trudy No, I hate those bondage games. You and BD . . . Yuck.

Clio Ow about some magic? (*She takes a bow and pulls out a hanky from under her collar. She entrances* **Trudy** *seductively with the hankies during the following.*)

Trudy You're always playing with hankies, what does that mean?

Clio I'm appy to take either role tonight. (*Clenches her left hand into a fist and stuffs the hanky down it. She blows into her fist like a conjurer and beckons* **Trudy** *to do the same.*) It's your treat, you pull. (**Trudy** *begins pulling from the fist and a white hanky appears.*) Um, a girl who knows what she wants, you'll do both of us, will yer? (**Trudy** *giggles, and pulls again, a mauve one appears.*) Um, naval fetish.

Trudy *begins to pull quickly and several coloured hankies appear.* **Clio** *grabs the string of hankies tight. She waves the last colour – yellow – at* **Trudy** *and laughs.*

Trudy My favourite colour.

Clio What, water sports?

Trudy I love anything to do with water. (*Spins into* **Clio***'s arms, bound by the hankies.*)

Clio Not this type, surely? Even I can't cope with yellow ankies.

Trudy You're frightening me. (*Pulls away, and the hankies fall to the floor.*)

Clio So name your game. What's your fantasy? Lighten up.

The rest of the scene is acted in physical theatre style.

Trudy *smiles. She does a cartwheel.*

Clio Oh no, none of that fancy stuff.

Trudy *continues to act physical, farcically, egging* **Clio** *on. She stands upright all of a sudden and pushes her chest out. She starts beating on her chest.*

Trudy (*Tarzan call*) Me, Tarzan.

Clio (*with surprise*) Me, Jane, be-ave.

Trudy Why not?

They act out a short Tarzan–Jane skit. **Clio** *breaks the fun.*

Clio I'm Samson and you're Delilah.

They act a short Samson and Delilah skit. **Trudy** *breaks the fun.*

Trudy I'm Romeo and you're Juliet.

Clio 'Slowly and wise, they stumble who run fast.'

Trudy Thumbelina, all the better to fuck you with.

Clio (*gasps*) I'm Sleeping Beauty.

Trudy King Kong. (*Walks in a King Kong style towards his Sleeping Beauty.*)

Clio (*screams*) Take me, take me, I'm Alice in Wonderland. (*Moves in slow motion, showing her delight at seeing* **Trudy** *exuding sexuality. She gently takes her hand, hair and reacts with delight.* **Trudy** *begins to feel awkward from the attention.*)

Trudy Tom and Jerry.

They act out Tom and Jerry. They play with the whip, sexualizing, using it as their tail, snatching the whip off each other. **Clio** *is excited and gets carried away as Tom.* **Trudy** *becomes excited too as Jerry; she stands up on two legs and roars like a lion.* **Clio** *picks up the whip and acts as a ring leader. They act out this scene.* **Trudy** *grabs hold of the whip and begins to crack it. She becomes intoxicated by its power. They pull the whip from each other, cracking the floor with it.* **Clio** *remains sexual in her whipping style, while* **Trudy** *becomes excited, dangerous, out of control, unsafe, going beyond boundaries. She begins to crack the whip at* **Clio** *and becomes more and more excited and carried away.*

Clio Stop!

Instant blackout.

Valerie Mason-John on *Sin Dykes*

Valerie   I'd like to say something about audiences and *Sin Dykes*. I was in *Sin Dykes*, but for me the audience was before the play even opened, because it was controversial; it was controversial because it had three Black women and three white women and it was focusing on S&M relationships. It was during that time where people had come with axes to chop up Chain Reaction. One of the reasons we did the frisking of the audience was to see whether people were coming in with dangerous weapons. And also because I always straddled that part. There were the Black-only spaces where I would go; but I was somebody who, because of the way I was raised, had white people in my life. So, I would have parties where there would be a mix, where Black and white people would come and it would be really quite mixed. So the audience, there was a tension and there was a buzz before the play even opened. Being in it, I think the most powerful part for me was playing Clio and having my white slave on a dog collar; because we could have switched it around, but it was like 'no', and that was the powerful part and the audience gasps.

Mojisola   I love that Tonderai's mouth just dropped open and you won't get that in the transcript.

Valerie   *Sin Dykes* is a Black British play and it's also talking about the issues. I was completely shocked when I was sent that clip about *Sin Dykes* from *That Black Theatre* podcast that what the characters were saying you could think they were talking about George Floyd. So, I would say that the play is definitely politically motivated, the politics was my news. If I was to see *Sin Dykes* performed again, I would want a trans character written into it; because back then the whole thing was about this Black–white relationship, but definitely I would have a trans character written into it now.

On diaspora programming

Mojisola Coming back to you, Rikki, we wondered about programming at Theatre Royal Stratford East. One of the things that amazed me as an audience member was the experience of going to see Christopher Rodriguez's play *High Heel Parrotfish*, which represented trans experience in Trinidad, and that being programmed side by side with *Bashment*. I felt like I was part of this season being warmed up by the programming for *Bashment*. I wondered about the Caribbean, and that moment in 2005 of those two particular performances sitting side by side, and how that was for you as an artist going to Jamaica for the first time doing that research and the kind of Caribbean connections. Any reflections about the intersection of those things and those islands being there at Theatre Royal Stratford East at that time?

Rikki You're right, it was a very special season because we were rehearsing while they were on. So, we were sitting up in the balcony watching that show and mixing with them in the green room, which was a very joyous thing. It was a wonderful moment and a moment that a lot of theatres wouldn't have been brave enough to do, especially back in 2005.

The Caribbean and queerness is so complicated. It was my first time going to Jamaica and my mum Monica was there at the same time. She was very defensive of Jamaica. And because I was there to do a thing about homophobia, and as a visibly queer person herself, she wanted me to not simplify it. And she was right. But it was very hard for me not to; I was so triggered by a lot of things that I really struggled. She reminded me that we were there and not dead, because I was getting a lot of stories about people being macheted to death and stuff. And it was so complicated the whole thing of, obviously, religion was a huge part of it and the colonialization of Western religions in people's minds and the shame that there was; because we're presented as sensual, so queerness is a betrayal of our sensuality, that we've been trying to strike a balance with in Western society – you know dancing, but going to church on Sunday, dancing on Saturday and dutty wining and going to church on Sunday with little lacy gloves on – was kind of that whole legacy I grew up with that feeling. And it was such an instructive experience to dig back into that and to have conversations with people and to see that their queerness was what they feared.

And that we've been taught that we were all queer in the oldest sense of the word, you know, weird, strange. Our dances, our bodies, our ways of using our bodies, our sensuality, all of that and in the kind of colonialism and in the case of the Caribbean, you know, outright centuries of slavery and plantation attitudes and all of those things are so deeply embedded in us, and in our slave traders who have the same battle with their own sensuality. British people have a famous battle with their sensuality and their sexuality. And there, you know, it was so complicated, and the Protestant fear of femininity and masculinity. And then the crossovers of that and how they inhabit each of us was just such a huge knot to untangle the entire time. And the thing that I learned from that trip and from that season was that the only way to counter it was to unashamedly inhabit my own, to inhabit my masculinity and inhabit my femininity, and inhabit my Britishness and inhabit my Africanness, and inhabit my

Caribbeanness, inhabit all of it; and to present myself and my plays, but not always my individual characters, as being absolutely an essential full human being. So in fact my characters too, I wanted them to be full human beings, no villains, blaming no one, all of us accountable, all of us potentially on the verge of complete and utter freedom and self-comfort in our bodies and in our souls.

And that is really what I learned there in those couple of years while I was doing that documentary putting it out, getting those responses, still recovering from the kind of tidal wave of fear that came when I made *Metrosexuality* (television series); I got a huge tidal wave of fear about my vision of the world, and all of that, and 2002–5 was where I really learned to stand up strong in myself and encourage everybody through the work by challenging everything head on to stand up inside themselves. And that is what I think our work is for. It's a very convoluted answer because it's a very convoluted question, but the simple answer is that every moment that you enjoy yourself in your body and in your work, and then you present that to the public, it's like the opposite to when you say you don't believe in fairies and the fairy dies. It's when you say you believe in this fairy that fairies come alive all over the place. And, you know, that's what I learned in that season, along with the things that didn't work in our shows as well as the things that did, and seeing audience responses to it, and the hunger they had to see that. It set me on this phase of my creative life.

Mojisola Thank you. Certainly, I feel like I grew into this after *High Heel Parrotfish* and going back for *Bashment*. *High Heel Parrotfish* made me celebrate my trans sisters in Trinidad and *Bashment* made me feel like, wow, just so brave. And that thing that you're saying about inhabiting yourself, because so much of my life I spent almost kind of half apologizing for my Danish side and thinking maybe because I'm a lesbian I'm not quite Black enough, and actually going, 'I am all of those things in the fullness of those things.'

Rikki Yeah, you don't have to apologize for your bougieness, or your intellectual side, or your ghettoness, or anything about you; you don't have to apologize because you're all of it, and we're all of it, and the minute we admit to being all of it without any shame, everyone gets the freedom to go, 'Oh I'm all of it too.' And that's why that *High Heel Parrotfish* thing is so powerful because at Carnival you let go of all of that, you're not trying to please God, you aren't trying to believe, you're just going back to your pagan roots. And then everything is pleasured.

Bashment

Rikki Beadle-Blair

For John Gordon

First performance at Theatre Royal Stratford East, 20 May–18 June 2005
Restaged 29 September–22 October 2005

Cast (in order of speaking)

JJ	Joel Dommett
Orlando	Anthony Newell
MC Eggy	Jason Steed
White Fang	Davie Fairbanks (originally played by Joe Marshall)
MC Venom	Ludvig Bonin
MC KKK	Nathan Clough
Karisma	Jennifer Daley
Sam	Arnie Hewitt
Daniel	Elliott James-Fisher (originally played by Luke Toulson)
Kevan	Duncan MacInnes
Bashment Compere	Arnie Hewitt
Arresting Officer, Judge, Prison Officer	Elliott James-Fisher
Musician	Joni Levinson

Creative team

Written and Directed	Rikki Beadle-Blair
Set and Lighting Design	Giuseppe di Ioriod
Sound Design	Gareth Owen
Music	Rikki Beadle-Blair
'How do you love me' performed by Rikki, Joni Levinson and Antoine Stone	
Bashment music performed by Antoine Stone and Rikki	
Engineered and Co-produced	Antoine Stone
Costume Design	Fola Solanke
Graffiti Art	John Gordon
Assistant Manager on the Book	Altan Reyman

During the rehearsals of the first production Rikki Beadle-Blair spoke about *Bashment* with Theatre Royal Press Officer Michael Siva and some members of the original cast

Michael What is this play about?

RBB It's about love for music, love for humanity, and the flip side of that, which is hate and self-hatred, fear of music and fear of humanity.

Michael What made you write *Bashment*?

RBB Being involved in this ongoing and growing debate about racism among Black people, racism in music, racism in Britain, and homophobia in music and Britain, in everyone. It's not just the obvious thing, which is homophobia, but it's also the racism that informs our opinions about these things. It wasn't just a simple thing of, 'Oh, there's a group of people and they don't like gay people'. The debate was so clouded by the way those groups of people were seen by society, the way that society saw itself. It was like the Russian babushka dolls – there was always something else inside the box inside the box inside the box. It was such a complex thing, and I wanted to start opening the boxes inside myself and understanding what I felt about the issue. So, it's a kind of internal debate between these fragments of me. Three years ago, I made a documentary for BBC Radio 4, *Roots of Homophobia*, in which I attempted to trace the homophobia that has recently become rampant in reggae music back to its source in Jamaica. It turned out to be a painful and complex journey, one that took me through the recording studios and churches of the Caribbean and brought me right back here to the British Isles where the laws and religious teachings that informed Jamaican attitudes came from. I debated the issues with my interviewees and even the most vehemently anti-gay told me I'd made them think. The documentary aired. It did well. I got amazing letters, I got awards. People said I'd got them thinking. But nothing really changed – the gay-baiting records multiplied – the 'kill the battyman' sentiments becoming even more casually confident even as they became more vicious. And then last spring, Brian Williamson, the prominent gay Jamaican activist, was murdered in his own home. And last summer Peter Tatchell's Outrage asked me to join them in a campaign against ragga music. I admire Outrage – they are the only ones doing something – and something must be done. But still I was conflicted and hesitant about where we would be going or where we were coming from, and why was I so ambivalent? Was it because I was Black? Was that reining in my gayness? As the press got wind of the issue and the column inches proliferated, I felt my uneasiness increase. I wanted to have a conversation with Outrage. But we were all so busy. Still I wanted to do something. So I wrote this play – to look for the truth to examine the complexity – and to try to do justice to our humanity – all of us – the queerest and the most homophobic (not necessarily mutually exclusive qualities), our humour, our honesty, our hatreds and our hopes. This is not my final word on this subject, but it draws on what I know so far and asks the question that nags at me every day about so many aspects of our lives: What on earth is going on?

Michael What are your personal views about the use of anti-gay lyrics in dancehall music?

RBB They are unnecessary and painful and hurtful, and dangerous, but there are so many things that are painful, hurtful and dangerous in society and yet they exist. Really, my journey has been to try and get past my knee-jerk reaction to those things. I need to get to: how can a record like this be selling so much? Why do people have these feelings? And that takes me to the bigger question. Why do people have these feelings about race, or about women, or about any group in society? Why do people think it's all right to withhold rights, or withhold their own acknowledgement of anybody else's humanity? It makes no sense and yet it can be so widespread. It's not just in Jamaica. It's in America, where they're trying to put anti-gay laws in place right now. Over here, we're just reaching the stage where gay people have equal partnership rights. The idea where somebody can even debate the equality of another human being is shocking to me. I keep thinking about that whole picture, rather than saying, 'Homophobic lyrics – we must stop them'. I want to know where the feelings are coming from and understand that and hopefully, somehow, ease the pain that's causing that.

Ludvig As a gay, Black man, how did you feel writing this play?

RBB I found it hard to understand why people beat each other up. I found it hard to confront, but it was good for me. I found the anger and the hatred really hard. Trying to get all my feelings about it, and the debates that I have, all into a play, that was hard. It wasn't difficult to do, but rather painful to do. It was a challenge, but a painful challenge. But the things that make me want to write are the things that I don't understand. Somebody said to me the other day, 'Everything you do has loads of drugs in it'. I thought to myself, no, it doesn't! This play doesn't, for instance. But I thought back to the last five or six things I'd written and there's loads of drugs in them. And I've never taken a single drug. But to me, it's my way of trying to understand it, to get it, appreciate it and not just put myself above it. Violence in there is not part of my life, but I want to understand it. I want to bring myself closer to people that I don't relate to.

Jason Which character in *Bashment* did you most enjoy writing about?

RBB There wasn't one in particular. There isn't a favourite character to write about, because they're all fragments of me. They're all parts of me.

Jason Is that how you write generally, in all your plays?

RBB Yeah, not consciously, but I've become very aware, very quickly, that they're all bits of me, arguing with each other. No matter how unpleasant what they say is, you can't write something more unpleasant than what you would think of. There's always something that's hiding in you that you're questioning, or challenging, or revealing.

Joel What do you want your audience to get out of it?

RBB I want them to think. I would like people to judge each other less, though you can't erase judgements. People do bad things, but I would like people to judge each other less and relate to each other more, because I think that's the answer to the conflict, to understand each other more.

Arnie Do you think that people coming to see *Bashment* will be coming more to see a musical than a serious play?

RBB I worried a lot about the title, but it's so strong, because it covers the music and it has 'bashing' in it, so it seems absolutely the right title. The celebration of music in the play is about my love for music, as well as my disappointment in the message that music can bring, or the way that people can use it. All the way through the play, the love of the music is expressed in the characters, though it's not a musical. I love writing musicals, but that's not what this is. It's a play about music, rather than a play done through music.

Joel Are you aiming to write a play that's naturalistic?

RBB I admire naturalistic film makers hugely. Ken Loach is a genius. But it's not me. That's not what I do. Dreams, to me, are the reality, and people tell the truth through their dreams. That's when you can't control what you're feeling. To me, theatre and art and film are like hyper-real things. Take Chagall's *The Birthday*. You have a girl, it's her birthday, she's holding a cake, he's kissing her, but he's upside down floating in the air and she's kind of off the ground, coming away from the cooker. To me, that's what captures what it's like to be in love with somebody and they've made you a birthday cake and you kissed them. You feel as if you're ten feet off the ground. It's not real, but it's honest. I'm not interested in naturalism. The thing of having them debating, I had to surrender to that to a degree and say, it's OK to do political theatre that involves discussion, because this subject needs discussion. The thing that's going wrong between the characters in the play is that they haven't experienced discussion up to now about it. I wanted to start the discussion. The characters would discuss the issue in the play; hopefully the audience would discuss it in the foyer, the critics would discuss it in the papers and people would start thinking about it.

Jason Who inspired you to write originally, back in the day?

RBB My mum. She taught me to read and write, before I went to school. So, when I was three, I started to read and I immediately wanted to be a writer. I think it was all those books in the library. There was a kind of magic world in the library and I wanted to just be a part of that world. All these people had so much to say, so many words and it was so exciting, I've still never written anything that's been in a library, but to me that's incredibly exciting. I just wanted to do that. Now, what inspires me to write is a good writer, especially American ones, but the thing that really inspires me are paintings and good songwriters. But what inspires me the most to write are actors, which is why I tend to cast things before I write them. I can go into situations where I don't know what I'm going to say, what I'm going to write, but I know that if somebody's passionate about their craft and if someone's a good actor, it makes me desperate to hear them say my lines, so I find something for them to say.

Michael Which part of Jamaica is your mother from?

RBB My mother's a big-town gal from Kingston! She was actually there at the same time when I did my documentary on her own little trip. So, I met up with her a couple of times. She was very, very, very excited that I was there finally, in Jamaica, and she wanted me to enjoy the beauty of the place and the people. She was concerned about the homophobia in the music, but she didn't want me to just see Jamaica in that light. She really wanted me to celebrate it, so it was quite difficult for her, I think. It was as complicated for her, with me being there and doing this documentary, as it was for me.

Michael Could you tell us a bit about your previous work?

RBB I did a TV series called *Metrosexuality*. It was about a community in West London, which was Black, white, gay, straight – every sexuality and colour in between. That's still playing all around the world. I've worked on a radio series of my own where I've played characters. Every day I'd play a different character, and I'd have a guest actor with me playing a guest character. Radio was great, because I could play anything and do anything, and what I looked like didn't get in the way. I played a dog once, my dog Angelica, and then I played a racist taxi driver who turned out to be Black. I did a movie called *Stonewall* for BBC and an American company. That was great, because that brought me to the attention to the Americans, and I was very lucky to have that. I'm the executive story editor for a TV series in America right now called *Noah's Ark*. I just wrote a musical down at the Ovalhouse called *Prettyboy*, and my company, Angelica, is resident over at the Actors Centre, and hopefully resident in other places as well. I'm looking for work, so we can word this like a personal ad, you know – 'Actor/writer/director/composer likes long walks and making art. Looking for theatres and film companies for a lasting relationship.' I just love to work, and I do a lot of work. I've got a big output in a lot of different areas. I can't be busy enough. Time is short. You've got to create.

Michael What plans do you have for the future after *Bashment*?

RBB I'm doing a stage version of *Stonewall*, which I'm adapting now for the Pleasance Theatre. I'm doing another two productions for the Axis Centre. One's called *Human*, which is a romantic comedy between people who have terminal illnesses. Hopefully, I'm going to do more plays here in London, and then I'm off to America. Of course, the thing I do every year is I work with young filmmakers in South Africa, helping them make their first films. I've done this for two years, making short films. Next year, I'm hoping to get three directors together to make a feature.

Michael How do you feel this play reflects Stratford East's commitment to develop new talent and new voices?

RBB This play is a poster for Stratford East's policies, which I applaud, because I was able to use a completely new cast. For most of these actors, it is their first professional theatre job. So, they're all unknown actors, who I've written the play for, and they've very kindly let me do that. And actually, this is only my second writing job for theatre. I've written lots and lots of television and radio, and film, and been paid lots of money for that! But this is only my second paid professional writing job in London for theatre. So, I'm new talent! We have a first-time costume designer, we have a racially diverse cast, and I think we're going to have a lot of first-time audience members as well. The subject matter of the play is something we deliberately chose to bring young people into the theatre, so they can see that it can be as relevant as cinema like *Bullet Boy* or the TV programmes that they watch and the music they listen to.

The way I work, by Rikki Beadle-Blair

Of course the exact details of the process depend on the project – when other companies ask me to write for them, especially when I am not the director, I usually work in the way that suits the organization or person who I'm working for. Invariably this means we talk, I write, they give notes and I rewrite and rewrite until they feel the script is ready to shoot, or be staged, or sent to Development Hell.

I have no problems working this way – in fact, it can be fun – but when I am the writer/director, as with this play, I prefer to cast the piece first and then write specifically for the cast. They are usually a combination of people who I have worked with for a long time, newish people who have done one or two productions or participated in readings and workshops along with brand new actors who have written to me recently and invited me along to see their work. If they capture my imagination and manage to keep themselves on my radar, I eventually call them up and ask if I can write a part for them. Once I have enough yesses (you'd be surprised how many people are too busy to have a play written for them), we get together and sit round a table. I tell them what the play is likely to be about (if I know) and then we chat, possibly about the subject matter, but more probably about a wandering range of random subjects . . . At the end of the first session the actors choose their characters' names and sometimes answer ten random questions about their characters – and then I go away and start to write.

We meet for the chats perhaps once a week for a month or two, and, hopefully, to read the latest instalment. It unfolds like a weekly soap, all of us curious to see what on earth will happen next. Suddenly, eventually I feel ready to bind the pages and we have a script, we have a play! Or at least a first draft. And we start to rehearse. And talk. And I rewrite and rewrite and rewrite, the poor cast highlighting their lines in script after script only to throw them away that same day.

So far, this process has not involved any improvising – though I'm not ruling it out for the future – but their presence and group dynamic is crucial to the development of the play. As I sample their 'personality DNA' I find that my usual themes and obsessions are informed with unexpected triggers that are sparked by the personalities, strengths, limitations and physical attributes of the actors I am working with. They are not playing themselves, by any means; they are often required to transform themselves quite dramatically and sometimes traumatically. They fill in extensive questionnaires in character, we do field trips to research accents and character histories as we try to create as total a synthesis between the actor and the character and keep on interrogating the script and myself and rewriting . . . The cast is a crucial element. They don't write the play – but it would be a totally different creation without them . . . Let me take this moment to thank every actor who has allowed me to write a part for them – You are my muses. My source of inspiration and revelation. And I cannot wait to see what you make happen next.

If you want to work with Rikki or ask a question – please email: RikkiBB@aol.com

Characters

JJ, *twenty-one-year-old Bristol-born white boy – low-key hip-hop styling – quiet, determined*
Orlando, *twenty-one-year-old Bristol-born and white – arty, bohemian, feminine, intelligent*
MC Eggy, *twenty-three-year-old East London-born African, muscular, ragga MC – protective*
White Fang, *twenty-year-old Jewish middle-class mockney who chats blackney – cocky*
MC Venom, *twenty-one-year-old East London-born African – compact fit ragga DJ – nervy*
MC KKK, *twenty-two-year-old East London-born Jamaican – wiry, ragga MC – explosive intense*
Karisma, *twenty-one-year-old, Yorkshire-born mixed-race girl – confident, unconventional*
Sam, *ageless feminine Black guy – dry wit and wisdom*
Daniel, *twenty-eight-year-old white lawyer – home counties – old-fashioned – uptight – shy*
Kevan, *twenty-one-year-old white art student – middle-class, northern – mouthy*
Arresting Officer, Judge, Prison Officer

The action takes place in East London today.

Pre-show – Audience Arrives to Find . . .

Three hanging punchbags. **JJ** *in his space –* **Eggy** *and* **Venom** *in theirs – kicking, punching, sweating, focused.*

Lights down on **Eggy** *and* **Venom**, *light still up on* **JJ**.

Orlando and JJ's Flat

One punchbag. **JJ** *is training.*

Sound: Key in the lock – front door opening then slamming.

JJ   Shit!

JJ *darts to bathroom, pulling off his training wraps . . .*

Sound: Bathroom door slams.

. . . just as **Orlando** *comes hurrying through, laden with shopping bags.*

Orlando   Oh God, oh God, oh God, oh God . . .

Muttering anxiously as he scurries, **Orlando** *pulls off his sarong and, struggling with a sandal, hops off to the bedroom.*

Oh God, oh God, oh God, oh God . . .

Sound: Bedroom door slams – bathroom door opens.

JJ *bursts back in, chewing his toothbrush and struggling to spray under his arms whilst pulling on his top.*

Sound: Car horn.

JJ   Shit! Orly! We're late!

Orlando (*offstage*)   I know! Five minutes!

JJ *hurries to the front door.*

Sound: Front door opening.

JJ   Five minutes, mate!

Sound: Front door closes.

JJ   Orly! Where've you been? I've been texting you!

Orlando   I know! I'm sorry!

JJ   Did you fall asleep in the park again? Like that time I found you face down on your laptop?

Orlando   That was a year ago! First day of the first term when we first came to London! I was resting my eyes!

JJ You were sleeping, Orly! In the park! You could have been mugged or raped or pissed on!

Orlando Stop – I'm getting an erection! I've been shopping!

JJ 'Shopping'? This is my big night.

Orlando (*offstage*) I know!

JJ This is the biggest bashment event on the calendar, babe.

Orlando (*offstage*) I know!

JJ Do you know what DJs and MCs up and down the country would give to compete tonight?

Orlando (*offstage*) I know!

JJ Do you know what it means for a white boy from . . .

Orlando (*offstage*) . . . 'Bristol to even get a sniff of this'? Yes, my lover, I know. Rude Boy have to 'come correc' innit'? and 't'row down on the 'Wheels of Steel'. Your face has to fit and your style has to blend. Which is why I've purchased . . .

Orlando *enters in a loud hip-hop/ragga-ish outfit.*

. . . this.

JJ That?

Orlando What's wrong with this?

JJ (*quickly*) It's fine.

Orlando What? This is dancehall stylee! OK, Rude Boy, bruk it down – from the feet up – What?

JJ Well . . .

Orlando Well?

JJ Sandals, Orly?

Orlando New butch sandals! Doc Marten sandals!

It's the painted toenails – I can clean 'em off in the cab.

JJ It's a packed nightclub, babe. People dancing and stomping. You'll be crippled. You can wear my spare Timberlands.

Orlando Fine. Timberlands. What about the rest of it?

JJ Top's a bit tight.

Orlando Yours is tighter.

JJ Mine's guy tight. Yours is . . .

Orlando . . . 'Gay tight'? (*Pulling at the top.*) Fine – we'll stretch it. – It's Gaultier, but we'll stretch it.

JJ   Orly, you asked.

Orlando   The trousers? Too tight?

JJ   Bit bright.

Orlando   Ragga is bright! (*Pulling CD from bag.*) I've done my research! Ragga is fucking blinding! Look at these lot – shirts in iridescent pink and retina-scorching orange, red gold n' green string vests, Moschino trousers pocked with glittering silver dollar signs, great big gold necklaces and great big fuck-off diamante earrings – they're fops, they're dandies, they're a gaggle of fucking Miami drag queens! Ragga is camp as fuck and this outfit is fucking fierce! . . . What?

JJ (*taking a photo*)   It'sssss . . . cute . . . You're cute.

Orlando   But? Cute ain't required? Maybe I'm not required then.

JJ   Orly, babe, we in't got time for this.

Orlando   I'm serious, JJ. I've blown a month's budget on dressing like Beenie Man and I've minced out of the bedroom looking like Queenie Man! I don't want to be a liability.

JJ   You are not a liability.

Orlando   And I'm not deaf. I've listened to the music, I've heard the lyrics and I know the score. Reggae artists don't like bottymen . . .

JJ   . . . Battymen . . .

Orlando   . . . Or cha-cha men . . .

JJ   Chi-chi men. Not all of 'em.

Orlando   Just the ones that sing about it.

JJ   It's just music, Orly.

Orlando   Just music? Rude Boy, the day we first met you told me that hip-hop was your heart and ragga was the blood pumping round you. And suddenly, when you finally notice they're preaching that we don't have the right to fucking breathe, it's 'just music'? They're trying to tell us something, love. If being a white boy in the dancehall is a hurdle to jump – being a gay boy is gonna be a fucking canyon. And when I'm around you're gay in great big pink neon lights – and The Music don't like it.

JJ (*stroking* **Orlando**'s *cheek*)   Orly . . .

Orlando   Look at you, touching another man's face and staring into his eyes . . . You're a great big faggamuffin.

JJ   Orlando – My lover – It's . . . just . . . music. Yeah, it's a powerful thing. A river of rhythmic blood runs through it. It's the voice of struggle – it's the beat of freedom and infinite possibility. But it's still just music. It in't perfect. It's like us, still growing, still learning – and to reach its massive potential it needs to face and be faced by its fear – Just like us. The Music needs this love – just like us. The Music needs the lyrics you inspire. The Music needs you. I'm gonna seize that DJ contest tonight – I'm gonna step up, claim our damn prize, thank my lover and walk out of there with you on my arm – and we're gonna change the world. Now let's fetch some Tims to protect those feet and catch that cab, what do you say?

Orlando   I say . . . Lyrics. I love you, Rude Boy.

He puts on the Timberlands. **JJ** *looks round at the clothes strewn along the ground and smiles – he pulls out his digital camera and starts to photograph* **Orlando***'s trail.*

Petrol Station/Eggy and Venom's Flat

Two punchbags – **Venom** *and* **Eggy** *box furiously.*

Julian Wolfavitz White Fang, *macked out in raggamuffin threads, is dialling as he enters and joins a queue formed by* **Sam** *and* **Daniel**. **Karisma** *at the till.*

Sound: phone.

Still wearing boxing gloves, **Eggy** *manages to answer his flip phone.*

Eggy   You're late.

White Fang   Eggy, man! I'm at the service station down the corner!

Eggy   Congratulations.

White Fang   I'm jus' in the queue, blood! Me reach in five! You lot set?

Eggy (*struggling to open a bottle of water*)   Mmm.

White Fang   Both me other bredrens there, yeah? Venom, yeah?

Eggy (*gulping water*)   Mmm.

White Fang   Is wha' you saying? Venom's there, yeah?

Eggy (*post-gulp breath*)   Haaaaahhh . . . Yup.

White Fang   What about KKK?

Eggy   What about him?

White Fang   Did he pitch up yet? Cheese and bread, man! Jus mek I speak to your cousin, yeah?

Eggy *taps* **Venom***'s shoulder and hands him the phone.*

Eggy   Talk this nigga off the roof, man.

Venom *tucks the phone into the crook of his neck as* **Eggy** *wanders off.*

Venom   Whaddup, nigga!

White Fang Is how you tell me 'whaddup' like you don't know what time it is?

Venom Why, what time is it?

White Fang Don't play, blood, don't play, you get me? I and I ain't in no mood, for real, blood. Pressure reach, blood – pressure reeeeach! Jus' answer me, blood – did KKK pitch yet?

Venom You mean he ain't with you?

White Fang (*closing his eyes*) I'm taking a deep breath now, Venom, man – to beg you me brudda, yeah? Get you n' Eggy showered, shampooed, press' n' dress' by the time me reach, me bredren, please, me beseech, it's pas' nine!

Eggy *returns with a pair of cold beers. Taking a beer,* **Venom** *hands the phone back to* **Eggy**.

White Fang This is our night, dread! This is the big Kahuna, you get me? Peoples dem a flock from far-flung corner a the country for this t'rowdown tonight and they ain't come to play, blood! You peoples need to scrape the crust out your eye and be at the door all alert and ready to chip and gone, ca' we pitch up late and it's over, end of! You hearing me, blood? You feeling me?

Eggy *rolls the cold beer across his brow and under his arms.*

White Fang Venom, you feeling me?

Eggy Yeah, man, seen.

White Fang You lot! I ain't playing, Egg-Man! This shit is real!

Eggy Yeah, blood, real, blood, feel you.

At that moment, **KKK** *bursts into the petrol station . . .*

KKK Yo! Sista! Gimme a Twix!

White Fang KKK located – back on track – ETA t'ree minutes – come correct to the kerb when I bell you, seen?

Eggy Seen, man, seen . . .

White Fang Is wha' y' wan'? Snickers or Mars?

Eggy Caramac.

Venom Kit-Kat and Flake.

White Fang I spoil you lot.

Petrol Station

Sound: cash register.

White Fang Yo, K!

KKK   Yo, sista!

Karisma *looks around, 'you can't be addressing me' style.*

KKK   How long you plannin'a blank a brudda for?

White Fang   K, bwoy, we ain't got time for this, man.

KKK (*still focused on* **Karisma**)   . . . What am I, Black or summink?

Karisma   See that there behind you? That orderly line of people stood patiently waiting? Here in civilization we call that a queue.

White Fang (*stepping forward*)   Alright, sis, alright darling, let's keep things moving, yeah? That's a Twix, a Kit-Kat, a Flake and a Caramac.

Karisma   That's Q and a U and an E and . . .

KKK   See, this here in front of you? This gleaming ebony proof that there is a God and he loves Black women? We call this a Black Man. And Black Man don't deal in queues – you get me, sis? Black Man have stood in 'nuff lines since time, you get me? Bread-line – dole-queue lines, immigration lines and police identification line-up. Well, Black Man broke away, seen? Black Man don't stand in line no more for nuttin'! Black man just step, from the back of the bus to the front, so, 'cause he knows he can count on his brudda and sista them cutting him a break. Or ain't it like that where you come from, lil' lassie?

Karisma   Sorry, I keep trying to catch a glimpse of this sister you keep talking to – or is she like your imaginary friend that only you can see?

KKK   Is who you a talk to so?

Karisma   Dunno, mate, who the hell are you? Next!

Sam   I suppose that must be me.

KKK*'s head turns with the deadly slowness of a Terminator as* **Sam** *moves forward on delicate feet to stand behind him.*
'Scuse me, brotha . . .

KKK   Damn. Shouldn't you be on top of some Christmas tree somewhere?

Sam   That position's reserved for fully qualified fairies – I'm just a trainee – working in the community to earn my wings. (*To* **Karisma**.) That's pump number three, a pack of Juicyfruits, some Red Rizla and a pack of Marlboro Lights, please.

KKK   You ain't mean to tell me you're serving this pussyraas bitch before me?

Karisma   No.

KKK   Hell no!

Karisma   I'll not be serving anyone before you . . .

KKK   Step off, batty boy . . .

Karisma   . . . 'Cause I'll not be serving you. Pump number three, pack of Juicyfruits, pack of Red Rizlas and pack of Marlboro Lights – that's sixteen pounds eighty-five pence please.

KKK and **Karisma** speak simultaneously.

KKK   . . . Listen, bitch, and listen good yeah . . .
Karisma   That's my name. Don't wear it out . . .

White Fang   OK, OK, ding ding, end of round one – everyone in their corner, yeah? OK, sis, what's your name, yeah?

Karisma   Bitch'll do fine . . .

White Fang   Sista, sistaaaa – help a brudda, out, yeah? Check me out trying to hang like Kofi Annan, trying to reunite the peoples, yeah? So, why doncha contribute to world peace, yeah and give us your name, yeah?

Karisma   Karisma.

White Fang   Now, that's a name. See how creative Nubian peoples can be? That's pure poetry, right there, fi real. Is your real name, yeah?

Karisma   Yes.

White Fang   Oh, sista gyal, you lucky still – you come from creative stock. My parents named me Julian, man – I mean, whassatabout? 'Julian'? Julian Wolfavitz – AKA White Fang, 'sup? (*Shaking her hand.*) See my man here christened Dijon Socrates Lawrence the third AKA inna da area as KKK – Krazy Kop Killa – Prob'ly you hearda 'im?

Karisma   Actually, no.

White Fang   Well, sista – fi sure you will. Inevitability in effec'. It's all about time, sis – Nature will take its course and soon, seen, ca' tonight my man here and him crew – the Ilford Illmanics – them a compete in the MC throwdown and mek I tell you as their promoter, manager, mentor what-have-you that said show is seized for real prisoners taken – castle captured, declare a damn ceasefire. See, what you a deal wit' here is a lyrical landscaper ready to tag his own Sistine Chapel – a fledgling legend on the edge of success and so he's just a lickle bit cranky, just a lickle bit wired. Ain't about you, sis, or this lickle chi-chi man standing here, it's about artistic temperament and the agony of genius, ca' all this Nubian warrior needs is just one itty-bitty lickle Twix to soothe his savage breast so the mojo will flow and another brother can rise. Contribute to world peace, sis support the arts, uplif' the race – and give the brudda a flippin' twix, yeah?

Pause.

Karisma   Next.

Sam   Still me. (*Searching in a very girly backpack.*) Do you take Switch?

Karisma   When your lyrical landscaper comes up with a phrase deeper than gimme a Twix – he can colour me impressed, alright? (*To* **Sam**.) Switch away, darlin' . . .

Just as the card is about to change hands, **KKK** *puts his hand over* **Sam**'*s.*

KKK Yo. Sista. Give me a Twix.

Daniel Excuse me.

All turn to see **Daniel**, *standing in line.*

Do you think you could take your hand off him?

KKK/White Fang Say what?

Daniel Sorry, that was rude of me – Do you think you could take your hand off him . . . please?

KKK Who the fuck are you – his boyfriend?

Daniel Sadly not.

White Fang Damn raasclaat batty boys, man – they're fucking everywhere! Babylon a' crawlin'!

KKK Nah, blood, He ain't gay, jus' posh. Ain't it, blue blood? You ain't a no gay pussyraas?

Daniel I prefer queer, actually. Well, I'm old-fashioned. Can't bear to stand aside while a brute manhandles a beauty. Just have to 'step up' – I believe that's the phrase? – step up, speak up and ask you respectfully to take your hands off him, please.

KKK You think I don't know what brute means? You think I don't know words and meanings? You think you can stand there and talk down like you so high and me so low? You drink spunk for breakfast up your dirty raas and you talk down to me? You don't know me. You ain't got no concept of me whatsoever. But what if I am just another ig'erant belligerent nigger n' I complete your picture of me and crush your bitch's paw in my fist like a biscuit? What if I fuck you both up and step over your bodies with my Twix n' gwan my way? What then?

Daniel I don't know. What then?

KKK I'm gonna arx one more time – Yo . . . sista . . . Give me a Twix.

Pause.

Karisma Magic word?

Pause.

KKK Please.

Karisma *produces a Twix – holds it out . . .*

KKK *produces a five pound note and holds it out to* **Karisma**. *The Twix and cash change hands.* **KKK** *bites into the unopened Twix and strides out.*

White Fang Keep the change, yeah?

He starts to leave just as **KKK** *strides back in to stand burning in the doorway staring at* **Karisma**.

KKK Think you're cute, innit? Think you got it all sorted – think you ain't ghetto. Just 'cause your upwardly mobile nigger daddy found a white bitch to be his baby mama and you grew up talking like the enemy you think you ain't ghetto, innit? Well, when you marry your nice lickle white boy with his nice lickle white job and his nice lickle white house in nice lickle Whitetown and you take your nice lickle mulatto baby out in his nice lickle white pram and all the nice lickle white mums arx you how long you been his fucking nanny you'll see just how cute you ain't and you'll know just how ghetto you are. And when that moment reach and you call your Gay Best Friend and he sends your call to voicemail – think of this moment, yeah, and remember – you coulda connected with a brudda. Someone coulda had your back. You get me? . . . Sista?

He walks out. After a moment, **White Fang** *walks straight up to* **Daniel**, *elbows him in the face and walks out.*

Bashment Basement Stage

Sound: Music blasting – bass pulsing – Lights whirling . . .

JJ 'Ear me now! Judgement day reach and t'rough the riddim me a' say creation a preach! Mek Man, woman and pickney, let the beats them a teach – you leaaaarn!

>See me 'ere like a lily 'pon the water
>White fi true
>White fi true
>Take me down like a lamb to the slaughter
>White fi true
>White fi true
>Close your eyes, seen, and open your mind
>See me there without prejudice and lies
>Your soul brudda and your partner in crime
>Hear me soul in the flows of me Rhyme
>Like the soil and the silt from the shore of the Nile River
>Dark fi true – Dark fi true
>Like the sweet sugar cane from heart of Mudda Africa
>Dark fi true – Dark fi true
>Feel me now, me brudda
>Father, sister, mudda,
>Time fi chugga, chugga,
>Dance the chugga chugga!
>Whine it! Chugga Chugga Chugga!
>Grine it! Chugga Chugga Chugga!

Share the humanity, me bredren, share the love! For in the eyes of the Music, we are all African! Unity! Peace!

Bashment Basement – Competitors' Area

Buzzing, **JJ** *goes to stand with* **Orlando***, who hands him a can of Red Stripe as they try to hang casual.*

Orlando Oh – my – God, Rude-Boy! How proud am I?

JJ Yeah? Was I cool?

Orlando I don't know about cool. Seemed pretty fucking hot to me.

JJ Orly . . .

Orlando Well, what can I do? You know I'm helplessly horny when you chat Blackney like that!

JJ Orly!

Orlando I know! Seen! Be cool! I'm being cool! Can we hi-five? Is that cool?

They hi-five. **Orlando** *swaggers as macho as he can muster.*

Cool, geezer! . . . What?

JJ (*grinning*) Nothing.

Orlando I look funny.

JJ You look great.

Orlando But do I look straight? Do I pass?

JJ I'm sorry, Orly.

Orlando What? Is it the eyeliner? – I thought I'd got it all off!

JJ Orly . . .

Orlando *pulls out a tissue and rubs at his eyes.*

Orlando Fuck!

JJ . . . Orly.

He reaches out and gently takes **Orlando***'s hand away. They break contact, quickly looking round.*

JJ I'm sorry. This in't you. But I'll make it up to you, I swear.

Orlando Yeah?

They smile.

JJ Ohhh yeah . . . Soon as we get home.

Orlando Oh God . . .

JJ Soon as we reach yard, man!

Orlando Oh God!

JJ Before the door even close, man! You gon' see how a thug makes love, lickle English bwoy.

Orlando Stop it, JJ. These trousers in't that baggy.

JJ Do you know how bad me wan' kiss you right now, lickle English?

Orlando Actually . . . I think I do.

JJ Wrap my arms roun' you . . .

Orlando JJ . . .!

JJ Wine and grine you . . . make you feel my lover's rock!

Orlando (*laughing*) JJ! Why is that so bloody sexy?

JJ 'Cause Blackness is realness – and realness is sexy.

Orlando So how come you ended up with the whitest boy on the planet this side of Prince Charles?

JJ You ain't white, Orly. You're blinding.

He looks around, holds up his hand – they share another hi-five, this time lingering a moment, fingers entwining . . .

Eggy, **Venom**, **KKK** *and* **White Fang** *come busting in.* **Orlando** *and* **JJ** *pull apart.*

Eggy Bo! Start the show! Niggas reach!

Venom Illmanics in da house! Mek the festivities commence!

Eggy Where the niggas at, man?

White Fang I dunno man, this is where them said congregate, yeah – lef' of stage innit?

KKK Something ain't right, bwoy, something ain't right . . . (*Up in* **JJ**'s *face.*) What the fuck you lookin' at?

JJ Whassup, blood – MC KKK, yeah? MC Venom – MC Eggy, Illmanic crew! Boss man, boss man, feel your work, legends man, legends! (*Offering his hand to* **White Fang**.) You the manager? Peace, blood.

White Fang (*giving* **JJ** *the hairy eyeball*) I know you?

JJ JJ.

Zero response.

They call me MC JJ. You guys here to check the show?

Eggy We're here to win it – where's the organizers and alla dat?

JJ Oh, they're probably up at the bar.

Venom   Damn, bwoy, how Black peoples come so lazy? Ain't no negro event ever start on time since the pyramids!

Eggy   For real.

JJ   Well, you know, this is the break.

Silence.

White Fang   The break?

JJ   Before the second round?

Venom   What the raas happened to the firs' round?

JJ   Firs' round done, man.

Venom   Done?

JJ   Firs' round gone.

White Fang   I'll fix it.

He exits.

Eggy   'MC JJ'?

JJ   Seen, man.

Eggy   From where?

JJ   Bristol – West Country boy.

Eggy   All the way to Eastside from West countryside, is it?

JJ   Innit. It's well cool to meet you, man, I love your work, Fi true. I feel that shit.

KKK (*looking at him darkly*)   You feel that shit?

JJ (*looks at him*)   Yeah, man.

KKK   You feel that shit?

JJ   Believe.

White Fang *returns.*

Eggy   White Fang! Whassuuuup!

Venom   So, is wha' them say, man?

Silence.

KKK   Well?

White Fang (*kissing his teeth*)   This system just corrup, man . . . Organizers them come like white man – fucking rigid! Them reckon first round done and gone.

Venom   So, wha'? We miss a round?

White Fang   We missed the whole thing, period. We bounced.

Venom   'Bounced'?

Eggy   'Bounced'?

Venom   You did stan' there and let them tell you we was bounced and never tell 'em nuttin' back?

White Fang   What you want me 'a tell 'em, man? 'It's cause we're Black'?

Eggy   'Bounced'? The Illmanics is bounced? How can that be? How can it be that the Illmanics is bounced and the little white pig-fucker farm boy is t'rough? Eh? Country? How you pull that trick?

Orlando   He was on time?

All head snaps to **Orlando**.

JJ   . . . Orly . . . !

All heads snap to **JJ**. *Then back to* **Orlando**.

KKK   And what the fuck is that?

JJ   That's Orlando. He's with me.

Venom   'With you'?

Venom, **Eggy** *and* **KKK** *exchange a look.*

Eggy   Is wha' the fuck a gwan here, man?

White Fang   So now we losing to a coupla chi-chi man?

Venom   That's too Babylon even for me!

Eggy   Nah, man they ain't queer boys – not and be ahead of our game. That ain't even a possibility still, you get me?

Venom   Too Babylon, man!

Sound: We hear the competition **Compere**.

Compere   Round two commencing – could MC JJ please take the stage?

JJ *looks at* **Orlando** . . . *The* **Illmanics** *watch them.*

Orlando   I'll be fine.

JJ   I want you to stand by the edge of the stage – where you can see me, yeah? Right here, Yeah?

Orlando   JJ, I'll be fine.

Eggy   Yeah, blood, he'll be fine.

KKK   He's got us to take care of him, innit, blood?

Compere   Last call for MC JJ!

JJ Right here, yeah? I'll be looking for you.

He steps onto the stage reluctantly . . . **Orlando** *looks round at the* **Illmanics** *and smiles nervously. The* **Illmanics** *smile back broadly.*

Sam's Place

Daniel *sits in a bean-bag with frozen peas on his nose . . .* **Sam** *goes through a book of CDs . . .*

Sam I think this calls for Nina. How do you feel about Nina?

Daniel I'm not sure we've been introduced.

Sam You'll love each other.

Sound: Nina Simone – 'That's all I want from you'.

Meet Nina Simone, my heroine. Nina, meet . . .

Daniel . . . Daniel . . .

Sam . . . Daniel . . . My hero.

Daniel Please to meet you, Miss Simone.

He hawks and spits blood into a blood-soaked tissue.

Sam Let me look at that . . .

He dabs at **Daniel**'s *nose,* **Daniels** *hisses and winces . . .*

Sam I've not said thank you, have I? Gratitude is somewhat of a dying art. Once a maiden would've awarded her knight her favour to wear.

Daniel And he would henceforth wear her colours with pride. (*Pause.*) I'm rather liking this.

Sam Really? That's impressively kinky.

Daniel I mean Miss Simone.

Sam Oh, the Nina! Always good for what ails you.

They listen a moment . . .

Well – I think you're all bled out for now.

Sam *takes the ice pack off to the kitchen.*

Daniel I do like your flat. You're very creative.

Sam And you're very diplomatic.

Daniel Seriously. I'm envious. Colour clearly doesn't scare you. My walls are all white with a hint of nicotine. Do you rent or buy?

Sam *returns.*

Sam   I squat. I'm a cluster of clichés I'm afraid. A slightly druggy, slightly draggy, dropout with an inadvertent tendency to draw drama like a magnet.

Daniel   You know it wasn't your fault, don't you? That your people don't appreciate you. It must be even more disappointing for you, when it comes from your own, like that.

Sam   As opposed to when it comes from your own?

Daniel   Well, you come to expect it from the white-trash element – The townies – the chavs . . .

Sam   . . . But never from the nice middle-class white boys. They just love the queers, don't they?

Daniel   Trust me, I've no illusions regarding the middle-classes – but they don't go queer-bashing on the streets

Sam   No, they go queer-bashing in the *Daily Mail* and the House of Lords. But the Blacks – surely they should understand oppression, shouldn't they? After all they've been through.

Daniel   Well . . . Shouldn't they?

Sam   After all, we're all on the same side, aren't we?

Daniel   . . . Aren't we? Shouldn't we be?

Sam   In a world where two and two made four we would be.

Daniel   And what does two and two make in this world?

Sam   A lynch mob. (**Daniel** *is peering at* **Sam***'s nose.*) I don't think it's broken.

Daniel   I suspect it's black eyes by dawn, though.

Sam   Oh, I always wake up looking like a raccoon – but that's the danger of sleeping in cheap mascara for you. Well, maybe I won't wash tonight and in the morning we'll be a matching pair.

Daniel *looks back at* **Sam***'s shyly smiling face . . .*

Daniel   Oh, shit.

Sam   Oh dear. Do we hear another sorry coming over the hill?

Daniel   I'm just not suited to this. One-night stands – sex – dating. Truth be told I'm a bit of a theoretical queer. Strong on concept, lousy in practice. I'm great at cybersex, cruising, wham-bams, a quick tug and a toss. But kissing confuses me. Sharing the cigarette, pillow-talk, love-tokens, dizzying romance, cosy domesticity – having and holding – I get flustered.

Sam   And colour scares you?

Daniel   It's not you. You are arrestingly lovely and instantly intriguing and henceforth on the regular occasions that I abuse myself in the lavatory at the uninspiring major league law firm where I force myself to work to advance my career, I shall invariably recall the trembling excitement of sitting on this bean-bag in your strange little burrow of a home – and smile and weave florid fantasies around what could have been if only I'd had the balls to ask you out. But if I fumble through a clumsy attempt to actually connect with you for real – I'll fuck it all up. And so – tragically – I cannot stay. (*Getting to his feet.*) I feel like a deserter in time of war. Who was it that said that we're forever responsible for those whose lives we save?

Sam   The Apaches. And look what happened to them.

Daniel *starts to leave.*

Sam   Wait.

Daniel *halts.* **Sam** *pulls off a sweatband off his own wrist and slips it onto* **Daniel***'s.*

Daniel   To treasure. Thank you.

He leaves – **Sam** *watches him go.*

Bashment Basement Stage

Orlando *watches from the edge of stage as* **JJ** *rocks the mic.*

JJ   Hear me now! Second-round reach!

   White boy come again fe snatch the crown!
   Whine it! Chugga Chugga Chugga!
   Grine it! Chugga Chugga Chugga!

The **Illmanics** *storm the stage.*

Venom   Niggas reeeeach!

Eggy   Now 'ear dis, now 'ear dis . . . this is not a tes' say this is not a drill!

KKK   This dancehall a requisition by the People dem Liberation Army known 'pon the street as The Illmanic Crew.

Venom   Resistance is futile repeat Resistance is futile – is time fe surrender!

Eggy   T'row up your 'and muthafuckas and assume the position!

Venom   Alla my niggas at the MC Trow-down Alla my homies outta Brixton Lockdown! Trow them gats in the air firing one round Shoutin'
Where my niggas at?

Illmanics   Yo! Where my Illmanics?

Eggy   My sweet bitches from the Barking Area!
My sweet hunnies all from Illford, see 'em dere? Tear out them weave from their scalp in hysteria screamin'
Where my niggas at?

Illmanics Yo! Where my Illmanics?
Niggas reach! East London!

KKK Looking cris, looking down, come fe claim the Black crown

Illmanics Niggas reach! East London!

KKK See how me dress to impress
How me step wid' out stress?

Illmanics Niggas reach – East London!

KKK Is a Black man ting – to look this fine a' take a brudda time, you get me? Make them white boys reach early and nasty up the place – Black man dress to represent the race!

Illmanics Niggaaaaaas reeaaaaach!

JJ Yo yo yo . . . Hol' on, yeah, hol' on . . .
Scuse me, brudda,
If you don't mind,
this is my moment,
This is my time . . .
Sorry, blood, yeah?
Nuff respect
But this is my stage,
And JJ's in effec'
How come Johnny Come Lately you say only white boys reach early fi true?
When rocking the house is a sea of Black faces all reach in dis place before you?
A wha' g'wan?
Ain't your mamma raise you to know that it's rude to intrude? A wha' gwan?
Ain't your papa tell you that every ting in the world ain' all about you?
A wha' gwan?
All your plans spannered
So you forget your manners
And now you step to a brother like you fixing fi fight?
Something ain't right, bwoy, something ain't right!

Eggy First t'ing, muthafucka, you bes' start address me as mister
'cause this nigga he ain't your brother no way and you ain't my sister
Make me laugh how you t'ink you stan' 'pon this stage like you some kind of wheel, star . . .
When your hairy-ass bitch has a dick for a clit 'cause your gyal is a geezer!

Venom But wait, dread, my boy here, he can't be a homo, me na understand!
For the dude to be batty, my nigga, he'd have to be screwing a man!
Yeah, I know his lickle bitch needs a shampoo and shave and he must be out of his mind . . .
but loving a dog – well it might be a sin,
But technically it ain't a crime

KKK Did you really think, wigga to real nigga, you could pull wool over this brutha's eyes?
That you and your pussy-raas punk boy could mug up the negroes and take home the prize?
If you tink you can fuck with this Black man then white boy your cornrows them fix up too tight
Just do what you do best and ben' over bitch, 'cause you really getting fucked tonight!

Illmanics A wha' g'wan?

KKK Alla dem so-call lyrical gangstas and bruk-ass MC pretender –

Illmanics A wha' g'wan?

KKK Alla dem nasty raas chi-chi men, batty bwoy nature offender

Illmanics A wha' g'wan?

KKK Them swallow man's dick
Then wan fi spit lyrics
Then they step to a brotha like them fixing fi fight?

Illmanics Something ain't right, bwoy, Something ain't right!

JJ So, the word's on the street, yo
The homie's a homo,
Illmanics feel sick
But what am I made of
That you're so afraid of
A guy who likes dick?
Now could it be what's really freaking you out is your ass gettin' kicked?
'Cause this faggot's proud to say I never found me a pussyrass I couldn't lick

Or maybe it's just that the babe on my arm is way finer than you'll ever own
Yeah, actually blood, if you all are such studs – how come Mister Lover-Lover's alone?

Could it be being bigoted don't make you blacker
It just makes you fucked-up and sad?
Or what's messing with your head the fact that last night, dread, I fucked both your mum and dad?
A wha' gwan?
What the big deal who I fuck with if I ain't fucking with you?
A wha' g'wan?
Is that what's really bugging you, boys?
Are you hungry for a lickle piece of JJ too?
A' wha' g'wan?
Should I be flattered?
Are your hopes shattered?
Is that why you step to a brother inciting a fight?
Something ain't right, bwoy, something ain't right!

All A wha' gwan – A wha' gwan – A wha' gwan – A wha' gwan – A wha' gwan – A wha' gwan – A wha' gwan – A wha' gwan – A wha' gwan? . . . Is wha' gwan?

Compere Illmanics – your disqualification stands – Will the Illmanics please leave the stage – your disqualification stands . . .

The **Illmanics** *slink off the stage* . . .

Compere T'ank you! MC JJ commence!

Bashment Basement/Halls of Residence

Orlando *and* **Kevan** *on their mobiles.*

Orlando Hey, Kevin.

Kevan Kevan.

Orlando Kevin's a perfectly good name.

Kevan It's yours if you want it – I'm sure it'll suit you. I, meanwhile, will be answering to the name Kevan.

Orlando Start again, shall we? Hey, Kevan.

Kevan Hey, yourself. So, you're still there?

Orlando Somehow, yes.

Kevan Surrounded by Black blokes in string vests, all rapping about the size of their dicks – God, I hate you.

Orlando Take a ticket and get in line.

Kevan They giving you attitude are they? Staring at you with angry burning hostile eyes?

Orlando (*drily*) Stop! I'm getting an erection.

Kevan I shouldn't worry too much. No one'll notice your little white Somerset mushroom in that jungle of tree trunks.

Orlando Kevan . . .

Kevan Sorry, I get carried away.

Orlando They are sexy though – in a scary way.

Kevan The best kind of sexy. Is loverboy about to win?

Orlando Well, I think he should.

Kevan But then you would – ooh, rhyme! I got skillz! With a z! Maybe I should come down there! Orlando, mate . . .

Orlando   Yeah?

Kevan   Do you want me to come down there?

Orlando   I'm fine. Don't want to overrun the place. That's the trouble with you honkies – Don't know when you're not welcome.

Kevan   'Honkies'? Do people still stay that?

Orlando   Probably. This is not the most politically correct environment. If I hear the n-word one more time . . .

Kevan   The 'n' word'? Forgive me, I don't speak coy. Do you mean nigga?

Orlando   Kevan!

Kevan   With an 'a'! It's OK with an 'a' at the end. That's just keeping it real. You just said yourself they're all saying it.

Orlando   Well, I can't get used to it, I'm sorry. Everytime I hear the word nigger I just hear the e-r.

Kevan   Ooops! Said it! And you've not been nicked by the PC police.

Orlando   I know it's me that's terminally unhip – they bandy it about round the place like it's nothing – there's a nigga in every sentence.

KKK, **Venom**, **Eggy** *and* **White Fang** *appear.* **Orlando** *does not see them.*

Orlando   Honestly! it's nigga this and nigga that . . . It makes me clench. I'm clenching right now as we speak.

Kevan   Well, don't give yourself contractions.

Orlando   Well, I can't be bandying words with you, I've got a man to watch! Laters!

Kevan   Peace out!

Orlando   Innit!

They hang up. **Orlando** *turns to find hisself face to face with the* **Illmanic Crew**.

Eggy   'Nigger'? Did I hear you say 'nigger'?

Orlando   With an 'a' – nigga with an 'a' – Anyway, I was just saying how I hate that word.

Eggy   How you hate niggas?

Orlando   The word. I hate the word. I love niggas – Black people – I'm from an estate when it was like eighty per cent Black. I don't hate anyone. We are all Africans.

The **Illmanics** *looks at one another then burst out laughing.*

Eggy   You just too funny, brudda man.

Venom   Ah, leave him, man . . . he's just a lickle chi-chi man. Make him gwan with him nasty self, yeah?

Eggy Oh, man, now you're just being scandalous and slanderous. How can an African be a chi-chi man? That just ain't logical.

*He slips an arm round **Orlando**'s shoulders.*

Eggy How can a righteous, conscious God-fearing, African man be a batty boy? Ain't no way. You ain't no batty boy, is it, Orlando, my nigga? You ain't dutty so? Is it?

Venom Man, leave him, he's cool. You're cool, innit, blood?

***Eggy**'s arms tightens round **Orlando**'s shoulders.*

Eggy 'Course he's cool. He ain't gonna come inna dis place and stand up in our face and bring nasty batty boy business inna di space . . . is it? Nah, man – It's you what ain't cool – bad-mouthing me bredren like him gay. Just wrong, innit, blood? You don't take dick do you, blood? Go on, put this fool straight – You ain't no dutty raas batty boy.

KKK It's OK, bredren. You're among fambly, now. You ain't gotta be politically correc'. Just say it yeah, and mek we let you gwan your way, yeah?

***Eggy**'s arms tightens round **Orlando**'s neck.*

Venom Just tell him you ain't a batty, yeah, dread, and he'll let you go.

Eggy You know it, cuz! He's right, blood, just tell me you ain't gay an' dat and you can go, yeah? You alright, blood? I ain't choking you am I?

White Fang He can't say it 'cause he's a queer. Innit? White boy? You are a dutty raas pussyraas, bloodclaat queer – Innit, chi-chi man? Innit?

Orlando Yes.

Pause.

KKK Is wha' you say? Yes? You said yes?

Orlando Yes.

White Fang And every night you suck that wigga wannabe's cock. Innit? And you love it, innit? You fucking love it. SAY IT! You fucking love it!

Orlando I . . . love . . . him.

*The **Illmanics** look at one another.*

Venom Love him? You fucking love him? A man? A bloke? A geezer? Fucking love?

KKK Now, ain't that a fucking bitch?

White Fang Nah, man . . .

*He punches **Orlando** in the face.*

White Fang/Eggy/KKK That's a fucking bitch!

*Stunned, **Orlando** slumps into **Eggy**'s arms. **KKK** back-hands him and sends him spinning into the centre of the stage. The beating continues, mimed, without any actual contact.*

KKK   Feel that shit!

Eggy *head-butts* **Orlando**.

Eggy   Suck that, bitch!

Venom   Oh, man, why you lot have to go and do that for? Now it's gotta be on for real – And we all gotta be in it! Aww, shit!

He punches **Orlando** *in the back of the head.* **Orlando** *drops to his knees.*

Venom (*flexing his sore hand.*)   Shit!

The **Illmanics** *take turns to kick and stamp on* **Orlando** *relentlessly until he lies on the ground in a pool of red.*

KKK   Pussy.

He exits.

Eggy   Faggot.

He exits.

White Fang   Queer.

He exits.

Venom *looks down at* **Orlando** *bleeding.*

Venom   Why'd you have to go and bring love into it, man?

He exits.

We hear the crowd roar. **JJ** *runs in holding his mic.*

JJ   Yeah, man! Orly? Where the fuck were you?

He sees **Orlando**.

JJ (*a whisper*)   Orly?

He drops the mic – BOOM – the sound FX echoes as he runs to **Orlando**.

JJ   Orly?

Lifting **Orlando**'*s face,* **JJ** *is confronted by a mask of blood.*

JJ   Orly! Oh no!

He pulls out his mobile phone and tries to switch it on, but his hand is shaking too much.

Oh fuck! Oh no! No, no, no . . .

He struggles to pick **Orlando** *up.*

JJ   Hold onto me, Orly, I've got you . . . Shit!

He slips in the blood, almost dropping **Orlando**.

JJ   Orly! I'm sorry, I've got you, I got you baby . . . I've got you . . .

He carries **Orlando** *out – leaving red footsteps.*

Petrol Station/Eggy and Venom's Flat

Sound: Till.

Karisma *is working behind the till –* **KKK** *bursts in and starts pacing. She watches him, warily.*

Eggy, **Venom** *and* **White Fang** *come running in the flat.*

Eggy/Venom/White Fang   Yeh man!

KKK   Yo, sista – gimme a Twix, yeah – please?

Karisma *hands* **KKK** *a Twix. He unwraps it. He bites it. He chews . . .*

Venom *and* **Eggy** *snatch up their PlayStation consoles and start to play . . .*

Sound: Video game.

Venom   Yeah baby yeah baby yeah baby, yeahhhhhh!

Eggy *throws down his console.*

Eggy   Shit, man!

White Fang *hands* **Eggy** *and* **Venom** *a beer each.*

Eggy   Stupid fucking queer, man . . .

White Fang   Stupid fucking batty man . . .

White Fang, **Eggy** *and* **Venom** *drink.*

Karisma   He was white.

KKK   What?

Karisma   My dad. Was white. My mum was the Black one. He worked in a tannery – skinning sheep. He was not a nigga. Nor was she – Nor am I.

KKK   'Was'?

Karisma *looks blankly puzzled.*

KKK   'He was'? 'She was'?

Karisma   When they were alive.

KKK *lunges at* **Karisma** *– kisses her on the lips.*

White Fang   You lot – I'm off home, yeah?

KKK *(breaking off the kiss)*   See you round, yeah?

As **White Fang** *and* **KKK** *heads towards their prospective doors they hear . . .*

Sound: Police siren.

Eggy, **Venom**, **White Fang** *and* **KKK** *all stop in their tracks.*

Police Station/Holding Cell

Venom, **Eggy**, **White Fang** and **KKK** *in a small room. They hold white cards.*

KKK Fuck – this – shit – man.

White Fang We'll be cool if we stick together, bredren.

KKK Fuck this shit.

White Fang It's all about unity, bredren.

Venom What you tell 'em man?

Eggy Nuttin'.

Venom Same here.

Eggy Didn't see nuttin', didn't hear nuttin', don't know nuttin', ain't got nuttin' to say.

White Fang Four bredren, one story. Safe.

Eggy Nuttin'. (*Raises his voice.*) The truth!

KKK Fuck 'em.

Sound: Voice-over speaker system.

Voice Numbers two, five, six and eight stand in line please . . .

They look at their cards . . . They are numbered 2, 5, 6 and 8.

KKK (*kissing his teeth*) Fuck you.

Venom That's us.

KKK Fuck that.

Venom, **White Fang** and **Eggy** *get in line.*

KKK And fuck you lot. Black man don't stand in line for no one!

Voice Number six . . .

KKK Fuck off.

Voice Number six . . .

KKK *gets in line.*

Voice Hold your cards in front of you . . .

A curtain of light comes up on the **Illmanics**, *causing them to squint slightly.*

Voice Turn to your left . . .

Illmanics *turn to face their left . . .*

Voice . . . and now right . . .

Illmanics *turn to face their right.*

Voice And front once more please . .

Illmanics *turn front.*

Light up on **JJ**, *his clothes covered in blood.*

JJ Number two, number five, number six and number eight.

The lights on the **Illmanics** *return to normal.*

Venom Well, that's us fucking kippered ain't it?

Eggy Shut up – he weren't there – we weren't there – no eye-witnesses, no ID. Nobody knows nothing. You get me?

KKK This is bullshit.

Voice Julian Wolfavitz – step forward.

White Fang Fuck! They mean me. (*Stepping forward.*) Yeah?

Voice Room three please.

White Fang You lot. Unity, yeah?

They touch fists.

Leave it wi' me, yeah? I'll fix this.

He goes off.

Sound: Door closing.

KKK This is beyond bullshit.

Voice Duran Hunter, please step forward.

Eggy *steps forward.*

Eggy This gonna take long? My mum's making curried goat and pigfoot this evening.

Voice Show your palms, please . . .

Eggy *shows his hands.*

Eggy And you know she don't like to reheat.

Light FX: Photo flash.

Voice Turn the hands over, please . . .

Eggy *turns his hands over . . .*

Light FX: Photo flash.

Voice Thank you. Step back.

Eggy Pleasure working with you.

Voice Marquis Campbell, please remove your shoes.

Venom *quickly removes his shoes.*

Voice Hold them out, soles facing up . . .

Venom *does this.*

Light FX: Three photo flashes in succession.

Voice Thank you.

Dijon Socrates Lawrence . . .

KKK . . . The third – and I ain't doing shit!

Sound: Door opening.

White Fang *hurries back in. Pale. The others look at him.*

Venom What man? What?

White Fang Fucking Bablyon got DNA, bredren.

Venom They got science? Shit, man!

Light change.

Interview Room

Sound: Door opening.

Daniel *enters holding four case histories. He shakes each* **Illmanic** *by hand.*

Daniel Mr Hunter, Mr Campbell, Mr Wolfavitz, Mr Lawrence.

Eggy And who the fuck are you?

Daniel Daniel Pearl. I'm your solicitor.

Eggy Excuse me?

Daniel I've been assigned by legal aid to defend your case.

White Fang You're fired.

Daniel *looks at them.*

Daniel Well, that was nice and quick.

White Fang Tell 'em to send a brutha in, a'ight? And make him straight while you're at it.

Daniel 'Make him straight . . .' Interesting . . .

He turns to go – **Eggy**, **Venom**, **KKK** *jump in his path.*

Eggy Wait wait wait, brutha, yeah?
KKK Where you going, brudda man, no need to be so sensitive, yeah?

Venom My nigga here jus' trippin'. We need us a lawyer, man – Fang, man, what the fuck?

Eggy How you gonna be dissing our only key to the gate, bruv?

White Fang He's redundant, man – muthafucka pure chi-chi!

Venom, **Eggy** and **KKK** *check out* **Daniel**.

KKK How you know him chi-chi? You shagged him or what?

White Fang Too much chronic blunt your faculty fi memory, blood – you don't recognize him?

KKK *looks at* **Daniel**.

KKK They all look the same to me, blood, know what I'm saying?

White Fang (*mimic king*) 'I prefer queer, actually.'

KKK Damn . . . For real?

White Fang For real!

Eggy Yo! 'this a private conversation or can any nigga join in?

White Fang We had an altercation with my man here and he himself reckons in public before witness dem that he is queer as a low-alcohol beer.

Eggy A 'true?

White Fang How's a battyman gonna defend this case and not sell us down the fucking river? I may be a freak, but I ain't a fool, you get me?

Eggy This true? You a battyman?

Daniel Well . . . I do prefer queer.

Eggy Fuck's sake, man! Ain't nobody got no shame no more? Gwan! Gone! And tell 'em sen' a righteous nigga up in here lickety-split, yeah?

Daniel Ah.

Illmanics What?

Daniel That may prove irksome. I'm afraid there's only one heterosexual Black man on legal aid in this catchment area – and he's snowed under with cases for a least a year.

Venom One Black man? Man, where all the other triflin' lazy niggas at?

Daniel All poached, every last one. Black solicitors are all the rage in the trendiest chambers currently. Ramsey might have space – Asian, plucks his eyebrows and calls everyone sista, very popular, but he might squeeze you in – There's a couple of Black women – I think one of them might be straight or at least bisexual – would you like me to make enquiries?

White Fang So why ain't you booked up? You the dregs or what?

Daniel Ah – I am that rare breed – the bright-eyed bushy-tailed and brilliant socially conscious lawyer, freshly defected to legal aid in an attempt to satiate my white liberal guilt – Still principled enough to present your case with utmost commitment to the rule of law without personal prejudice. However, as you are so sure that a heterosexual Black lawyer will be more sympathetic to your position – I must humbly bow to your collective decision. Good day, gentlemen.

He is about to hit the door.

Venom   He called us niggers.

Daniel *stops.*

Venom   Alla us. He called us all niggers . . .

KKK   . . . We overreacted, but he provoked us . . .

White Fang   . . . And we're really, really sorry.

Courtroom

Sound: Voice-over speaker system.

Voice   Let the accused stand . . .

The **Illmanics** *face front.*

Voice   Taking into consideration that three of the four perpetrators of this deed have no previous recorded convictions – along with your claim that the recipient of your attack provoked you by first mistaking you for drug-dealers and then subjecting you to a torrent of appalling racist abuse, I hereby accept your eleventh-hour plea bargain of guilty to the lesser crime of Actual Bodily Harm and I hereby sentence Hunter, Campbell and Socrates to two years in Her Majesty's Prison. As for you, Wolfavitz, I have taken into additional consideration the submission from your solicitor that considering your background and education, this situation was not typical of your previous character and that you were to a great extent playing a naïve game of follow-my-leader. You are sentenced to eighteen months. Bailiff take them down.

Sound: Banging gavel.

Voice   Stay in line. Step forward.

The **Illmanics** *step forward.*

Voice   Remove all your clothing except your underwear. Rule number one. You will not speak in the hallways – you will not speak in the showers – you will not speak unless in your cells, at meals or in the recreation areas – in fact no one will speak unless spoken to and given permission to reply. Is rule number one understood?

By now in their underwear, the **Illmanics** *nod.*

Voice   Bend forward . . .

The **Illmanics** *bend forward.*

Voice   Lower your shorts.

As they start to lower their shorts . . .

Blackout.

Orlando and JJ's Flat

JJ is sorting through the piles of clothes on the floor and putting them into a laundry basket.

Sound: Doorbell.

JJ *pulls out a knife that's hidden in the laundry . . . he approaches the door.*

JJ   Who the fuck's that?

Kevan   JJ? It's only me!

Hiding the knife, **JJ** *opens the door.*

Sound: Two locks opening and a bolt being drawn back.

Kevan *enters holding up a newspaper.*

Evening paper. Massive editorial – page of letters and emails. The nation up in arms.

He puts the paper on the laundry. **JJ** *takes the laundry out without reading it . . .*

Kevan   Most reckon it should've been attempted murder and they should be serving life. Apparently 'cause they've already served ten months on remand, they'll be out in like six months with tags on their ankles. Mental. Who'd have thought it? The whole nation on the side of a couple of dirty queers – 'cept for one fucked-up old judge. Is Orly about? I brought his favourite beer.

JJ   Orly's asleep.

Kevan   Oh. Sorry. (*Putting the beers back in the bag.*) . . . Sorry . . . you want me to fuck off . . . Sorry . . .

JJ (*stopping him*)   You know what? Let's forget sorry. (*Taking the beers from the bag.*) Sorry's all used up. (*Hands a beer to* **Kevan**.) Fuck sorry.

Kevan   Fuck sorry.

They open their beers – they drink.

JJ   And when Orly's ready, he'll be ready. Just tell him nobody cares how he looks, OK? He can never be anything but beautiful. Anyway. Fuck sorry.

He drinks.

Kevan   Do you think maybe you should have been there?

JJ   Mmm?

Kevan   For the sentencing. Like made a special appeal to the judge or something? I dunno. Forget it.

JJ   Orlando was coming home that day. I in't never leaving him alone again. Shit, yeah, probably should have been there. . . I in't never where I should be.

Kevan   You were with Orly. Fuck sorry, yeah?

JJ   Fuck sorry.

They drink. **Orlando** *calls from offstage.*

Orlando (*offstage*)   JJ . . . ?

JJ (*jumping up*)   Orly?

Orlando *wanders in, dressed for bed.*

Orlando   JJ!

JJ   I'm here, Orly babe, you can go back to bed! What you doing up again so soon?

Orlando   I had another nightmare . . .

JJ   Ohhh, baby . . . it's OK . . .

Orlando   I dreamed that my head was ice cream and you was an Alsation . . .

JJ   . . . let's get you back to bed, yeah. . ?

Orlando   . . . And you kept licking my face and swallowing me!

JJ (*hugging* **Orlando**, *laughing despite himself*)   Orly!

Orlando   Bit by bit, my ears, my eyes, my eyebrows, my nose – I was a dog's dinner!

JJ (*rocking* **Orlando** *in his arms*)   Orly, Orly, Orly, silly Orly. It was just a dream. This is real. See, I'm me and you're you – You in't ice cream, Orly, and I in't a dog – We're real.

A puddle of pee spreads round **Orlando**'s *feet* . . .

JJ   Oh, Orly!

Orlando (*super-innocent*)   What?

JJ *nips off.*

JJ   You know what! We've discussed this!

JJ *comes back with rubber gloves and a rag to mop the floor* . . . **Orlando** *spots* **Kevan** *staring in shock.*

Orlando   Keevie?

Kevan   Hey you.

Orlando *throws his arms round* **Kevan**, *kisses, hugs and rocks him.*

Orlando   Keevie, Keevie, Keevie . . . I've missed you, missed you, missed you. Where you flippin' been, man?

Kevan   Missing you.

Orlando   I'm sorry, Keevie – I've been sick. I weren't allowed to come to school for ages and ages – But I'm nearly better now – I just have to take my headache pills and I'm cool. Oh, my gosh! JJ! Can Kevan stay?

JJ   Kevan doesn't want to stay, silly, he's got things to do.

Orlando   Please, please, please! He can sleep in our bed, there's loads of room! Can he, can he, please?

JJ Kevan, do you want to stay?

Kevan Sure.

Orlando Yeaaahhh! I'll find my spare pyjamas!

Orlando *runs out.* **JJ** *looks at* **Kevan***.*

JJ You OK?

Kevan You must hate them so much.

JJ *starts to wrap his hands to box.*

Kevan Not all of them, just the ones who are like them. The ghettoey ones.

JJ This didn't happen cause they were Black, mate.

Kevan Maybe not. But that's why they're getting away with it, isn't it? That's what was behind the judge's ruling. In the end you should have known how they'd react to a pair of batty boys. So it's your fault. They're not supposed to know better and you are.

JJ Kevan, we can't think like this, man.

Kevan Can't we? Why can't we? Why can they? They're allowed to feel what they like because they're still recovering from slavery, is that it? We're not slave-owners. We're not racists. But does that mean we have to be fucking punchbags just 'cause we're liberal white queers? OK – they don't have to love us back but do they have to hate us?

JJ *starts boxing with the punchbag . . .*

JJ Kevan, one of them was white.

Kevan He was white once he got to court – but when he was stamping your lover's brains out, what colour was he trying to be, then? It's all so fucked-up and us letting 'em get away with this just fucks it up all the more. This feeling, man . . . what are we supposed to do with it?

JJ I don't know. You sure you can handle staying the night, man? I know what Orlando means to you.

Kevan You mean I've always been a little bit in love with him.

JJ It's cool. Who wouldn't be?

Kevan It's was never just Orlando. It was you and Orlando. Orlando and you. I was in love with the idea of you. What you stood for. You were Orly and JJ.

JJ We're still Orly and JJ.

Kevan That's not Orly, though is it?

JJ Don't be fooled, mate. He's lost a few years, but it's Orly, alright.

Kevan So, you're gonna still live together?

JJ Orly and JJ for ever.

Kevan Are you really ready to be someone's dad for ever? What about his parents? Don't they want him with them? You have told 'em?

JJ His mum put the phone down as soon as she heard my voice. I'm the Satan who lured her boy to Sodom.

Kevan Jesus, what's wrong with people?

JJ People hate queers. Even nice white people. I should write and thank her. Imagine if she had wanted him back? I couldn't handle losing Orly entirely, man – it'd fucking fry me.

Kevan And what about sex?

JJ *keeps punching . . .*

Kevan You're twenty, JJ. Orly's – what, seven, now?

JJ He's still beautiful. You said it yourself, he can never be anything but.

Kevan But you can't make love to a child, mate.

JJ I know. But this my life. Orly and JJ.

Orlando Keevie!

JJ He's coming! (*To* **Kevan**.) I'll catch you up, mate, OK?

Kevan OK.

He goes into the bedroom – **JJ** *batters away at the punchbag – his punches underscoring the next scene . . .*

Prison Block

Eggy *in one cell,* **Venom** *in another. Both lying on their bunks.*

Eggy Yo! V! V, man!

Venom Eggy? Whattup?

Eggy Whattup you, cuz? Been calling you. Never seen you in the yard this morning. You cool?

Venom I'm cool, cuz. They just changed my recreation shift.

Eggy Bastards! Sorry, man. I tried to get us in the same cell and that. Babylon just cold.

Venom Cold, man! They took my cross, you know that?

Eggy MUTHAFUCKAS!

Venom Eggy, man, ain't you gonna wake your cellmate and that?

Eggy My cellmate's well sleeping. Can't you hear him snoring? He's like a Hoover! Listen!

Venom *listens –* **Eggy** *makes snoring sounds . . .* **Venom** *laughs.*

Venom Crazy Black bastard.

Eggy How's your cellmate?

Venom   Gone.

Eggy   Gone? You on your own?

Venom   He's dead, man.

Eggy   Dead?

Venom   Suicide, man. Woke up this morning and my man was just hanging there.

Eggy   What, by the neck? Shit man, and you never hear nuttin'?

Venom   He was always quiet, man. Kind of a ghost even before he passed, I s'pose.

Eggy   Damn. So, you cool sleeping in that same cell n' that?

Venom   Ah, nigga, I'm strong, don't worry about it, still. I ain't the one killed hisself, is it? (*Looks around.*) I dunno – bwoy, you see some things tho, in this life, ain't it?

Eggy   For real, cuz.

Venom   How the fuck did we end up like this, cuz? How'd we end up here? Caught up in all this ragga business? We ain't even Jamaicans, man. Always trying to keep up with the Windians man. Ain't we the real Africans, though? It all started with us and here's us trying to hang – straining to chat like them from their tiny island. It's all wrong-side up, man.

Eggy   Don't do that, man. We never do that.

Venom   Do what?

Eggy   We don't turn on our own. Every Black man is a brother.

Venom   What about coppers? And queers?

Eggy   They forfeit their Blackness.

Venom   And it's in the Bible ain't it? Thou shalt not . . . summink . . . I don't know, man, I swear . . .

Eggy   For real, cuz . . . Marquis, man, I'm sorry you ain't in with me, yeah? I ain't saying you're soft – I just wish . . . anyway, we just have to be strong and hold on – we ain't here for ever. We can come through.

Venom   Yeah, man, we can come through.

Eggy   Stay strong, African man.

Venom   Stay strong . . . Come through . . .

Orlando and JJ's flat

JJ goes over to pile of large-format photos and lays them out on the ground, overlapping the prints to complete a collage of **Orlando**'s *sleeping naked body.* **JJ** *lays down and, with an arm and leg draped over pictures of sleeping* **Orlando**, *closes his eyes . . .*

Interval.

Prison Interview Room

Eggy *waiting.*

Sound: Door opening.

Enter **Venom**.

Venom   Whattup, my bredren!

Eggy   Cuz! Still ugly!

They go into an elaborate handshake and bump a shoulder.

Bwoy, how you get skinny so?

Venom (*mimes toking*)   Ganja diet, innit?

Eggy   Bwoy bad! Staying lean, stayin' mean!

Sound: Door opening.

White Fang *enters – he has a black eye.*

Eggy/Venom   My nigga!

White Fang   My boyz!

They go into an elaborate three-way handshake.

Eggy   How's the runnins over in C wing? You some buff nigga's bitch, yet?

White Fang   Yo, fuck you and the dick you rode in on, ai'ight? I'm in a cell of four white muthafuckers, man.

Eggy   Aw, now, nigga, that ain't right!

White Fang   You feelin' my pain?

Venom   Jus' wrong, bro! Is them do that to that to your face, blood?

White Fang   They see me come in with you lot and they had a problem. I had to regulate innit? S'all under control.

Sound: Door opening.

KKK *enters.*

KKK   Black peopllllllles!

Venom/Eggy/White Fang   Negroooooo!

They exchange a labyrinthine four-way handshake.

Eggy   Reunioooon!

Venom   Illmanics in the houuuuuse!

White Fang   Duck – and – cover! Drop and roll!

KKK   Fuck all that, man.

Venom   Yeak, fuck alla dat, man – Fang, me bredren, is wha' the plan?

White Fang   Plan, blood?

Venom   For the appeal or whatever – it ain't you what arrange this rendezvous?

KKK and **Venom** *look at one another.*

KKK   He don't know?

Eggy   V, man, you don't know?

Sound: Door opening.

They all look round. **JJ** *enters.*

Venom   Awww, man! You gotta be fuckin' kiddin' me!

White Fang   Welcome to 'Meet the victim'!

Venom   You know what, fuck this, man.

Eggy   You heard the man. What you got to say, Country?

JJ *pulls up a chair. He sits and looks at them.*

Venom   Ain't what he wants to say, man. It's what he wants to hear.

Eggy   Wha' y' wanna hear, wigga boy? Apologies? Want us to break down in tears and beg for forgiveness? Hang our heads in shame? You wan' see niggas on their knees?

White Fang   He wants us to turn back time and cure his bitch, innit?

Eggy   Is it? Jonesin' for your butt boy?

Venom   Nah, man, he just wants to hear the S word.

KKK   Nah, he wants us to feel the S word. He wants us to restore his faith in 'umanity. Regret the buzz we got from smashing his bitch's face. Repent the high we got from destroying his dream. He wants to believe again that Black folks ain't all bad. He wants to feel OK for still loving us despite everything – for still wanting to be us. He don't want to face the fact he ain't a real nigga and he's just a tourist. He don't want to meet the people who live here and deal with reality. He wants to live in his dream world and for it all to all make sense. Innit, wiggaboy?

Eggy   Is that it, white boy? Is that the miracle you're here for?

JJ   I just wanted a look at you. (*Pause.*) . . . Thanks.

He gets up and, without a look back, leaves.

Eggy   That's it, batty bwoy! Gwan wit' your nasty-raas self! (*Turns back to the others.*) Well, that was fun . . .

Illmanics   . . . Next!

Orlando and JJ's Flat

Orlando *comes scampering in, giggling – We hear* **Sam** *offstage.*

Sam (*offstage*)   Ten! Nine! Eight! Seven!

Breathless, **Orlando** *looks around frantically. There is only a chair.*

Sam *enters – eyes still closed and feeling his way . . .*

Six! Five-Four-Three . . .

Orlando *squeals and wriggles under the woefully inadequate chair.*

Two!

Orlando (*to himself*)   . . . Shhhhh! Shh shh shhhhh!

Sam   One.

He opens his eyes . . . He looks around – **Orlando** *squirms and stifles a giggle . . .*

Sam   Hmmmm! Why is it so dark in here . . .? I must get my eyes seen to . . . I can barely see a thing!

He sits on the chair. **Orlando** *is beside himself with barely repressed glee.*

Sam   Now, where is that wily little Orlando? I tell you, he's just too clever for me – I just give up – I'm off home to finish waxing, these eyebrows are galloping out of control . . .

Orlando *crawls out excitedly.*

Orlando   Here I am!

Sam   Where?

Orlando   Here!

Sam (*turning in circles*)   Who's that? Who's talking?

Orlando (*racing round him*)   Me, me! I'm here! Here I am!

Sam (*hugging* **Orlando**)   Oh my God! There you are, you master of disguise!

He sees a puddle under the chair. Reaching round he feels **Orlando***'s bottom and finds a wet patch.*

Oops – a touch damp in the rump – It's wipin' time! (*Pats* **Orlando***'s butt.*) Panties off, Principissa –

Orlando *starts to take off his trousers –*

Orlando   Awww, flip! Have I sat in something again?

Sam   No, love – you've pissed yourself. Don't sit on the floor, you'll make another puddle. Chop chop, we don't want nappy rash . . .

Orlando (*feet struggling with trousers*) They won't come off! My shoes are too big!

Sam OK, sit down then . . . it's fine.

Orlando *sits.* **Sam** *takes* **Orlando**'s *trousers off over the shoes.*

Sam Here we go, Houdini – here's how we take our trousers off whilst keeping our shoes on – a skill every man should master . . .

Orlando You're so clever – you can do everything. Are you going to stay here and live with us forever and ever?

Sam Young man, you've known me a month.

Orlando I love you, Sammy.

Sam Sam. You like me. You love JJ.

Orlando Yes. But when I tell JJ he looks sad.

Sam That's men for you – can't handle commitment. Just keep telling him anyway 'til he smiles. You have to wear 'em down.

Orlando *leans forward and gives* **Sam** *a deep lingering kiss.*

Sam *rolls up* **Orlando**'s *now-removed trousers.*

Sam Mmm. You've been drinking milk again. You know it give you the runs.

Orlando *starts to take off his pants.*

Sam Er, no! Keep the underwear on for a moment, 'til I fetch some clean ones, alright?

He hurries out . . .

And save the kisses for JJ OK, darling? They're all for JJ.

Orlando Excuse me.

There is a tone in his voice that stops **Sam**.

Orlando Sam, it it?

Sam Yes, Orlando?

Orlando *is suddenly somehow his own age again.*

Orlando What's wrong with me?

Sam You've had an accident, love, and you've been sick.

Orlando It's something in my brain, isn't it?

Sam You've got brain damage. But here you are – miraculously cured!

Orlando But it won't last, will it?

Sam You come and go.

Orlando Yes, I think I remember, almost. You're pretty . . . are you seeing JJ? No. You're the home help. Sorry . . . (*Looking round.*) It's summer now, isn't it?

I love summer, don't I? They're never long enough in London. When you see JJ will you tell him I miss him? Just in case I forget?

Sam I will – but try and remember, eh?

Orlando Ooh . . . I stink . . .

Sam I'll fetch your clean knickers.

He exits.

Orlando My bum's sore . . .

A child again, he sprawls out on the ground in frustration . . .

Sameee! My bum's sore!

Sound: Door opening. **Orlando** *leaps up.*

Orlando JJ!

JJ *enters.* **Orlando** *descends and peppers him with kisses.*

JJ Orly? Where's your trousers?

Orlando Hey, JJ. What do you say? Do you want to play the gay boy way? Orly and JJ sittin' in a tree – k-i-s-s-i-n-g . . .

JJ Where's Sam? Have you scared him off?

Sam!

Orly, babe . . . Sam!

I got something for you . . .

He produces a sparkler and lighter.

Orlando Ohhh . . .!

JJ *hands the glittering and fizzing firework to* **Orlando**.

Orlando Ohhhhhhhhhhhhhhhh! Jay Jaaayyyy!

JJ Orly – you're soaked! Sam!

Sam *enters.*

Sam Present, sir!

JJ Orly's soaked.

Sam I'm running a bath. Orly, come!

JJ I'll do it.

Sound: Doorbell.

Pause.

Sam Seeing as I don't live here, I'm guessing that's for you.

JJ Take Orly to the bathroom, will you, please.

Sam *leads* **JJ** *off to the bathroom.*

Sam Come on, skunky bum . . .

JJ And lock the door, yeah?

He approaches the front door.

Who the fuck's that?

Daniel Mr Johannson? I'm Daniel Pearl. I represented the defence at the recent trial.

JJ 'Daniel Pearl'?

Daniel I'm sorry to have bothered you at home.

JJ *opens the door.*

JJ What do you want?

Daniel Justice. I know you believe that if your partner's attackers had been jailed for life justice would have been served – it would not. As repellent and depressing as they are, those ignorant bullies are not what has caused you this unspeakable suffering. They are merely the carriers of a disease that struck your lover down. I used to believe this disease was society. Struggling to make sense of this senselessness, to fathom this brutality – until yesterday, while searching for the BBC World Service on my car radio – recently replaced after my sixth break-in – I came across an extraordinary sound – bass, drums, chanting voices – hypnotically rhythmic. I never dance, but here I was nodding to the beat – So seductive, so stirring, so bloody sexy. And then an extraordinary voice two parts earth and one part sweet molasses chanting a familiar phrase. One I've heard in interview rooms and young offenders units countless irritating times. And now here it was, pumping through my body, over and over – hijacking the very pattern of my corruptible heartbeat – until I found myself chanting too. 'Chi-chi man, chi-chi man – chi-chi man fe dead.' I've googled chi-chi on the net – Do you know what it means? Termite. Cockroach . . .

Daniel/JJ . . . Vermin.

Daniel And I was singing along. With words I barely understood. And then I looked to my right and I saw that the kids in the next car – shaven heads, tracksuits, diamond earrings, you know the type – were singing along with me. Tuned into the same station and singing the same words. Our brains were being colonized – infected. I think you should take out a civil case against the composers, producers and performers responsible for these records. They are the disease. We can be the cure. (*Pause.*) And that, perhaps, might be something like justice.

Orlando *enters in a towelling robe, wet head and wet feet . . .*

Orlando   JJ. JJ!

JJ   Stay in the bathroom, babe, I'll be there in a minute . . .

Orlando   Look at my footsteps! I'm Robinson Crusoe!

JJ   Man Friday, Orly.

Sam   More of a wet weekend, I'd say . . . Come on, soggy, let's sort out your toes before you get trenchfoot and fuck up my CV. (*Seeing* **Daniel**.) Oh. Hello.

Daniel   Hello, Sam.

Orlando   Hello!

Kevan *arrives.*

Kevan   Hey you! How'd it go? (*Seeing* **Daniel**.) Oh, hello. Who are you?

Sam   This is Daniel.

Orlando   Hello, Daniel!

Daniel   Hello, Orlando.

Kevan   Daniel?

JJ   He was the defence lawyer in . . .

Kevan   I know who he is. What's he doing here?

Daniel   I wanted to have a quick word.

Kevan   How about cunt? That's a quick word.

JJ   Kevan.

Kevan   Come to gloat have you? Fucking cunt!

JJ   Kevan. (*To* **Daniel**.) Come in a minute, yeah?

Daniel   Thanks.

Daniel *and* **Kevan** *step into the flat.*

JJ   Sam, could you get Orly dressed, please?

Sam   Come on, little mermaid. Let's get you fit for dry land.

He leads **Orlando** *off.*

JJ   So you think it's that simple? The music.

Daniel   Music is influential. That's why there are national anthems. And hymns and football chants.

JJ   So, if there were no football chants there'd be no hooligans?

Daniel Music can be a rallying cry.

JJ Music can be a lot of things.

Daniel What is it to you?

JJ It's everything. It never made me hurt anyone. Before I found Orly, music was the only thing that could help me.

Daniel Did it help you be queer?

JJ This was before I knew I was queer.

Daniel And when you finally did know did the music help then? Or hinder?

Kevan What the fuck are you two talking about?

Daniel Music. What does it mean to you?

Kevan To me? Depends on the music.

Daniel *opens his backpack and pulls out an iPod and pair of portable speakers. He starts to hook them up . . .*

Daniel . . . May I?

JJ *shrugs . . .* **Daniel** *deftly completes the connection and presses play – we hear an infectious ragga tune . . .*

Daniel What does this music mean to you? First thoughts and words that come in your head . . .

Kevan Black music. Ragga. Dancehall. Dance music. Sexy.

Sound: iPod.

Vocal Boom! Go a gat in a batty-bwoy brain!

Daniel *presses pause.*

Daniel Did you get that?

Kevan Boom something?

Daniel *reads from the CD cover.*

Daniel Conveniently it's the title . . . 'Boom! Go a Gat in a Batty Boy Brain.' JJ? 'Gat'?

JJ Gun.

Daniel 'Batty boy . . .'?

Kevan I know what batty boy are.

Daniel . . . And I think the word 'brain' is universal – 'Boom go a gat in a batty boy's brain – Bang goes a gun in a queer boy's brain.'

Sam *enters, unnoticed, as* **Daniel** *releases pause.*

Vocal Gwan, pull a trigga inna Nigga brudda name.

Daniel 'Go on, pull a trigger in the name of Black men . . .'

Vocal Sen' a chi-chi man a hell wit a . . .

JJ *snaps it off.*

Daniel 'Send a chi-chi man to hell with a spike in the eye.'

Kevan Jesus Christ, JJ. That's fucked-up.

JJ It's just music.

Kevan Is that what they're all saying?

Daniel When I was sixteen the first Lenny Kravitz album was my bible. It was more than music.

JJ And if he told you to go out and shoot people, would you have done it? No Kevan, that's not what they're all saying.

Kevan Just some of them? That's fucking insane, JJ.

JJ The world's insane, Kevan – there are nutcases everywhere – Some of 'em make records – Some of 'em make brilliant records – Freedom of speech can be fucked-up but that's democracy. (*To* **Daniel***.*) You haven't answered my question.

Daniel If Lenny Kravitz had told me to go out and shoot people, would I have done it? . . . No.

JJ And why not?

Sam 'Cause he's a nice well-educated white boy. And they're a bunch of impressionable jungle-bunnies who don't know better.

Daniel You know that's not what I mean.

Sam And do you know what you mean?

Daniel Have you listened to this music?

Sam I've heard it.

Daniel And you find it acceptable?

Sam I find it . . . painful.

Daniel So, are we going to just let them hurt us?

Sam Some people find the sight of two men kissing painful – are they right to make it illegal?

Daniel No, they find it offensive.

Sam No, they find it painful.

Daniel Those are their issues – These are our lives. Are you suggesting challenging Black people on homophobia is racism?

Sam Are you planning to picket any white artists?

Daniel Like?

Sam Like Eminem? Multi-platinum selling homophobic Eminem? 'Sexy' white-trash Eminem who doesn't do interviews with gay magazines who write about him anyway Eminem?

Daniel Eminem doesn't advocate murder.

Sam Isn't there a line in there about raping a lesbian? Oh, wait – I forgot – that was a joke. He's funny.

Daniel OK . . . maybe we should consider suing Eminem.

Sam Here's the thing, Daniel. Black people expect to be under attack. If you go after the handful of Black people who are making any money, all we'll see is another white man trying to take our power. It won't work.

Daniel 'We'?

Sam We.

Daniel Sam. You're gay.

Sam And Black. Or didn't you notice?

Daniel I noticed. You're Black. And the enemy is every colour under sun. Today they happen to be Black, tomorrow they'll be something else.

Sam 'The enemy'.

Daniel Not because they're Black – because they're trying to hurt us. If I was here today talking about rock music would you join us?

Sam I don't know.

Daniel Well, join us. Work with us. Help us.

Sam 'Us'?

Daniel *looks round at* **JJ** *and* **Kevan**.

Daniel Me. Join me.

Kevan Us.

Sam I won't be the golliwog on the dust-cart.

Daniel Sorry?
Kevan Do what?

Sam I won't be the mascot. Proof that you're good non-racist white folks.

Sam   OK.

Sam   I'll go educational but not oppositional.

Daniel   OK. um. What does that mean?

Sam   Each one, teach one. Outreach.

Daniel   Oh. OK.

Kevan   Now, let's not overdo it, OK? Not everyone needs a hug, you know – some people need a slap, and some of them are Black.

Sam   And some of them are not.

Kevan   Don't you ever just want to open a can of kick-ass?

Sam   You mean now?

Daniel   OK, you two . . .

Kevan   What happened to 'By Any Means Neccessary'?

Daniel   Gentlemen, please, whatever the colour, the enemy is not in this room. Perhaps we could agree to deal with these issues on a case-by-case basis?

Sam *and* **Kevan** *shrug.*

Sam   OK.

Kevan   Cool.

Daniel   JJ?

All *look at* **JJ.**

Prison Hallway

Venom *is mopping the floor . . .* **White Fang** *passes slowly holding a tray of food, head bowed, his face badly bruised.*

Venom (*whispering, not looking up*)   Yo! Yo, blood!

He dares to move closer.

Yo, Fang me brudda. Whassappening? Why ain't you speak with me, blood? Yo!

White Fang   Come away from me, man.

Venom   Is wha' you say?

White Fang   Come away from me – we can't speak, man. They're watching.

Venom   Fuck them, man, they can't hear.

White Fang   Not the screws, man.

Venom   You mean them cell-mates you got?

White Fang Yeah, man. They got a problem with coons, man, innit? They ain't feeling 'em for real.

Venom Fang, man . . . What the fuck you just call me? What's that on your face, bruv?

He makes a move towards **White Fang** *– who drops the tray with a metallic crash to reveal that he is carrying a large chisel . . .* **Venom** *stares at it.*

Venom Man, what the fuck you doing? We're spars, man – we're brothas!

White Fang (*loud*) I know you, nigger? I fucking know you? (*Whispers.*) Walk away, blood . . .

Venom Fang, blood . . .

White Fang I'm begging you bruv . . . Walk.

Venom You know I can't step with every muthafucka watching, man . . .

White Fang Then you know I gotta fuck you up.

Venom We ain't gotta play this game, blood, we can stand together, shake hands and stay strong. We can represent. (*Steps forward.*) . . . Blood . . .

White Fang Nigger!

He punches **Venom** *clean in the face.* **Venom** *goes down.* **White Fang** *leaps into a straddle position, chisel held in both hands above his head . . . panting, but never striking, panting panting . . .*

Venom *grabs the tray and hits* **White Fang** *in the side of the head, and in a second their positions are reversed.* **Venom** *straddling* **White Fang** *with the chisel held aloft.*

White Fang Do it! Please man, for me, man!

Venom For you?

White Fang They've seen me fail, man. They'll fucking crucify me! Just the eye. In the eye, yeah? Please man, I'm fucking begging you, man! Release me, man!

Venom Julian, man . . .

White Fang *punches* **Venom** *in the face.*

White Fang White Fang, you fucking coon! WHITE Fang! (*Punching.*) You fucking ignorant fucking jungle bunny!

Venom (*agonized*) Fuck, man . . .!

White Fang Fucking monkey! Fucking baboon! Fucking gorilla monkey coon!

Venom *stabs down, the knife hovers above* **White Fang***'s eye.*

White Fang (*makes sounds like a monkey*) Oo oo oo oo oo oo oo oo . . .

Venom *stabs down.*

Blackout.

Exercise Studio

Five punchbags suspended from above.

Daniel, **Sam**, **Kevan**, **Orlando** *and* **JJ** *dressed to exercise.* **Orlando** *wearing headphones and dancing.*

Daniel Welcome to the first gathering of Lashback – a self-defence group for lesbian, gay, transgender, bisexual and questioning queers of all persuasions. Obviously right now the only representatives are, well . . .

Sam . . . Gay.

Daniel . . . but with our imminent non-confrontational initiative against the death-mongerers of ragga as our first major public platform I believe that this David can grow to become a Goliath that can defend us and our sisters and brothers from the omnipresent threat of unprovoked attack. Kicking butt in the name of Love.

Others Kicking butt in the name of Love!

Sam (*to* **JJ**) JJ, sister, where d'you want us?

JJ Well, firstly, we need to assess everyone's basic fighting ability. Everyone by their punchbags, yeah? Orly, babe . . . (*Removing* **Orlando***'s headphones.*) You wanna play?

Orlando OK!

Daniel, **Sam** *and* **Kevan** *stand by their punchbags.*

JJ OK! The punchbags is the enemy – you have to defend yourself – do what you can – go!

He starts punching – nobody else moves.

You're facing a drunk hard-faced bastard who's about to punch your face in with a knuckle-dustered fist – what do you do?

Orlando *opens his arms and hugs his punchbag.*

Sam Aw bless! Some people never learn.

JJ Sam – what would you do?

Sam Me? Well, there's a trick I learned from my grandmother – who be know as the Battling Bitch from Brixton . . . (*Doing as he speaks.*) They're facing you down, you maintain eye contact, but gradually lower your centre of gravity as if curtsying in supplication and subordination, until you can slip off your shoe – (*Slipping off shoe.*) – and batter! The fucker! (*Attacking punchbag with shoe.*) Round! The face! (*Running off.*) And run! Non-confrontationally of course . . .

Kevan With only one shoe?

Sam Not very graceful when you're in heels – but hey, survival is the ultimate glamour.

JJ Okayyyy, now – ball the fist up – do not tuck the thumb inside – you don't want to break it – aim to connect with this part of the fist here – stand far back enough for the arm to be almost extended on impact – pull back . . . and punch!

All – except **Orlando** *– punch – with a satisfying whack.*

Kevan/Sam/Daniel (*pleasantly surprised.*)   Oh! Mmm! (*etc.*)

JJ   Feels good, don't it?

Kevan/Sam/Daniel   Mmm!

JJ   Now just picture whoever releases your anger, yeah?

He leads them in a rhythmic punching.

– a mugger – (*Punch.*) – a homophobe – (*Punch.*)
– abusive ex –

Big punch.

– school bully – (*Punch.*) – teacher . . .

Kevan (*punching hard*)   Bastard!

JJ   Kevan?

Kevan (*punching hard*)   Bastard! Bastard! Bastard! (*Frenzied.*) Fucking fucking bastard bastard!

JJ (*stopping him*)   Kevan!

Kevan *pants . . .*

JJ   Well done – take a breath – you OK?

Kevan   I'm great – this cunt is dead though! (*Battering punchbag.*) Dead! Fucking cunt! Nasty! Dirty! Homophobic! Cunt!

Daniel   I applaud your ability to access your anger, Kevan – but the c-word is offensive to many lesbians and gay men.

Kevan   Cunt! Fucker! Cunt! Cunt! (*Crying.*) Cunt! Cunt! Cunt! Cunt!

Orlando *puts his arms round* **Kevan** *– who breaks down, weeping . . .* **Orlando** *rocks him in his arms . . .*

Kevan   Bastard . . .

Silence – except for **Kevan**'*s weeping . . . then . . .*

Sam   Nice cup of tea anyone?

Daniel (*snatching up his wallet*)   Good – on me?

Sam   On you sounds great!

Sam *and* **Daniel** *exit.* **JJ** *gently prises* **Kevan** *and* **Orlando** *apart, handing* **Kevan** *a towel . . .*

Kevan God, I'm turning into such a total cry-baby.

JJ *slips* **Orlando***'s headphones back over his ears.* **Orlando**, *still holding onto his hands, dances round him . . .*

JJ What's going on, Kevan?

Kevan What's going on? You're going to stand there with Orly right beside you and ask me what's going on? We're being massacred! (*Breathing.*) . . . Oh shit. I'm sorry. It's just knowing they get released so soon. And there's you so . . . fucking . . . staunch – I don't know if I'm pissed off with you or in awe. Maybe I just need a boyfriend.

JJ Well, I can recommend that.

Kevan Sorry. I suppose we're both a bit out of practice. Maybe we should help each other out.

JJ Oh?

Kevan Maybe go for a drink before the demonstration on Friday?

JJ *looks blank.*

Kevan Friday? We're picketing that gig by that reggae dude – Lego Man?

JJ Lion Man.

Kevan Yeah, him. We could go to that bar in New Cross just before, check out the babes and have a flirt – what do you reckon?

JJ Kevan, I know the picket is needed – Statements have to be made – life has to be lived – and cute boys need to be loved. But I don't know if I can do anything except love Orly and the music.

Kevan How can you still love that music, after all it's done?

JJ It's not the music.

Kevan If it's not the music, then what is it?

JJ These are the questions that chew me up, 'til it feels like there's nothing left over.

Kevan Nothing? Not even a little bit? I'm a student, I'm used to feasting on crumbs. We're both here, mate. Why do we have to be alone?

JJ I don't know. Maybe we don't.

Kevan So, it's a date? . . . ette?

JJ It's a datette.

Kevan What is that Orly's listening to?

JJ Just some random tracks I downloaded for him . . .

Kevan *goes over to* **Orlando** *and lifts a headphone for a quick listen.* **Orlando** *gives* **JJ** *a kiss.* **JJ** *replaces the headphone.*

Kevan Lion Man?

JJ Don't tell Daniel. (*Grins apologetically.*) Orly loves it.

Prison Visiting Room

Karisma *waits* . . . **KKK** *enters. They look at one another.*

KKK You came, then.

Karisma I wonder which of us is more surprised.

KKK You remember me? Who I am?

Karisma Your name's KKK and you like a Twix?

KKK Your name is Karisma and you don't take no shit.

Karisma (*looking round*)   Never been in a prison before.

KKK You're lucky.

Karisma How long you in here?

KKK Too long.

Karisma What you here for?

KKK We don't ask them questions in here.

Karisma OK . . . What am I here for?

KKK *shrugs.* **Karisma** *produces a letter.*

Karisma 'Dear Miss Karisma, I'm sorry, but I do not know your full name so please forgive my overfamiliarity. I also hope you can forgive my writing to you at your place of work, but I wanted to inform you that I am now a resident of Her Majesty's Prison and to ask if you could find the time and the generosity somewhere in your heart to come and visit me. You are probably wondering why – If you visit I will explain. Regards, Dijon Socrates Lawrence the third aka KKK.'

She folds the letter and waits.

KKK I tried hating you – dismissing you. Demonizing you. But you'd taken over a room in my brain and you were holding a part of me hostage. So I gave in and writ you. I never thought in a million years you'd actually come.

Karisma So why'd you write, then?

KKK In a place like this fantasy's what gets you through it.

Karisma So you're not gonna ask me to be a drug mule? Bake you a cake with a file in it?. . . Show you my tits while you wank furtively? Well, I'm disappointed. I was looking forward to being outraged. Is it that shameful?

KKK Shameful?

Karisma What you've done? Is that why you can't tell me? Are you ashamed?

KKK Ain't I tell you? We don't talk about them things in here.

Karisma I ain't in there.

KKK No, I am. And you're out there – judging me. (*Turns away.*) Well, thanks for coming, yeah? Fucking bitch!

Karisma (*pause*) You're welcome.

She gets up, turns and starts to leave . . .

KKK Gwan, skank, fucking run! Run like everybody else runs. Run from the fucking devil – gwan! Run from your own shame!

Karisma *stops.*

KKK Yeah, woman. Your shame. The shame you feel when you look at me. Another Black man in jail. Another Black man bringing down the race. Another Black man with no shame. (*Pause.*) I ain't got no shame. I don't know why. Weren't I born with none? Was it kicked out of me? Did I lose it on the way? Or did you get my share? Are you walking out the door with my only hope for redemption? Are you gonna forget me? Am I done? Am I over? The lost cause? Is that what I am? Is that me?

Karisma *looks at* **KKK** *– then sits down.*

Karisma Don't tell me – you're innocent.

KKK Who's innocent in this world? You? The truth is, sista, I'm a liar. I tell lies. I lie to my mother 'bout where the bling comes from. I lie to my babymother 'bout where I been. Even them rare days when there's nothing to hide, I lie just to keep in practice. I am a fucking lie. P'raps the reason I writ you and no one else is to see if I could deal with another living person and not bother with lies. Let's face it, your expectations so low of me you can't be disappointed. (*Pause.*)

I was in a fight.

Karisma A fight?

KKK An attack. I attacked someone. Hurt 'em bad. Brain damage.

Karisma Why?

KKK He was gay. He was white. He was there. I disgust you. You hate me, innit?

Karisma I don't know. Did you hate him?

KKK I didn't know him. Actually . . . Yes! Man and man together – it just – it ain't right. That's in the Bible.

Karisma Know the Bible well, do you?

KKK I know that part.

Karisma You a Christian, then?

KKK 'S how I was raised.

Karisma Finally, something in common. I was a big fan of Jesus growing up. He said such cool things – 'If thine eye offend thee, pluck it out.' 'Judge not lest ye be judged.'. . . Not a word about homosexuality, funnily enough as I recall – 'cept maybe 'Blessed are they that are persecuted for righteousness' sake'?

KKK Gays ain't persecuted – they're promoted. They're all over the TV and that. They got sitcoms! Where's our sitcoms? They practically got ads saying, 'Be gay! Be funny! Give straight men make-overs like we can't dress ourselves!' What if everyone was gay? The human race would die out innit? It's our purpose to breed. Our imperative.

Karisma How many kids you got?

KKK Four.

Karisma Don't think there's much chance of the human race dying out with you around, mate.

KKK Look, you ain't gonna convince me it's cool and dandy for one man to kiss on another man like it's normal, 'cause you know it ain't.

Karisma I think it's beautiful.

KKK It ain't natural.

Karisma What's natural? This plastic chair we're sitting on? The food we eat? Shaving? Tampons? Cars? Laser surgery? I've seen you in your tracksuit – not a natural fibre in sight.

KKK It all comes from nature in the beginning though, don't it? Plastic, nylon – it all has to come from somewhere before it's refined, yeah? So it's all natural yeah? (*Realizing what he's said, kissing his teeth.*) Think you're well cleverer 'n me, innit? This chi-chi man weren't natural. Him act like a gyal.

Karisma And you don't like girls?

KKK Now you're just talking stupid. You know what I'm saying . . . Man is man, and woman is woman. That's how the system works . . . You want your man to be a man don't you?

Karisma I want everyone to be themselves.

KKK Well, I'm a man who don't like queers – that's me. What? You want me to apologize? You know how hard it is to be me? To be a man in this world? In this life? A Black man? You don't know. You can't know. Black woman's pain don't compare, you hear.

Karisma I'm not qualified to compare.

KKK Well, I am.

Karisma Oh really.

KKK Yeah really. Nuff spare time inna dis place, yunno. I been reading – researching. Black women's four times more employed, five times more likely to do well in school. Nine times less likely to end up in jail.

Karisma And Black woman should apologize for Black man's failure in the system?

KKK She should be aware of how the system is failing her man. She should get it. She should support her soldier.

Karisma 'Soldier'?

KKK This is a war, woman! And you want me to indulge some white boy's privilege to be soft? He was there – up in our club – up in our music all up in our face – what did he expect? A kiss and a cuddle? Or what he got?

Karisma So, that's what you've brought me here to tell me? That you've got no soft side?

KKK You what?

She eyes **KKK**'s *painted nail – he snatches it out of view.*

Karisma No gentle side, no graceful side – No elegance yearning in you?

KKK What the fuck you talking 'bout?

Karisma Just a wall of man with no way in and no keyhole of tenderness anywhere?

KKK What you trying here, gyal? You trying to mess with a brotha's mind?

Karisma I don't know. Is that why I'm here?

Sound: Buzzer.

KKK Shit.

Karisma Time's up.

KKK Already. Muthafuckas don't give you nuttin'. You ain't coming again?

Karisma You inviting me?

KKK I never had a chat like this before. Prob'ly you went college, yeah? Conversation's normal to you.

Karisma Trust me – this is all brand new.

KKK (*unsure*) So . . .?

Karisma So?

KKK So next month? If I try and come up with a little sump'in to show you? Like, on the feminine side?

Karisma How could a girl resist?

KKK I'll work on it.

Interview Room

KKK *sits in silence, watching . . .*

Sound: Door opening.

White Fang *enters, his face battered.*

KKK   Yo.

White Fang   'sup.

He sits.

Sound: Door opening.

Eggy *and* **Venom** *enter –* **White Fang** *turns away as* **KKK**, **Eggy** *and* **Venom** *exchange handshakes.*

Eggy   Bruv . . .

Venom   Bruv . . .

KKK   Whaddup . . .

Sound: Door opening.

Enter **JJ**.

JJ   Was it the music?

Silence.

Eggy   You had me at hello.

The **Illmanics** *smile to themselves – but make no eye contact.*

JJ   Was it the music that made you do it? Did you chant lyrics while you beat his brains out? Was it church? Did the preacher inspire you to despise people who fall in love without your permission? Did you learn it in school? In the playground? At home? Where does it all come from? The laws in Jamaica and Africa? Brainwashing you? Where does the rage begin? Or did someone come out of nowhere to crush your life underfoot when you weren't looking? Should I be in the hate already? See, I envy you. I want to feel nothing just like you do. I wanna laugh about you being in here just like you do. I wanna not give a fuck about all this. I want to hate.

Silence. **JJ** *gets to his feet, goes to the door.*

Sound: Door opening.

Sam *comes in.* **JJ** *walks back to the centre of the room.*

JJ   This is Sam.

Sam *holds open the door.*

Sam   Come on, trouble . . .

Orlando *runs in, playing aeroplanes.*

Orlando   Eeeeeeeeeoooooooooow! Eeeeeeooooowww!

JJ   This is Orly.

Orlando   Eeeeeeeooooooooooowwwww! I'm an airplane!

JJ You're an excellent airplane, Orly – but I just want you to meet some people, OK?

Orlando OK.

JJ You know how you like meeting people, Orly. You like making new friends, yeah?

Orlando (*smiling bashfully*) Yeah.

JJ Well, this is Marquis . . .

Orlando Hi!

JJ That's Duran.

Orlando Hi!

JJ Dijon Socrates the third . . .

Orlando Hi!

JJ And Julian.

Orlando Hello! (*Looking round.*) Everyone's so sad!

He heads towards **Venom**, *arms open.* **Venom** *darts away.*

Venom DON'T FUCKING TOUCH ME, YOU FUCKING QUEER!

Eggy Oy! Leave my boy, yeah?

JJ *steps in front of* **Eggy**, *gently pulls* **Orlando** *to him.*

JJ . . . Orly.

Orlando I'm sorry, JJ. I just wanted to give him a cuddle.

JJ I know, baby – it's cool. Sam . . .

Sam (*taking custody of* **Orlando**) Come away from the bad men, lovely.

Eggy So this is your secret weapon is it? The spastic and his mammy?

Sam Is who you a' call mammy, bwoy?

Eggy Who the fuck are you calling 'bwoy', Mammy?

They kiss their teeth.

JJ I just wanted you to meet Orly.

Eggy Bullshit. You just wanted to fuck us up and you brought along Aunt Jemima here to prove that you ain't a racist! Well, I got news for you, white boy – that ain't Black – that's a fucking coconut!

Sam Sing us another song while you're on the chain-gang. I'm a coconut because I'm gay?

Eggy Because you're a traitor to your race. I bet your father's well proud of you, innit?

Sam And I bet your mamma's well proud of you, Prisoner eight-six-six-six-one-zero – innit?

They kiss their teeth.

I told you this was a waste of time, JJ. What the hell are we doing here?

Eggy Yeah, what are you doing here? Ain't you had enough yet? Coming here – arxing questions – like answers exist. What the fuck it you really want to know? Why did this happen? To you – the niggalover? Why do niggas hate niggalovers? Why do niggas hate queers? Why do niggas hate everyone – even other niggas? Cause that's what niggas do. Niggas hate.

JJ Not all, man.

Eggy All.

JJ Not all Black people are niggas.

Eggy See, white boy, that's what you ain't been getting. Everyone's a nigga. Every last one of us. Ain't you? Why did you wanna be a MC – all the way out there in cow country? Because you wanted to be a nigga? Or because you knew you were a one?

Silence.

What was it you related to? The passion? The rage for how fucked-up and uneven and unfair this world is? The rage for how it makes you feel? You come here talking 'bout how you wanna feel the hate. Bullshit. You already feel it. We all feel it. We're all niggas and we all hate queers. Including you.

JJ Me?

Eggy Yeah – you.

Sam Yeah . . . You.

Eggy Aren't you here with all us? Under the same laws – and the same religions?

Sam You watch your hands in conversation and wonder how gay you look – You build up an armour of muscles, like a billboard, that advertises your masculinity. And still you wonder what earthly use you are if you don't procreate – you wonder what it is that made you queer – was you born like it or did your mother rock you wrong in the cradle – have you got a woman's brain in a man's body? What the fuck are you? Why the fuck are you? You march and you chant and laugh in the face of those who spit and shit on you and tell yourself you can be gay and proud and still be a man –

Eggy – That you can be Black in this world and still be a man –

Sam – but there's the doubt –

Eggy – and there's the hate –

Sam – and there's your nigga.

Eggy Here's your nigga. Different muscles . . .

Eggy/Sam   . . . same nigga.

Eggy   Trying to be a man in a world that says you can't. Trying to be here in a world that says you ain't.

Sam   And the best you manage is to be a cartoon.

Eggy   Yeah. It's the music. And the preacher and the playground and the parents – and yeah, them laws back home that was put in place back in the day by the British Empire – The same laws that was in place inna dis 'ere country not so long ago. It's alla dat – and more. There ain't one reason why niggas hate queers – there's every reason.

Sam   'Cause we're all queers . . .

Eggy   . . . and we're all niggas. Struggling to be men. unable to handle you and your boy there fucking. Forget all this men loving men bullshit – it's the fucking that's the mind fuck. Men getting fucked – too close to the situation a nigga's living – you feel me, nigga?

JJ (*pause*)   Yeah. I feel you, nigga. (*Pause.*) Thank you.

He raises his fist. **Eggy** *looks at it.*

Eggy   For what? Helping you find your hate? It was always there, man.

JJ   For helping me find my truth.

Eggy *looks around at the* **Illmanics**. **White Fang** *is staring at the wall, disassociated.* **Venom** *is looking at the floor.* **KKK** *is watching, still as a cat.* **Eggy** *is alone.*

Eggy   And what's that, then?

JJ   That hate is weakness. And lovers can't afford to be weak.

Eggy   Now, I know you ain't calling us weak, man . . .

JJ   'These are the words of my master, keep on telling me, no weak hearts shall prosper. And whosoever diggeth a pit, Shall . . .'

Venom   'Fall in it . . . Shall bury in it.'

Eggy   So, you know your Marley.

JJ   He's my prophet, man. 'I don't fear their humiliation – Just to prove my determination –'

JJ/Venom   'I don't yield to temptation –'

JJ/Venom/Eggy   'I haven't learned my lesson in revelation.'

Eggy   'The road of life is rocky – and you may stumble too – and while you point your finger – someone else is judging you.'

JJ   'Would you let the system make you kill your brother man?'

JJ/Venom   'No, dread, no . . .'

JJ   'Well, the biggest man you ever did see was . . .'

They look at **Orlando**.

Venom 'A baby . . .' 'Open your eyes and look within – are you satisfied with the life you're living?'

'Most people think Great God will come from the sky – Take everything and make everyone feel high – but if you know what life is worth then you will look for yours on Earth . . .' (*Deep painful breath.*) We goin' a Hell, innit, man?

Eggy Hush, man.

Venom We're already gone, innit? We're already there. 'Let them all pass their dirty remarks – there's only one thing I'd really like to arx – Is there a place for the hopeless sinner – who has hurt mankind just to save his own.' Our grandmother she come to see us in here just one time. I had to beg her never again. To see her cry like that – so heartbroke. (*In torment.*) I wanted to die, man, I wanted to fucking die!

Distressed, **Eggy** *starts towards* **Venom**, *but cannot hold him.*

Eggy Cuz, cuz, cuz . . . Hush . . .

Venom Oh fuck, man . . . we're there, man, burning for sure. For sure . . . lost, lost, our souls is lost . . .

Orlando *walks up and puts his arms around an unresisting* **Venom** *and rocks him.*

Venom How do we reach forgiveness from here, man? Which way redemption?

JJ Wish I knew, man. For real. Wish I could find forgiveness myself. But I can't hate you and I can't forgive you. All there is – is this.

Eggy Hit me, man.

JJ *looks at* **Eggy**.

Eggy Hard as you like. We gotta do something innit? If we want to move on. Hit me.

JJ You wanna move on?

Eggy Look at us, man. Look where we are. We got to move on – or die or something. Yeah. I wanna move on. I wanna feel – whassit – remorse. I wanna be sorry. And you want vengeance, don't you? So just hit me, yeah? For all of us.

JJ I ain't gonna hit you, man. But thanks for asking, yeah?

Eggy Well, listen if you ever change your mind – you know where I am. Or if you wanna talk about anything, music or Marley or whatever, that's cool. Cool?

He raises his fist.

JJ Cool.

JJ *and* **Eggy** *touch knuckles – fist to fist.*

Visiting Room

Karisma enters to find **KKK** *waiting.*

KKK You came back.

Karisma And you're still here.

Karisma *holds out a photograph.* **KKK** *looks at it.*

Karisma Recognize these two people? Look closer. See it yet? My smile in his face, her eyes in mine?

KKK I see it.

Karisma This was taken a week before he killed her. With his bare hands. She was getting texts from a man at work. He thought she was encouraging him. By the time I came home and found 'em he'd hung himself. Now tell me you're qualified to judge a Black woman's pain. Don't worry, I'm not going to cry.

KKK I'm sorry.

Karisma No, you're not. You don't know them.

KKK I know you.

Karisma No, you don't.

KKK I want to. And I want to be sorry. I'm ready to be sorry. See, I been thinking.

Karisma Thinking? What next? Feeling?

KKK . . . about my feminine side. You wanna see it?

Karisma Oh go on, then, seeing as I'm here.

KKK *yanks his pants down for a moment to expose a pair of silky knickers.* **Karisma** *screams in delighted surprise.*

Karisma Why Miss Jones, you're beautiful. Where'd you get them? Agent Provocateur?

KKK I bought 'em on eBay.

Karisma God bless the internet. That good am I? One visit and you're converted from lager lout to ladyboy? No wonder I can't keep a man.

KKK Don't worry about it – I had these before you.

Karisma Oh.

KKK It's the thinking that's new . . . not the feeling. And all down to you. And I've been listening. Studying. You can cry now if you want. For your parents. I'll know what to do.

Karisma Which is?

KKK Well, I can't hold you – not in here. But I'll want to. And I won't let you cry alone.

Karisma What happened to the soldier?

KKK He's found something new to fight for.

Karisma Well. You really have been studying.

KKK And learning. We are all niggers and we're all queers.

Karisma Now I'd wear that t-shirt.

KKK (*grins shyly*) Gyal, you something else, you know that? Always got a line.

Karisma And you've got a pretty smile.

KKK *produces a huge smile.*

KKK And you ain't got a man?

Karisma All the best men are queer.

They smile.

Orlando and JJ's Flat

Sound: Car horn outside.

JJ *rushes in still dressing and deodorizing,*

JJ Orly!

He opens the door, calls out . . .

One minute, yeah? Orly!

Orlando I'm doing wee-wee!

Venom *comes out of the toilet.*

Venom He's doing wee-wee.

JJ He does that a lot.

Eggy *enters with a backpack.*

Eggy We know.

JJ His number twos can be a bit unpredictable as well.

Eggy/Venom We know!

JJ So, you've got a couple of changes of clothes, in case, yeah?

Eggy (*holding up backpack*) Er . . .

JJ And you've got both my mobile numbers, yeah?

Eggy JJ, man . . . Chill.

JJ Yeah, I'm chilled, chilled, seen, seen. Only one ice cream, yeah, or he'll eat 'til he's sick.

Eggy It's cool, blood. I've got a kid myself, take her out every Thursday – I know the runnings.

Orlando (*offstage, approaching*)   Marky! Marky!

Orlando *appears in the bathroom door.*

Marky Mark!

Venom   Marquis, Orly. Marquis. Did you flush?

Orlando   Come and check out this poo first (*Indicates eighteen inches.*) – it's this long!

Venom   Lead me to it, man, can't wait . . .

Orlando   Come on, before it sinks!

JJ   Orly . . . Orly . . .!

Orlando   What, JJ? Me and Marky are busy.

JJ   How about my goodbye kiss?

Orlando *rolls his eyes, gives* **JJ** *a kiss then breezes off.*

JJ   No hug?

Orlando   I haven't washed my hands.

JJ   I love you!

Orlando   I know.

JJ   And if he has one of his moments, if there's even a glimpse of the old Orly, you'll call me, yeah? I don't want to miss it.

Eggy   You're on speed-dial, now gwan!

JJ   Peace.

They brush fists.

Eggy   Peace. Go!

Sound: Car horn.

JJ   Shit!

He runs out . . .

Sound: Toilet flushing.

Orlando *runs in laughing,* **Venom** *is trying to catch him.*

Venom   Orly, man! Orly! Fuck's sake . . .
Orlando   Can't catch me! Can't catch me!

I'm slippy as a eel!

Eggy   What the fuck are you doing, cuz?

Venom   Trying to get him to wash his hands, man! Orly!

Eggy   Orlyyyy!

He holds out a lollipop – **Orlando** *heads straight for it.*

Orlando   Mmmmmmm . . . !

Eggy (*snatching it out of reach*)   Dirty hands don't hold lollipops!

Orlando *runs to the bathroom.*

Eggy   What in hell are we doing?

Venom   Fuck knows, man.

Sound: Tap running . . .

Venom   What if he pisses himself, man?

Eggy   You'll handle it, cuz.

Venom   Me? You're the one what's got kids!

Eggy   Yeah, but he ain't my kid! I don't hardly touch them – I ain't gonna be wiping sweetboy's arse am I?

Venom   You don't touch your kids, man?

Eggy   Your daddy touch you? No, me neither, and we turned out fine, innit? I love 'em an all dat but touching 'em just ain't neccessary. Fuck this, man, why you sweating me? I thought we come out of prison, still.

Venom   Takes more than a key, cuz. If you don't want to do this, why we here?

Eggy   So you don't go to Hell.

The Crossbar

Kevan *is waiting in a cute outfit holding two beers.* **JJ** *arrives – stands in the doorway, watching as* **Kevan** *finishes a beer.* **JJ** *turns and leaves.* **Kevan** *turns to the door – no* **JJ**. **Kevan** *starts on the second beer.*

Outside the Click Club

Daniel *giving out flyers.*

Daniel   Music not murder! Ragga not Rage!

Sam *hurries up.*

Sam   I'm here, I'm here – Music not murder! Beats not beatings! Sorry – Poor Daniel – you shouldn't have been left to take on the enemy alone.

Daniel   Actually, everyone's been cool.

Sam   Well, what about those?

He points to red stains on **Daniel**'s *shirt.*

Daniel Oh, those? Just tomatoes. There's been a couple of drive-bys . . .

Sam They were jealous of your cute outfit.

Daniel Of all the words in the English language you could select to describe me, I don't think anyone would choose cute.

Sam Then let's see if we can come up with a new word specially for you.

Daniel Oh dear. I'm just going to fuck it all up again, aren't I?

Sam We'll see.

Kevan *storms up and snatches a bunch of flyers.*

Kevan Music not murder! Rhymes not crimes!

Sam/Daniel (*exchanging a look*) Hi.

Kevan Hi – Music not murder! Tracks not attacks!

Sam Are you OK?

Kevan Oh, I'm great. Just wicked. No fucking boyfriend, no fucking life, but hey, no brain damage! 'OK'? I'm downright lucky! Music not murder! Verses not hearses!

Kevan, **Daniel** *and* **Sam** *move on as* **Venom** *and* **Eggy** *enter in a hurry,* **Venom** *holding ice lollies.*

Eggy What the fuck have you done with him?

Venom I only turned away for one second to pay the ice-cream geezer – Orly was right behind me being Tinker Bell sprinkling magic dust.

Eggy 'Tinker Bell'?

Venom You know – Tinker Bell! Peter Pan's fairy friend!

Eggy Fuck's sake!

Venom What we gonna do, man? He ain't never gonna believe it was an accident is he?

JJ Accident?

Eggy JJ, bruv!

JJ Accident? (*Looks round.*) Where's Orly?

Eggy JJ, bruv, it's cool . . .

JJ Cool?! WHERE THE FUCK IS ORLY, YOU MURDERING BLACK BASTARDS? ORLY!

Eggy JJ! Hear me, yeah?

JJ *stares at* **Eggy** *wild-eyed.*

Eggy Orly is fine. He is here – somewhere – and we will find him, bruv. We will find him.

Eggy, **JJ** and **Venom** *run off in separate directions*

Eggy/JJ/Venom ORLY!

Orlando *enters giggling, trying to find somewhere to hide.*

Orlando Ninety-seven! Ninety-eight! Ninety-nine . . .

He almost collides with a silhouetted figure. Light reveals a hooded **White Fang** – *he wears an eye-patch.*

Orlando Julian?

White Fang *hurries away* . . . **Orlando** *goes after him.*

Orlando Julian! Julian! You caught me! You caught me! Here I am! You won!

White Fang What the fuck are you talking about?

Orlando The game! You found me and you won! You are so clever! Duran and Marky'll be so jealous!

White Fang Who?

Orlando You know. Duran and Marky – Eggy and Venom.

White Fang Are they here?

Orlando Somewhere. (*Whispers.*) I think they're lost. What's wrong?

White Fang *goes to leave.* **Orlando** *darts in his way again.*

Orlando Aren't you friends no more?

White Fang Will you just fuck off out of my way, please?

Orlando Why are you scared?

White Fang What the fuck do you want from me?

Orlando I want to be friends.

White Fang Friends? You really have got brain damage.

Orlando I want to know what happened to your eye. It wasn't Duran or Marky was it? I'm sure they never meant it. Did they hurt you, Julian?

Venom *comes running in.*

Venom Orly, my brother! Where the fuck?

They exchange an elaborate handshake.

Orlando Whassup, bredren!

Venom *sees* **White Fang**.

Venom Fang?

Orlando We've been playing, Marky – Julian won. Marky Mark, did you hurt Julian?

Venom What?

Orlando You heard – If you did anything to hurt him, even by accident – you should say sorry. And you two should kiss and make up.

White Fang It wasn't him. I did it all myself.

Orlando You cut out your own eye? Why?

White Fang It offended me. I was banged up with a bunch of white blokes who didn't like niggers.

Orlando But we're all niggas.

White Fang Speak for yourself. I was just an honorary nigga – a nigga once removed. When I found myself needing to stab me a fellow negro in order to appease the Caucasian hordes – I couldn't do it. I'd rather cut out my eye than deface his precious blackness. Blackness was next to godliness and I was just a pale-faced little Jewboy. Joke is – it's not as if I even liked niggers really. Yeah, I wanted to be seen with 'em – like a chav wants to be seen with a pit bull on a chain – yeah, I thought I wanted to be one – they made victimhood so much funkier than us. We were all angst, they were about attitude – we kvetched, they rapped. They were cool. My grandparents met in a concentration camp and yet five years after the war they had their own shipping firm in Wapping. Black people are still recovering from slavery three hundred years ago – but to me they were cool – when the truth is that being a nigger is just so three hundred years ago. My liberal parents would die if they heard me talk like this – if they hadn't already disowned me. My dad's flash law firm takes legal aid cases and my mum does social work at a women's prison – they listen to Aretha and Otis – they love Mandela, Malcolm X, Martin Luther King and Oprah – oh, they love the schwartzes – but the blacks don't love 'em back. 'Cause they know the truth – don't you, MC Venom? You know that white liberals are just racists without balls. We can worship you, we can demonize you – but we can never stand beside you without adoration, envy, contempt or fear. Innit? Blood? . . . Peace.

He leaves.

Orlando Peace out, my nigga!

Venom Let's just get you home, little man, yeah?

Eggy *comes striding up.*

Eggy Fuck's sake!

Eggy *and* **Venom** *head straight for* **Orlando** *and scoops him up between them.*

Orlando Bredren!

He initiates the elaborate handshake, **Eggy** *declines.*

Eggy Yeah, yeah, fairy boy, let's go!

He grabs **Orlando** *by the hand, realizes himself and lets go.*

Kevan Oy!

He heads over to **Eggy**, **Venom** *and* **Orlando**.

Kevan What the fuck do you think you're doing?

Eggy Wondering who the fuck you are.

Kevan Who the fuck am I? Who the fuck are you?

Daniel *and* **Sam** *head over to join them.*

Daniel Kevan – Duran, Duran – Kevan . . .

Kevan I'm his friend, who the fuck are you? Come on, Orly.

Eggy Who the fuck am I? Just the nigga who's gonna hospitalize you, muthafucka.

Daniel OK, Duran, there's no need for for this . . .

Venom He's right, Eggy man – ain't no need to escalate, alright?

Kevan 'Eggy'? Fucking 'Eggy'? OK, you know what, take your fucking hands off him, alright?

Daniel Kevan.

Eggy Or what?

Kevan Or I'm gonna have to be the muthafucka who hospitalizes you, nigger.

Eggy *and* **Venom** *share a look of disbelief.*

Eggy/Venom 'Nigger'?

Kevan Nigger! N – I – G – G . . . E-R!

Daniel/Sam . . . Oh dear.

Venom Oh, you silly white bitch – gwan!

He swings jokily at **Kevan** *who dodges.*

Daniel/Sam/Eggy Whoa!

Eggy Whooo, it's oooon!

Kevan Come on, come on, best shot!

Sam (*rescuing* **Orlando**) I'll look after you, pet – no charge.

Kevan Best shot, best shot! You think white men can't jump? Think again, yeah? KnowhatImean? You get me?

Daniel OK, time gentlemen . . . Kevan . . .

Kevan You fucking get me?

He punches. **Daniel** *goes down.*

All (*not* **Orly**) Shit!

KKK's Flat

Karisma *hurries into the romantically lit room – she holds two glasses of wine and wears a man's suit.*

Karisma   Sweetheart!

Sound: Car horn.

KKK (*offstage*)   I know! One minute!

Karisma *opens the door, calls out.*

Karisma   One minute mate! Babycakes! How long you gonna be in that bathroom? Taxi's outside!

KKK   I know!

Karisma   . . . Bleedin' women . . .

KKK   Possess your soul with patience, man . . .

He enters in a dress and full make-up.

. . . Beauty takes time, you know what I mean?

Karisma *stares.*

Karisma   Oh my God . . . Dijon . . . All is forgiven.

KKK   Dionne. Tonight I'm Dionne.

Karisma   You're beautiful.

She goes to kiss him . . . **KKK** *turns his head.*

KKK   Mind the lips!

Karisma *takes his hand and kisses it . . . they entwine arms and drink.*

Sound: Door unlocking.

Eggy (*offstage*)   Raaatid, man! Don't drop the muthafucka!

KKK *and* **Karisma** *stare at one other wide-eyed.*

Karisma   Bathroom!

KKK *nips into the bathroom just as* **Eggy**, **Venom**, **Sam** *and* **Kevan** *burst in, carrying an unconscious* **Daniel**, **Orlando** *sprinkling them with fairy dust the whole time.*

Eggy   Crazy white faggot weighs a ton, man!

Sam   Why aren't we at the hospital?

Venom   These is nearer, innit?

Eggy   You know how long an ambulance takes to reach New Cross?

Venom   Fucking hell, little man, is wha' you have to hit him so hard for?

Kevan   You started it!

Eggy   You got anger-management issues, man!

Daniel   Uhhhh!

Sam leans over Daniel.

Sam   Daniel?

Daniel lifts his head and kisses Sam deeply. Eggy and Venom look away.

Eggy   . . . Fuck's sake, man!

After a few moments, he peeks, looks away.

Fuck's sake!

With a gasp, Daniel loses consciousness again, head hitting the ground with a bang. Sam pulls himself together.

Sam   Water.

Venom   Bathroom.

He starts toward the bathroom, Karisma blocks the way.

Karisma   Bathroom's occupied!

Eggy   And who the fuck are you?

Karisma   Dionne's girlfriend.

Eggy/Venom   'Dionne'?

Karisma   Dijon! I'm Dijon's girlfriend.

Venom   He only come out of prison this week!

Daniel coughs.

Sam   Water!

Daniel   I'm fine!

He pulls Sam into another kiss, Eggy recoils.

Eggy   Fuck's sake! Water!

Karisma   Kitchen! It's only upstairs!

Venom   Fuck that! Dijon! Open the door, blood! It's me!

Karisma   Dijon's sick! I'll go up and get it . . .

Venom   Dijon, man!

KKK opens the bathroom door and comes out.

Venom   Dijon?

Kevan   Dijon Socrates Lawrence the third? AKA Krazy Kop Killer?

Venom   Lord Jesus Christ, Babylon reach!

KKK   Hey, you lot, whassup?

Eggy   'Whassup'? 'Whassup'? You stan' there looking like a down-low J-ho and you have the nerve to arx us 'whassup'? What the fuck is goin' on?

Karisma   None of your business. You don't have to explain yourself, Dijon.

Eggy   And who the fuck is this irritating bitch? Your boyfriend?

Orlando   His lover.

All look at **Orlando** *– who has suddenly grown up again.*

Am I right? That's your lover? (*Approaching* **Karisma**.) I'm Orlando. Pleased to meet you.

Sam   Shit! JJ!

Sam, **Eggy**, **Kevan** *and* **Venom** *whip out mobiles and speed-dial.*

Karisma   Pleased to meet you. I've heard so much about you.

Kevan   JJ, mate! Where are you?

He ducks out of the room.

Karisma   I'm Karisma.

Orlando   And this is Dionne?

KKK   Well, I couldn't decide between Dionne and Diane.

Orlando   Why not both? Dionne Diane Socrates Lawrence . . . The first.

KKK   You do know who I am, yeah? You know what I've done?

Orlando   Do you believe that's who you are? What you've done?

KKK   What else can I be?

Kevan *re-enters.*

Kevan   He's down the road at the Click Club – he's on his way.

KKK   I'm sorry. For what I've done. And ashamed. I'm ashamed. So sorry, so ashamed . . .

Orlando   Why be ashamed, when you can do something else? And become that?

KKK   Maybe that's what I'm trying to do.

Eggy   So what, you're gay now?

KKK   No blood, I ain't gay.

Karisma   Trust me, he ain't gay.

Eggy   Trust you? You turned him into a woman!

KKK   I ain't trying to be a woman, bredren.

Eggy   You can't call me bredren dressed like that, man!

Sound: Car horn.

Karisma   I better pay that taxi off.

She exits.

Eggy   You were going out like that?

KKK   We were going to a ball.

Eggy   A ball? OK, Cinderfella, I admit it – I do not get it. Help me understand, yeah? What the fuck?

KKK   Ain't you got a feminine side?

Eggy   If I have, it don't look like that, alright?

Venom   What does it look like?

Kevan   A lady truckdriver, probably.

Eggy   Fuck off! That's his job! I dunno, do I?

Orlando   Actually, you do.

Eggy   I do?

Orlando   You do. It looks like love.

Eggy   Like what?

Venom   He says it looks like love, cuz.

Eggy   You lot just come away from me, yeah? Alla you just too damn sissy!

Venom   So what if it looks like a lady truck driver? A lady's a lady, innit?

Eggy (*to* **Venom**)   You stay out of it, you get me? You alright, dread? Ain't concussed or nuttin'?

Daniel   I'm fine, thanks.

Kevan   I'm sorry I hit you, mate . . .

Daniel   So am I. Sort of . . .

He kisses **Sam**.

Eggy   Fuck's sake!

Karisma *enters with* **JJ**.

JJ   Orly?

Orlando   JJ?

Eggy   Oh God.

JJ *grabs* **Orlando** *in his arms.*

Orlando Where've you been, Rudeboy?

JJ Looking for you, Orly.

Orlando I'm just here.

JJ Yes. You are. Oh God, Orly. . . There's so much I want to ask and now it's all flown away. Orly. I miss you, Orly. I love you.

Orlando There's something wrong with me, isn't there?

JJ There's nothing wrong with you.

Orlando Yes there is. I'm sorry.

JJ There's nothing wrong with you, Orly. You're perfect.

They kiss.

Eggy Oh man!

He turns away to find **Karisma** *and* **KKK** *kissing.*

Eggy Oh man!

Daniel *and* **Sam** *kiss.*

Eggy Fuck's sake! (*Eyes meeting* **Venom***'s.*) What the fuck you looking at?

Orlando *laughs and breaks away from* **JJ***.*

Orlando urrrr! **JJ**! He put his tongue in my mouth!

JJ Orly?

Orlando JJ kisses bo-oys! JJ kisses bo-oys!

JJ No, Orly . . . only you.

Orlando (*whispers*) It's alright . . . We won't tell! (*To the others.*) Will we?

JJ It's OK, I don't mind . . .

Orlando *wanders round the room, looking up at the walls.*

Orlando JJ kisses bo-oys . . . Man, look at all these records! Hundreds and hundreds and thousands and millions! Whose are they?

KKK They're mine.

Orlando Yours? Wow! You must be a millionaire! Can I play one?

KKK Sure.

Orlando *tries to scrunch a record onto the turntable.*

Venom Let me, yeah?

He puts on the record, scratches it flashily and spins it.

Sound: Music – Lion Man.

Orlando Ohhh! Lion Man! (*Dancing.*) Let's dance! Everyone has to dance! (*Looks round.*) What's wrong?

JJ *steps forward and stops the record.*

JJ It's Lion Man, Orly. He doesn't like us.

Orlando Well, then, we just have to love him more, innit?

JJ It's too disappointing, Orly. You get into the rhythm, you're dancing happy for that first minute and then the lyrics kick you in the teeth.

Orlando Well, before the lyrics there's the music, JJ. And the music is innocent, isn't it?

JJ Maybe . . . yeah.

Orlando Then if we just dance to the music, so are we. Let's dance, JJ – Just for a minute, yeah? Is wha'y'say, star?

JJ I say . . . lyrics.

He re-starts the record, **Orlando** *dances round him.* **JJ** *watches a moment, smiling, and then starts to dance with* **Orlando** *– swept up by his lover's joy.* **Venom** *is nodding his head, watching them.* **Eggy** *gives* **Venom** *a warning punch in the arm.* **Venom** *ignores him, moving out of range, nodding some more.* **Karisma** *holds a hand out to* **KKK** *– who takes it, allowing her to draw him into a winding, grinding slo-dance.* **Venom** *is starting to move more now, getting into the rhythm . . .* **Sam** *crooks a finger, beckoning* **Daniel** *to his feet. He takes* **Daniel***'s hand and leads him into a step . . . and they dance.* **JJ** *reaches out to pull* **Kevan** *in to dance with both him and* **Orlando***. Reluctant at first,* **Kevan** *can't resist being infected by* **Orlando***'s smile and he starts to dance.* **Venom** *heads for his cousin, he grins at him.* **Eggy** *kisses his teeth, looks away, then looks round, shaking his head but before he can edit himself – he is smiling.* **Venom** *laughs – pointing at him.* **Eggy** *gives in . . . He starts to move – and everyone is dancing.*

Music break . . . and as the lyric kicks in . . .

Blackout.

End.

Rikki Beadle-Blair on *Bashment*

Rikki I was asked to write a play for Theatre Royal Stratford East by the new artistic director who was coming in at the time, who was Kerry Michael; he was just taking over from Philip Hedley who had been there a long time, about twenty-three years; and Kerry was moving from being deputy artistic director to full and he asked me to write a play. I'd seen a play that Kerry had directed as he was starting his tenure called *The Battle of Green Lanes*, which was a play about a bisexual Turkish boy, and the tension between Greek and Turkish people in North London. The thing that really struck me was when the character's bisexuality turns up, his best friend is gay, is Greek, and the audience's response was so loud and not positive. That's something I grew up with, hearing audiences responding to my work and other people's work. You get these pockets of resistance to humanity and sometimes it becomes abusive – there's hostility. When you're writing for a theatre, the theatre is a character in the play. And so I really wanted to write for that audience. I'd just done a documentary for [BBC] Radio 4, about homophobia in ragga music, and I'd gone to Jamaica, to speak to people in churches, on the street and so on. My mum's from Jamaica and it was my first time in the country, and it had been this kind of visceral experience. So, coming back from that and putting it on the radio, I wasn't done with the subject.

It felt like this was a great way to actually have a conversation with the audience, which is why I started writing plays in the first place. I wanted to write books at first, but then I realized that plays, particularly seeing working-class theatre and Black theatre, the audience is not quiet, they respond – it's like panto – they're back and forth with the audience. I knew they'd be like that at Stratford East; so I wrote a play specifically with the audience as a character. I cast first and then I write the script for the actors, though they're not playing themselves. Team Angelica was going then and I asked some people from out of Team Angelica and some new people and then I started writing them a play; all the way through, I knew that the audience was going to respond in certain ways. In the first preview, I went backstage and the cast were all staring at me traumatized. 'What's happening out there? There was shouting?' And I said, 'But you knew they were going to do this; all the way through rehearsal I was telling you that they'll react like this here and react like that there, you have to keep going.' Some scenes, they were like, 'We can't keep going because they're so noisy, how do we keep going? They can't hear us.' So we have to develop all these techniques to do that. Of course, after three or four days, the cast became completely used to this audience being this other character and they started to be able to play with the audience really and start realizing that the audience was part of the symphony; so they were realizing that it's our job to conduct them through this journey. I've had that kind of experience with other pieces, but with *Bashment* it was the peak experience of that, because the audience was so into it; and the audience would often have arguments amongst each other. Somebody is queer bashed in it and I hit them hard with it, there was a lot of blood and it's a big shocking moment. Some audiences would cheer the bashing and so other people in the audience are traumatized; they would start fighting; I would have to go out sometimes in the interval and give out free copies of the book to calm people down and just be this ambassador. Then what you would see is big sections of the audience going from hostility and also a lot of humour. When white people come and see a show with a lot of Black people in the audience they're surprised by what we laugh at. Because like other minorities, we've learned to deal with a lot of pain, and a lot of trauma through humour and through laughing at things. So, it's very odd for them because they're like, 'How can you laugh at this?' So, it was a really interesting mix of audience responses and it was my job really to guide them from hostility and dismissal to empathy and to conversation and then to love.

The triumph of the show was always at the end. All the way through there's two male lovers and if they went anywhere near kissing each other, the audience would start getting crazy. And then at the end I had them dutty wine with each other,[1] and the audience went insane every single night and were thrilled to see it. Obviously, they were shocked as well but then I had them kiss and I think I hit them with like nine same-sex kisses one after another, from different characters. One of the characters who's very macho is being able to be somebody who is cross-dressing and has a whole kind of feminine side that he has repressed in his life; and the audience were kind of on the ropes reeling at this point. But then that amazing ending where they would always give a standing ovation to the cast and particularly the gay characters. The audience have gone on this journey. What was disturbing about it was that you've taken them on this huge journey and every night you'd leave the theatre exhilarated by having taken this audience on this incredibly difficult journey together. Then the next lot come in the next night and they're back at zero and just thinking, 'How many people think like this? How many coach loads of people are there like this that we have to have this conversation with?' Of course, you know, the answer is, there are continents full of people that need to have these conversations. But what I learned from the documentary, and that show and other shows, is that they want to have that conversation, and that if you connect with people in a way that's honest and authentic and you don't back down from your points of view whilst respecting theirs, and then hold up a mirror to them, they will see themselves, and they will see our faces on top of one another, and they will get there, and it's an endless battle. But eventually I have seen the tide change so much from that show and from twenty years ago, seeing and making shows in the 1980s and 1990s. It's a completely different world. We have so far to go. But what that has taught me is that we can get there.

Mojisola I remember being in an audience in *Bashment* and as a lesbian, as a queer person, riding those tides, riding those waves, and thinking 'Will I get out of here safe? Am I OK?' And seeing a whole massive transformation in a huge crowd of people in the audience – *Bashment* is more than a play, like so much of our work is.

---

1 Dutty wine is a Jamaican dance style of gyrating to music from the reggae dancehall scene. Dutty wining became even more popular with the release of Tony Matterhorn's song of the same name.

Nine Lives

Zodwa Nyoni

Author's note

When a friend of mine was deported in 2013, I wanted to understand the process of claiming asylum in the UK. I read research studies, media reports, blogs and articles from the Home Office. Though useful in building a picture of the discourse around refugees and asylum seekers, I was still not connecting to the human experience. I contacted City of Sanctuary, who put me in touch with Meeting Point, a drop-in session for refugees and asylum seekers in Armley, Leeds. It was here that I met the people who so far had been depicted as statistics, who truly lived in the constraints of policy. Each person had their own story to share. In the last year there has been a surge of dehumanizing reports in the public domain regarding refugees and asylum seekers, in addition to negative uses of the word immigration. This play hopes to connect us all back to the human stories. It aims to counter generalizations about migration and assumptions about refugees and asylum seekers.

Nine Lives was first performed at Òran Mór on 19 May 2014 and was 'A Play, a Pie and a Pint' commission by West Yorkshire Playhouse and Òran Mór. It was revived for a national tour in 2015, with the following cast and creative team:

Ishmael   Lladel Bryant

Director   Alex Chisholm
Composer   Jonathan Girling
Mbira (soundtrack) Kudaushe Matimba
Sound Designer   Ed Clarke
Stage Manager   Emaleigh Pightling
Design Associate   Emma Williams
Producer   Milan Govedarica
Marketing and Press Lizzie Forbes-Ritte, Purple Marketing lizzie@purple-marketing.co.uk
Outreach   Harriet Morgan-Shami
Evaluation   Alice Mukaka, University of East London

Characters

Ishmael, *Zimbabwean asylum seeker, twenty-two years old, living in Armley, Leeds*
Cath, *café owner, mid-fifties, with broad Yorkshire accent*
Brian, *café owner, mid-fifties, deeper-tone voice, also speaks with a broad Yorkshire accent*
Young Nigerian Man, *Nigerian asylum seeker, eighteen years old and cheerful*
Ricky, *white, fifteen years old, streetwise truant with a pit bull*
Bex, *white, nineteen years old, born and bred in Armley and single mum to four-year-old Bailey*
Cyrus, *Iranian refugee, early fifties, Christian, heavy-set and married with children*
Miss Marie Monroe, *drag queen and host at a night club in Leeds*
David *(voice-over), former Zimbabwean radio personality, late thirties, Ishmael's former lover*

Note
All characters are played by the same actor (except David, whose voice is pre-recorded). Changes in characters are marked by indented stage directions and text.

Scene One

The stage is empty and dimly lit. Enter **Ishmael** *carrying a suitcase. He wears jeans, T-shirt, trainers and a track top. He puts down the suitcase centre stage, looks around and then takes a light bulb from his pocket. He screws it into the holder above his head. The light snaps on. It startles him. A soundscape of an angry mob marching fades in.*

Ishmael *starts running, The sound crescendos. He runs faster and faster, until breathless. He stops. Soundscape fades into mbira music.* **Ishmael** *speaks with a Zimbabwean accent.*

Ishmael
Some of us were running.
Some of us were fleeing.
Some of us know wars that will never cease.
Some of us were persecuted.
Some of us were stripped and beaten.
Some of us have scars that will never heal.
Some of us are broken.
Some of us were thrown into prisons.
Some of us were sent back.
Some of us were dispersed.
Some of us were alone.
Some of us felt invisible.
Some of us felt time slow in our wait.

Music starts to fade. He takes off his jacket and folds it. He place sit on the floor.

Burnstall Heights, Flat 46, twelve floors up, third door on the left. Temporary accommodation, not home. This is Section 95, not leave to remain. This is where you will wait. This is all that you'll get.

There's a stranger in my house, or I think that I am the stranger in his house. He tells me not to touch his things and never speaks to me after that. This conveyor belt of a system moves us from place to place. You'll never know who you'll find here. You'll never know how long they have been here, in these concrete cocoons where we live in limbo. We'd be perfect metaphors for change if we didn't emerge so scarred. Something happens to us in our metamorphosis. We shed the past to acquire new inflictions. Oh, it is traumatic to be an immigrant.

Beat. The sound of a clock ticking fades in. It gets louder and overbearing. **Ishmael** *paces. The tick slows down.*

By the end of the first month the walls have started closing in. During the day I worry that the nightmares will come true. I fear sleeping in case the laws will change overnight and this country will vomit me out. They don't tell you how long the wait will last. The hands of the clock have gone limp from my avoidance. There is no use in keeping time. (*He picks up his jacket.*) I start taking walks.

Street noises snap in.

Malts pub. Full pint glasses at eleven a.m. Laughing. St Bartholomew's. Stained-glass windows. Pink tracksuits, red tracksuits, black tracksuits. Young girls on phones, babies on hips and pacifiers in mouths. Mike's Carpets boarded up. Fridges dumped in streets. Pit bulls on leashes. Grandmothers with brooches pinned to their coats. Music blaring out from car speakers. Fish and chip shops. Tattoo shops. Charity shops. Betting shops. Turkish shops. Russian shops. Tower blocks. Back-to-backs. British Heart Foundation. Cancer Research. St George's Crypt. Town Street. (*Beat.*) Barbra Taylor Bradford written in stone. Alan Bennett written in stone. Stanningley Road. Number 16. Prison walls. Greggs. Bodybuilder. Two for Ones. Mosque.

I want to learn everything. I want to remember it. I want it to remember me. I want it to climb inside me and build a home. I don't want to feel strange and distant in this place. I don't want the nightmares of the past.

Pause. **Ishmael** *pulls out his phone. He dials a number but it goes to voicemail. The answering machine is heard.*

Male Voice   Hi, this is David. Please leave a message.

Ishmael *appears frustrated. Street noises fade.*

Scene Two

Café sounds fade in. **Ishmael** *moves the suitcase upstage right and uses it as a chair.*

Ishmael   I've started checking Facebook. I give up bread and milk to save enough for two hours on the computer at Cath's Café. Cath is married to Brian. Brian always stays in the kitchen. I've never seen his face. All I've ever seen is a forearm with a tattoo of a white flag and red cross passing plates of full English breakfasts. As each plate comes through, Cath is forced to peel herself away from the weekly *Take a Break* that's spread open on the counter. I sit in the corner every Thursday. For the hours that I'm there, their marriage unfolds for us to hear.

> *He stands and changes to* **Cath**.
>
> (*Calls out.*) Bri, you're not gonna believe it. Listen to this, grandma falls in love with long-lost grandson. There are some right sickos are out there? I bet they're Americans.
>
> *Changes to* **Brian**.
>
> Yes, love. They can only be Americans.

Back to **Ishmael**.

They go back and forth arguing about who guessed it first.

> *As* **Cath**.

I mean, what you doing falling in love with your grandson? Jeremy Kyle's low but that'll even be too sick for him. There's gotta be a limit even for the bottom feeders.

Back to **Ishmael**. *He sits. The sound effects fades.*

He tells her not to be so judgemental. They start back up arguing again. Cath's Café has been open for twenty years.

Beat.

I scroll down David's page checking for updates. His last post was an interview that he did with Star FM. It was the last time I'd heard his voice before all the trouble began. Above it were posts telling him to never come back. Good riddance to them all. A disgusting import from the colonial days. Un-African. Ungodly. (*Beat.*) I write him messages. I write him many messages asking him to tell me if he's alright. (*Pleading.*) If you don't want to do it here just call me. Are you in England? Please.

Pause.

He hasn't replied. He hasn't read any of the messages.

Frustrated, he stands.

The fear didn't give me time to plan. I ran out of Harare. I ran out of Zimbabwe. I ran out of South Africa. I arrived at Heathrow with the little that I had, but they said it wasn't enough. They ask me to prove that I am gay. (*Beat.*) They ask me, what does a penis feel like? Why do I like it? (*Visibly upset.*) I need to tell them we weren't dirty. I need to tell them we were so much more. I need David.

Pause. He sits and composes himself.

I look at my page last. I haven't called anyone. Still after two months, I don't know what to say to them. My friends Muzi and Deejay post every day.

Where are you, bro?

Hey, why didn't you tell us?

They are, were, my boys, since we were this high. (*He gestures.*) We never thought we'd exist past the good times. We were the blood brothers.

He stands and mimics swordfighting.

The three musketeers riding together for life! The boys all the ladies loved! (*He laughs. Beat.*) I wanted to tell them.

When I was fifteen, I knew for sure. But, I was worried about them treating me differently. At seventeen, I was worried they wouldn't see a man. At twenty-one, I was worried what drunk mouths would say. I spent years practising what I'd even say to my father.

He plays out the conversation.

Listen, can we talk? I think I'm . . .

Maybe he'd understand. Or maybe I'd die right there on the spot. No, not his only son. Not the one who's supposed to carry his name. Not in this family! Not in this house!

I thought about telling my mother. But maybe she'd die right there on the spot, and then be resurrected to drag me to church to receive a healing.

He rushes to the suitcase and opens it. He pulls out traditional African dancing shells. He shakes them back and forth and cries out.

Yeessss, Lord!

Cleanse him!

Heal him!

Saaaaaave him!

Pause.

They needed a good son. I tried to be a good son for as long as I could.

Beat. He returns the shells to the suitcase. Inside he finds a flyer. He takes it out.

In the library I find a flyer for a place called Sanctuary Point. On Mondays, in a church between 5 p.m. and 8 p.m. there is a gathering of others like me. The words 'hot meal' call out to me. It's not been easy rationing £36.62 a week for food, clothes, toiletries, transport and chasing an overstretched London solicitor who has all of my files. He stopped representing me when they moved out of a convenient radius. I've been living in my head for so long I wondered if I'd remember how to speak to another person.

The sound of voices and children playing fade in.

A church is an empty place without its people. Its Monday's congregation fills it with the sound of children playing, keyboards tapping, the smacking of snooker balls, foreign tongues, broken English and the hope to piece it all together.

The woman at the desk signs my name in and points towards a queue forming by the little kitchen at the back of the room. I make my way, but before I arrive I'm stopped by a voice calling out:

Changes to **Young Nigerian Man** *and calls out.*

My brother! Welcome!

Back to **Ishmael**.

A young man walks towards me with such elation as if we are long-lost childhood friends reunited again.

As **Young Nigerian Man**.

Come, come.

Back to **Ishmael**.

I hear Nigeria in his voice. He takes my hand into his and for a moment, I'm reminded of the warm touch of another. Our handshake is fast and acrobatic. It is as if we are performing a traditional dance of salutation. We sit together and eat our meal of rice and curried chicken. He tells me:

As **Young Nigerian Man**.

There are four more Nigerians, one Ghanaian and six Libyans. But you are the only Zimbabwean. Don't worry you will meet them all.

Back to **Ishmael**.

But I do worry. I worry about the moment when one of them turns to ask me the reason for my claim. I know that, even in our collective misfortune, my brothers and my sisters could still shun me. A citizen of the unwanted being excluded by the excluded. Would I lie to them?

The sound effects fade. The lights dim.

I stay at Sanctuary Point until the drop-in session ends. I walk back to the flat thinking of what I'll do until the next Monday. I wonder if the young Nigerian man will be there again next week.

The night's darkness was over me when I got back. I pressed the button for the lift. It was slow coming down.

Sounds of a dog barking snaps in. **Ishmael** *cowers.*

I didn't see him coming. I heard the dog barking and the snap of the leash. I cowered into the corner. Urine and fear filled the small corridor. The boy laughed and released the growling dog again.

Changes to **Ricky**.

This here is Blade. Short for Razor Blade cos of his teeth, innit. He's a good pit bull. I'm Ricky. (*Beat.*) We saw you up near our street, walking all lah-di-dah from church. It's all good for yous lot, innit. Free food, free clothes and free laptops. Hey, maybe you can borrow us one of those laptops one day. You know, give back to the community and all that.

Back to **Ishmael**.

Ricky couldn't have been more than fifteen years old.

As **Ricky**.

Blade ain't eaten today. I ain't got money to feed him. Are you going to feed my dog?

Back to **Ishmael**.

The dog was already digging its nose into my spilt food parcels.

As **Ricky**.

Are you going to feed me? What else you got?

Ishmael *quickly empties his pockets and holds his hands up.*

   As **Ricky**.

   Cheers, mate. We'll be seeing you same time next week.

Back to **Ishmael**, *who collapses tearfully on to the floor.*

I don't go back to the drop-in centre. I don't go out at night. I don't go out for eight days. I don't want to know the streets anymore.

Fade in mbira music.

Some of us found others, like us.
Some of us found them seething.
Some of us were called leeches.
Some of us were dirt beneath their shoes.
Some of us broke our African names.
Some of us erased our histories.
Some of us conjured up secret identities.
Some of us couldn't recognize ourselves anymore.

Music fades out.

Scene Three

Inside **Ishmael***'s flat. The lights brighten.*

Ishamel   The sun comes out for the first time in a long while. I decide that today I will bravely leave the flat.

Outdoor playground sounds fade in. **Ishmael** *moves the suitcase centre stage.*

I walk to a little park and sit on a bench. I watch the leaves as they fall. A little boy comes running up to me making the sound of a racing car. He rolls the wheels of his toy along my arm and takes off running again before his mother can catch up.

   Changes to **Bex**. *She calls out to her son.*

   Bailey, get the fuck back here! (*Beat.*) Hiya. You know he takes them toy cars everywhere, drives me crazy (*Pulls out a cigarette. Beat.*) I ain't seen you here before.

Back to **Ishmael**.

I tell her it's my new favourite place. Its beauty has long been lost to her because she says:

   As **Bex**.

   (*Surprised.*) Dogshit park is your favourite place?

Back to **Ishmael**.

It's the space. It doesn't feel like we're all squashed together.

> *As* **Bex**.
>
> It's always looked the same to me. What's your name?

Back to **Ishmael**.

The lie rolls off my tongue before I can even catch it.

> *As* **Bex**.
>
> It's nice to meet you, Sam. I'm Bex and that's Bailey.

Back to **Ishmael**.

Bailey runs up to her and buries his face into her thigh. He pulls at her Nike jacket, beckoning her to bend. He speaks softly. His words are secrets only for his mother's ears. Her bleached blonde hair falls forward revealing a letter B tattooed on the back of her neck. Bex pulls out a lollipop from her pocket, Bailey snatches it and runs back to the swings.

> *As* **Bex**.
>
> People think I'm lying when I say he never shuts up at home. You got kids, Sam?

Back to **Ishmael**. *Outdoor playground sounds fade out.*

In two weeks we see each other three more times in the park. Sam is funny. Sam is studying business at college. Sam wants to be rich man one day and never have to worry about struggling. Sam likes Tinie Tempah. Sam doesn't have a girlfriend, it's a bit complicated. Sam has an older brother. They used to wrestle a lot when they boys, play-fighting nothing serious.

> *As* **Bex**.
>
> My mum never wanted more kids. She said I was handful enough. I think about giving Bailey a little brother one day. I like the thought of my two boys looking out for each other, you know.

Back to **Ishmael**.

(*Joyful.*) I have become someone with her. When Bailey falls asleep holding a sausage roll in his hand, I realize that I have become someone that she can trust.

> *As* **Bex**.
>
> You don't mind do yah, carry him home for me?

Back to **Ishmael**.

As we walk I ask her about his father.

> *As* **Bex**.
>
> (*Annoyed.*) Dickhead ain't worth talking about. He left before Bailey were born.

Back to **Ishmael**.

I put Bailey down on his bed, he curls up and sticks his thumb in his mouth.

As **Bex**.

(*Lustful.*) Listen yeah, you can stay for a bit if you want. Relax, Sam, you don't have to be so nervous. I'm not asking you to marry me. *Strictly*'s on tonight.

Back to **Ishmael**.

She clears away the clothes on the sofa. In the mess there's a new fire engine still in its packet. She holds the toy in her hand like it's something rare and precious.

As **Bex**, *with an innocence and love about her.*

I was hiding this. (*She sits.*) It's Bailey's birthday in a couple of weeks. It's not like he bloody needs another one, but I like how happy he is when he's playing with them. Here, sit down. (*Slides to one end of the suitcase. Beat.*) I'm thinking of giving him like a right big party and inviting all his friends. I'm going to get balloons with a big '4' on 'em and put them round the house, hang them out the window, so that everyone knows that something special is happening. I'm going to make a right fuss over him. I do it every year. God knows why I ain't in debt over that boy.

Back to **Ishmael**.

I tell her that I think it's lovely that she loves him so much. She pulls the toy closer to her chest and sighs, deep and heavy.

Beat.

As **Bex**.

(*Solemnly.*) Bailey's dad didn't even want him. He wanted me to get rid of him. But I couldn't, you know. It just seemed cruel to get rid of something that was, you know, like, living. I remember the day so clearly.

I woke up real early, I put on my school uniform and told my mum that we had a school trip. When I got to the hospital, they put me in a room with another girl. She was moaning and wriggling all over the bed. Her sister kept telling her that she was going to be alright.

I was only fifteen then, so the nurse asked me if someone over eighteen was going to come and pick me up. They couldn't let me go, afterwards, without an adult. I was like yeah, yeah sure, my boyfriend's coming. When she left the room, I called him a bunch of times but it kept going into voicemail. I couldn't believe that he weren't there. He'd been the one saying that we couldn't keep it. I waited and waited and when the nurse came back, she was, like, listen love, I've got to start. I've got other patients to see.

(*Beat. Angered.*) It hit me then. He really didn't care about me.

She jumps up.

I jumped out of bed and I was like no! No way am I doing this. The nurse thought I'd proper lost it. I thought there's no point. If he doesn't want to be with me to raise it and he doesn't want to be with me to kill it, then why am I even with him?

I'm not better off anyways. But if I keep it, at least then I'll have something that cares about me.

So I put my clothes on, went down to his mam's in Chapletown and started banging on the door.

(*Shouts.*) Leon!

Leon, get the fuck out here!

Leon, you think you can just leave me on me own!

His mum flung the door open. I thought she was going to kill me. She was all, like, my Leon this and my Leon that. He's a good boy, what will he be doing with a little white girl like you? (*Beat. She sucks her teeth.*) She didn't even know me. She had no fucking right to talk to me like I was shit. Well, your son is having a baby with this little white girl. Her jaw fell to the floor when I said that. Oh, Nana, he ain't told you that? Tell him I didn't do it and I'm finished with him. I wasn't even gone two minutes before Leon called screaming down phone. He was a right proper coward when it came to his mam. She'd always threaten him, like, you mess up I'll send you to Jamaica one way, mate. I told him straight, grow up, Leon, you're going to be a dad and hung up the phone.

Pause. She sits.

Yeah, I knew we'd never get on from that point.

Once, his mum tried to have Bailey taken off me. She told the NSPCC that I wasn't a good mum cos Bailey had a bruise on his leg. He was two years old and was always running about. They investigated and in the end they believed me, he'd just fallen down. That's when I stopped her seeing him. I told Leon he could come over whenever he wanted, but he never did.

I thought it was alright because Bailey already had a nan. But then, my mum got a new boyfriend. He never really wanted us around. He'd never had kids so he couldn't cope with Bailey crying all the time. I came back from doctor's one day and found all of mine and Bailey's stuff packed up. He stood at the door saying we couldn't stop at my mum's house anymore. She didn't say owt. They'd only been together two month. I thought forget it, do what you want, Charlie will put us up. And she did, she's always been a good mate. Three month we were there and then we got this flat. Our own little place. Mine and Bailey's place. Just the two of us.

Back to **Ishmael**.

She finally looks up and pulls herself back into the room with me.

As **Bex**.

I talk a lot don't I?

Back to **Ishmael**.

I don't mind, I tell her.

As **Bex**.

Well, I think we're gonna be right good mates, you and I.

Back to **Ishmael**.

She puts the remote in my hand and heads to the kitchen.

As **Bex**.

You want some tea? I've only got fish fingers and wedges cos that's all Bailey will let me buy. Is that alright? I was gonna tell you something actually. A mate of mine, Garry, sells fridges. He's done his back in and is looking for someone to help him with deliveries. I can't imagine it's much but it's something. He's hardly breaking bank so it'll be the odd job here and there. D'ya want me to ask him? (*Beat.*) Sam, did yah hear me? (*Beat.*) Sam?

Back to a panicked **Ishmael**.

I didn't know what to say. How would I explain Sam being trapped by Ishmael? Sitting in her flat with her truths laid out in front of me made my lies a heavy stone in my heart. Selfishly, I wanted to sit with someone and be just normal. Bex saw me. (*Fade in mbira music.*) I tasted something that I was not allowed to have. I quietly slipped out of her flat.

Some of us wear our secrets,
Like a cloak around our shoulders.
Some of us don't know how to act,
When they label us aliens.
Some of us don't know how to be,
When limbo comes with every morning.

Music fades out.

Scene Four

Inside **Ishmael***'s flat. He moves the suitcase upstage left. He removes his jacket and places it behind the suitcase. As the music fades he's startled by the presence of his flatmate.*

Ishmael I don't see shadows around when he walks. There are goodbyes with no words and at times I forget that he's even in the flat. Our life together is a constant attempt not to meet, not to touch and not to connect. But his body tells a story. (*Crosses the stage.*) Hard steps on floors, humming in the bathroom and deep breaths at night. I want to know who this tale belongs to. All day I listen out for him. When the shuffling and thuds stop, and the front door slams shut. (*Creeps towards the suitcase.*) I sneak out of my room, tiptoe towards his door. I knock, and wait. Then push the door open, just enough for me to peek in, scan for a letter and finally learn his name.

Ishmael *opens the suitcase and pulls out a picture frame with a picture of a man, wife and two children.*

Cyrus comes into the kitchen. There are no boundaries today. He looks me straight in the eyes and says:

Changes to **Cyrus**.

What do I tell them? What do I say to my wife? No more appeals. Denied, last time. They send me back. I don't want to go. Two years they have me wait and just like that they say it's over. My family is waiting for me to bring them here. We all suffer in Tehran. There, there is no life. They don't want us here but we cannot go back.

Back to **Ishmael**.

I don't have any answers for him. I don't have any answers for myself.

As **Cyrus**.

You wait and see, they do to you what they do to me. You apply, they reject, you appeal, they reject, you beg, they tell you there's nothing more they can do. Well, they won't get rid of me. My friend tells me if they take you to the airport you cry, you scream and you fall on the floor. Pilot won't fly with crazy man. They not allowed. I do everything by the rules and hope for fairness but it not work. So I make trouble. I don't care.

Back to **Ishmael**.

I see his anger building. He clenches his fist and punches a hole into the kitchen door.

As **Cyrus**.

This is England, but in here it is slum. She fix nothing because she think we nothing. We don't deserve anything, not even her kindness!

Back to **Ishmael**.

I don't even have to ask, I know he means Angie, the landlord. The one who makes us feel like we've fallen into a crack and no one is looking for us. When I first met her I held out my hand and said, hi, I'm Ishmael. She grunted. She doesn't need to say it, but I know it. She owned everything in this flat, including my dignity.

As **Cyrus**.

Kitchen sink have mould when I move in. Carpets stained, I get down on my knees and scrub. My bed break six months ago. She give me stick, wood from fence outside and say here, fix it. Go, go see bedroom. The wall is wet. It's been wet since I come here two years ago. I tell her and tell her my daughter Susan have asthma, it is bad for her. She says, I see no children here. I tell her, they're coming! She laugh at me. She laugh at my children. She laugh at my appeals. She laugh at my rejection. She laugh at my deportation. I hold my tongue and she laugh. I say please and thank you and she laugh. I read my Bible and she laugh. She comes in with own key and check your room when she want. I suspect she take what she want, but who will believe foreigner over British. She come in bathroom, to check shower with me inside. Home Office give people like her money to rent property.

One year ago, I get my first rejection and they give me Azure card. She free to do what she want with money but I can only use card at authorized places. I cannot use bus with no money. When they give me I ask, how do I get back to Border Agency office to report? The first time I go, I walk two hours to Kirkstall. I get there late and the officer give me a warning. I tell him I had to walk far but he doesn't care. I swear they teach them not to be human.

Two years they treat me like this. Two years I walk. Two years I shop where they tell me to shop. Two years I buy what they want to me to buy. Two years lady at the till laugh at me when card don't work. She talk in microphone to everyone in Tesco and call manager. I don't know what this card is, she say. (*Shouts.*) Yes, you know! (*Beat. Visibly upset.*) I come here every week. (*Beat.*) Everyone in line look at me like I ruin this country. She make me feel small.

Pause.

Look at them out there, living their lives. They don't know, the dogs at the gates are not how they protect this country. They do it in this flat, my friend. They do it in here. (*Points to his chest.*) They break spirit and make you want to give up before they tell you to go.

Pause. Back to **Ishmael**.

The days following the flat is quiet. We are both alone with our thoughts, knowing the inevitable is soon. One morning, Angie opens the door, followed by three men. They barge into his door and start packing his belongings. He tells them that this isn't right. They don't stop. I don't go out to look.

He cowers by the suitcase and hugs the photo.

I pull the blankets over my head.

As **Cyrus**.

Let me dress. Just let me dress.

Back to **Ishmael**.

And just like that, he was gone.

Silence. Fade in mbira music.

Some of us didn't cheat.
Some of us held on to our integrity.
Some of us held on to our honesty.
Some of us had dreams turn into boulders.
Some of us were begging for a taste of your liberty.

Ishmael's *phone rings. The music ends abruptly.* **Ishmael** *tosses the picture into the suitcase. He searches for the phone in his jacket pocket. He answers.*

Male Voice It's me, David. Don't talk, Ish, just listen. Stop sending me messages, OK? I know what you want from me but I can't help you. Remember it was my house that was burned down. I barely made it out. I got my asylum, Ish. I want to start again. Please just let me go. Don't ruin this for me. I hope everything works out for you, but I don't want to deal with all that stuff again. I refuse to see another application form. I refuse to answer any more of those questions. I had to explain what I do with men and why I like it. Never again! I've been degraded enough. Plenty people pay others to support their claims. Just do the same and take it to the Home Office.

Ishmael I'm not going to lie. I was your secret and you left me to face it on my own. I can't be sent back now, not after running. My family, my friends, the police will all be waiting. What will I tell them? Just tell the Home Office that you know me. Be my evidence. Help me.

David *hangs up.*

Ishmael . . . Hello? . . . David?

Beat. Mbira music fades in. **Ishmael** *is angry and upset.*

Some of us were joining lovers.
Some of us left lovers.
Some of us, were discarded by lovers.
Some of us felt love wither inside.
Some of us felt raging storms crashing against our chests.

The mbira music fades out.

Scene Five

As the mbira music fades out, dance music slowly fade in. **Ishmael** *puts his phone back into his jacket pocket and sets it aside. He turns away from the audience and opens the suitcase. The music builds.*

He pulls out a pair of pink-glitter stilettos and turns to the audience. He looks down at his trainers and back at the heels. He looks hesitant. He sits.

Ishmael The city is different at night. There are creatures that wake and take over in the darkness. I want to know what it's like to become.

He starts taking off his trainers.

Inner beings escaping from their cages. Free to be. I want to escape my body.

He slips on the heels.

I know that it's there. I haven't been brave enough to go. I've thought about what I'd see there. I've thought about who'd see me there. I've thought about the people back home. I've thought about what they'd think if they saw me right now. My elation soaring on the back of their pain. I've thought about being their shame. I've thought about being their black sheep. I've thought about whether they'd know me now. Back home is not like over here. Here there are neon lights. Here there are queens. Here there are rainbow flags drawn high.

The dance music blares out. Disco lights flash.

Body, beat, mission, Monday, bubbles, paint, night, glitter, rave, collar, cuffs, cabaret, music, body, flesh, uppers, downers, him, she, me.

The music fades a little. Beat.

It's nothing like I have even know. It is more than I have ever seen. He, she takes me by the hand. She tells me to dance, to let go. I'm awkward. Is this what it feels like to not be afraid? Is this what freedom feels like? Is this how it feels to be yourself? (*Beat.*) She leans in and speaks in a language that is only made for us:

> *Changes to a sensual* **Miss Marie Monroe**.
>
> Don't be strange, darling. Just let, it, all go. In here, it's all fun. I'm Miss Marie Monroe. Zhoosh your riah, slap on some lippy, powder your eeks, grab a bevvy and dance! Come on, turn my oyster up!

Back as **Ishamel**.

I'd been holding it in for too long. It needs to come out, to break out. I give in. Let it be, let me be me.

He laughs and dances with joy.

Some of us wanted to stop being afraid.
Some of us wanted to find ourselves.
Some of us wanted to belong.

The dance music gradually fades. **Ishamel** *stops dancing and takes the heels off. He opens the suitcase and put them back.*

Scene Six

Inside the suitcase **Ishmael** *finds a letter from the Home Office. It takes him by surprise. His mood becomes more sombre. He opens it nervously and reads. There's a look of disappointment on his face. He quickly puts on his trainers and jacket. He puts the letter in his pocket and pulls out a toy car from the suitcase. He straightens himself. Outdoor playground sounds fade in. He moves the suitcase back to centre stage.*

In four months Bailey looks like he's grown enough for a year. I'd missed Bex. I wanted to tell her so much. I wanted to tell her what had happened since the last time. I wanted to tell her why the last time had happened.

Ishmael *rolls the car towards the audience.*

> *When it stops he snaps into* **Bex**.

What you want? You know what, I don't even want to know. I mean honestly, what sort of person just walks out like that. It was weird. You could have at least said that you were going. You made me feel like as if I'd made you up. I thought I was going crazy. I started to think after you were gone that I really didn't know anything about you. I mean I knew stuff, but nothing that really mattered. You could have been a murderer for all I knew. I thought you were going to come back and kill me in my sleep. You don't just do that to people. Bailey actually liked yah. You don't show your face around here for months and you think it's alright to just turn up with your little presents. (*Shouts.*) Bailey! Bailey. bring it back. Bring that bloody toy back here! Put it in the bin over there! I said put it in the bin! He's going to put it in the bin when we get back home. You might as well go. I wasn't trying to shag you if that's what you think. And I'm definitely not going to shag you now. I was just trying to be your friend.

Back to **Ishamel**.

I ask her to sit down. I hand her the letter.

He places it on the suitcase.

She doesn't understand.

He paces as he tries to explain himself.

My name is Ishmael and I have to leave. I tell her to wait, to let me finish. (*Beat.*) I shouldn't have lied, but I didn't want to be who I was. Ishmael can only dream of the life that Sam has.

He sits beside the letter.

You were my friend, but I didn't know how to be your friend. You reminded of what it's like to feel good. You reminded me what it's like to be a person and it's silly because you didn't do anything. You just sat next to me and said hi. Not many people said hi. Not many people made me feel good. They sort of look past you, look through you, and the ones that see you only see what label you have.

This letter says I'm a reference number. I'm an applicant. I'm circumstances. I'm categories. I'm outcomes. But it doesn't say that I'm real. It doesn't say that I exist. That I laugh. I cry. I dance. I dream. I wonder. I want. I think. I question. It doesn't say that I'm a person, Bex. I went to this club and whilst I was there I felt alive. I chose to be there, proudly. Everything has been out of my hands. Everything still is out of my hands, but for that moment I tasted it. I tasted choice and it was good.

Pause.

But I can't have that again. They refuse, Bex. It's not as easy as you think it is. You've got to prove yourself and if that fails, you've got to start again and that's your last appeal. I'm going for my last chance. I don't know what will happen. (*Beat.*) I know you don't think it's much but I'd rather have this park, this place as it is now, as my own. At least then I can hold it. Waiting to be allowed to live is like flickering in and out existence. Sometimes you're not even sure if you are real. You made me feel real. That is all I wanted to say. I'm sorry that I lied.

She doesn't say anything. I can't tell from her face if my apologies are enough. She just stares at me. (*He stands.*) Then, she takes the letter, folds it, puts it into my pocket and holds out her hand.

As **Bex**.

Hiya, Ishmael. Nice nice to meet yah, I mean properly yah.

Back to **Ishmael**. *He smiles. Mbira music fades in.*

Some of us leave pieces of ourselves,
In all the places that we've been.
Some of us are still counting
How many battles we have to face.
Some of us, are just at the beginning;
Hoping to call somewhere,
Home again.

Ishmael *picks up the suitcase and leaves. Music and lights fade.*

End.

BURGERZ

Travis Alabanza

19–20 October
Ovalhouse (previews)
23 October–3 November
Hackney Showroom
13–17 November
Royal Exchange Theatre, Manchester
18 November
Homotopia, Hope Street Theatre, Liverpool

Writer and Performer   Travis Alabanza

Creative team

Director   Sam Curtis Lindsay
Designer   Soutra Gilmour
Associate Designer   Isabella Van Braeckel
Lighting Designers   Lee Curran and Lauren Woodhead
Sound Designer   XANA
Movement   Nando Messias
Dramaturg   Nina Lyndon
Production Manager   Shaz McGee
Assistant Production Manager   Cat Ryall
Stage Manager   Beth Lewis
Assistant Stage Manager   Vita Ingram-Anichkin

Cover and publicity images
Photographer   Elise Rose
Make-up   Umber Ghauri
Styling   Mia Maxwell
Creative Direction   Vasilisa Forbes

Preface

At the point of publication I'll be twenty-three. I have no university degree. And I didn't really know what an artist was until I moved to London when I was eighteen. What I mean to say is: I don't really know how any of this works. What I do know is that *BURGERZ* needed to be written, it needed to be performed and it needed to be heard.

This play could be described as something that is looking at one incident, but instead I believe it is more accurate to say that *BURGERZ* has become an emblem for so many other incidents, deaths, acts of violence and harm that the trans and gender non-conforming community have to face every single day. *BURGERZ*, for me, is about archiving the pain in our reality. It is about complicating the narrative. It is about writing down that these things exist, and that we cannot keep pretending they do not.

So many other trans people could have written this truth. So many other members of our community mentioned how they have had food thrown at them, dodged insults, faced beatings, been harmed – and so many of those mentioned the deathly silence surrounding their attacks. In this current moment, in 2018 in Britain, the public are being consulted on the Gender Recognition Act. Trans people are having to withstand countless attacks from media, public and private sectors. The news is filled everyday with debates about whether or not trans people are a danger to society – but no one is talking about the dangers we face from the rest of society.

I conducted a series of dinners called 'Tranz Talkz' across the country. I sat around a table with strangers, bonded only by our transness, eating burgers and chips and asking them questions about their life. Every single person said they were anxious outside. Most said they edit themselves before they leave the door. Almost all said they were harassed. My Facebook feed has at least one status a day from a trans and/or gender non-conforming friend detailing their attack. I check in with my trans friends and hear weekly about the struggles they faced from their transphobic doctor, or boss, or family. This has the power to fill me with sadness and remorse, but more often I think about how this reminds me of our resilience as a community. A resilience we should not have to harbour, yet we still manage to do so.

BURGERZ is about the violence. It is about the hurt. It is about telling you that this pain and that hurt exist and that society is complicit in this.

But also, with that, I hope it is a text that reminds you of our resilience.

With love, and a call to action,

Travis

Dedicated to all the trans people, all the gender non-conforming people, all the outsiders and the others that have had their life stopped, halted, ended, constrained due to violence.

You/We/I deserve more.

A warehouse with a giant box centre stage. The doors of the box open to reveal **Travis** *wearing overalls and boots.*

A burger was thrown at me in broad daylight in April 2016 on Waterloo Bridge whilst someone yelled the word tranny. I think over one hundred people saw and I know no one did anything.

A pause.

If I become obsessed with how the burger works, how it flies, how it smells and how it lands then maybe I will have some agency over it. Maybe I will feel like I was once in control.

Imagine that burger now. Imagine it in front of you. The most typical burger you see. The emoji. The archetype. The original. The real burger.

A pause.

The burger bun. A piece of dough.

A piece of dough is just a piece of dough until you figure out it is supposed to be part of a burger, to make the bun. Then, there are many things you must do to it to make it right. Make it work. Turning flour and yeast to whole things, heating things, changing things. Altered to circles through knives and cuts. Kneaded and poked, stretched out and pinched, moulding and ploughing the dough, prodding it into shape to eventually be the bun that will eventually hold the burger.

The burger bun must be round. Top heavy, bottom light, one bigger than the other. Always one bigger than the other, big holding small in place. Top to bottom. We are not aiming for equal.

Imagine that burger now. Imagine it in front of you. The most typical burger you see. The emoji.

The archetype. The original. Real burger.

The burger bun.

Once made, cut into half, burger in mind, always burger in mind, bread cut, cursed for not being quite right. A patty placed in. We imagined beef, do not pretend you did not. Or moreover that it would be weird if I placed chicken in there now. Sure, we accept a veggie pattie, or even aubergine in high-end food places in East London served in old car parks – but do not lie that you imagined that first. You saw the patty. Real burger equals real patty equals real beef equals real . . . burger. Placed inside.

Pause.

This is where people believe the burger has some freedom. We've got the bun, the beef, the patty – and now, we finally feel we have a choice. That the burger becomes your liberal playground, toppings are where you can make you . . . You! The burger that liberals want. Now it's your turn to jazz it up, place whatever on top, go wild, it's your burger, it's your life! But let's not pretend we didn't all have ideas for how this burger should look. Expectations. Lettuce, green. Tomatoes, sliced, I guess red. Cheese, thin. Mayo over the top. Onions, maybe. Some other garnish. Sure, some freedom – but we did know what to expect. We had this burger planned, and imagined. All I see now is the dough that is the burger bun, attached at the waist to the patty, to the salad, to the expectations. And if I change too much about how this burger was imagined, it will be ridiculed. Sent back to the kitchen.

Pause.

'HOT DOG OR BURGER?'

'HOT DOG OR BURGER, LOVE?'

'HOT DOG . . . OR BURGER, LOVE?'

I can't remember what I chose or I do not want to mention it, partly because I'm not sure it was a choice.

'You often have to choose between burgers and hot dogs in life, Travis – it would be odd to have both.'

'But mum, last time I saw a burger stall was at that tacky Christmas fair with you, they sold hot dogs there, and you didn't find it odd.'
'Yeah, you're right. But they were in separate containers. Clearly labelled.'

Pieces of the same dough could be made into a bun for a burger or a bun for a hot dog, but once it's made into another it's very hard to change back. People would still know it was always a hot dog bun first.

People might only see buns as something to hold burgers, that is until they hear about hot dogs, and then there is this whole other world where you had hot dogs as your priority, your archetype, your emoji – and figuring out about hot dogs meant that you looked at burgers completely differently. My mum never really cooked or made hot dogs in the house, so all we ever knew was how to choose burgers, but if I grew up with my dad then I'd pick hot dogs every time, without question. Then twenty years or so down the line I'd be making some show called *HOT DOGZ* with a Z.

Pause.

It's ridiculous that we place two things next to each other and expect ourselves to be able to make a choice, or to lie and tell ourselves it is a choice when there are two things placed next to each other. As if something containing only two could ever be a choice. That is not a choice. That is rather jumping to which death you think may be less painful.

HOT DOG OR BURGER?

Die quietly or die loudly? Splitting things up into two arbitrary categories has never worked ever since the beginning of time.

Then you went there with your fucking utensils, your fucking cutlery, your fucking recipe books with no fucking seasoning and decided that we all had to choose between a fucking burger and a fucking hot dog, but it wasn't a choice, because you looked at me, and you said in one minute this person is a fucking person that eats burgers. As if I couldn't be that and more, as if I couldn't catch my breath, for a minute.

As if burgers isn't something that happens violently after it, as if burgers isn't violence in its definition. As if the burger isn't violent in its creation. As if violence doesn't happen to hot dog and burger choosers, as if it starts when you are choosing between hot dog and burger, as if choosing . . .

Travis *realizes they are losing composure. They pause. Regain poise.*

They get out a very large box and get inside, changing out of their overalls and into a dress and heels.

The first time I tried on a dress . . .

I was young, even younger than now, not embryonic, but you know, not this time. I was ten years old, at my gran–

Travis *looks out into the audience.*

What am I doing?

I don't remember the first time I tried on a dress. Oops, that's it, go on, remove my trans card. I don't remember.

A pause as they look out into the audience.

Well look:

Tried on a dress at nine, black sparkly; seven years later beat up for wearing one exactly like that.

Played a witch in a school panto, found a bit of my gender, football team made fun of it, got an A-star.

Can't tell you the first time I got called a faggot but can tell you every time I've ever been called beautiful by a stranger.

Didn't base my gender off of female celebrities, was more interested in emulating aliens.

A recipe book falls from the ceiling and slams onto the floor.

I need to make this burger.

Travis *pushes out a kitchen island hidden in a box.*

Maybe it is about knowing when you need help. Recognizing when you could continue to struggle on your own, but would breathe lighter with someone else. It feels weird because I do not know you, but I do not think that is a prerequisite for help.

I've never made a burger from scratch before. I'm not a very good cook; in fact, I rarely ever cook.

I need to do this, I just know it will be hard.

They look out to the audience.

So I'm wondering if there is anyone here that would help me? Cooking experience helps, but isn't required, a lot of us learn on the job.

You do not need to have brought your own ingredients, or utensils, or kitchen, I've done all that.

They reveal the kitchen.

You would have to come up here, for a while, be OK with sticking around. You'd have to be OK with talking in front of strangers . . . I'm still getting used to it.

I could get you a drink, we'd give you a cushion for your chair.

To themselves.

Wow, look at all these things I think I have to bring in to get someone to help.

To the audience.

Just bring yourself, all of it.

So, who will help me make a burger . . . anyone?

Travis *waits for some people to put their hands up.*

I never thought I'd say this, but I need a man. I think we have some shit we gotta work through. I need a white man.

I need . . . a cis white man . . . to help me. Make a burger.

They identify a volunteer.

This feels scary, you . . . I think I want your help. Can you take my hand? Commitment is scary, right? How do you feel?

Travis *brings them on stage and gives them the recipe book.* **Travis** *then brings out a stool and a cushion from a box at the back. They get out their own stool. They go into a drawer and get out an apron and hand it to them. They sit down together.*

Would you like a drink? I can get you white wine, red wine, rosé wine, G&T, vodka Coke (diet as well), water, sparkling or still, Heineken, Carlsberg or . . . an orange Capri Sun.

Travis *serves the requested drink.*

I need to do some of this on my own, but it's just nice to know that you could be here to help. I can't cook, so, it helps to know someone is there.

Could you tell me what the first page says?

Man *reads from the recipe book.*

Man
Wash your hands.

Travis *pauses. Looks round for a sink. Realizes/remembers there isn't one.*

Travis
Budget for a sink would've been . . .

Then goes into the drawer and gets out some hand sanitizer. Squirts twice on their hand. Gestures to the **Man**, *squirts it on theirs, and rubs it* *together. When they have finished they put the sanitizer away and gesture to turn the page. The page will have instructions for the* **Man** *to read.*

Man
Travis, before you can make the burger, it is important you decide the type of box the burger must go in.

Travis
Type of box? Hold on, I thought I'd start cooking now, what do you mean?

Man
Travis, before you can make the burger, it is important you decide the type of box the burger must go in.

Travis
I'm sorry. But . . . but how do I pick a box for something that isn't even made yet? That doesn't seem right.

Man
Travis, before you can make the burger, it is important you decide the type of box the burger must go in.

Travis
But . . . I mean, even with that logic. This seems unfair. I mean, say even if I pick the beef burger, which I know I will, it's the most typical one, then I do not know what shape it will come out. I do not know if I will change my mind whilst cutting it, spontaneously pick a different shape last minute, or . . . or what if in the pan it changes shape, or my knife slips. Do I then still have to try and squeeze it in the box I've already picked? Like, a reminder that I really can't cook so to predict a shape of anything at this point feels really beyond my skill set.

Man
Travis, before you can make the burger, it is important you decide the type of box the burger must go in.

Travis *pauses and looks at the many boxes. They find a box containing boxes and the text is spoken as they explore this.*

Travis
What came first? The burger or the box for the burger? Man or woman? Or the cages made for man or woman? The person free from man or woman? Or the person in charge of capturing the person free from man or woman? Gender or violence? That last one was the same thing. When I think about boxes I think about order, about containment and the need we have to tidy things. I think about how when things are tidy, it is always those that are messy that are punished. Colouring outside the lines was never rewarded, only shunned.

Do you feel boxed in?

All the times I had been encouraged not to wear this, all the times the flick in my wrist had been straightened, or the raise in my voice had been muffled. We are policing people before they even know the person they are. We are punished for when we fail.

Last week on a tube a mother called me an abomination to mankind, and I said isn't that an oxymoron? Isn't man already an abomination?

Two weights hang in equilibrium, they force us to stand with one toe upon them, and if you unbalance them there is this fear that the scales will smash and so will everyone else's compliance and you will be punished accordingly. This is all about order. It's about structure. It's about regulation and to be unregulated is to be dangerous. There are billions of people in this world and somehow we will decide two boxes to fit all these people in. As if fitting billions of people in two boxes could ever be comfortable. We will decide who you are before we know you, decide which box to place you in, and then not let you change even if we can tell it was the wrong box.

Sorry, what was the instruction again?

Man
Travis, before you can make the burger, it is important you decide the type of box the burger must go in.

Travis *opens the box to reveal two identical burger boxes. They continue to search other boxes for boxes.* **Travis** *speaks this next text through the boxes until they are hidden.*

Travis
It seems silly to hide in the very things that try to contain you. Two thousand years ago there were Gods that looked like me. And maybe you. Worshipped in their plurality. Existing. Not cast aside. Castrated. Cast away. But seen in their plurality as a strength, not a hindrance. Hijra – South Asian. Bakla – Philippines. Kathoey – Thailand. Two Spirit – Native American. Quariwarmi – Inca. Femminiello – Italian. Up until the nineteenth century Italian 'lady boys' had their rituals seen as a gift, they were seen as elite. People believed they were connected to the ancient practices of Hermaphroditus. The Sister Boys and Brother Girls of the outback, indigenous tribes, once celebrated.

Travis *climbs into the back of a large box.*

And I wonder how we ended up here? I wonder how I ended up as the person struggling to decide which burger goes in which box, having to even make this burger for this box, having to think this whole time about burgers and boxes – and you became the people in charge? Who will decide if this was good enough? Done the correct way?

We hear the sound of an electric turkey carver start. **Travis** *cuts the cardboard box to get through.* **Travis** *pops through, now holding a box (similar to the one they put away but way more* **Travis***).*

I've got the box. Can you tell me the next step?

Man *reads page two of the instructions.*

Man
Mince.

Travis *struts across the stage, finds the big mincer, puts on latex gloves and gets out a chunk of meat. The meat is minced.* **Travis** *then places the mincer away.*

Travis
I'm ready for the next instruction.

The page is turned.

Man
Spice.

Travis *grabs the spice rack from the kitchen and places it on the table.*

Travis *goes to add spice to the mince, then stops.*

Travis
I REALLY should not be adding my own spice to this mince.

Looks at **Man***, to gesture they need help.*

Will you stand behind me?

It's quite important that we get this right. Not enough spice and things can really feel quite bland. This burger can't be bland. Will you shake some in and I'll tell you when to stop.

Man *shakes some spice in.*

Keep going. I know you are nervous, we are always nervous when adding spice into the mix. Stop. Stop. Not too much. We need enough to know it's there but not enough that we notice it fully. Keep going. Bit more. Go on. We need just enough that we can brag about this being a spicy burger afterwards, but don't name any of the spices on the ingredients list – it's better to leave it out. Keep going. A bit more. Is that too much for you? Does it feel too present? I would say pick up another spice but you know if there's two types of spices in one mix then shit really fucking hits the pan. Go on. Stop. Take a breather. I know all this work is hard on

you. It must be so exhausting. To constantly
have to respond to people's requests for more
fucking spices. I can tell you're tired. So in
a minute I'm going to say 'go on', and you
will add the last bit of spice. Then you will
take your seat. Later you will go home. And
write a long Facebook status about how good
you feel that you did this, and that when this
burger is made you will make sure everyone
knows it could not be made without your
invaluable, groundbreaking, spice-related
work. People will comment on that Facebook
status and tell you that you are such a good
person, and if you ever make a mistake in
the future, people will say, 'This person could
have never made that mistake because one
time they added spice to this fucking burger.'

Go on.

Man *adds the spice and goes back to their seat.*
Travis *begins to mix the mince with their
hands, intensely, eventually forming a patty.*

I can often feel a room become heavier as
soon as race is brought up. A sticky, dense
feeling where the room becomes . . . almost
hotter. The temperature kind of rises and I
feel we suddenly have less space. Steam always
rises to the top. Of course, I do not feel this
shift or the rise in heat . . . the steam; some of
you do not either, because for us, it never left.

I was caught stealing once when I was
fourteen. I should have just said I was trying
to integrate myself in British tradition!

The third time I met someone online to have
sex he left because he said, 'I thought you'd be
more masculine because you're Black.'

I think often about what happens when we
die. I wonder if hell is just a place where we
watch white people in a club try and find
rhythm, whilst they continuously dance to
'I'm Coming Out' by Diana Ross as they
awkwardly off-beat gyrate their hips in your
face whilst impersonating the Black sassy
women they met last week.

It's not just that before colonization gender non-conformity existed in different forms, it's that colonization and race continue to completely affect how gender continues to be formed. To think it is only trans people that are misgendered is the whitest way to think about bodies. Black bodies have known what it means to be de-gendered, hyper-gendered, misgendered since the beginning of your slavery. You know in these hate crime adverts they always advise the poor trans person to call the police, and I always want to ask back, 'Why would we bring more trouble to our door?' And then I remember we aren't all in the same house . . . are we?

Travis *has formed the patty and placed it down.*

To the **Man***:*

Are you still OK with staying with me? Can I get you another drink?

They serve a drink if requested.
Travis *goes to put the spice rack away and feels something else under the table: the burger buns. Feels them. Brings them above the table and begins to play with them until they place them on their chest.*

I never really wanted breasts. I don't think. I mean, I'm not sure. I probably had the same urge to have breasts as I occasionally get to shave my hair. Fleeting. It's not always present, and it comes and goes. But there comes a moment when I start to wonder, if I made more effort, stuffed more things into me, turned some things over me, chopped some parts up, would you start to believe me when I say that I am hurting?

If I got these breasts, and changed my face, and blended into the walls, would we start to hear me when I scream? Would I even need to scream? I wonder how many bodies have forced parts onto themselves in order to be seen as fixed, legitimate, so they no longer need to stop traffic.

Why when I say I'm trans does someone ask, 'What will you have done?' 'What is next?'

As if trans can never be a destination. As if trans is synonym for broken body.

As if I cannot say I'm trans and someone say, 'You do not need to change. I will protect you the way you are.'

Travis *to the* **Man**:

Can you get me the tape? It's in the top drawer.

They gesture to the **Man** *to bind the burger buns on top of* **Travis** *as they say the text.*

I imagine myself with breasts a lot more now.

Feeling them over my chest.

Stuffing my top to see how the weight would feel.

I cannot tell if this is something I really want, rather something I need. I do not know if that matters.

Travis *takes off their buns in an instant. Back to the task at hand. They place a new bun on the surface. Cut it. Get out the lettuce. Onion and tomato.* **Travis** *takes the lettuce and the tomato, and slides the onion over to the* **Man**. *Carefully gives them a knife.* **Travis** *begins to chop. And the* **Man** *starts cutting the onion too. The next three questions are asked in gaps whilst the* **Man** *is cutting the onions with* **Travis**. **Travis** *allows space for natural conversation to form.*

When was the last time you cried?

What does it feel like to be a man?

Are you scared of being outside?

Travis *will signify when they finish by stopping cutting and saying:*

Thank you.

When they have finished, they place the three chopped items in three clear bowls.

What's the next instruction?

Man
Cook.

Travis
Oh yes . . .

Travis *starts as if to cook, but then brings back out the hand sanitizer.*

'For old times' sake!'

They wash their hands one more time.

Travis *gets out the pan and places it on the hob.*

Travis *starts the timer that is preset to three minutes.* **Travis** *starts by placing the burger in the pan.*

Travis *tries to focus on the cooking. As the cooking amplifies, you can hear the noises of the past and present.* **Travis** *tries to remain focused on cooking.*

No one will sit next to me. My eyes go from floor, to their eyes, to door. Their eyes never leaving me. It was the Victoria line, Oxford Circus southbound to Brixton and someone had finally occupied the seat next to me.

Things felt closer. I had my headphones in, but I had no music on; a melody is a privilege for those that do not need to be aware.

'What the fuck are you?'

I wanted to reply: 'A person, another human, someone who deserves respect.' Or I wanted to hear the six other people that heard say something too.

We all stayed in silence. His hand was on my inner thigh for the rest of the journey.

Heat intensifies.

Dalston Overground station, it was after a gig, a man followed behind me breathing down my neck.

Heat intensifies.

Busy shopping mall. Group of girls laugh at me. Someone tries to trip me down the stairs. They say it's an accident.

Travis *goes to add salt.*

Travis *to the* **Man***:*

Taxi driver pulled up to pick me up, saw what I was wearing, and said I was disgusting and drove off.

I'm on a bus back home and a group of school children get onto the top deck to join me. Instantly they notice my pink skirt, matching pink jumper and pink eyeshadow. A young girl smiles at me and I smile back. I forget for a moment about all the other stares that day.

Her friend sees the exchange and is scared by the possibility. 'Why is that man dressed like a girl?' The teacher sees: 'It's rude to point, lower your voice.'

The kids continued to point and laugh.

I became a spectacle, an object of other people's ambitions.

'When I grow up, I want to be just like you, but I'm too scared to say that so I'm just going to point and laugh.'

To the **Man***:*

Have you ever been pointed and laughed at in public? Or had a whole room stop as you walk in?

The timer buzzes. The burger gets flipped.

Travis *to the* **Man***:*

Can you get me a glass of water, please?

11 November. 'Children sacrificed to appease trans lobby', an article written by Janice Turner in *The Times*. I was the subject of that article.

I tried to go into a single-stall changing room in Topshop and I was kicked out cos I made the other customers feel uncomfortable. They lied in the press and said that I changed the rules of Topshop and I was the reason they were now 'gender-neutral' – ignoring the fact there'd been gender-non-specific changing rooms nine months before 11 November. There were photos of me in every major newspaper, misgendering me, pulling apart my appearance, telling me I was an imposter; people were tweeting at me saying they wanted me to die thousands of times a day; in the street people would come up to me and call me a freak; a group of mums told the theatre I was working in at the time that I should lose my job, and my mom saw photos of me on *Good Morning Britain* whilst doing the dishes. She sent me a text saying, 'I don't understand what's happening, but would you like to come home for dinner?'

The heat rises.

Everyone's busy debating whether or not I'm a snowflake whilst a group of lads throws snowballs at me and my friends. It didn't feel like a game.

Anti-trans billboards go up around Liverpool the same week that one of our sisters is murdered in the streets.

They're debating our existence on the television again, whilst a trans friend was held up at knifepoint the day before.

I think about the first time I was slapped round the face.

The bus, the tube, the mall, the shop, outside my house, online, in my house, in my bed, at the doctor's, at the airport, in the newspaper, on the stage, in the bathroom.

Harassment isn't just one moment. It doesn't just start and stop.

I walk outside. The world will say I have privilege. That I have the choice to avoid it.

And I want to yell: 'What choice.' 'What choice gives me the honour to hide myself on the streets.'

It is not in split seconds, it is in every single pain in my body I am still yet to discover. It is the pain my doctor notes from my head never looking up, it's the UTI my friend has from never feeling safe to use the bathroom, it's the anxiety that has induced in my head to look for eyes when they are not there, it is the continuous cloud surrounding me, it's me grabbing at my body and not knowing which parts need fixing. It's trying to breathe when the whole room feels like it is closing in, it's crying and not knowing for which moment, it's grabbing at your body wanting something to work. It's not knowing what changes I am making for myself, or for you. It's knowing I was not born in the wrong body, rather born in the wrong world, but still grasping at my chest, longing for something to change, for me to change, for me to do better, it's wanting to gi–

We reach a point of climax with both sounds, as the timer goes off.

Travis *walks away from the kitchen.*

The timer remains beeping.

To the **Man***:*

Can you turn it off?

The power of the kitchen and of the hot pan is killed off. **Travis** *leaves the kitchen to walk away.*

If I walk out of this room right now, leave you and leave like this, like how I want to be, in these clothes, in this gender – I will be beaten, I will be bashed, I will be shouted at, I will be hurt. And you will go home. We have gotten into this cycle. Where bad things happen and we have to go on stage and perform for them in order for us to be believed. We have to be polite, bring in lights, bring in costume, make you laugh, bring in a show, and hug the very people that have their hands around my neck. You have your hands wrapped around my neck. I asked you here. You've helped me. But I can still feel the hands.

I'm so confused.

I need you, but I can't tell what that looks like.

Am I doing this wrong? Have I done this wrong? What are we asking for that seems more than just breathing? What is the debate in breathing? What debate? What debate is left? Who is left? It feels like both of us can't do this alone.

I just want to figure out who I am outside of violence. I just want to make this fucking burger and be done with it. To finish it. To make this burger and be able to have you believe me, understand me, want to be there, without me having to ask.

They look in the pan.

It feels like we were always set up for failure?

Through the past speech **Travis** *has been getting further and further away from the* **Man**. *A shift in sound as* **Travis** *reaches the top of a box. The back doors of the giant box are opened.* **Travis** *breathes.*

And sometimes I close my eyes. Sometimes, when I am being shouted at, thrown abuse, followed home, shaken up, or the world feels like too much to hold on my shoulders, or I am too tired for the weight of my lids
– so I just hold them tight. And closed.
And I think about the dream that I had last night. Where I was no longer here. Dead in this time. But not in an awful state, just peacefully somewhere else. Close my lids and imagine I am no longer feet-on-ground, but in air, floating. And I'm floating next to my ancestors in the Philippines. The Baklas. And we are both floating in a time before we were punished. Floating in and out of genders, the Bakla turns to me and speaks in their own tongue. 'We have been creating these words long before they were shouted at us.'

The Bakla holds me in their arms and lifts me above the weight of my shoulders, and places me on the finger of the Femminiello, just above the atmosphere. The Femminiello looks at me in my eyes.

'Why are you scared?'

'How can you hold all of me on just one finger?'

'Darling, we have held so much more for centuries. We were not always treated like dirt, we were once seen as blessed. Of course I can hold you on my finger, that power never leaves you.'

The Femminiello spun me around, one hand painted the other dry, and threw me over sidewalks of jeers, and mirrors of back pain and late nights, into the bed of a Hijra named Jaan, and in no words Jaan tidied the blankets around me, placed my eyes next to the pillow and tucked me in.

'Goodnight.'

'Are you not afraid?'

'I once was. When they first came over here, said "male or female" and we said "no". They called us a criminal tribe. I was afraid. Then I was scared. But when you close your eyes at night, and remember that we have survived all of this, that we have been here, have existed, have lived beyond the jeer, then you can breathe easier.'

'But the pavements feel so lonely . . .'

'Isolation is the best tactic of oppression. But I need you to open your eyes, your ears, your heart, and remember that we have been there too. You are not new, you are not the only one, the streets will make you feel like there is no one else, but remind yourself of the lands before they were walked on.'

Jaan blew out the candle, as the Femminiello closed the curtains, and the group of Baklas gently pushed me back down to the ground.

I opened my eyes to hear you say faggot, and remembered that there was more than this moment.

The mood shifts back to reality. **Travis** *is back down at the kitchen. Looks at the* **Man**. **Travis** *asks:*

What's next after cooking?

Man
Assemble.

Travis *and the* **Man** *assemble the burger.*

Travis
Burgers are really messy. The texture of
them can be quite coarse, invasive, sticky
– sometimes they cost nine pounds
and other times they cost three-twenty-five with
chips and a drink. It depends where you get
them from. I know burgers aren't everyone's
favourite food, I don't think they are mine
either, but I didn't think people hated burgers
enough to waste them. I don't mean
waste as in not eat all of the last tiny bits and
put the scraps in the bin. I know people don't
always eat the very last bite, or maybe leave
the onion, or maybe the lettuce. I mean fully
waste them. Like a whole burger. Like to buy
a whole burger and then to not use it is to
waste it. To not eat the rest of your burger but
instead to throw it.

The burger is assembled. The **Man** *sits back in their seat.* **Travis** *sits across from the* **Man**.

I became obsessed with how a burger feels
and smells because I needed to re-create an
intimacy with it that wasn't forced. I needed
to get to know it so I could pretend that we
had a choice to meet each other. If I become
obsessed with how the burger works, how
it flies, how it smells and how it lands, then
maybe I will have some agency over it. Maybe
I would feel like I was once in control.
But truth is – there isn't really a way to do
that with this. Whenever I get down to it,
whenever I really say it out loud, whenever I

utter the words to someone else, or myself or even as I do it now, they still don't feel like my words to tell. It still feels exactly as violent and as horrible as when it happened. I can't lie and say I have any control.

A moment passes.

When I realized the burger had hit me I realized it was too late to dodge. I'm not good at dodging things. Especially unplanned things.

A burger was thrown at me in broad daylight in April 2016 on Waterloo Bridge whilst someone yelled the word tranny. I think over one hundred people saw and I know no one did anything. To be trans and Black and gender non-conforming is to both be accustomed to the violence whilst also dissociating from the reality. I am a human being who was kind of not shocked when a burger was thrown at me by another human being. No one did anything.

I am yearning for one time, for me to say this, and to hear someone shout out in the room, 'I'm sorry.' For someone to shout, 'No, for fuck's sake, that happened.' For us to find this violence so repulsive that our bodies launch forward involuntarily to hug someone. But I do not think we are shocked. No one did anything.

I gave everyone around one minute to come up to me. To shout at him. To touch me. To look at me. To see me. To remind me that I was human. But everyone was still walking. I had to touch the mayonnaise on my shoulder for me to make sure that it was real, because if you looked at everyone else, it would have you thinking nothing in the world had changed. I guess nothing had changed though, if we really want to think about it. The world was working exactly how it had been made to. No one did anything. Mothers with their children, men in their suits, students with their feminist tote bags.
No one did anything. And I'm left scared,

I know that burger could be a fist, a knife, a choked neck, but what I do not know is if you will be there? You have never proved us wrong. No one does anything. No one did anything.

The man who threw the burger at me did pause though. We both did. For a split second. I wondered if he was going to scream, 'I was afraid, I am hurting so I hurt you.' Maybe he was waiting for someone to hold him back, to tell him off for the action I still do not know if he planned to have. But he saw the world had not noticed, and continued with his day.

Travis *gestures for the* **Man** *to sit, this time not to the stool on stage, but back to their seat. We allow this moment to happen. They look at the* **Man** *as they leave.*

No one did anything.

But someone else did notice. I remember there were two people's eyes I saw after the burger had been thrown. The man, and a lady across the street. Her eye caught mine for two seconds. She saw me holding back tears. She saw what had happened. She saw the man, and then saw me, and then she looked down. And she carried on walking. With everyone else, who carried on walking. And I'm not going to say anymore that no one did anything, because walking away is action, is action that you choose. Because doing nothing is not neutral.

I often think about that woman. I often wonder if she went home and cried too. If she saw the safety I was mourning, and cried for how much worse hers could be. Maybe she thought that if she touched me she would catch it too. As if we exist on a ladder, and in that moment she realized she was not at the bottom, but that my hand could grab her and pull her down if she offered to wipe the mayonnaise off my dress.

Maybe she caught my eye like you just caught mine.

Travis *gestures to a* **Woman** *in the audience. Gestures for them to come up on stage. When they do, they stand opposite* **Travis**.

Travis *hands them the opened recipe book. The* **Woman** *reads:*

I vow to protect you, more than others have before. I vow to protect you, as in the plural, as in more than just you. I vow to realize that in my safety, in my comfort, in my silence, comes your danger, hurt, and entrapment.
I vow to know that I cannot possibly be free, whilst you, the plural, are still hurt. I vow to know that I cannot remain silent when others are hurting, to recognize that silence is part of the hurting. I cannot, on my own, make them stop. Make them turn away. Make them look less. But I know that I can wake up.
I know that I can do better. I vow to make sure that everyday I go outside I realize that I am not alone, that I am together, with you, the plural, and me, the plural – that there cannot be singular anymore. That we have tried singular, and we continue to fail. My freedom is not just tied to yours, but is not freedom without yours.

Travis *hands them the real burger in the box.*

When I throw this burger I will throw it, not to hurt you again, but to acknowledge that I have hurt you before. That my hand may not have thrown the bun, the beef, the patty, but my silence still burns. I did not need to throw the burger with my own hand to still hear it hit. I throw this burger, to bring this vow of words into action. An action born out of violence with a hope to turn into some promise. A promise to do better. For each other. For others. I will say sorry. We will count to three, together. I will throw this burger at you. It will fall to the ground. And I will go back to my seat. And you will leave the stage. And I will go home. So will you. But outside, we are now together.

I'm sorry.

One . . . Two . . . Three . . .

The burger is thrown at **Travis**.

End.

On gender non-conformity

Mojisola There are some themes recurring in terms of this idea of pre-colonization and seeking those things out and one of the uplifting and celebratory things – and by the way, Tonderai, I don't see *Zhe* as a piece of work of shame, it was a moment in rehearsals, but I hope I haven't traumatized you! The piece grew, I saw it many, many times, but I felt it's such a celebratory piece and one thing that really stays with me, stayed with some of the young people that I brought to see *Zhe*, was the word 'choza'. And I wondered if you had any reflections on that?

Tonderai Gosh yeah, and you know, I'm writing a novel and there's one character who I was looking for a name, and I just couldn't get the name so I said, well, just for now I'm just going to use Choza, which was a word my mother used. What used to happen in the townships a lot is that a lot of the women would go to South Africa and buy things and then come back and sell things and so I played with girls; I just was one of the girls. And this woman went to South Africa, and came back and said: 'Oh, I know what you are, you're choza.' She said: 'A choza is someone who's not a boy and is not a girl, they're just sort of there. So, you're Choza.' And to this day, my brother and sister call me Choza. And it's something that my mother always finds difficult because, 'You are a boy, aren't you?' Now she says 'aren't you?' She puts a question at the end of it, which I think is really great.

So Choza was just that fluidity and I thank God that when I moved to England my brother and my sister kept that alive at home. And before I was Choza, I was Zeffee, I was little Zeffee, because there was this sort of understanding that there was something about a spirituality, a way of thinking and understanding the world, that was to do with a genderlessness, which gave you wisdom or gave you almost like an understanding of both of those things. And my grandmother and everyone identified me as possessing those qualities before I understood my gay identity. So, the first thing obviously that happens when you move to London, and you go to a boys' Catholic school, they just said 'you're gay' and I absolutely couldn't believe it. I was like, 'What is this thing that sounds terrible? How am I this thing? What happened?' Because growing up people had identified that there was something, but it wasn't sexual, it was just about that identity being almost a call back to something or somebody. And as a result, I think I've always been self-possessed, even as I was bullied, I was self-possessed, because my father recognized me as Zeffee and my siblings also saw this Choza thing, which was so real, and so powerful and so strengthening. There is no other word for me to give this character that I'm working on, but that name which goes again to reclaiming the spaces that we are reclaiming.

One of the things that we also need to do is to reclaim historically what was lost, because as we know it's been now said many times that the Victorians brought in this kind of strict scrutiny of gender and also sexuality. And I just don't know if we've claimed it enough back as ours, as part of every Black person's heritage is this understanding of spirituality and reality, gender as this sort of multi-universal thing, connected to the soul of someone. Yeah, and for me definitely that's something that I want to explore. And when I think of certain individuals as characters, I'm now not really looking at them in terms of their gender, either. I'm also thinking about what spiritually does this person represent? In Zimbabwe, there's a lot of these beliefs that are not so strange. You know when we announced Mbuya Nehanda was the great female iconic character in Zimbabwe who the Victorians tried to hang, they tried to hang her several times and they just couldn't succeed because her neck was just so strong. And finally, they thought they could and she said before she allowed herself to be hanged, because she allowed it to happen in the end, she said 'my bones will rise again'. And it's believed that she came in the liberation struggle to help people. And one of the reasons why Grace Mugabe and Mugabe kind of all fell apart was that she started to insinuate that she was the second or third coming of Nehanda and everybody was like, 'OK, that's enough get them off.' But there was spirituality, which is a part of the country, part of the idea of how we look at ourselves as people, which is so fundamental. Hopefully we can get to the point where we understand these stories far more potently than we do at the moment because they're shrouded, because of Christianity going in there.

Mojisola   Travis, I see you reacting to some of what Tonderai was saying; I was wondering what your nods were about?

Travis   I have that line in *BURGERZ* where I've got the white man on stage and I say, 'You know, thousands of years ago there were gods that looked like me' and I point to me and then I pause and I shrug to the white man and I go 'maybe you', and it always gets a laugh because the man looks so offended because he's used to being seen as the godlike image of people. *BURGERZ* was the first time I was given time in a rehearsal room, and paid time. I love what Tonderai said. It helps when there's money because as someone that doesn't have a degree, I spent a lot of the first two weeks just going to the library and reading about all the histories of gender non-conforming, and for lack of better word trans, but I don't even like using that word because it's a new word to describe an ancient thing. I was like, 'How do I put this into *BURGERZ* because *BURGERZ* was very much grounded in my reality. At the section, I was, like, 'I've got it, they're going to be my respite.'

There's a process with *BURGERZ,* which is that every time that talking about harassment was too much in the room or talking about the real things, I go, 'Can we just go and learn about the femminiello in Italy?' or 'Can we go and learn about the baklâ in the Philippines?' So we'd go and dive into a book. That's why, in *BURGERZ*, it's the only time I leave the stage and go above and leave the man on the ground with the cooking, and the only time the lights change, and it's the only time we brought in a movement choreographer to teach me flowing in my movements, because I wanted this section to be just about me. So it's the only time also that the lights go off the audience, and it's the only time where I'm told not to look at the audience members. Because I felt like I couldn't escape a gaze in *BURGERZ* and I got halfway through making the show and I was like, 'Ooh, how does this land about gaze?' I was like, 'This bit will have nothing to do with anyone but me and my joy in finding it.' I think there is such a power when you find out that you're not a new discovery. That's like a very joyful moment to go, 'Bish, you ain't new! You're not new.' And that's the journey. I met so many older trans people that let me have my moment of thinking I was new. And then when they caught up with me the next time they were so joyful that I found out: 'Bish you found out you ain't new.'

Lynette   I was also thinking about where the T is in Black queer theatre and then as I was thinking it, I started to reel off all of these plays. There's cross-dressing in *Moj of the Antarctic*, androgyny in *Zhe*, intersex in *STARS* and gender non-conforming in all of them. It's actually there, so it's interesting hearing that.

Travis   And if I could add, I think that what I'm finding at the moment when I'm researching things is that there's the new T, the T on the new T and the new formation of trans. So, what I'm really learning and what I'm trying to go away from is that this lie that there wasn't Black transness is because we were using different words to describe our gender, and if we categorize transness in this white Eurocentric way we're always going to think we weren't there before. But what I've had to learn really quickly and harshly is that I was looking in the wrong places. Maybe why I was nodding so much at Tonderai speaking is I'm like, 'Well those words [e.g. choza] are never going to turn up in the Stonewall summary of statistics of trans people of colour.

Temi   Travis, you did this performance, and I can't remember what the song was but you spoke a bit about how queer people have always been sacred, and then that came back in *BURGERZ*. I think that was such a big part of *The High Table*; and where you get to with it is that colonialism erased that; actually, it wasn't that we were these secretive people in society, but actually we were sacred, we were part of religious practices. The fact that we might not fit into a gender binary was a sign that we're spiritual and had greater wisdom rather than that we were denigrated in any way.

The High Table

Temi Wilkey

The High Table had its world premiere at London's Bush Theatre on 7 February 2020 with the following cast and creative team.

Cast

Teju — Stefan Adegbola
Mosun/Yetunde — Jumoké Fashola
Musician/Co-Composer — Mohamed Gueye
Leah/Adebisi — Ibinabo Jack
Tara — Cherrelle Skeete
Segun/Babatunde — David Webber

Creative Team

Playwright — Temi Wilkey
Director — Daniel Bailey
Set and Costume Designer — Natasha Jenkins
Lighting Designer — José Tevar
Sound Designer/Composer — Enrico Aurigemma
Movement/Associate Director — Gabrielle Nimo
Dramaturg — Deirdre O'Halloran
Costume Supervisor — India Askem
Casting Director — Ruth O'Dowd
Production Managers — Marco Savo and Ian Taylor for eStage
Company Stage Manager — Adriana Perucca
Assistant Stage Manager — Crystal Gayle

With assistance from Bush Theatre's Project 2036 cohort (2019–20): Set Designer QianEr Jin, Sound Designer Darius McFarlane and Lighting Designer Devon Muller. With further thanks to Wabriya King (drama therapy and safeguarding support), Oladipo Agboluaje (Yorùbá pronunciation guidance) and Esi Acquaah-Harrison (dialect and accent coaching). With special commendation to Nkechinyere Nwobani-Akanwo.

Acknowledgements

It's been said before, but it really does take a village.

Thank you to the ancestors that came before me and all the queer black elders who inspire me in life as well as art. Especially Uncle Cyril, Le Gateau Chocolat and Mamma D.

To the Royal Court Writer's programme, without which I'm not sure this play (or my playwriting career) would have ever started. Thanks to everyone in my group, especially John King and Elin Schofield. And to Joe Ward Munrow, Ellie Horne and Louise Stephens, for their early notes and encouragement.

To John R. Gordon, Rikki-Beadle Blair and, of course, Tom Wright. Thank you being my first and greatest champion, teacher and advocate.

To all the actors from the readings and full production, thank you for giving my words life and my mind more dimensions: Rebekah Murrell, Ike Ononye, Mensah Bediako, Susan Aderin, Nicholle Cherrie, Sheila Atim, Sule Rimi, Cyril Nri, Sarah Niles, Stefan Adegbola, Jumoké Fashola, David Webber, Ibinabo Jack and Cherrelle Skeete.

To everyone at the Bush! For believing in this story and for making it sing. Lynette Linton, Deirdre O'Halloran and, most especially, Daniel Bailey. Thank you all so much.

To everyone at Birmingham Rep for making this possible. Especially to Amit Sharma.

To the wonderful Lily Williams alongside Chloe Beeson, Emma Green and Mark Starling.

To everyone that read the play along the way: Lolita Chakrabarti, Doreene Blackstock, Lucy Prebble, Elayce Ismail, Natalie Ibu, Jess Edwards, Milli Bhatia, Adjoa Andoh and Suzanne Bell.

To Dom O'Hanlon, Sophie Beardsworth and everyone at Methuen Drama.

To the writers that paved my way and ignited the inspiration for this play: Lena Waithe, Wole Soyinka and Yrsa Daley Ward.

To my family. Blood and chosen. Thank you for all your support. Mum, Dad, Toni. And Travis Alabanza, Tom Ross-Williams, Celine Lowenthal, Tom Rasmussen, Nkenna Akunna, Jack Parlett, Ellie Kendrick, Paapa Essiedu, Rozzi Nicholson-Lailey and Paul Adeyefa.

Characters

Tara, *twenties, bride to be.*
Omotara (Yoruba) 'Child is the worth of family'

Leah, *twenties, Tara's fiancée.*
Leah (Hebrew) 'Weary'

Teju, *mid-forties/early fifties, Tara's uncle.*
Tejumade (Yoruba) 'Fix your gaze on the crown'

Segun, *mid-forties/early fifties, Tara's father.*
Segun (Yoruba) 'Conqueror'

Mosun, *mid-forties/early fifties, Tara's mother.*
Mosunmola (Yoruba) 'I move close to wealth'

Yetunde, *mid-forties/early fifties, The Ancestor of the North.*
Yetunde (Yoruba) 'Mother has returned again'

Babatunde, *mid-forties/early fifties, The Ancestor of the West.*
Babatunde (Yoruba) 'Father has come again'

Adebisi, *twenties, The Ancestor of the South.*
Adebisi (Yoruba) 'The crown has given birth to more'

Notes

(–) Signifies an interruption.

(/) Signifies where a character interrupts another with overlapping speech.

(*) Signifies a pause, either due to the use of music or an atmospheric shift.

The text uses a mixture of English and Pidgin English.

Teju and the Ancestors should speak with Nigerian accents.

The mother and father should speak in Nigerian accents, though slightly Anglicized.

All other characters speak with British accents, though Tara may often adopt a Nigerian accent at will.

Multi-roling may be necessary. Suggested pairings are:
Segun *and* **Babatunde**, **Mosun** *and* **Yetunde**, **Leah** *and* **Adebisi**.

Settings

Tara, Leah and family
London, England. Present

Teju (and Segun)
Lagos, Nigeria. Present

The Ancestors
The North Star. On the edge of the present

Scene One

The North Star.

Opening song:

> Ẹ káàbọ̀ si irawọ (ariwa)
> Ẹ káàbọ̀ si irawọ (ariwa)
> Ẹ káàbọ̀ si irawọ (ariwa)
> Ẹ káàbọ̀ si irawọ (ariwa)

> Show them, show them
> Show, Show them.
> Show them. (Show them)

> Show them, show them
> Show, Show them.
> Show them. (Show them)

> Hmm! Without burnt offering. Hmm! Without blood sacrifice.
> Hmm! Without burnt offering. We go show you, show you.

> Hmm! Without burnt offering. Hmm! Without blood sacrifice.
> Hmm! Without burnt offering. We go show you, show you

> From the North to the South, from the East to the West.
> For your front, for your behind. We go show you, show you.
> From the North to the South, from the East to the West.
> For your front, for your behind. We go show you, show you.

> Ẹ káàbọ̀ si irawọ (ariwa)
> Ẹ káàbọ̀ si irawọ (ariwa)
> Ẹ káàbọ̀ si irawọ (ariwa)
> Ẹ káàbọ̀, káàbọ̀ Kaabo.

* * *

Babatunde   That didn't sound right.

Adebisi   Ah-ah! I thought I sang it well.

Yetunde   We just didn't have the fourth harmony. That's all. It was good!

Adebisi   Are there usually four of us?

Babatunde   Who are we missing?

Yetunde   Babatunde. So, you don't know how to greet?

Babatunde   Sorry, Ma.

Adebisi   Hello, Auntie.

Yetunde   Good to see you, Adebisi. I haven't seen you at one of these before?

Adebisi It's my first.

Yetunde Ehe! So you've finally come to join us at a council.

Adebisi Yes now, by force.

Yetunde You shouldn't have left it so long. You've been dead for a while. The afterlife isn't just for rest, you know.

Babatunde What do you think we've been summoned for?

Yetunde Maybe there's a newborn to bless. Or some kind of a family feud.

Babatunde Lai lai! I don't want a feud. They're too lengthy. Let's pray it's a blessing.

Yetunde Feuds don't take too long.

Babatunde They do! The last summoning I was on, I was here for decades.

Adebisi What?

Yetunde He's exaggerating.

Adebisi I can't stay here for a decade! I'm meant to be resting.

Yetunde They never feel that long. Their days are a few minutes to us. It'll be over before you know it.

Babatunde I just hope it's not a feud.

Yetunde What's the rush?

Adebisi He's probably just tired. Coming here all the time, when he should be resting. We can't all be veteran council members like you.

Yetunde Well, some ancestors like to help their descendants.

Babatunde And what thanks do we get for it? Do any of our descendants ever thank us? They don't even summon us anymore!

Yetunde Only in recent times.

Babatunde The gods have to gather us together themselves. Can you imagine?

Yetunde That will change.

Babatunde Hmm! I thought I would have at least been reincarnated by now. I've been coming to these councils enough.

Adebisi Is that the only reason you do it? Because . . . I do not want to be reincarnated yet!

Yetunde The afterlife isn't so bad.

Adebisi Why do you like it so much, Yetunde? You haven't been back to Aiye for centuries.

Yetunde What rubbish! It's not even been two centuries.

Babatunde That's a long time now!

Yetunde Baba, weytin you go talk? You self. You were only living one generation after my own.

Babtunde But I've *tried* to be reincarnated.

Adebisi And I only just died!

Yetunde You didn't *just* die!

Babatunde I've been trying to get back to Aiye for a long time! You! You just sit up in Orun-re-re, resting like there's no tomorrow.

Adebisi Don't you want a tomorrow life, Yetunde?

Yetunde Shh! Stop.

Pause.

I thought I heard something. One of our descendants –

Adebisi Are we able to hear them?

Babatunde Yes, but it's not a direct line. When they used to pray, it would hit our ears clear as a bell. Now it's harder. We're having to eavesdrop on them, like children hiding under the stairs.

Yetunde We can still divine what they need, from under the stairs! We're still their ancestors. We have our judgement, our discerning ears.

Adebisi What kind of thing do you hear?

Babatunde Hmm! Well – you didn't hear it from me but . . . you know Fola?

Adebisi Yes. What has she done?

Babatunde She wants to marry . . . an Igbo man.

Adebisi Hey, gods!

Babatunde I know.

Yetunde Ah-ah! I think she should now! She should marry who she wants –

Adebisi An Igbo man?

Babatunde Impossible!

Yetunde Look at you people. Me, I died before you both. Before those yeye borders were drawn, when our tribes actually meant something!

Adebisi They still mean something!

Yetunde I should be the one, of all of us, to be against Fola's marriage. He's a good man. They're in love. What's the sense in keeping them apart just for the sake of tradition?

Adebisi Because traditions are important! They're who we are –

Yetunde Says Mrs Convert!

Adebisi Eh?

Yetunde You! When you were on earth you abandoned our traditions to go and serve the white man's god.

Adebisi That was different. We had to. They would beat us for worshipping the old gods.

Babatunde Shh! Did you hear something?

Adebisi No.

Babatunde Hmm! I wish I could summon up a drink while we wait.

Yetunde Baba!

Babatunde Being so close to Aiye is making me itch for my senses again. For the taste of palm wine. The scent in a lover's hair.

Adebisi What happened with the council for that one, Yetunde?

Yetunde For Fola?

Babatunde Yes. Did they bless the wedding?

Yetunde Of course now! We blessed it sharp sharp. We weren't going to stand in their way. Just because of their tribes. That council was very quick.

Babatunde Where is this fourth Ancestor? We always arrive at the same time.

Adebisi Why do we need four?

Babatunde There's always an Ancestor of the North, East, South and West.

Adebisi Which one's which?

Yetunde I'm the North. I've been dead the longest.

Babatunde Not if the Ancestor we're waiting for is your elder.

Yetunde Well then, I am the North until further notice.

Adebisi Where are they? When will they come?

Yetunde Na wa for this one! I don't know how you can be *long* dead and still be doing African time –

They are interrupted. They all breathe in.

Babatunde Are you getting this?

Yetunde Yes.

Adebisi I can hear them.

They are silent.

Scene Two

London, present. The Akindeji dining room.

Tara   She should marry whoever she wants! The rest of the family will come around.

Segun   Not this family.

Tara   Once they see how happy they are together. They'll have to. That's what it comes down to. If you really love someone, you want what's best for them. Even if it's not what you initially hoped for.

Segun (*beat*)   Lai lai! Marrying an Igbo man? God forbid! What is so wrong with our Yoruba men that she must be marrying outside of her tribe?

Mosun   Leave them, Segun! They're in love.

Leah   What's so bad about Igbo people?

Segun   Well, Lisa, I'm glad you asked –

Leah   Leah.

Segun   What?

Leah   My name's Leah.

Segun   Oh yes. Of course.

Leah   It's fine.

Segun   I'm sorry –

Leah   No, go on. It's fine.

Segun   The thing about Igbo people is. They no go season their food!

Mosun   Ah-ah!

Segun   Their pounded yam is hard. Like stone.

Mosun   Wey you go talk?

Segun   It's true now!

Tara   He always gets like this after a few drinks.

Segun   They eat people.

Leah   What?

Tara   Dad!

Segun   Igbo people eat people.

Mosun   What rubbish!

Segun   I said what I said.

Mosun   This is nothing but tribalism. He's a good Christian boy. If he was Igbo and *Muslim* I would understand, but he's a Christian –

Tara   Why should it be a problem if he's Muslim?

Mosun   The Lord says 'There is neither Jew nor Greek, slave nor free, male or female for we are all one in Christ Jesus!'

Leah   Amen!

Tara   Amen?

Mosun   If he's a Christian, his tribe no dey matter!

Tara   Since when were *you* moved by the Spirit?

Leah   'Neither male nor female!' That's what she said!

Tara   I'm not sure she meant it like that.

Mosun   I'm just waiting for the day you bring home your own special somebody Omotara. Yoruba or Igbo or even Hausa sha! It won't matter.

Segun   That's if she even marries a Nigerian. What if she go marry an Oyinbo?

Mosun   Me I don't mind. He can be African, Oyinbo, whatever! So long as we can still have a proper Naija wedding, and we eat jollof rice and plantain and moy moy at the reception.

I'm just praying for the day that I'm seated at the high table, spooted well well in my aso ebi. Gele crowning my head. Diamonds go be shining on my ear, on my necks, my wrists. Watching you dancing with the man you love.

Leah   Tara.

Mosun   Fola said this man 'he kisses the ground she walks on'. That's what I want for you.

Beat.

Did you enjoy your food, Leah?

Leah (*beat*)   Yes, thank you.

Mosun   I was worried we hadn't made enough. Tara called to say you were coming after I'd already started cooking. I hadn't expected you.

Leah   Sorry about the last-minute addition.

Mosun   No now! You are welcome. She so rarely comes over anymore. I thought there might be something wrong.

Leah   No, nothing wrong!

Tara   It's actually the opposite, we wanted to tell you something. Some really good news.

Segun's *phone rings.*

Segun Sorry.

Mosun Is that him?

Tara Who?

Segun No.

Tara Uncle Teju?

Segun No, it wasn't him.

Tara Did you see him when you were in Nigeria?

Segun Yes.

Tara How was he?

Segun He's fine. He was fine.

Mosun How is your work, Leah? Aren't you a . . . lawyer?

Leah Yeah, it's good thanks.

Mosun I always wanted Tara to be a lawyer.

Leah I think Tara has something she wants to tell you.

Segun Who wants another drink?

Mosun I think she could dress herself up a bit more. Don't you think? Dress like you. Catch herself a man!

Leah Don't you have something to say?

Mosun I'm sure you've got yourself a fine man to spend your time with. Pretty girl like you.

Leah No actually.

Mosun You don't have a boyfriend?

Leah (*beat*) No.

Mosun Are you looking?

Leah Not really.

Mosun Well, I guess you two will be old maids together then!

Leah That's one way of putting it.

Mosun You know, some mothers would put pressure on their daughter. But not me. I just put my faith in God. The right man will come along soon.

Tara Mum.

Mosun Yes, Tara?

Tara That's what me and Leah came here to talk to you about. There's no easy way of saying this, but I'm really happy about it and I hope you will be too.

Beat.

Leah and I are getting married.

Pause.

Segun You and . . . you?

Tara Leah. Yeah.

Segun But . . .

Tara I've been trying to tell you.

Segun When did this . . .?

Leah I proposed. Nearly nine months ago.

Segun And you didn't think to . . .?

Leah Well, exactly.

Tara I've been waiting for the right time.

Leah And I've been telling her that there's never going to be a right time . . .

Mosun No.

Tara (*beat*) What?

Mosun I said, no!

Tara We're not asking your permission!

Mosun You said you were a bisexual.

Tara (*beat*) So?

Mosun We thought you would end up with a man. Get back together with Samuel.

Tara That ended years ago!

Leah Tara said she told you about us.

Tara I did!

Leah Then why are they talking about it like it's the first time they've heard?

Tara I did tell them about you.

Mosun I don't think so.

Tara I sat you down, two months after we got together, right here at this table. I told you I loved her. That being with her felt like a miracle.

Mosun I don't remember.

Tara You can't ignore it anymore.

Mosun We didn't raise you like this! You never even looked at a woman before she came along.

Leah That is definitely not true.

Mosun You turned her head!

Leah If you think that, then you really don't know her.

Mosun Don't you think life is hard enough?

Tara What are you talking about?

Mosun As a woman. As a Black woman. We don't need anything else on top.

Tara It's not 'on top'.

Mosun You know / what I mean.

Tara / It's underneath. Enmeshed.

Segun We just don't want you to struggle.

Tara I won't.

Leah Or, you know, she will! But I'll be there.

Segun OK. Look, Omotara, you've made your point. We've heard you. If this is what you want, then we can't stop you. But marriage! It's . . . it's too far.

Tara Leah's everything to me.

Segun Omo, please.

Tara What?

Segun You're upsetting your mother.

Tara By telling her how happy I am?

Leah I'm sorry.

Tara Why are you apologizing?

Leah This must be a lot to handle. They've barely met me and then we tell them we're getting married!

Segun Thank you!

Leah I wish it could have been different. But what we're trying to say is that we're getting married in three months and we'd really like for you to be there.

Pause.

Mosun No. We can't.

Tara (*beat*) Dad?

Mosun The Lord says, the Bible says –

Tara I don't care what the Bible / says, Mum.

Mosun / It is an abomination!

Tara Dad? Can you fucking say something for once?

Mosun You will not use that language under my roof –

Tara Oh, but calling my relationship an 'abomination' is fair game?

Mosun It *is* an abomination.

Leah Come on, we're going.

Tara Fuck this.

Mosun Get out!

Leah We're going!

They leave.

Mosun My God. I knew something was up. As soon as Omotara said she was bringing her. Insisted! This is serious, Segun.

Segun I know.

Mosun Serious, serious, serious.

Beat.

She doesn't even look like a man.

Segun What?

Mosun At least if she was one of *those* lesbians we could get away with it. With the wedding pictures. God! My mother is going to faint. She's going to have a fit. Omotara has killed her grandmother! We should call Omo, we should tell her that.

Segun I don't think it'll help.

Mosun Ah! I thought it was over. She hadn't mentioned it for so long. I thought it had ended. Now this?

Segun Wishful thinking!

Mosun Well, no more thinking. That's not enough. Time for prayer. No weapon formed against us shall prosper. I will disrupt this wedding with the mighty name of Jesus. How are we going to have grandbabies? Segun. My only child.

How could she do this to me?

Segun I don't think this is about you, darling.

Mosun I never thought this would happen. I knew when she moved in with her it was serious. But I thought she would come to her senses eventually. Me, I just took it to the Lord. God, what are we going to tell people? Segun?

Segun Why does this thing always follow me? Just when I think it's gone it comes right back.

Mosun This is different.

Segun It's like I'm cursed.

Mosun Ah-ah! Don't say that. We are blessed and highly favoured! This, her wedding, doesn't mean anything. It's just a road bump. We will get past it.

Segun Maybe I was wrong.

Mosun No.

Segun Maybe I should have done more for him.

Mosun You did everything you could.

Segun What if, this thing with Omotara . . . what if it's some kind of punishment? Divine justice.

Mosun Stop that, Segun. God wouldn't punish you for your brother's sins! You tried to help him.

Segun But I should have stayed longer. Not booked that early flight home. Maybe I could have reasoned with him.

Mosun What were you going to do? Camp outside his compound? If he didn't want your help then you couldn't force it on him. You'd already spent enough money getting there in the first place!

Segun But he was in danger.

Mosun He knew the risks! Segun, I don't care what he said. I'm not saying it's right. The laws back home, they're too harsh. But he knew the risks when he went there.

Segun But if he's not safe?

Mosun He is. He was exaggerating. Emotional blackmail. It's just another kind of 419. You did the right thing. He couldn't come here. Once he's stopped his sulking, he will call you. Don't worry about him. We've got more important problems. Three months? Chai! We need to start fasting and prayer from this night! Now, now! I won't even do the dishes.

Segun What?

Mosun Yes o! They can wait till morning. This is an emergency.

Beat.

Are you coming up?

Segun Yes.

Mosun No weapon formed against us shall prosper. Amen?

Segun Amen.

Scene Three

The North Star.

There is a slight bewildered pause. **Yetunde** *stands apart from* **Adebisi** *and* **Babatunde**.

Adebisi What on earth?

Babatunde I could barely hear a thing.

Adebisi Is it always like this? I know you said it was hard but –

Babatunde It's usually better than that.

Adebisi It was like a bad radio. Did they have those when you were last alive? Like . . . the frequency was off.

Yetunde Back when, way back.
Way back, way back when
When I lived, I lived with –

Babatunde There must some kind of interference.

Adebisi What is she doing?

Babatunde I don't know.

Adebisi Yetunde?

Yetunde Back when, way back
Before, before
They scatter our ways.
Before, before
They set foot in Nigeria.

Babatunde A beg, just leave her! We need to figure out what they were saying.

Adebisi I think I heard something about getting married? Omotara, she must be getting married.

Babatunde Yes now, maybe all we need to do is bless the wedding! Did you hear who she was marrying?

Yetunde Before they even *called* it Nigeria.
Named it, *named* it,
a land not theirs.

Adebisi Probably another Igbo man!

Babatunde Well, that's simple. Let's bless it and get back.

Gave it the wretched name,
the wretched, wretched name
Of nigh-nigh-nigh-geria.

Adebisi Ah-ah! Yetunde, can't you be quiet? This is no time for song. We're in the middle of council.

Yetunde Back when, way back
Before the white man came.
In my time. My time.
My time.

Beat.

It was different then. We were sacred then –

Adebisi We all know that Yetunde! It's a shame our descendants don't call on us like before, but this is hardly the time to be doing clappa clappa about it. We have work to do.

Yetunde Tara is marrying Leah. The woman she brought to dinner.

Adebisi What? No!

Babatunde I didn't hear that.

Yetunde I did.

Babatunde You're wrong. It's just the interference.

Yetunde I am the North, I've been dead the longest and I've served on these councils the most. My ears are finely tuned to Aiye by now. I heard it.

Adebisi Well.

Babatunde Alright.

Yetunde So, like you said, all we need to do is bless the wedding and go.

Adebisi We can't do that.

Yetunde And why not?

The sound of static.

Babatunde What is that? What is going on?

Adebisi Is this normal?

Babatunde Have you ever heard it before, Yetunde?

Yetunde No.

Adebisi How do we make it stop?

Yetunde We can stop it by blessing this marriage, leaving this place and going back to Orun.

Adebisi We can't do that.

Yetunde Why not?

Adebisi We cannot bless this ye-ye marriage.

Yetunde What is ye-ye about it? Na your head be ye-ye, Ade!

The static stops.

Babatunde Oh, good. It's stopped.

Yetunde *exits.*

Adebisi What's gotten into her?

Babatunde Me, I don't know! But we better follow her. Make her see sense. We need to get this summoning over with.

Scene Four

London, **Tara** *and* **Leah***'s home.*

Tara You're lying.

Leah Nope. I can't do it.

Tara I don't believe it. No! How have you got away with this?

Leah I've never been able to.

Tara I swear you were doing it at Bree's wedding!

Leah No.

Tara You smiled at me when it started!

Leah That's all part of how I get away with it. You've got to look excited when it starts. Then no one notices when you're not doing it.

Tara What do you do when it comes on?

Leah I just . . . go to the loo.

Tara Is that what you did tonight?

Leah Yeah! I needed to go.

Tara How could you?

Leah But also, it was good timing. I either go to the loo or I just sit it out.

Tara Leah. You can't sit out the electric slide!

Leah Yeah, but I can't exactly get up and do it badly either. It's embarrassing! I'm scared they'll revoke my black card or something –

Tara We *should* revoke your black card! At your big age? You've never learnt it?

Leah I've tried picking it up a few times but I just get lost and I go backwards when I should go forwards or I step the wrong way and then I step on someone's toe and then everyone's so annoyed at me because I'm messing up the flow.

Tara But it's so simple.

Leah Tara. You know I'm dyspraxic.

Tara It's just a jazzed-up two step.

Leah You're actually being really ableist right now!

Tara Come on.

Leah What?

Tara Let's go. I'm teaching you. No wife of mine is sitting out 'Candy'. Not on *my* wedding day. Impossible.

'Candy' by Cameo starts playing.

Leah Are we really doing this now? It's like . . . 2 a.m.!

Tara It doesn't matter.

Leah Turn it down a bit.

Beat.

You have to promise not to laugh.

Tara I cannot promise you that.

Leah I want to go to bed!

Tara I'm mirroring you. OK?

Leah *nods.*

Tara Now step to the right, step to the right. Then to the left, then to the left! EHE! And back and back and forward and back. I think I could do this before I could walk.

Leah How is that possible?

Tara I was probably bopping along to it in my pram. At every wedding, the birthday, family barbecue. I bet I was doing it in the womb. When my mum was stepping to it, with my dad sliding to it beside her, then behind her and then beside her again. It's that deep muscle memory. Like generational trauma. What's the opposite of trauma?

Leah Shut up! I'm trying to concentrate.

Tara It's in your sinews, babe, your bones. Your blood. It's electric. No need to concentrate! You just surrender to it.

Nothing like it. Stepping and sliding in unison, everyone putting their little spin on it. Their little twist. Styling it out! It's magic. That synchronicity with everyone in the room. All of your friends, your family. Til the sax solo takes over and fades out above your heads, into the sweaty air.

Leah *stops. Watching her enjoy the dance.* **Tara** *notices, switches the script and takes her by the hand. They dance together for a bit. Then* **Leah** *breaks away.*

Tara What's wrong?

Leah Nothing.

Tara You were starting to get it before. It was good!

Leah   Yeah?

Tara   I told you it was easy. All you needed was some one-to-one tuition . . .

Leah   Are we going to dance like that at the wedding?

Tara   Yeah! That's the whole point.

Leah   I don't mean 'Candy'. I mean, you know, proper. Like that.

Tara   Yeah. If you want.

Leah   We never dance like that.

Tara   OK.

Leah   We didn't tonight.

Tara   What happened to being dyspraxic?

Leah   What about it?

Tara   You said . . .

Leah   That's not why we don't do it.

Tara   We can dance however you want, babe.

Leah   OK.

Beat.

Is it alright that they're not going to be there?

Tara   Who?

Leah   You know who.

Tara   God. Yeah, it's fine.

Leah   Yeah?

Tara   I mean . . . yeah.

Beat.

They probably *will* come.

Leah   You think?

Tara   Maybe.

Leah   They haven't RSVPed yet

Tara   That doesn't mean anything.

Leah   I don't think you can count on them coming.

Tara   Can we go to bed?

Tara *turns off the music.*

Leah   You don't want to talk about it?

Tara No, I'm just . . . I'm tired. All this dancing!

Leah OK.

Tara And teaching. Teaching is exhausting!

Leah Fine. Let's go to bed.

Tara We're going to practise more in the morning though! And every day before work, until the wedding day.

Leah What?

Tara Yeah! When I'm finished with you, you're going to be sliding in your sleep.

Scene Five

The North Star.

Yetunde Babatunde Oluwaleti Gbenga Akindeji!

Babatunde Do not use my full name, Yetunde.

Yetunde You are going to agree to this. I will pull rank if I have to.

Adebisi You can't pull rank!

Yetunde I can! I am the most senior Ancestor of this council of guidance –

Adebisi No!

Yetunde Am I not the Ancestor of the North?

Adebisi That doesn't mean anything. Baba said it's just nominal –

Babatunde It doesn't mean you're in charge here, Yetunde.

Yetunde My last life pre-dates yours, not so?

Adebisi That does not denote rank here.

Yetunde Oh? It does not? Please – Babatunde come and collect your niece because I don't know which land and which people she dey hail from –

Babatunde Yetunde.

Yetunde She is clearly no relative of mine.

Babatunde Listen to us!

Yetunde Is it not at the deepest core of our values in the Yoruba tribe to respect our elders? To respect the wisdom of our forebears –

Adebisi Yes! In Aiye!

Yetunde And in Orun too –

Babatunde We are not in Aiye or Orun now, Yetunde.

Adebisi In matters like this, in matters of guidance, we need to take the proximity to our descendants into consideration –

Yetunde *Proximity?*

Adebisi Yes, now!

Babatunde Ade arguably has a closer tie to Tara. Being her great-great-grandaunt.

Adebisi And Babatunde! He has a direct route to her lineage, being her great-great-grandfather.

Yetunde I am her great-great-great-*great*-grandaunt. Great x great equals greater! Great-*est*. I am surely the one to be trusted with this decision –

Adebisi I disagree.

Yetunde Yekpami-oh! Gods, come and smite them for this rubbish.

Adebisi Aunty, we're already dead.

Yetunde A beg, you should dead them again jo!

Babatunde We cannot bless this marriage, Yetunde.

Yetunde Why not?

Babatunde Because it is not . . . normal. It is not our way.

Yetunde Eh?

Adebisi She cannot conceive. She cannot have children with this – this her girlfriend.

Yetunde She can. Not in our time, but now –

Adebisi It is unheard of. It is not African.

Yetunde Who are you to say what is and is not African? Mrs English textbook –

Babatunde Alright –

Yetunde Mrs Bible before bedtime.

Babatunde Yetunde –

Yetunde Daughter of Empire!

Babatunde That's enough.

Yetunde You would not know what was African if it looked you square in the eye and spat in your face. We are blessing this marriage. It is what the gods would want.

Adebisi The gods are not here. They have chosen us to decide what to do.

Yetunde You are a disgrace. Both of you. You're a disgrace to our lineage.

Adebisi What do we do when this happens? When we disagree?

Yetunde We do not normally disagree. Every other summoning I've been to we've thought in one accord. It's been quick. Simple. Done the blessing, or given the healing or the sign that our descendant needed. Then we go home.

Babatunde Well, we'll have to put it to a vote. And I'm afraid it's two against one, Yetunde –

Yetunde No! We are missing one Ancestor. We cannot conduct a vote without all of us present.

Adebisi That's not our fault. There must be a problem with the system. There's only been three of us for this long. We cannot wait for another Ancestor to arrive.

Babatunde Even if they did come, and they happened to vote your way, Yetunde, it would still be a tie.

Yetunde Not so! For you must count the will of the descendant.

Adebisi We don't know when they're going to come! We don't even know *if* they're going to come.

Yetunde That may be so. But we are not leaving here until they join us.

Adebisi This is madness! I want to go home. To my rest.

Yetunde This is your first council. The first time you've ever bothered to turn up for your ancestral duties. Don't talk to me about rest.

Babatunde We need to get back.

Yetunde For what, Baba? What are you hurrying back for?

Babatunde Because Papa Elegba said once I complete this council, the gods might finally grant me my tomorrow life.

Yetunde Oho! So this is why. You're putting your own selfish, carnal needs above the struggles of your descendants? Just so you can get yourself back to Aiye?

Babatunde Please, Yetunde.

Yetunde This is what you are rushing for? Well, if it is so important to you to get back, then we should get this over with. We should bless this wedding, Baba. Vote with me.

Pause.

Babatunde No. I'm sorry, I can't do that.

Yetunde Then I guess we're staying here.

Adebisi This is absurd! I'm going to the edge. To call on the gods.

Yetunde Leave them be!

Adebisi They will not be best pleased with your nonsense.

Yetunde Just because you can't get your way!

Babatunde I'm going to go too.

Yetunde Baba! You can't. You two are breaking up our council.

Babatunde This fourth Ancestor, they might be lost. I'm going to call to them across the spine. The sooner they get here, the sooner we can go home to Orun.

Yetunde Which is all you two care about.

Adebisi And all you care about is being close enough to Aiye to smell at life without actually having to live it!

Yetunde What?

Adebisi That's why you're always serving on these councils without ever applying for reincarnation! (*Beat.*) Well, some of us don't like to be close to Aiye. Some of us need to rest.

Come on, Baba!

A thunderous sound.

Yetunde You see? You see what you've done? You've angered the gods.

Babatunde I've never heard that before.

Yetunde This is what happens when you disrespect your elders.

Babatunde Look at what you've done!

Adebisi What does it mean?

Babatunde What if they take away our right to reincarnation?

Adebisi They wouldn't do that.

Babatunde You disrespected the North!

Adebisi You said it was nominal!

Yetunde Hmmm!

Babatunde You just cost me my life, Ade. My tomorrow life! All because of your loose tongue.

Adebisi You don't know that.

Babatunde Ah-ah! Why couldn't you just keep your mouth shut, for once?

The thunderous sound develops. **Teju** *enters. He is covered in dust and looks as though he's just woken up.*

The Ancestors look at one another, stunned.

Scene Six

London, **Tara** *and* **Leah***'s home.*

Leah I want to tell you about it but also I don't. You know?

Beat.

I wish we could have just gone together. Like, I want to know what yours is like but also . . . I don't. I want to be surprised! But what if they clash or if they're too similar?

Beat.

What if they're exactly the same.

Tara They won't be.

Leah You should have seen my mum's face. Honestly, when I put it on . . . I didn't even have to look in the mirror. I knew it was the one cos she just started crying straight away. Tanya said she was being moist! But Mum just kept saying she was so happy. 'I'm just so happy!' Bless her.

Beat.

When are you getting yours?

Tara I don't know. I was going to wait until I'd sorted out our natives.

Leah Haven't you taken the material to the tailor?

Tara No. Not yet.

Leah Why not?

Tara I wanted to see how many people RSVPed. On my side. Usually everyone wears the same, so the guests can match. Do you think it'll be weird for us to wear attire if there aren't any Nigerians there?

Leah No! We can get our friends to wear it. My family.

Tara Your sister's had that baby pink bodycon picked out since before we were engaged. Tanya's not changing her outfit for anyone.

Leah I'll talk to her. Have they still not called?

Tara No.

Leah Why don't you ring them? It's been over a month.

Tara I'm not making the first move! They're the ones in the wrong.

Leah Yeah, babe, but you didn't give them much time to come around to the idea. See it from their perspective. You bring around some random woman and say you're going to marry her. That's a lot to take in.

Tara You had met them before.

Leah Barely!

Tara At graduation.

Leah That doesn't count. That's before we were together.

Tara But you weren't a stranger.

Leah I was as good as a stranger to them. You could have at least told them when I proposed! Or invited them round when we moved in together. You know, something!

I honestly feel sometimes like if I hadn't gone with you that night, you never would have told them.

Tara   I would have!

Leah   After we'd been married for ten years, with three kids. Three secret kids!

Tara   No!

Beat.

Three? I thought we said two –

Leah   Yeah, two, depending! Depending on how we do it. I just said three for dramatic effect.

Tara   You say everything for dramatic effect.

Leah   You think I'm being dramatic? You think it's too much to ask to have your girlfriend – your *fiancée* tell her parents about you?

Tara   That's easy for you to say!

Leah   What?

Tara   You've got no idea what it's like. Your parents practically threw a party when you came out.

Leah   No they didn't!

Tara   Your mum's there crying happy tears while mine's calling me an abomination and you're really trying to tell me how I should handle things?

Leah   That's not fair.

Tara   No, Leah, it's *not* fair! After I came out, the first thing I said to Bree was 'at least they didn't disown me!'. And that was probably only because I came out as bisexual. It was probably just because I gave them some hope that, eventually, I'd maybe settle down with a man. That it was just a phase. Now they've actually got to face up to who I am . . . this might be it!

Leah   It's not.

Tara   You don't know that.

Leah   They wouldn't disown you.

Tara   You don't know them.

Leah   Well, whose fault is that!

Tara   Unbelievable.

Leah   I'm trying to understand, Tara. But you haven't even once tried to see it from my side. Do you think it was easy for me walking into your house like that, your family home, and feeling like a stranger? Acting like I was just your friend.
I know it's been hard for you with them. I see that. But it's been hard for me too.

Tara I tried. So many times! But they didn't want to know. Every time I mentioned you, it was met with this silence. So I stopped talking about you, about most things! Anything emotional. It was either that or stop speaking to them all together. And I couldn't do that. They're all I have. I know it sounds like I kept you from them but it was the only way. It's not like you and your family. We're different. My life with you was just a separate thing. They became separate worlds.

Leah And now I'm forcing them together.

Tara I want to. I don't want to do that anymore.

Leah OK. I'm sorry for getting on at you.

Tara It's alright. Sorry meeting my parents was so shit.

Leah I kind of like them!

Tara Yeah?

Leah Before the shouting match, I was thinking we might make a nice little family.

Tara I chose a song today.

Leah Did you?

Tara Yeah, it was easy. I was kind of pissed you even had to ask! I didn't need the options on a spreadsheet.

Leah It was a hard choice!

Tara No it wasn't.

Leah I only made an Excel shortlist because you made zero suggestions when I asked you.

Tara That's because you asked me when I was working!

Leah OK fine. What did you choose?

Tara 'Weak'!

Leah Love it. Why?

Tara Because . . . that was our first kiss!

Leah No it wasn't!

Tara Umm . . . yes it was!

Leah Our first kiss was outside. There wasn't any music. Unless you're counting the music playing in the house? But I don't remember what that was.

Tara That one doesn't count.

Leah I hate it when you say that.

Tara It wasn't proper. Because of how I freaked out after!

Leah Yeah but it still happened.

Tara It's not a good first. For our story. Our proper first kiss was two weeks later to 'Weak'. When I came and met you and we got that train south. And I apologized and told you how I felt and played you this song on my headphones. One in each ear. Cos I'd been playing it on repeat for days

. . .

She starts singing the pre-chorus of SWV's 'Weak'. Starting from 'Cause my heart starts beating triple time . . .'

Leah And then you kissed me!

Tara Yep!

Tara *sings the chorus from, 'I get so weak at the knees . . .'*

Leah (*gently interjecting*)   With our headphones in.

Tara *continues singing.*

Leah On the train!

Tara *continues to sing and then* **Leah** *joins in, in harmony, for the last line of the chorus.*

Leah I don't think you've kissed me anywhere like that since.

Tara I listened to it this morning though and it's quite long! We're going to have to come up with more moves than just swaying side to side.

Leah That's dead! We've got to switch it up. I want to be dipped. Twirled. Pirouetted. The whole shebang.

Tara Yes, ma'am.

Leah Maybe we could go to a class!

Tara Like a dance class?

Leah We could come up with a whole routine!

Tara If you want.

Leah Really? OK great. I'll book it tomorrow. Will you help me twist my hair before bed?

Tara Yeah. Where's the oil?

Leah It's in the bathroom.

Tara I'll go get it.

Leah Thank you.

Scene Seven

The North Star.

Babatunde (*slowly*)   Kí l'orúko ò re?

Adebisi   It's not working.

Babatunde   Kí l'orúko yín?

Adebisi   He doesn't understand Yoruba or English.

Yetunde   I think he understands.

Babatunde   Nibo ni o ti wa?

Yetunde   He just can't speak.

Adebisi   Ah-ah! This is not normal.

Yetunde   Maybe he's been dead for too long.

Adebisi   No. You've been dead for millennia and you can still speak fine!

Babatunde   Maybe it's because he's never been summoned before.

Adebisi   That's not it. This is my first!

Beat.

Kì lo de? Why can't you talk?

Teju *opens his mouth. Nothing.*

Yetunde   Leave him.

Babatunde   We can't leave him. He's our only way out.

Adebisi   Well, he doesn't need to speak. We can explain the situation to him and he can either nod yes or no.

Babatunde   Are you sure he understands?

Yetunde   I will explain it.

Adebisi   Why do you get to?

Yetunde   Because I am the eldest, the North –

Adebisi   You do not know that. This one, he might be from before your time.

Babatunde   Before the dawn of linguistics.

Adebisi   What's the protocol for this?

Babatunde   Protocol? There's no protocol! The gods have sent us a mute imbecile Ancestor who probably got lost on the straight line from Orun to the North Star, talk less of making an informed decision.

Yetunde   Ah-ah! Stop. You know, he can understand you.

Babatunde I don't care! This foolish fool is all that's standing in the way of my tomorrow life. He's wasted enough of our time! Turning up late. Now he can't talk!

The sound of static.

Adebisi This sound again!

Babatunde It must be from Aiye.

Adebisi For gods' sake, not now! We know what we're here for now. Why must we be still listening to Aiye? We need to concentrate on this! We need to hold the vote.

Yetunde I don't think it's from Aiye, Ade.

Adebisi Eh?

Yetunde I think it's him.

Babatunde No. It can't be. He's just an Ancestor. He's not a god.

Yetunde That may be so, but I think he's doing it.

The static rises.

Scene Eight

Lagos, Nigeria. Some weeks earlier.

Teju Segun! How now? Thank you for coming.

Segun (*beat*) So you couldn't pick me up from the airport?

Teju I'm sorry, my brother.

Segun Hmm!

Teju I couldn't – I can't leave the house.

Segun Why not?

Teju How was your flight?

Segun It was fine. It was a flight, they're all the same.

Teju Can I get you something to drink?

Segun No. Why are all the blinds down?

Teju No reason.

Segun You don't like sunlight?

Teju I . . . I slept in late. I just got out of bed.

Segun Hmm! When you should have been picking me up from the airport. How are you anyway?

Teju I'm fine! Segun, I really appreciate you coming here.

Segun Fine?

Teju I'm sorry if I scared you.

Segun What do you mean you're fine?

Teju I just mean that I'm OK. That I'm not as bad as when we spoke.

Segun Teju, if you're fine, then I'm really wondering why you asked me to book a last-minute flight to Lagos. Barely any notice!

Teju I'm sorry.

Segun You sounded like you were crying blood! I was shaking when I heard you. A grown man, crying like that! And when I tried to call you back, no answer. I was calling and calling you. Days like that. You couldn't pick up your phone?

Teju No.

Segun Why not? Eh? Mummy couldn't get through to you. You've had her worried sick. She even had her house girl bring her here and she still couldn't find you.

Teju I didn't know.

Segun You would have known if you looked at your phone! Getting an elderly woman to come chasing after you. For what? You only responded to my messages when I said I'd booked my flights. Which kind of rubbish be this, Teju?

Teju I needed to talk to you.

Segun Talk? Talk koh? I had to book off work. Pay through my nose! What was so important that you couldn't just tell me over the phone?

Teju I couldn't . . . I couldn't do this over the phone.

Segun Do what? Teju?

Teju (*beat*) Wunmi has left me.

Segun Wunmi?

Beat.

OK. Why?

Teju She was upset. I . . . I did something.

Segun I didn't know I'd be flying over from London to be doing marriage counsellor! I thought it was an emergency. You said your life was in danger –

Teju It is.

Segun What did you do?

Teju I . . . I went somewhere.

Segun To where? Ah-ah! Teju, why are you snailing my time?

Teju I'm trying, Segun. This thing no be easy to say –

Segun (*beat*)   Did you have a mistress? Because that thing . . . that one be small small. Hey! In this country it's strange if you no fi get mistress. I'm not saying I approve. Wumi is a good woman. She deserves better. But this is not so much now! So much to be calling me over, to travel na London.

Teju   No be small ting wey I go talk, Segun –

Segun   Then weytin be the problem?

Teju (*beat*)   I'm sorry.

Segun   For what? Please, Teju! Just tell me what is going on. Are you in trouble?

Teju *nods.*

Segun   What's wrong? What's happened?

Teju   I go tell you.

Segun   Good!

Teju   But you have to . . . I need you to just sit there and not talk. Do you understand? Do not say anything. OK?

Segun   Why not?

Teju   Please, Segun. Please.

Segun   Alright.

Pause.

Teju   Do you know the Stone Bar, just up the highway, near Victoria bridge?

Segun *goes to speak then simply nods.*

Teju   On Sunday, I was there.

Beat.

I just went in for one drink. Wunmi and I had fought. We're always fighting these days. If I'm honest, I can barely look at her sometimes.

I was at this bar having a drink, just minding my own, not looking for anything. When this man, he came and took the seat right next to me. There were many other places for him to sit. I did not look for him oh! But somehow . . . he found me.

He had very high cheekbones. Fair skin. We spoke for a while. He was funny! It didn't feel like we were just meeting. It was like we had known ourselves for a long time. He kept calling me 'my brother', 'my brother'. I liked it. But also . . . it didn't feel right to me somehow.

After we'd been talking for a while, he invited me to this party. 'Private party,' he said. 'Very private.' And he winked at me. I swear, Segun, I didn't know what that wink meant. I didn't know. But, I can't tell you why, I left my car and I followed him there.

This party, it was in a hotel. And there were many, many men there. Just men. All different ages. I thought this was a little strange but Wale – that was his name – he had such reassuring eyes. He offered to buy me a drink and I said yes. And as he walked to the bar I noticed that there were a couple of men behind him, to his left, who were . . . kissing. Out in the open.

I felt afraid for them. I didn't know how they'd forgotten themselves like this! I checked to see if anyone else had seen them and . . . It was everywhere. Pairs of men: holding hands, dancing, slow, with their arms around each other. One man was just stroking the back of his lover's head, on the sofa, looking into his eyes. It felt like I was looking into their living room.

I couldn't believe it. Right here in Lagos! So many men like this.

Beat.

Like me.

Wale came back. He smiled at me, gave me my drink and, with the other hand, led me to the dance floor. He was looking at me so deeply. Like he could see into my future. My past. As if he could see everything I'd ever denied myself and longed for and lost, all in one moment. He pulled me in closer. We were dancing now. Chest to chest.

I hadn't been touched by a man like that. Not since university. Not since . . .

I think he was about to . . .

Then we heard the shouting. We all heard it, before we saw. The police came in. So many of them. They were screaming so loud. Shouting words I won't repeat. It was biblical.
Beating us – three men to one: battered on the floor. I tried to run. One of the men from the sofa, he was bleeding on the ground. From his head, I think. It didn't look like he was moving.

And I couldn't find Wale. As I ran, I searched for him. But I couldn't find him. He let go my hand, as soon as we heard the voices. Before I knew what was happening. The music kept playing. I can still hear the song. It was 'High-life'. So sweet. In all the screaming, the running, the beating, the music kept playing. I couldn't find him anywhere. Then I felt the blow. Hard. To the back of my head.

When I woke, I was in jail. They put me in for the night. I had to call Wunmi to come and collect me. The police told her why I'd been arrested. And . . . well, after she came to get me, she dropped me off here, didn't say a word and left. I haven't seen her since.

Beat.

The sound of static.

Scene Nine

The North Star.

Yetunde Did you hear all that?

Babatunde Every word.

Adebisi So he's from the present?

Babatunde That isn't possible.

Yetunde Teju? Do you understand us?

Adebisi He must be. He must have only just died.

Yetunde I'm so glad you've come. I'm so very glad you're here.

Babatunde That doesn't make any sense.

Yetunde We have an opportunity here. You've ascended to the afterlife. Do you understand me?

Adebisi Why wasn't he sent to Orun re-re?

Yetunde You've bypassed your resting place to come and make this vote.

Babatunde This must be a mistake.

Yetunde The gods do not make mistakes. Omotara is getting married. Your niece. Much beloved. She's getting married to the woman she loves and we're here to decide whether to bless the wedding.

Adebisi Babatunde and I are voting no.

Yetunde But with your vote, and Tara's will, it doesn't matter. We can go ahead and bless it.

Adebisi This is unfair!

Yetunde How?

Adebisi He's not supposed to be here! The gods wouldn't send him here straight from death.

Babatunde Plus, he's biased.

Yetunde No he's not!

Babatunde I'm sorry, Yetunde, but he is, you know he is. He's . . . you know, one of them.

Yetunde And so? Are you not biased yourself? Don't we all have personal affinities? Misguided and well informed.

Divine and damned. Just and unjust. Tejumade here knows his mind. Don't you? You know what is right. I know speaking is difficult but, please, just nod your head for me. That's enough.

Adebisi No, he'd need to say it. Verbally.

Yetunde That's not what you said before!

Babatunde Well, things have changed.

Yetunde What is wrong with you? You are her ancestors, you're meant to be her divine protectors. How can you withhold her right like this?

Adebisi This blessing is not her right.

Yetunde It is! It's their chance for happiness and good fortune. To harmony. Everyone deserves that.

Adebisi Not everyone, Yetunde.

Yetunde We cannot leave their love to the wilds of fate! It may not survive.

Adebisi If it was for *everyone* the gods would give it to them automatically. They wouldn't need us! There'd be no council of guidance, no summoning, no vote –

Teju I vote . . . no.

Yetunde What?

Babatunde What did he say?

Teju I said, I vote no.

Interval.

Scene Ten

The North Star.

Yetunde (*beat*)   What do you mean you vote no?

Teju   I vote no.

Babatunde   But . . .

Yetunde   Kilonshe?

Adebisi   I know I should be pleased but . . . I can't say I'm not surprised!

Yetunde   Do you understand what we're asking you?

Teju   Yes.

Yetunde   Then how could you do this?

Adebisi   Maybe, despite his preferences, he respects the sanctity of marriage.

Yetunde   You don't need to do this.

Adebisi   The union intended between a man and a woman.

Yetunde   We're not in Aiye anymore Teju. There's no need to pretend here. We have the power to change Omotara's future. Why don't you want her to be happy?

Teju   I don't want her to struggle. This marriage. It'll only end in heartache.

Yetunde   No. It doesn't have to. Things are different for her.

Adebisi   To be honest . . . it doesn't really matter why he's voted. The point is he's voted. It's over. We are not blessing the wedding!

Yetunde   Teju, please.

Adebisi   Which *means* we can finally leave this place and get back to Orun-re-re!

Babatunde   Thanks the gods!

Yetunde   Please reconsider.

Teju   What is the afterlife like?

Yetunde (*beat*)   What?

Teju   You said that this isn't it. This is in-between. What's it like?

Babatunde   It's . . . it's . . .

Adebisi   Nice.

Babtunde   If you've just died.

Adebisi   Yes, it's very peaceful.

Yetunde   Teju, let's stay on topic.

Babatunde   It's a bit like a hotel.

Teju What?

Adebisi What's a hotel?

Babatunde It's comfortable! Luxurious even, but people are always saying you wouldn't want to stay there for ever.

Adebisi No.

Babatunde We're looking forward to returning to earth. To Aiye.

Adebisi Well, most of us are!

Teju I didn't think it would be like this. I was preparing myself for . . . I braved myself for hell.

Yetunde What happened to you, Teju?

Babatunde Ah! You don't need to tell us. I'm sure it's a painful memory to recall.

Yetunde Can you show us?

Babatunde Let's just get you back to Orun. Safe and sound.

The sound of static.

Babatunde No!

Yetunde Thank you.

Adebisi Not this again. Ah-ah! I don tire.

Yetunde Too bad.

Adebisi But –

Yetunde You better shut up your mouth!

Scene Eleven

The sound of static. Back to Lagos, Nigeria, some weeks before.

Segun Can I talk now?

Teju Yes.

Pause.

Segun You got out of jail.

Teju Yes.

Segun So that's it.

Teju No, Segun. They're asking for money.

Segun Who are?

Teju The police. They said if I give them the money, they will drop the charges and they won't take it to trial.

Segun (*beat*) How much are they asking for?

Teju Five million.

Segun Five million Naira?!

Teju Yes, Segun –

Segun That's big money, Teju.

Teju I know.

Segun And this is why you called?

Teju I didn't know what else to do.

Segun You'd be better off finding that money and using it on a lawyer, my brother.

Teju I can't –

Segun You would be fine in trial. Being there isn't illegal. It's just . . . it's just if you were having . . . doing –

Teju If I was engaged in homosexual acts.

Segun Yes. So they can't prove anything. You can't be convicted for dancing! If that's true? If that's all you were doing?

Teju It's not about being convicted, Segun. This is Nigeria. If I'm up for trial, I'm guilty. It becomes public. I could lose my job. I may already have lost Wunmi. I can't go to trial, Segun. It would ruin me.

Segun Five million Naira?

Teju Yes.

Segun That's over ten thousand pounds, Teju.

Teju I'm not asking you to give me the money.

Segun (*beat*) Then what exactly am I doing here, Teju? Why have you dragged me halfway across the world?

Teju I want to escape.

Segun Eh?

Teju I need your help. I want to come to London.

Segun (*pause*) Oh.

Teju I'm not afraid of going to jail, Segun. Before any of that comes the beatings. I have seen it before. The face of a man, published in the newspapers. Branded a homosexual. Not two days later you hear that they've been beaten. Within an inch of their life. Sometimes to death. I'm not safe here, Segun. Prison would be horrible but this thing, it could kill me.

Segun Teju –

Teju Let me come to London. I've been reading about seeking asylum. If I can just tell them what's been happening, if I can prove that I'm in danger –

Segun I don't know.

Teju I wouldn't be a burden to you. It would just be for a few months. I wouldn't stay in your house for long.

Segun And then what? What would you do? Get a job? Without a visa? It's not so easy, Teju. You can't just start a new life –

Teju Why can't I? You did.

Segun It's different for me.

Teju How?

Segun I'm a doctor.

Teju So? They no get-ee professor na England?

Segun You'll be lucky to even teach in a primary school. To be a janitor. They don't care for our qualifications na England!

Teju I don't care. Anything is better than this, Segun. Anything would be better than looking over my shoulder. Shaking through my body every time the doorbell rings.

Segun What about Wunmi?

Teju She's already left me to the dogs –

Segun I'll give you the money.

Teju What?

Segun Five million Naira, was it?

Teju Yes, but –

Segun I won't be able to write a cheque but I can transfer the money to my Nigerian account and take it out for you. Just this once.

Teju But it won't be once, Segun. You know the police in this country. Na Lagos! They're ruthless. You think if I give them this money once they wouldn't blackmail me again?

Segun You don't know that –

Teju They'll hold me to ransom for years. For the rest of my life if they want to! Your money won't help me long term.

Segun You can be discreet, can't you? For God's sake, Teju! Just stay away from men like that, this Wale and that your Isaac. These wayward men. Stay away from temptation.

Teju Isaac?

Segun Just pay them the money and keep your head down. Don't go to any parties like that again and everything will be fine. You can call Wunmi, straighten things out. If you weren't doing anything there they can't prove it and the rumours will pass. You can't uproot your whole life because of one foolish party. This thing will blow over. These things always do. Everything will go back to how it was.

Teju Segun, how did you know about Isaac?

Segun You . . . you mentioned him, just now. When you were talking about Wale.

Teju No I didn't. I said university. I didn't mention anyone's name.

Pause.

You knew? All this time. You knew about me and Isaac.

Segun I saw him, one morning, sneaking out of your dormitory. There'd been rumours about it. You two were very close, people would say. You were hardly discreet! I was actually coming to your room to speak to you about it when I saw him.

Teju Did he see you? When did this happen? Did you say anything to him?

Segun Yes, Teju! I told him to stay away from you. I told him to stop carrying on like that with you. Or . . .

Teju Or?

Beat.

Or what Segun?

Segun I said he'd regret it.

Beat.

Teju You threatened him? He never spoke to me again. Never. I thought it was something I'd said or something I'd done.

Segun I was trying to protect you.

Teju He never so much as looked at me again. After waking up together that day. Laughing in the morning. Then silence. Because of you –

Segun It was for the best. Teju, I mean it. God knows where you would be now if I hadn't done it.

Teju I'd be exactly where I am.

Segun What?

Teju But with some company, maybe –

Segun You don't know that.

Teju You want me to keep pretending –

Segun Not pretending, Teju. You don't need to *surrender* to this thing. You have a choice. I'll give you this money. Get the police off of your back.

Teju Then what?

Segun Wunmi will come around.

Teju Then what?!

Segun You just . . . keep your head down.

Teju I don't want your money. You're offering me a plaster when I need surgery. I need to get out. If you don't want to help me then you can leave –

Segun I'm trying to give you five million Naira –

Teju Leave, Segun!

Segun *Five million!*

Teju I mean it, Segun –

Segun You're mad! Just because I won't help you get to London.

Teju *goes to the door.*

Segun I flew across the world for you, with no information, barely a week's notice. I've come here to help you. Like I always do! Bail you out, like I always do –

Teju (*firmly*) I'm asking you to leave.

Segun (*beat*) Alright. I'll call you tomorrow. I'll come by, with the money. In cash. With a good night's sleep, your mind will change.

Teju *is silent.*

Segun Goodbye.

Teju *stands for a moment. Lost.*

Scene Twelve

London, **Tara** *and* **Leah***'s home.*

Tara Hey.

Leah Hi!

Tara How was your day?

Leah You missed it.

Tara What?

Leah The dance rehearsal.

Tara Shit! That was today?

Leah Yeah.

Tara I'm sorry.

Leah   Where were you? I took the afternoon off work.

Tara   Did you still take the lesson?

Leah   No.

Tara   I'm sure you could have! You needed it more than me . . .

Leah   Is that supposed to be funny?

Tara   What's up with you? I've said I'm sorry. It's just a dance.

Leah   It's romantic.

Tara   I know, babe, but it's our wedding day. We could do the Macarena and it'd be romantic.

Leah   You promised.

Tara   And I'm really sorry I missed it. I'll make it up to you.

Leah   What were you doing?

Tara   I was sorting wedding stuff.

Leah   Did you check the seating plan?

Tara   Uh . . . no. I didn't get around to it.

Leah   I left it on the table.

Tara   I'll look at it in a bit.

Leah   What's wrong with you?

Tara   Nothing!

Leah   Can you just check it now, please.

Tara   Looks good to me.

Leah   Properly.

Tara   Fine.

Beat.

Where's the high table?

Leah   All the tables are round.

Tara   So?

Leah   So a round table can't fit on the stage.

Tara   I'm sure we can find a rectangular table somewhere.

Leah   I just . . . without your parents there. It feels . . . exposing.

Tara   So they're not on the seating plan?

Leah   No. They still haven't RSVPed.

Tara Yeah, but they were never going to RSVP.

Leah They're not going to change their minds.

Tara They're African, you don't even need to be invited to a wedding in Nigeria. You just turn up.

Leah I don't think they will, babe.

Tara Well, you don't know that.

Leah I do. They're not coming. We need to move forward as though they're not coming. Or else it'll hold us back.

Tara I need to finish this.

Leah I've tried talking about it and you keep brushing it off. And you don't help! With any of the wedding stuff. I feel like I'm doing all of this alone.

Tara I've been busy!

Leah You've been waiting for them to call. And it's not going to happen.

Tara Leah, can you just leave it?

Leah Do you even want to marry me? Do you even want this?

Tara (*pause*) Yes.

Leah You paused.

Tara So? I'm allowed to pause.

Leah Not when you're sure.

Tara I just, I don't know who's going to be there on my side of the aisle. If they're not there, if they're really not coming, who have I got?

Leah You've got loads of people. All our friends!

Tara *Our* friends. What about mine? Me and mine.

Leah It's not about yours or mine. It's about us! That's the whole point.

Tara I'm not going to have anyone standing behind me. No one's going to be up there with me. I went shopping for my dress today. And I had no one to go with. I had to book an appointment late and Bree couldn't miss work and I couldn't find anything that fit right and I couldn't decide what design I wanted and I looked in the mirror and there was no one standing behind me. There wasn't anyone squealing or crying or drinking Prosecco in the afternoon with me. I didn't have anyone to celebrate with.

Leah You should have said.

Tara It was fine.

Leah I would have come with you.

Tara You know that's not the same.

Leah You should have booked an appointment further in advance.

Tara Leah.

Leah Sorry.

Tara You've got everyone around you. Someone to walk you up the aisle.

Leah You said you didn't want that!

Tara I do! I do want it. I thought I could do it without. But . . . what does it really mean without your family there?

Leah It means you love me and you want us to share a life.

Beat.

Tara?

Tara I can't.

Leah What are you saying? You don't want to do it?

Tara I'm really sorry.

Leah Wow.

Tara What are you doing?

Leah I'm going.

Tara Where?

Leah I don't know. I'll stay at Mischa's.

Tara You can't leave.

Leah You just told me that you wanted to cancel our wedding, Tara.

Tara We can talk about it.

Leah I don't think there's anything else to say.

Tara Don't go.

Leah I'll pick my stuff up in the morning or, God, I don't know, I'll get Mischa to.

Scene Thirteen

The North Star.

Adebisi Wait . . . I don't understand any of this! Why didn't he just take the money?

Yetunde What did you do? Teju? Did you go to London anyway?

Babatunde Yetunde, with respect, if he went to London I don't think he would be here now.

Yetunde I want to hear it from him. How did you die?

Babatunde It doesn't matter. He's dead now and he's voted. We need to go back.

Yetunde   Why did you vote this way? You don't have to.

Babatunde   We must respect his decision.

Yetunde   I can't.

Babatunde   Why not?

Yetunde   I need to understand.

Babatunde   What's wrong with you, Yetunde? Why is this thing pepe-ing you so much?

Yetunde   Why won't you bless this wedding?

Teju   I can't.

Yetunde   What happened to you, Teju?

Teju   He turned his back on me. All that time he knew and he turned away from it. He didn't want it near him.

Yetunde   But you could have still travelled to London?

Teju   For what?

Yetunde   For your safety. For a better life!

Teju   Without Segun it was too hard. I wouldn't have anywhere to live. Nowhere to go. They would have put me in a detention centre. I couldn't work and I couldn't receive any money while I waited for my asylum claim. I would have just been moving from one cage to another.

Yetunde   He might have changed his mind.

Teju   No. That day I realized. He thought just like my father. Him and Segun were the same. Daddy always knew. I know it. He would have beaten it out of me if he could.

Yetunde   What did you do after your brother left you?

Teju   I went back to the Stone Bar. Every night. For weeks. I kept hoping Wale would come in. I thought, somehow, he'd know to meet me there, and he'd come for me. It felt obvious. Maybe we could run away together? Start a new life. It was foolish. I didn't even know him. The police kept coming around, hassling me for money. I felt as if everyone knew, or if they didn't, the news would travel soon. I stopped going to work. Definitely couldn't go to church. I only left the house to go to the bar. Hoping. Started drinking. Wale never came. I didn't know where to go. Once, I even went to the hotel, where the raid happened. I sat at the reception for hours. I was so alone.

Yetunde   It's not like that for Omotara.

Teju   No. But you can't get far in this life without your family behind you.

Yetunde   You can.

Teju   I don't want this for her.

Yetunde It's not easy, but you can!

Teju It isn't worth it. I don't want her to be like me. Living in fear. Getting beaten in the streets.

Yetunde She won't.

Teju You're telling me people like us don't catch beatings for London?

Yetunde She won't be alone! Did they come for you? Is that why you're doing this?

Babatunde You don't have to answer that.

Yetunde He does! Teju! How did you die?

The sound of static rises very quickly. The Ancestors are still. Then the static becomes one high pitch note and cuts to silence. The Ancestors turn and look at **Teju**.

Scene Fourteen

London, **Tara** *and* **Leah***'s home.*

Mosun It's very small, isn't it?

Tara Mum.

Mosun You'd think you could afford a bigger place by now! You're nearly thirty.

Tara We've had to save a lot. For the wedding.

Mosun Right. Are you renting?

Tara Yeah.

Mosun Pouring your money down the drain.

Beat.

Who's your caterer?

Tara What? Uh . . . Aunty Gloria.

Mosun Hmm. Good luck. That woman will rob you blind!

Tara What are you doing here?

Mosun Your father sent me.

Tara OK. Why?

Mosun Where is she?

Tara Leah?

Mosun Yes.

Tara She's not here.

Mosun Is she at work?

Tara I don't know. I don't know where she is.

Mosun Who puts your shelves up?

Tara What?

Mosun Who does the gardening?

Tara We don't have a garden!

Mosun What do you do when a chair breaks?

Tara We have a balcony but –

Mosun Or your toilet's clogged?

Tara What? We fix it. One of us fixes it.

Mosun You need a man around the house.

Tara Dad doesn't do any of those things!

Mosun That's because we can afford to get someone to do it for us. By the looks of things, you can't.

Tara Did you want to say something? Or did you just come here to take the piss?

Mosun Yes. Your uncle died.

Tara Oh. Right. Which one?

Mosun Uncle Teju.

Tara What? How? He's younger than Dad.

Mosun I just thought I should tell you.

Tara He can't be dead.

Mosun He is.

Tara How did he die?

Mosun He killed himself.

Tara What? Mum. Are you serious?

Mosun Yes, Omo. The police found him at a gay party in Lagos and then, when your daddy refused to give him the money to pay them off and move to London, he took himself to the outskirts of a little village near Warri and topped himself apparently. Took them days to find him. Agbaya!

Tara A gay party?

Mosun Their mother is in pieces. This will probably finish her off, poor woman. Your father's going to have to fly over there again to take care of her. And Wunmi!

Tara He's gay?

Mosun   Was. Yes, he was gay.

Tara   Did you know?

Mosun   We didn't know for sure. Your dad always had his suspicions but he married! We thought he'd put it all behind him. Sounds like he shot himself on the road side. Miles away from the village. From Lagos! What a mess. I feel sorry for the person who found him like that. And the talk! That's the worst thing. Your grandmother is having to fend off so many questions. The whole neighbourhood is spreading rumours about him. About their family. It must be awful.

Tara   Why didn't you tell me?

Mosun   It was none of our business. It only would have encouraged you.

Tara   What do you mean? It's not infectious! He couldn't make me more gay.

Mosun   You had a choice.

Tara   What?

Mosun   You could have chosen something else.

Tara   This isn't about me.

Mosun   You said you were bisexual! You didn't need to do this thing.

Tara   That's not true.

Mosun   You're my only one! You're all I have. I sacrificed everything for you. To come here and look how you repay me.

Tara   I can't live my life indebted to you!

Mosun   And why not?

Tara   Because it's ridiculous!

Mosun   I'm your mother. You owe me everything.

Tara   Not this. Not who or how I love.

Mosun   You shouldn't live like this! See what happened to your uncle. This thing, it never ends well.

Tara   I think you should go.

Mosun   No, Omo, we need to talk about the funeral. The travel.

Tara   I'm not going. I'm not going anywhere with you.

Mosun   You mean you're going to miss your uncle's funeral? This is important. This is family.

Tara   I can't go there with you. If that's how he died. I don't want to.

Mosun   Well, your father will be very disappointed.

Tara   I don't care.

Mosun   Eh?

Tara About either of you. About what either of you think.

Mosun What do you mean?

Tara I'd like you to leave, Mum.

Mosun You're being very rude.

Tara I'd really like you to go.

Mosun Alright.

Tara Hope you have a safe flight.

Mosun It means we'll miss it.

Tara What?

Mosun The wedding. We thought you could come back early. But your father and I, we'll need to stay on. We weren't going to come to the wedding anyway but . . . I just wanted to say . . .

Tara OK. That's fine. It doesn't matter now.

Mosun Yes.

Beat.

Don't let Gloria charge you extra for doing nothing!

Tara OK.

Mosun That woman is a viper.

Tara Yes, Mum.

Mosun And make sure to take lots of pictures.

Tara I will. We will.

Mosun Good.

Tara Bye, Mum.

Mosun Bye, darling. I love you.

Tara Yeah.

Scene Fifteen

London, outside Mischa's home.

Tara Lee?

Leah Fucking hell.

Tara Sorry!

Leah You scared the shit out of me!

You can't just lurk outside my house, Mischa's house, like that –

Tara I wasn't lurking –

Leah How long have you been here?

Tara Only like . . . ten minutes.

Leah This is messed up, T.

Tara I'm sorry. I know you said you needed some space but –

Leah So you turn up outside my house?

Tara Mischa's house.

Leah You better hope she's not in. She's not your biggest fan right now.

Tara Mischa?

Leah She thinks you've messed me around.

Tara Fuck Mischa.

Leah Tara!

Tara (*beat*) I hate Mischa.

Leah She's my maid of honour!

Tara She's your ex-girlfriend!

Leah We're lesbians. We stay friends with our ex-girlfriends. It's normal –

Tara It is not normal. I'm not friends with any of my ex-girlfriends –

Leah That's because you don't have any ex-girlfriends!

Beat.

What are you doing here?

Tara Did you get my messages?

Leah I *saw* them. I haven't listened to them because, like I've *said*, I'm trying to take some space.

Tara My uncle died.

Leah What?

Tara My uncle Teju. Suicide.

Leah Oh my God.

Tara That was why I was calling –

Leah Tara, I'm so sorry.

Tara I found out . . . my mum told me he was gay.

Leah (*beat*) What?

Tara Yeah. He was gay . . . and I didn't know. The police found out. He was up for trial over there.

Leah In Nigeria? Jesus.

Tara I feel like if I'd known I could have helped him.

Leah You don't know that.

Tara If they'd told me.

Leah I don't think things are ever that simple, babe.

Tara All this time, I had someone I could talk to. In my own family and I didn't even know. If someone had told me, maybe he would have felt less alone.

Leah There was probably a lot of other stuff going on for him. Just because you didn't know, doesn't mean that if you had you could have *saved* him. That's not how any of this works.

Tara I feel like I've lost him twice. Like I'm mourning a relationship I never had.

Leah I'm sorry.

Tara Yeah.

Pause.

I miss you. I'm so sorry about everything. I was an idiot.

Leah No.

Tara I want to marry you. I do. I don't give a shit what my parents think, whether they come or not.

Leah We can't do this now.

Tara I mean it, Lee.

Leah Babe.

Tara I can't lose you.

Leah You won't.

Tara I don't want to end up like him.

Leah You're in shock. You're grieving. I don't want to make this huge decision in the wake of all of this. I don't want it to be a knee-jerk reaction –

Tara It's not.

Leah You don't know that.

Tara Yes I do.

Leah I said I needed space and that hasn't changed. I'm sorry.

Tara Please! I need you.

Leah But there are things I need! Things that . . . I don't know if I'm getting them from you.

Tara What are you talking about?

Leah I just . . . I spent so many months waiting for you to suck it up and tell your family about me. About our wedding. And the moment you finally did, you freaked out and call it off!

Tara And I've said I'm sorry!

Leah I know, but . . .

Tara What do you want me to do? Do you want me to beg? I'll get down on my knees. Whatever you want. I want this.

Leah I'm sorry about your uncle. It's awful. I can't imagine! I'm not trying to hurt you. But these aren't the right circumstances for starting again.

Tara Why not?

Leah Because we can't get married because your uncle died. We can't do that. I still need some space. I love you and I'm so glad you came. I want to be there for you. You can call me anytime. But we just can't get back together like this.

Tara But we will get back together? Eventually?

Pause.

Leah I'll talk to you soon. Call anytime.

Tara (*beat*) OK.

Leah *exits.*

Scene Sixteen

London, the Akindeji home.

Tara Why didn't you tell me?

Segun Omo.

Tara You made me think I was the only one. My whole life!

Segun I'm sorry. I don't have time right now. I need to organize my flights. The funeral.

Tara You made me feel like I was different from everyone!

Segun This isn't about you, Omotara. My brother has just died!

Tara You made me think that there was something wrong with me. That I was wrong!

Segun You are! It is!

Tara There we go.

Segun I'm busy right now.

Tara You've finally said it!

Segun This isn't the time for this.

Tara You always made out like you were the more tolerant one. But you're worse than Mum! At least she wears it on her sleeve. Why didn't you help him? Mum said he was on trial.

Segun I did! I offered him money.

Tara Why didn't you bring him here?

Segun It wasn't a good idea.

Tara Why not?

Segun I was doing what I thought was best.

Tara You thought it was best for him to stay in a country where his existence wasn't legal?

Segun It was just one party, Tara! One mistake in over twenty years. I thought he could restrain himself –

Tara It wasn't about a party, Dad. If Uncle Teju was gay, he wasn't safe there.

Segun He wasn't gay!

Tara What? Mum said.

Segun He wasn't! He'd just slipped up, once – in the past. And again, with this party. I thought if he worked hard enough, he could put it behind him.

Tara Wow.

Segun He didn't need to do it again, Omo! He could repair his marriage. Start afresh. He had a choice.

Tara I can't believe you!

Segun This was just a setback.

Tara Why would he choose it? Why? In Nigeria. Where he could be sent to jail – beaten to death. Why would he choose to be gay?

Segun I don't know! I didn't understand –

Tara Even if you didn't understand it, you could have helped him. Let him back come to London with you.

Segun It was too much! I had just arrived in Lagos, that day. And, with no warning, my brother was telling me that he was gay and that he wanted to come to London, to start a new life. If he came here, he'd become someone else. Someone I didn't recognize. I didn't want him living that kind of lifestyle on my doorstep. In my house. What would I have told people? The people at church?

Tara   What lifestyle? You mean my lifestyle?

Segun   No.

Tara   You thought if you left him in Nigeria it would all go away. And you wouldn't have to deal with it. Just like with me. You didn't want to look at it.

Segun   I only wanted what was best.

Tara   You wanted what was best for you! For your reputation. You were trying to keep it a secret to protect yourself!

Segun   I was protecting him!

Tara   And how did that work out?

Segun   It's not safe, Omo! Anywhere. It's not safe for you to be like this. I was trying to protect my family! That was all I wanted. To stop him putting himself in danger.

Tara   You put him in danger, Dad! You kept him in danger. Your silence is dangerous! Do you understand that? You isolated him. Drove him to desperation. Whatever Uncle Teju was, whatever he felt for other men, it wasn't something he had to restrain in himself. It shouldn't have mattered to you. If he'd come here he would have been safe. And because you couldn't face up to the truth of who he was, he's dead.

Segun's *breathing becomes erratic.*

Because of you, he's dead.

It becomes clear that he's having a panic attack.

Dad? Are you ok? Dad, sit down.

She holds his hand.

It's going to be alright. Just breathe, Daddy. Deep breaths. Breathe slowly.

Eventually he settles.

Segun   It keeps happening. Your mother thinks it's because I haven't slept. Since the news came. Every time the phone rings, I can't breathe. It feels like it's all happening again.

Tara   With Uncle Teju?

Segun   Yes. When they said it. It was so matter of fact. The way they told me. He's gone. What have I done, Omo? I turned my back on him. On my own brother. I killed him.

Tara   No.

Segun   I did!

Tara I'm sorry. I'm sorry I said that.

Segun Whenever I try to sleep, I see his face on the day that I left him. I left him there to die.

She takes him in her arms.

Tara It's alright, Dad. It's going to be alright.

He smiles. Gathers himself.

Segun Your mother says you're not coming with us. For the funeral.

Tara No.

Segun Because of the wedding?

Tara Not exactly. The wedding's off. I think maybe Leah and I are over.

Segun Oh.

Beat.

I'm sorry to hear that.

Tara Are you?

Segun Yes, really. Do you still love her? Do you want her back?

Tara Yeah. But I think it's too hard. I've not been who I should have been in our relationship, because of all of this.

Segun She'll come around.

Tara I don't think so.

Segun We'll see.

Scene Seventeen

The North Star.

Babatunde It's over, Yetunde.

Yetunde No.

Teju I'm sorry, ma.

Adebisi The eyes of the gods are upon us.

Yetunde This doesn't have to be how it ends.

Adebisi Once his stone is cast, we will be delivered into Orun-re-re in a matter of minutes.

Yetunde No!

Adebisi Stop it, Yetunde. You're corrupting our vote.

Yetunde It's people like you that did this to him.

Adebisi How dare you.

Babatunde We need to take him home. He's been through enough.

Yetunde You're the reason.

Babatunde He needs to rest.

Yetude Teju, you must not do this thing.

Babatunde Yetunde.

Yetunde Please.

Babatunde Let it go.

Teju I'm doing what's best. I don't want her to end up like me.

Yetunde She won't.

Teju Perhaps if I hadn't tried it, with Isaac. If we hadn't been together. Then maybe I wouldn't have got a taste for it.

Yetunde That's not how it works, Teju.

Teju How would you know?

Yetunde I . .

Teju I'm trying to take care of my niece.

Yetunde You don't even know her fiancée!

Adebisi Look, we're splitting donkey's hairs. Save your breath. We're going back to our rest.

Teju You wouldn't understand.

Yetunde I wouldn't?

Teju No, you wouldn't.

Yetunde Teju, you need to change your vote.

Teju Why?

Yetunde Because . . . because . . . (*A beat.*)

She begins to stamp. Rhythmic and urgent, as she did in the beginning.

Teju What is she doing?

Babatunde Oh no.

Adebisi Here we go!

Yetunde
  Back when, way back
  Way back, way back when
  When I lived, I lived with –

Teju Is she alright?

Yetunde
  Before, before
  They scatter our ways.

Teju What is she doing?

Adebisi We don't know. But whatever it is, it's not going to work, Yetunde!

Yetunde
  Before, before
  They set foot in Nigeria.

Babatunde The gods will be coming for us soon. It's a waste of your –

Yetunde
  Before, before the white man came.
  In my time. My time.
  My time

Beat.

  It was different then,
  We were sacred then.

  Back then, way back
  Way back, way back then
  Way back when I lived, I lived with
  My shadow.

  My shadow, they called her.
  The people of my village.
  Of my small, small village.
  The people, they called her
  My shadow.

  When the sun go rise, when the sun go sink
  We went hand in hand, til the sky went pink

  Back then, way back,
  Way back, way back then
  Way back when I lived,
  When I lived I loved her.

Teju What are you talking about?

Yetunde I'm talking about my time, Teju. In my time, there was none of this ye-ye oyinbo judgement. In my time there were boy-brides of Sango. Boy-brides! The god of thunder himself would take boy-brides in his ceremonies!

Babatunde That is different. That was for religious practices –

Yetunde (*quoting her own song*)
  It was different then,
  We were sacred then.

  People like us, we were sacred then.

Babatunde You're telling us you're gay?

Yetunde (*beat*) They did not have this word in my time.

Teju You're like me.

Yetunde Yes, Teju. I'm like you and Omotara. In my time, women would take women for husbands.

Adebisi That's not true.

Yetunde In my time, in my Nigeria, before it was even called Nigeria, we understood: You go want who you go want.

Adebisi I don't believe you. Polygamy, yes, but –

Babatunde Why didn't you tell us?

Yetunde I didn't want you to think I was biased. For the blessing. I didn't want you to try and take my vote away.

Adebisi She's lying!

Yetunde When the white man came with his missionaries and puritanical nonsense, it scattered our people. They polluted our ways. They stopped us from being who we were, who we *are*, from loving who we love. They tried to stamp out our ways, our rituals, our beliefs. They scraped our culture with their dirty nails and it's still bleeding today.

Adebisi Homosexuality, in our people, it was never accepted!

Yetunde Who you think go write your history book, Ade?

Adebisi I'm not listening to this rubbish. I'm going to the edge, see if the gods have left a trail for us.

Yetunde (*forcefully*)
  Fire doesn't crackle
  It dey roar, it dey roar
  No dey crackle am, crackle
  It dey roar, it dey roar.

  Back when, way back
  When the first, the first
  The first of them came
  When they first made settle
  On the *edge* of our land,
  On the *edge* of our village.
  Just the edge of our land.

They were kind, so it seemed,
They were kind. O, they were kind
So it seemed, they were kind.

They were spreading their word,
'The word of God'. Through interpreters,
Telling of 'The word of their God'.

And slowly, slowly, the people dem change.
The people, my people,
the people dem change.

Our elders, they tried
To stop, to stop
Stop the tide of the people
As they began then to change.
But the talk of our customs,
Of our blood, of our soil
Speaks much, much softer
Than the brimstone and hell.

Me and my shadow, we stayed close to our home,
As we felt the tides turning, we stayed close to our home.
We ground our yams and we harvested our wheat,
We prayed to our gods, then massaged each other's feet.

Back then, when we made love then,
As we felt the tides change
It became, not for pleasure,
Not for pleasure anymore.
Not for pleasure, no more pleasure,
Not for pleasure anymore.
But for hot reassurance as we felt our lives slip.

As we felt the tides change, 'neath the soles of our feet.
We made full-bodied, head-back, sweet-sweat love.
Such full-bodied, head-back, sweet-sweat love.

*

On the night when they came, they did not play the drums.
Like when we sacrificed a ram or a goat to the gods.
On the night when they came for us, they did not play the drums.
No they did not play the drums, they did not play the drums.

I *heard* the fire before I smelt it, I smelt it –
I *smelt* the fire before I saw it, I saw it –
I *saw* the fire before I felt it, I felt it –
I felt it, I felt it – O gods how I felt it!
I saw it, I saw it tearing through our home.

Mine and Funmilao's home,
My shadow and me,
Just our ordinary home.

Ohhh, fire no dey crackle,
It dey roar, it dey roar
No dey crackle am, crackle
It dey roar, it dey roar.

They had us surrounded,
The white men at the front.
Rallying their troops,
Of the people that we loved.

And I looked into her eyes,
As the fire it dey catch,
As the smoke it go rise,
As our throats it go touch.

I looked into her eyes,
Amidst the panic,
Between our screams.
And I knew she would not run.
She would not run, she would not run.

Outside to them
She would not do it.
She would not run, she would not run.
Outside to them.
Surrender.
She would not do it.
So nor would I.

And we held each other, as the flames licked our feet.
And we screamed chest to chest, in the caustic heat.
We held each other as our house burnt down,
As our life and our dreams, they were razed to the ground.

We held on to each other
In defiance, as we died.

When it was over, our spirits rose
With the smoke, to the sky.

Babatunde You never told us. I thought you died from disease.

Yetunde I did. Na Hatred now. You no dey hear? Powerful sickness. It swept through my village and killed me. And my love.

Teju Where is she now?

Yetunde Funmi? She's in Orun-re-re.

Teju Do you ever see her?

Yetunde No.

Teju Why not?

Yetunde It's not really a place for . . .

Babatunde It's a place for rest. Solitary. Quiet. It's not built for companionship and all its bloody humanity. For bickering or laughter or –

Yetunde Touch.

Babatunde Yes.

Yetunde That's for us to find in Aiye again. When we return.

Teju Then why haven't you?

Yetunde We are waiting.

Adebisi For what?

Babatunde Is that why you've never applied for reincarnation?

Adebisi What are you waiting for?

Yetunde We want to go back when we can be together, truly together. Like before. On our own land. On our own soil. We want to go back when the sickness has passed.

Adebisi Oh.

Teju Right.

Yetunde Teju, I want us to bless this wedding. I want to give Omotara a chance at the life I couldn't have, the life we couldn't have. Please. *Please.*

Pause.

Adebisi I vote to bless the wedding.

Yetunde What?

Adebisi I've changed my mind.

Babatunde I vote to bless it too.

Yetunde (*beat*) Why?

Adebisi (*beat*) Tara deserves more than what the stars laid out for you. For you both.

Yetunde Thank you.

Teju Well . . . it doesn't matter how I vote now!

Yetunde But we care how you vote. All the same.

Pause.

Yetunde Teju? What do you think?

Teju I can't. I can't vote for this. I'm sorry.

Adebisi (*suddenly*) Hello!

Babatunde Eh?

Yetunde Why not?

Adebisi How are you?

Babatunde Ade, this isn't really the time to be making small talk.

Adebisi How's life after death treating you?

Beat.

This is weird. But you were the one . . .

Tara *enters and says this with* **Adebisi** *in unison.*

Tara *and* **Adebisi** That told me Yoruba people used to speak to their dead. Still do. So that's what I'm doing. I hope you can hear me.

Babatunde What's going on?

Tara I want to ask you so many questions! I have so much to ask you about.

Yetunde She's speaking to us.

Tara I want to know when you first knew . . .

Yetunde (*to* **Teju**) A descendant calling upon the dead!

Tara And I want talk to you about Leah. I wish I talked to you about her when you were here. I want to ask you what I can do to get her back and tell you about the first time I kissed a girl and ask you how it felt when you realized you were gay. I want to ask whether it felt like you were coming home to yourself. Or if it felt like a betrayal.

I want to ask how you knew and if you ever loved anyone and how it felt when you died and why you did it and if I could have helped!

I want to . . . I want to talk to you. But this isn't really the same.

Teju *goes to touch her.* **Yetunde***, kindly, stops him.*

Tara I've really fucked things up with Leah! You'd love her I think. I wish you could have met. I wish I'd told you about her sooner. Maybe if you'd known, it would have made you feel less alone. Did you feel alone? I don't know how to show her I'm serious. I wouldn't have cared what Mum and Dad said. If I had your blessing! That's the funny thing. If I'd known. It wouldn't have mattered.

Pause.

Yetunde Teju? It's not too late.

Teju Yes. I vote to bless the marriage. I take my stone and I cast it down for love.

Adebisi   Praise the gods!

Teju   For the life I never had.

Yetunde   But the life that could be.

Beat.

Next time.

Babatunde   That is very nice but . . . the wedding's off. All our dilly-dallying here has scuppered things for them in Aiye. It's not happening. How can we bless them if they're not getting married?

Adebisi   Is there anything we can do?

Yetunde *starts stamping.*

The same rhythm we have heard from her before.

Slowly, the Ancestors all join in. Following **Yetunde***, they surround* **Tara***. The rhythm reaches a climax and suddenly stops.*

Tara   I don't know if this is you Uncle T. But I feel like that star's winking at me.

The Ancestors breathe in. Then, they breathe out. **Leah** *enters.*

Leah (*beat*)   Who are you talking to?

Tara   No one.

Beat.

Hi! I didn't expect to see you. It hasn't been a week yet –

Leah   Your dad came to see me.

Tara   What?

Leah   He booked an appointment at my firm.

Tara   At work?

Leah   Yeah!

Tara   When?

Leah   This morning.

Tara   But he was flying today.

Leah   He said! He was worried he'd miss his flight but apparently talking to me was more important.

Tara   Why? What did he want?

Leah   He wanted to try and get us back together.

Tara   Really? I'm sorry. I didn't ask him to do that.

Leah I didn't think you had.

Beat.

I've missed you.

Tara I've missed you too.

Leah I thought you'd be in touch again. What with your uncle –

Tara I wanted to give you some space, like you asked for.

Leah Oh. Thank you.

Tara (*beat*) I'm sorry.

Leah You don't need to apologize.

Tara I've not held my head up high with you. I thought it was just stuff with my parents but it's everything! Every time we're outside our four walls. I've not been beside you. Properly.

Leah No. You have. I've not been patient! I've been rushing us through our whole relationship. Our first kiss. Our first date. I've been pushing you from day one and it's not fair. I shouldn't have proposed.

Tara But I want you.

Leah And I haven't believed you. After we first kissed and you freaked out. I've been testing you ever since and that's not right. I'm sorry.

Tara It's alright.

Leah Your dad wants us to get married. Promised he'd come back in time for the wedding. He said he wanted to get to know me. Wanted me to be a part of the family.

Tara I want that too.

Leah I'm not sure about marriage though.

Tara Oh.

Leah I don't know if we need to! You're already my family. You're the first person I want to speak to in the morning.

And you're the only person I enjoy arguing with. Bickering with! I love you even when I fucking hate you. That's family! I don't think we need a piece of paper to prove that –

Tara So what are you saying?

Leah Maybe we don't need to do it! I went a bit mad with all the wedding stuff for all the wrong reasons. Probably some internalized hetero-aspiration shit. But we don't need that. We can just . . . be together. *Stay* together. Loudly!

Tara I hear that. But . . . I want to marry you. I want to mention you to people I've just met and call you 'my wife' and I want people to know what you mean to me.

'Girlfriend' just doesn't cut it anymore.

Leah Well, you can still call me your wife! If it's just the title . . .

Tara No, babe, I want all of it. The whole thing! I want to wear the rings and wear the dresses and throw a party that celebrates us. Who we are and all we've been through and how well we take care of each other. I want to take both your hands in mine and vow, before the whole world, that it is my intention to love you forever. I really want that.

Beat.

Do you?

Leah (*beat*) I do.

They kiss. It starts tentative, then becomes rapturous.

Above them the Ancestors begin the ritual.

Yetunde We bless this union in the mighty names of our forefathers,

Babatunde We bless your union with the wisdom of our foremothers,

Yetunde We grant you both favour from the hands of our great forebrothers and foresisters,

Adebisi Our foresiblings and our forebearers.

Teju All of our ancestors behind you. Each day.

Yetunde We pull the planets into alignment, by the power of the gods.

Babatunde We place each star above you to gaze kindly upon your love.

Teju We bless you.

Adebisi We bless you.

Babatunde We bless you.

Yetunde Amin.

*

Babatunde I think our work here is done.

Yetunde Until next time.

Babatunde May I say, it's been a pleasure working with you all.

Yetunde It has?

Babatunde Of course now! What's a little bickering amongst family?

Adebisi Nothing.

Yetunde Well, I hope we meet again. In service to our descendants or in Aiye itself.

Adebisi Whichever, suits me.

Yetunde   We should take Teju to his rest. To Orun-re-re.

Teju (*beat*)   Do you think I will like it?

Babatunde   Yes. It's a place of perfect peace.

Yetunde   It'll get you ready for your return.

Adebisi   Next time, it will be better for you. I'm sure of it.

Beat.

Come on!

Babatunde   I will guide his right arm.

Adebisi   I will guide his left.

Yetunde   And I will order his footsteps. Across the spine of the sky.

Babatunde   The so-called 'Milky Way' –

Adebisi   It's the well-treaded path to eternity Teju –

Yetunde   We'll walk it with you, like we did your father before you.

He turns around. He looks forward. They go.

Epilogue

Tara *steps outside. She is in full Nigerian wedding regalia. In Aso Ebi and gele.*

The wedding reception is still going on indoors. She seems to have come outside for some air.

She looks up at the sky. Takes a moment. With her drink in hand, she lifts it up to the Ancestors.

Pours a libation. Smiles.

Moments later, **Leah** *comes out. Also in aso ebi and gele. She walks up quietly behind her. Hugs her from behind.*

They kiss.

Blackout.

Temi Wilkey on *The High Table*

Temi I hadn't written a play before. I applied for the Royal Court Introduction to Playwriting Group and the ten-page scene that I wrote was a funny version of my coming out; it was actually really funny, because it was actually a really funny situation, but also horrific, my parents didn't respond very well. I got into the group and then I had to write a full play. So, I wrote the first draft of *The High Table* for that. At the time of the first draft, I was in a relationship with someone that I thought I would probably end up marrying, but I didn't feel like I could have a conversation with my family about them. Also, the conversation is quite interesting, where I think a lot of African parents or family members living in this country are sort of broadly OK with some people being gay but 'not in my house' was the sort of vibe I got from my family. I used to babysit for these two queer women who are married, and my mum was really fine about that because you know, 'I know Gee, she's at my work, but not you.'[1] I thought it was a really interesting, contentious, position to be put in, and I thought it might make a good play.

Rikki Did you anticipate the audience response? The audience response every night was ecstatic for that play, people got up and danced at the end, it was a complete and utter celebration. Did you expect it? Did you envisage it? Did you feel that when you were writing it?

Temi I knew that I wanted to end it with the Electric Slide when I first wrote the scene where they do the Electric Slide.[2] But when I was speaking to the director Dan [Daniel Bailey] about it we were like it's almost like you have to make the play good enough that people will do that. So, I didn't really anticipate that. I spent a lot of time in the run-up to it being on worrying that Black people would hate it, that queer people would hate it, that Black queer people would hate it, I don't really know why but it was just I was just so sure that I would let down all the communities that I was somewhat representing. There was a hope that that would be the response but I don't think I really thought it could happen. Or I did, you know, it's that the gap between the critic part of yourself as a writer and the fantasist dreamer part of your brain. So I think the critic didn't think it was possible but the fantasist was always hoping that would be the response. I guess the play's written to hopefully elicit that.

Mojisola Brazil has come into the conversation through Topher and Travis, Zimbabwe through Tonderai and reference to Jamaica through Rikki; of course, right now we are in the diaspora – Vancouver, Berlin, London. But we're really interested to hear more about that connection and the importance of ourselves as Black queer diasporic creatures, and the place of Africa, ritual, tradition and Yoruba culture in *The High Table*.

Temi I really love what Tonderai was saying about making work to heal yourself and heal others and I feel like that's a big part of why I wrote the play. When I was asked earlier about why I wrote the play, I was, like, 'I don't know, you just write don't you.' But actually it is mainly to heal yourself; and I feel like when you write it sends you on

---

1 The name has been changed.
2 A line dance that has regained popularity at parties where it's performed to Cameo's song 'Candy'.

a journey towards the things that you don't know that you need and I feel like I needed, without knowing, some kind of connection to my ancestry and connection to rituals that were wiped away by colonialism; but then also a deeper understanding about the relationship between queerness and colonialism. And that's the sort of Ghanaian image of the Sankofa where you look back to go forward. I think in something that I'm trying to write at the moment, in the sense that, when you're mourning something that you've lost because colonialism has had such a huge impact on the cultures and their rituals and the identity that even within specific African countries aren't able to hold on to. But then also the celebration, the joy of creating something else and creating a new culture, and I think that's why the Electric Slide was such a big part of the play, because it's our own tradition, it's our own diasporic tradition.

Rikki Were you tapping into the queerness of ancient mythologies? Because there's a lot of gender shifting, and queer connections, queer romances and passions and crimes that happened between the gods and legendary figures in mythologies. Was that a big part of what you were looking at?

Temi Yeah, there's a line in *The High Table* about how the God of Thunder, Shango, would have boy brides in his ceremonies. And so, I think actually where the play probably originated way back was I imagined a relationship between an African king and their male servant, which was informed by that.

Mojisola Temi, I was so excited because I was thinking, actually it's an invitation also for people to go off and research that and go 'what, boy brides, Shango? Female husbands, really?' I remember having an argument with a Nigerian theatre scholar telling me there's no homosexuality in Igbo culture. But there are female husbands in Igbo culture. If it's in a play, you can go off and go, 'Wow, let me look into that.'

Lynette Temi, *The High Table* was your first play, but I know that it was a play that was part of the Pass the Baton initiative at the Bush Theatre. Jackie Kay's *Chiaroscuro* was shown a few months before yours. Did you see *Chiaroscuro*? Had you already written your play by then?

Temi Yeah, I read it many years before.

Mojisola Were there any particular kind of formative moments as an audience member as a reader in terms of your own development?

Temi It's different for me because I wasn't in it, even though I act. Because there's so many characters, and I didn't want to be in it. I thought as it was my first play, I wanted that emotional distance. And I kept imagining an actor that I'd be playing with saying that they wanted to change the lines, or struggling with the lines, and me being in the scene and not being able to have two hats on. We've already touched on the audience coming up and dancing to Electric Slide. But the thing I'm probably the proudest of, I wasn't actually there for, the stage manager relayed it to me. It was the night that my mum came and she brought ten aunties. So, it's basically like having eleven mums in the audience and it was horrible. There was some kind of poetry event going on next door, so it was really loud and you couldn't hear my words, and my mum was there and I just wanted to die. The stage manager told me that a few nights prior, two men had come (and it's interesting that we've been talking about Black masculinity a bit) because they were both quite straight presenting, whatever you want to call that, but this is her words; she was watching them watch the show. And, obviously, the play's about two queer women wanting to get married, but later you find out that one of the characters who lives in Nigeria is gay. And she said that apparently as they watched that character's monologue, she saw them melt into each other, and it was almost like they were allowed the space to be intimate. People who are partners that maybe on the street wouldn't be that intimate with each other were able to fold into each other; and that really meant a lot to me, especially because I was freaking out about my mum. That's probably the audience response that meant the most to me.

Rikki   That was everywhere in that show. I don't know if you didn't see it then. Because people at your show were breathing. Like, they've been waiting to exhale. Then that feeling of 'I'm in the majority here, this is my space, and other people are coming to my house to hear my stories.' It was a hugely powerful thing for so many people in that audience.

Lynette   Did you say that you didn't want to perform in it because you wanted to keep a separation between the writing of the play and the performing of it? That's interesting because other people performed – *Zhe* [Tonderai], *Brown Girl in the Ring* and *Sin Dykes* [Valerie], *Moj of the Antarctic* [Mojisola] and *BURGERZ* [Travis]. It's interesting to see the difference between performing your own work, doing something that comes from an experience that you had or you want to respond to, and then writing the play.

Rikki   Would you act in it now, Temi, now that it's done?

Temi   Yeah. It was only because it was my first play, and it was such an important thing, it was eight characters, and I wouldn't be able to trust that the play would be as good as it could be if I were in it. Now it's done, yeah, definitely.

STARS

Mojisola Adebayo

STARS was developed during a residency with idle women in 2016, thanks to Cis O'Boyle and Rachel Anderson. It was first performed as a staged reading at Ovalhouse Theatre downstairs on 29 June 2018, with the following creative team.

Creative Team

Co-Producer/Writer/Performer (playing Mrs and all characters except DJ Son) – Mojisola Adebayo
Co-Producer/Music Supervisor and Producer/DJ Performer (playing DJ Son) – Debo Adebayo
Director – Rikki Beadle-Blair
Director during Research and Development process – S. Ama Wray
Animation Artist and Illustrator – Candice Purwin
Set and Costume Designer – Rajha Shakiry
Costume Designer (during R&D process) – Claudine Rousseau
Lighting Designer (Ovalhouse) – Pablo Fernández Baz
Voice Director – Andrea Ainsworth
Stage Manager – Alison Pottinger
Consultant on Intersex – Valentino Vecchietti
Consultant on FGM – Rasha Farah of FORWARD
British Sign Language Interpreters – Jacqui Beckford and Izegbuwa Oleghe
Emerging Artist Mentees – Natalie Cooper, Sonny (Junior) Nwachukwu, Dike Okoh, Lettie Precious
Artistic Access Workers – Conrad Kira and Karen Tomlin

STARS, produced by Tamasha Theatre Company and ICA, premieres at Institute of Contemporary Arts, London, Spring 2023.

Note

Female performer plays Mrs, and the GP (and all the characters except the DJ Son).

Pre-show

Music: 'Space is the Place' by Sun Ra. Audience are ideally seated in-the-round or horseshoe to accentuate the storytelling feel. Set not yet fully revealed.

Opening Ritual

A suggested ritual, feel free to experiment: on house clearance there is silence, haze, a mystical, starry feeling. Enter one male followed by one female performer. He is dressed in robes and hat that resonate with the culture of Dogon, Mali, as do all the visual elements of the show. He whirs a bullroarer over his head; the humming sound represents the voice of the sacred star, Sirius B/Po Tolo, signifying the arrival of the Nommo. The female performer represents the Nommo – an African androgynous anthro-amphibian space traveller. She is dressed in costume/headdress/mask inspired by Dogon culture. The two walk slowly, ritualistically, into the ominous dimly lit space. Arriving centre stage they turn full circle with the bullroarer. Whirring subsides and the two performers are still, facing each other. Lights go black and hand-drawn animation of the Nommo story is projected with voice-over and creative captions (artistic surtitles) below. The animation in the play connects in some way all to **Maryam/Mary**, whom we meet later. The animation are **Maryam/Mary**'s drawings; they are what she sees or imagines or even dreams, whether or not we see her in a particular scene. All words spoken in the play are creatively captioned, either embedded into the animations or projected on the set during spoken text, all to support access for people who are D/deaf or hearing imapired (especially as music plays throughout the show). Audio description is also available on headsets and touch-tours are offered for people who are blind or visually impaired. Relaxed performances are also offered at specific performances. All efforts are made to make sure the production is inclusive to all.

Nommo animation/voice-over
(*Both performers, calling, slow, in sync.*)   Nommo . . . Nommo . . .
Once we were two
When two was one
Space duo, in solo
We Nommo
Both female and male,
Of land and of sea,
From Po Tolo
Comes Nommo
Of Sirius: B.
Beings of twin
Fish-like-body-persons
With feet and fins
Scales and skin
Rainbow chameleons
Ancestral aliens
This is a tale of tails . . .

Scene – Funeral/New Dawn

During the animation/voice-over the two performers carefully remove their costumes (used again at the end of the show) in the darkness. At the end of the animation upbeat music, e.g. Hudson Mohawke's 'Scud Books', kicks in, powerfully contrasting the scene. Female performer is now revealed as **Mrs**, *our protagonist, a Black (or Black mixed heritage) woman of around eighty years old, from south-east London. Male performer is her son, a DJ in his thirties.* **Mrs** *and* **DJ Son** *are dressed for a funeral.* **DJ Son** *is holding an urn; he hands it to* **Mrs**. *They embrace, sadly.* **Mrs** *watches* **DJ Son** *walking away. He enters his radio studio, raised and upstage left. He prepares to play a dance music radio set (mixing live) throughout the entire show, no pause. This is a concept album for the stage. Suggestion of a London council-flat kitchen of an elderly lady is revealed, downstage right. Significant items: fridge, washing machine, radio, kitchen table perhaps with sixties lampshade that looks a little like a space shift hovering over the table, two chairs. However, set is non-naturalistic. The play is* magic in its realism. *For example, all props that are revealed can come from inside the fridge.* **Mrs** *goes into her kitchen, places the urn on the table, looks at it, a determined look.*

Scene – Flash Forward to GP

A flash-forward in time. 'Scud Books' cuts out immediately as we find **Mrs** *sitting in the chair of the* **GP**'s *surgery, down centre stage. She faces the audience. 'Perotation 6' by Floating Points plays.* **Mrs** *is over eighty years old and speaks with a south-east London/cockney accent of her time, which is more precise and clipped than the cockney accent of today. Although she is Black, her voice is like any white Londoner of her time.* **GP** *is in her thirties, white English received pronunciation. All live spoken text is projected in creative captions, displayed from the DJ's radio studio.*

Mrs   Me husband died
And it's taken my whole life
But Dr,
I've never had one
And I want one
Before I die.
I want to know what it's like.
What is wrong with me?

GP   Anorgasmia

Mrs   She said.
Ain't that a flower?

GP   Also known as 'Coughlan's Syndrome'.

Mrs   Nice Irish name.

GP   An inability to orgasm. Sometimes because of lack of adequate stimulation, sometimes it's caused by trauma: fight, flight, freeze. Sometimes –

Mrs – Sometimes, I feel I almost might, when I have a forbidden thought . . . and then I . . . sneeze. Do you think it's connected?

GP I really don't know about that Mrs . . .

Mrs Could there be a cure?

GP Have you ever tried . . . self-help?

Mrs I had a lavender bath and candles.

GP I mean, perhaps with an electrical device? Not in the bath of course, that would be dangerous. Was there anything else Mrs . . . We are passed our ten minutes and you are well past menopause so perhaps you'd like to find a hobby instead? And I'd like you to book in for a dementia test – it's just a precaution . . .

Mrs Dementia?
Hobby!
Electrical device?!
I need to find a *cure*.
My orgasm has got to be out there
Somewhere!

Scene – Kitchen

Mrs *is back in the kitchen looking at the urn on the table as before. There is also a goldfish bowl filled with water (the goldfish is not real), a radio, an ashtray, a packet of cigarettes, a lighter, the* Mirror *newspaper, reading glasses and a mug of tea on the table.* **Mrs** *sits. Turns on the radio. Sips tea. Listens to* **DJ Son** *speaking softly, unassuming, through the mic.* **Mrs** *proudly mouths his tag line (below),* 'Taking you through the night, sci-fi style. Frequencies open.'

DJ Son This is Michael Manners, the original AfroCelt on NTX.

Mrs That's my boy . . .

DJ Son Show's dedicated to Terry Manners. Taking you through the night, sci-fi style. Frequencies open . . .

He plays 'West G Cafeteria' by the Space Dimension Controller. **Mrs** *listens, takes out a cigarette, clocks it is the last one in the box, lights it, watching the urn.*

Mrs (*quoting Mr, her dead husband*) 'What now, Mrs?' What now . . . (*Music underscores.* **Mrs** *sits, takes her reading glasses, opens the* Mirror *newspaper and reads her horoscope.*) 'Planetary activity in Leo, and today's new moon marks the start of a personal adventure – even at the onset of winter. Despite the fact a pursuit of yours turned out to be a flight of fancy, you should accept an invitation from afar, without hesitation. Keep doors open. Breathe new air. Throw caution to the wind.'

(*To the fish in the goldfish bowl.*) Well, cat, what do we make of that? (*Listens in her mind to cat, the fish, who she hears saying,* 'Time to give up smoking'. *Cat's text can*

also be captioned.) Agreed. (**Mrs** *draws deep on her last cigarette. Stubs it out. Takes a deep breath, she might cough. Sips tea. Pauses at a newspaper article.*)
'Government plans to send refugees into space.
Five years after Brexit – Project Spexit: Space exit'
(*Imagining.*) Immigrants on Mars . . .
Asylum on Saturn . . .
Aliens meet the aliens . . .

(*Reading an advert next to the article.*) 'Whether you are an exile or an expat, you can apply for Project Spexit in partnership with the Virgin Space Travel Programme. Budget planet relocation (one way) or luxury space holiday (return). Terms and conditions . . . apply online now!'
Wow.
'www.' . . .

Disappointed as she is not online.

Don't no one use pen and paper anymore . . .

DJ Son   This is Space Dimension Controller with 'West G Cafeteria'.

Mrs   Cat food! How rude, I am forgetting myself.

She gets fish food from the fridge. The fridge stores all props. She empties the container of fish flakes. There are only a few flakes left. She feels guilty for neglecting 'Cat'.

Whatchu lookin at me like that for? Shops shut. You'll have to wait 'til morning . . .
(**Mrs** *hears 'cat' suggesting, 'How about a sprinkling of the old man?'* **Mrs** *reacts shocked.*) I can't do that!

She hears 'Cat' saying, 'Well, he ate fish didn't he?'.

You're not wrong about that, Cat.
Mr probably finished off several of your relatives,
Beer battered with vinegar and chips,
Licking his lips,
Pissed. (*Picking up the urn, impersonating Mr. NB: Here and throughout the play, the performer should embody action that is described, act out the memories, keep it live.*)
Staggering back to manhandle his Mrs every Friday, Saturday, any day, any night
So –

DJ Son *and* **Mrs** (*simultaneously without awareness of each other*)   – what goes around . . .

DJ Son   comes around.

Music. **Mrs** *empties the ashes from the urn into the goldfish bowl. The fish gobbles the ashes.* **Mrs** *laughs.*

DJ Son   'Fight'. This track is one of mine on Native City. Memories of my old man, Terry.

She hears her son, shame. Then to the audience, her confessors.

Mrs What must you think of me?
(*Justifying herself.*) Sixty years of 'honour and obey'
I was a zombie, a slave,
The *living* dead, that was me.
He don't feel nothing now do he?
He don't feel nothing at all.
So nothing's changed there.
There's not a husband, a father
Only a jailer.
But I've served my time in this space.
I've known my place.

She starts saying the line along with the music, enjoying the freedom.

Yeah I've served my time in this space,
I've known my place.
What *now*?

DJ Son 'Travlin' by Norm Talley . . .

Sound of doorbell. Animation projected: through a spy-hole, on the landing of the council block, we see a girl, around eleven years old, of African descent, ringing the doorbell, desperate to use the toilet and **Mrs** *letting her in. Animation could become abstract to convey time passing. The moon (symbolizing* **Mrs**'*s husband) disappears. The sun (symbolizing the girl) rises. Quick change into* **Mrs**'*s comfy in-door clothes.*

Scene – Mrs and Maryam Become Friends

Another doorbell. **Mrs** *is brighter, in comfy clothes, slippers, now smoking a vape. The girl* (**Maryam**) *is at the door.* **Maryam** *is polite, confident, innocent, matter-of-fact; she speaks RP English but as a second language, with perhaps the faintest memory of somewhere in Africa.*

Mrs Hello again, little friend.

Maryam I brought you chocolates, for my birthday. (*Hands a box of Celebrations chocolates.*)

Mrs It's not my birthday.

Maryam I know, that's why I said it, *my* birthday.

Mrs Oh, happy birthday. Aren't you the one supposed to be getting presents?

Maryam I got lots of presents. I got . . . holiday.

Mrs Oh . . . going anywhere nice?

Maryam Been already. Came back for big school starting. Was saving Celebrations but Mum said I should give them to you to say thank you.

Mrs What for?

Maryam Yesterday's toilet.

Mrs Oh right. No need to thank me, just being neighbourly but . . . come in and have a Celebration anyway.

They go inside. **Mrs** *goes over to the table with the girl, who is scared of the fish.*

Mrs Make yourself at home. He's all right, he don't bite. If my furry friend Feena was still alive she'd likely have a scratch but this cat's safe in his bowl.

Maryam *looks confused.* **Mrs** *empties a few of the chocolates on the table.*

Mrs (*referring to the chocolates*) What's your favourite?

Maryam Number 3: Galaxy. Number 2: Milky Way. Number 1: Mars. I love planets and stars.

Mrs You wanna apply for that Spexit.

Maryam Doing a project for school. And when I grow up I am going be a space woman.

Mrs Oooh a little Lieutenant Uhura. I always felt a bit like her when I worked at British Telecom. (*Like Uhura.*) 'Hailing frequencies open, Captain.'

Maryam What?

Mrs *Star Trek*.

Maryam No, *Star Trek* not real. I am going to be real, like Mae Jemison.

Mrs Who?

Maryam First Black woman up there. But I will be first from my country. (*She points up.*)

Mrs (*like* E.T.) 'Phone home' . . .

Maryam Huh?

Mrs *E.T.*

Maryam I don't know what you are talking about.

Mrs (*like Tom Hanks in* Apollo 13) 'Houston, we have a problem.'

Maryam I know. I need more science.

Mrs You better have a Mars then. I'll put the kettle on.
(*To the audience.*) And that's how it started.
We finished off the Celebrations
Every afternoon after school
While she worked on her stars project.
Then she'd have a pee and I'd a vape and a cup of tea.

Short animation as **Mrs** *picks up* **Maryam**'s *stars project book and flicks through the pages. We briefly see fragments of* **Maryam**'s *drawings, writing, diagrams.*

'What are you doing in there, Mary?'

She said she liked the quiet,
She says she liked my toilet,
The woolly loo-roll holder – she reads astronomy.
Feeling sorry for the grieving old lady
She'd fetch me the *Mirror*, daily.

Girl But *Metro* is free?

Mrs Sometimes you gotta pay for quality, Mary.
Her name ain't even Mary,
Her name is Maryam
But no one at school can say it right
And Mary sounds less Muslim.
She went to Catholic school see,
The primary attached to my parish
And after that soldier got his head chopped off in Woolwich
It was easier to be a Mary than a Maryam.

Mrs *says the rosary several times throughout the play.*

> Hail Mary, full of grace
> The Lord is with thee
> Blessed art thee amongst women
> And blessed is the fruit of thy womb, Jesus

DJ Son Here's Rhythm is Rhythm with 'Strings of Life' . . .

Scene – Memories of Church and Children

Mrs I got born again for ten minutes
Searching for 'the final frontier'
When Mr was having his affair with Venus
(*calling towards flat in the opposite block*) from over there!
I was lonely and they give you free chicken on a Sunday.
But Venus eventually had enough of his drinking n' pissing in the bed so he came back and shat in ours instead
And I went back to mass.
I dunno,
Maybe I needed to believe leaving him was a sin,
Maybe I'm scared of it:
Freedom.
And being Catholic is much more straight-forward than being a happy clappy,
All those dancing socks-in-sandals –
You know where you stand when you're in Rome

Mrs *re-plays her time in a born-again Christian church. Goes into the audience.*

I could just never fall in the
Evangelical hall,

I've never been very good at being ecstatic.
I look around one revival
And it's like they're all having seizures,
Trembling, heaving and talking in tongues:
'Mymamamazgottasuzukimypapasgottahondamypapasazgottasuzukimamamassgotta hondaaaaaIwannaHyundaiIwannaHyundai IwannaHyundai . . .'
But I don't go nowhere
I'm just stood there
And no matter how hard the preacher push-push-pushes (*attempting to 'slay' someone 'in-the-spirit', she reaches towards a carefully chosen audience member*) my head
I just can't let go of my bones.

Returning to the stage/on the bus.

When it's all over I have chips and curry sauce on the bus back to Woolwich.
My kind of communion.

Chris always waits for me to leave the service
Pretends he's going the same way,
He's one of those hippy holys . . .

Chris Jesus got me off heroin – hallelujah.

Mrs Praise the Lord.

Church was full of unhappy wives and people with addictions,
Chris gets me talking on the bus about unlikely attractions
How he likes –

Chris older women and there's nothing against it in the Bible, Old Testament or New . . .

Mrs And as I dunked my chips in the curry sauce I confessed to him that I – sometimes feel drawn to women and my husband's my biggest regret.
He went silent.
I hadn't a clue it was me Chris had a crush on.
Not very Christ like
I was fucking forty-four he could have been my son!
(*Wistful.*) But my son hadn't yet come
I imagined him to be waiting on a star . . .
And when by some miracle at forty-six I managed to hatch one good egg (*Picking up the radio.*)
And my little boy finally arrived! (*Clutching the radio to her chest.*)
And I squeeeeeeeze him close to my breast for eighteen years until he says –

DJ Son (*suffocated*) I can't bear it anymore, Mum.

Mrs And he leaves me.

To study music at uni and then spinning his discs around the world . . . (*Quoting Spock, as if saying goodbye.*) 'Live long and prosper', son.

He's got his own radio show now. (*She pauses to listen then speaks into the radio as if her son is tiny.*) Done all right for yourself haven't you, my little Mikey . . .

DJ Son No one calls me 'Mikey', Mum. (*Quoting his business card.*) Michael Manners: Music Producer. DJ. Broadcaster.

Mrs And I think –
(*Sudden rage, directed at her son.*) Weren't it me that ripped
To arse-hole from fanny squeezing your big head out of me
Then clawed my way through the menopause with you screeeeeaming at me?
Weren't it me that worked day *and* night shifts all them years
to put music in your fingers and ears?
Weren't it me that stood in the way of you and Mr's fist
So you wouldn't know what you had missed?
– I can call you what I like, you arrogant little shit!
And then I caught my thought.
Mother Mary forgive me.
'Yes of course: Michael.
Cuppa tea?
Where's my manners?
I forget.'
Yeah, he's done all right for himself, Michael, considering . . .
Where was I? –

DJ Son 'Lunar' . . . track's by Acre.

Mrs Back to the bus with Chris
Who's half the man my son's grown up to be.
Prick goes and tells someone giving him 'spiritual counselling'
That he's got an obsession for some kind of . . . (*whisper*) lesbian.
'Course it goes around the congregation like a bush fire.
They haul me in to an 'emergency house meeting' (*acting out the memory*)
I have to take a shift off
Semi-detached in Greenwich
Ornate iron-gate, original tiling,
I think to myself, now that's a lot of tiling.
They sit me down at the big oak kitchen table,
And without so much as a 'howdy-do' or a 'Hallelu'
Pull down the velux (*pronounced veloo*) blinds announcing –

Playing church elders:

Church Elder One Your body is a temple and you haven't kept it clean.

Church Elder Two That is why your husband treats you –

Mrs the way he did.

Church Elder Three That's why he turns to other women and drink.

Mrs Even implied that is why my first child

Church Elder One   was still born . . .

Mrs   My Gabrielle.
My wingless angel,
Who I love, I don't care that she was disabled,
Who I love, even though Mr said –
(*Suddenly as* **Mr**, *cockney*.)
Mr   She was better off dead.

Mrs   The *bastard*.
The born-agains said –

Church Elder One   Your womb has an omen, Satan has a hold.

Church Elder Two   That is why you cannot conceive.

Church Elder Three   Believe-believe-believe.

Mrs   And they try to squeeze the

Church Elder One   deeemon of lesbianism out-out-out!

Mrs   of me. Declaring it –

Church Elder One   entered in through horoscopes,

Church Elder Two   sci-fi films

Church Elder Three   and pagans in your *African* ancestry.

Mrs   Out comes a saucepan (*re-playing with the goldfish bowl*)
Le Creuset (*pronounced le-cru-zay*) no less
A big heavy orange one
Very middle class
All place their White hands on my Black head, shoulders, breasts and press-press-press
And there's me, leaning over the saucepan,
And there's them, expecting the

Church Elder One   EVIL SPIRIT

Mrs   to come out in my vomit
But all I can manage is a little bit of spit.
(*Ironic.*) Such a disappointment (*returns the goldfish bowl*).

Never felt quite right with the Evangelicals after that.
And then when Mr finally pulls his penis out of Venus
And they all go

Church Elder One   Praise be! Our prayers have been answered.

Mrs   And I get pregnant with my son and the elders call another house meeting.

Church Elder Two   Just in case there's another demon.

Mrs   And then that Freddie Mercury from Queen dies
And the Leader stands up in the Sunday celebration and says

Church Elder One   Mercury got what he deserved, AIDS, the curse –

Mrs   I says no.
Enough!
None of this sounds like gentle Jesus or Mother Mary to me
And I love 'Bohemian Rhapsody'
Now Freddie could take you to outer space . . .

'Bohemian Rhapsody' mixes in momentarily with animation from **Maryam***'s stars book.* **Mrs** *flicks through the book, enjoying the music, Mercury's voice rings out, 'Mama . . .'*

Scene – Maryam and Mrs Observe the Neighbours

Mrs *and the girl watch the neighbours from the window.* **DJ Son** *mixes in 'Moondance'.*

Mrs   Mary changed my night to day.
This flat is the deck of the Starship Enterprise.
(*Quoting* Star Trek.) 'It's life, Maryam, but not as we know it.'

DJ Son   'Moondance' on Tribe.

Mrs   We're watching the whole constellation of the council estate.
We survey 'neighbour planets' over kitchen plates.

Animation of planets/people described below.

She talks me through it all while I have a vape.

Mary   The universe accelerates.

Mrs   But looks like our estate is going backwards . . . Look at him, on his phone by the railing, raging (*impersonating the young blood from the estate*), 'it's the system, it's the system . . .'

A game, naming the neighbours after planets:

Mary   Jupiter. Hothead. Full of gas. Could have been a star . . . Look, Neptune is going out. Only after sunset you see him . . . dark rings around his eyes.

Mrs   Probably working shifts. And look who's coming across the playground.

Mary   Saturn.

Mrs   Stunning.

Mary   Big rings in her ears.

Mrs   Afro-centric Empress (**Mrs** *calls*) yes my sister! Saturn!

Saturn   Greetings, Auntie!

Mrs   *Auntie?* (**Mrs** *is disappointed, realizing how old she appears.*)

Mary Look, sitting on the bench, Uranus!

Mrs Don't be rude.

Mary Mrs, your jokes are older than you. Uranus looks like his face flipped over. And see, Pluto coming home with her shopping. Pluto's not a real planet. She's a dwarf.

Mrs Don't call her that. She's your height and you wouldn't like it. Gets laughed at but gets on with it. (*Calls out to the woman of short stature passing, with her thumb up.*) Respect! (*The woman looks up.*)

Pluto (*a little cynically*) Hi.

Mrs And look who it ain't. (*Kisses her teeth.*)

Mary Venus? She is really hot. (**Mrs** *grunts.*) And he is really cold, my favourite.

Mrs Where?

Mary The homeless man in big winter coat and bright red face. All year round.

Mrs (*singing from David Bowie's 'Life on Mars'*)

'Oh man, wonder if he'll ever know
He's in the best-selling show
(*Calling out of the window.*) Is there life on Mars?!' (**Mary** *is laughing and applauding.*)

Mrs (*to the radio*) Let's have a bit of Bowie, Mikey!
Those were the days. Just never thought I'd outlive him.

Mary Your husband?

Mrs No. David Bowie! South London's finest.

Mary Nah, Stormzy. Much better.

Mrs (*like Stormzy*) 'You're getting way too big for your boots.'

They laugh.

Mrs No . . . I always knew I'd outlive Mr. He was weak.

Mary But he loved you?

Mrs He might have done. He just didn't know how. Love is what you do, innit?

DJ Son I'm playing this one on a promise. Here's 'Falling Rizlas' from Actress . . .

They listen to the music for a moment.

Mrs Who am I then?

Mary Earth.

Mrs Me? Planet Earth? No.

Mary Yes. You are.

Mrs Why?

Mary   Because, you are mostly blue and covered in clouds.

Mrs   Oh.

Mary   And Mr, he is like the moon, always following you around, even though he is dead.

Mrs   Blimey.

Mary   And Mrs, you are not a healthy planet (*pointing to the vape*). This is not good for you. I read it in *Metro*.

Mrs   Heavens. Anything else, Dr Spock?

Mary (*a joke*)   Dr *who*?

Mrs (*quotes* Dr Who)   'Geronimo!' (*Laughs, conceding defeat to* **Mary**.)

I'm not exactly . . . 'Mother Earth' then.

Mary   Sorry.

Mrs   It's all right. You're probably right. But you little one are the sun, brightening up my day.

Mary *smiles. Then a sad pause.*

Mary   If I am the sun
Maybe that is why
I burn.
If I am the sun,
Maybe that is why
If you looked at me
You would close your eyes . . .
Perhaps I will build a rocket
For my school project
So I can fly closer
To myself
And then I will keep on flying
(*Line sung like acoustic version of Jamila Woods's song 'Way Up'.*)
After myself
To a little star in the dark
'Po Tolo'/Home
From where the 'Nommos' come . . .

DJ Son   'Bouramsy' from Lil Silva.

Nommo Story Part One – Animation Interlude

Animation. **Mary** *is recounting the story of the Nommo to* **Mrs**, *while she is drawing them for her stars school project. We see the drawings. Text in voice-over/subtitles.*

Mrs   So, the story goes . . .

Mary   The Nommos
Were migrants from across the cosmos
Sailing the sky to planet Earth.
Descendants from a star that you and I cannot see –

Mrs   With naked eyes at least –

Mary   Sirius B.

And for thousands of years,
Sirius A we could see
But Sirius B was known only
To the Dogon of Mali.

Mrs   Cousins to the Pharoahs?

Mary   Who knows.
The Dogon call Sirius B, 'Po Tolo'.
'Po'?

Mrs   – star?

Mary   Tolo – the tiniest white seed you can scatter in a field . . .
The white scientists could not see this star.

Mrs   Nor could the Dogon, it's too small, too far.

Mary   But their fathers were told of Po Tolo
By?

Mrs   – the Nimmos!

Mary (*correcting* **Mrs**)   The Nommos!

Mary   Ancestor aliens sailing to Africa in a space ship from Sirius B.

Mrs   Seriously?

Mary   They say Sirius B orbits Sirius A every half of a century . . .

And Dogon paint all they know of the cosmos from the Nommos
On the walls of houses,
Celebrating with rituals, sculptures, dances!

Mary   Dogon art exhibits in New York, London, Paris

Mrs   Making Picasso a modernist and careers for anthropologists.

Mary   And then one day
Through a big telescope

Mrs   Old blue eyes said
(*impersonating an English scholar*) 'Indeed Sirius has a B that cannot – *nakedly* – be seen'
And he took a photo,

Mary   In 1970.

Scene – Maryam's Revelation

Mrs European scholars –

Mrs *as the scholars.*

Scholar One What a wonder!
The star really is very, very, dense
Just as that remote tribe said
And it is as white as snow . . .
But how could these old Black Africans know?

Scholar Two Their cave paintings reveal the vastness of the universe!
Before *us* they knew of Jupiter's moons!
And the rings of Saturn – they could see!
And Sirius B *does* orbit Sirius A every fifty years *precisely*.

Scholar Three They knew that the planets revolve around the sun
And that the earth was born from a big *big* bang.
While we were still drawing maps of the earth as flat
And believed the horizon was the end of it.
When we were still too scared to set sail,
For fear our boats would fall off into hell,
When we still believed the sun revolved around *us*

Scholar Two And the dark creatures of the earth were wicked primitive savages.

Scholar One While we were burning witches and heretics

Mrs It seems these Africans were intergalactic!

Mary The Dogon knew all about Sirius

Mrs How could that be? . . .

Mary We told you! We were told by? . . .

Mrs (*getting it right this time*) the Nommos!
Extraterrestrial Afro-hermaphrodite anthro-amphibian migrants!

Mary Both male and

Mrs female.

Mary Of land and

Mrs of sea.

Mary Like humans and

Mrs fish!

Mary With feet and

Mrs fins!

Mary Scales and

Mrs skin.

Mary Ancestor aliens!
Rainbow chameleons!

Mrs This is a tale of tails . . .

DJ Son Toumani Diabate: *Salaman*.

Scene – Maryam's Revelation

Mrs She said

Mary it burnt

Mrs Like no temperature you could touch,
When she was cut,
In the summer holidays.
Her eyes clenched shut.
Hands pressing her head, shoulders, legs . . .

Mary It was so painful.

Mrs Shameful.
But she insisted –

Mary they did it because they love me.

Mrs Her parents.
That's why she wouldn't – (*Grabbing her mobile phone.*)
'Let me phone the police! I should call social services!'

Mary No! Please, Mrs, don't say, they might take me away . . .

Mrs And I know it's selfish but
I was afraid they might take her from me too . . .
So 'it's our little secret'.
Why she liked to use my toilet.
Why it took her fifteen minutes to pee.
Why it –

Mary (*through pain*) stings.

Mrs And she transports herself –

Mary to the stars!

A monologue from **Mary**, *sitting on the toilet, clutching a book called* STARS *by Andrew King, reciting what she has learnt to distract herself from excruciating pain.*

Mary 'Every atom of your body
Was once part of a star.'
Part of a star . . .
Part of a star . . .

An atom is smallest matter
That 'cannot be cut'.[1]
Cannot be cut.

Can never be cut

To the stars you must return,
Maryam,
To the stars you must return . . .

Mrs So that was why she shuffled her feet across the estate
Why she wouldn't drink
Why she was loosing weight
No matter how many Galaxys she ate.
She said (*recovering from the pain momentarily*)

Mary When you look into the stars you look into the past . . .
But you can't change it.

Mrs If I could,
I would . . .

DJ Son *rewinds the track and plays forward again with Bouramsy over Nommo animation interlude two.*

Nommo Story Part Two – Animation Interlude

Text is in voice-over/captions as with part one.

Mary But,
Just like Earth and Moon are partners in destiny
Just like Sirius B is one part only of a shining binary
With Sirius A –

Mrs The Dog Star – man's brightest friend
This starry story also has a companion:

Mary The Dogon *also* believe in one God,
In the sky

Mrs sounds familiar

Mary Amma,
Who wanted the Earth as His celestial . . . (*hesitating, shy of the subject*)

Mrs (*sexual*) partner

Mary But he could not . . . (*hesitating*)

---

[1] From Andrew King's, *STARS: A Very Short Introduction* (Oxford: Oxford University Press, 2012), pp. 1 and 29.

Mrs 'mount her'

Mary Because her . . . (*hesitating*)

Mrs 'mountain' was too big
(*Aside just for the adult audience.*) It got in the way, he couldn't get it in.

Mary The wilful single mother Earth gave birth
To a jackal, a devil instead!

Mrs Whom Amma rejects as he could not possibly be the father.

Mary The devil/jackal runs around bringing the world into disorder.
So Amma created the Nommo as messengers, saviours of the world!
But even though the Nommo are

Mrs transmitters of all the Dogon know,

Mary To the people, Nommo look . . . (*hesitating*)

Mrs troubling,
As doubling androgynes,
Their bodies ugly and fishy with excessively fleshy differing . . .

Mary So Dogon believe to stop the world from all this disorder

Mrs Brought to the world by the reckless devil-jackal son of un-mountable mother,

Mary A boy must be made to look like a boy and a girl must be made to look like a girl and we must look like Nommo –

Mrs – no more!

A duel of duals has ensued since then
Repeated the world over
In religions, traditions, medicine.
Justified
With knives,
Scalpels, razor blades and needles in hand
To make a woman a woman

Mary and a man no less than a man . . .

Mrs This is an old tale of tails . . .

Mary But, once we were two

Mrs When two was one

Mary And some of us want to go home.

End animation.

DJ Son – Here's 'Bright Star', the Sunset Remix.

Track plays.

Scene – Why?

Mrs Why? . . .

Mary Tradition.

Mrs Yes but why?
Tradition.
Later she said:

Mary Mrs, I asked my mum about that thing.

Mrs Did you? What did she say?

Mary She said English people don't understand and I should never talk about it. I'm not talking about it, OK, Mrs?

Mrs OK.

Mary She said it happened to my brother too, when he was thirteen, but I was younger and braver. I got bigger party, I got new dress and Elsa dolly from *Frozen* you know 'let it go, let it go . . .' OK I am too old but still everybody happy, everybody give us money – much more than my brother!

Mrs That's different, Mary, what they cut off the boys ain't the same.

Mary It's not true. My mum said, little girls have a bit, little boys have a bit, both gets cut, because if we didn't, boys grow into girls and girls grow into boys and no one knows who is who.

Mrs It don't grow into a willy, Mary . . .

Mary (*upset*) And then I ask why they close me, why I cannot pee why it hurt so much, Mum? . . . (*Recovering.*) She says it happen to her too, and to my grandmother and to every lady body I know in my family since the beginning of time. She say it make us clean and calm. Pure and perfect girl for marriage.

Mrs Mary, it's not right.

Mary But my mum said!

Mrs Mary, what you got, what you *had*, down there, no one is supposed to touch unless you want them to, and when they do it's supposed to feel . . . (**Mrs** *isn't sure how it's supposed to feel.*)

Mary It's supposed to feel? . . .

Mrs Nice.

Mary Nice? (*i.e. is that all?*)

Mrs (*realizing the inadequacy of 'nice'*) Like the best thing in the whole world!

Mary What is the best thing in the whole world?

Mrs I dunno. Ice cream. It's supposed to feel like ice cream in the summer down there. It won't make much difference to your brother, Mary, except he'll probably never get his winkle caught in his zipper.

Mary I don't understand.

Mrs Neither do I.

Mary It is supposed to feel nice? It just hurts . . .

Pause.

You feel nice? With Mr?

Mrs You can't ask me that!

Mary Why you ask me, questions then?! I am not a girl anymore, Mrs. I know things now.

Mrs I don't feel nothing, he's dead.

Mary No, before he went to heaven? . . . What was it like, on your wedding night?

Mrs He's not in heaven Mary, there's not a hell big enough for him and it was never like ice cream. I only married him because I thought I had to after what happened in the fridge.

Mary Fridge?

Mrs This ain't about me, Maryam. You and me, dear, it is not the same.

Mary Why?

Mrs Because you're just a child and I'm an old girl. I'm a soft old bourbon in the bottom of the biscuit tin. I've had my chance at happiness, you ain't!

Mary I have happy chances, lots of them. You are making me sad! I am going to be a space woman. Like Nommo! My Mum and Dad love me. They're not like you and Mr! This our culture. If I didn't get cut no husband would want me. And what will happen to me if no one will want me in this far away country where no one says hello, how is your mother, father, sister, brother? . . . My family love me . . . It's just . . . Owwwwwwww . . . I have to pee.

Mrs She shoved past me and then left straight after that. (**Mrs** *gets her vape. Smokes a little.*). Didn't stop for chocolate or a chat. Came back the next day but wouldn't cross my doorstep. Holds that doll from *Frozen* in a shiny green dress. Thrust it in my face –

Mary (*with doll*) Look!

Mrs 'Let it go, let it go . . .' You coming in?

Mary Underneath – LOOK!

Mrs What is it?

Mary Nothing. Nothing there. Just like me. I am pretty.

Mrs You are pretty, Mary.
You need to pee? Come inside –

Mary – NO! Mum says (*recalling her mother*), 'Maryam, come. Why only *you* goes to her house? Hmm? You know people in this country always doing funny funny things to children. I see it on TV every day. Maybe she is a paedo. Maybe she is a witch. Stay away from that old woman. OK? Come here. (*Cuddles her daughter/self.*) Good girl".

Mary Maybe I am cut but you are cut too, Mrs. Cut-off and covered in scars. But I am going to the stars. I am being a space woman, the first woman from my country and I don't need this dirty thing. My mother and my father they brought me here, they (*quoting her father*) 'sacrificed everything and provide everything'. I don't need anything. And when I grow up I will provide them.

Mrs That's right. That's right. Look, come inside and let's –

Mary No, no, no! There is nothing for me inside. There is nothing for you! Just a cigarette that is not a cigarette, a cat that is really a fish, science that is fiction, the *Mirror* with no reflection – just made up stars and a son who hides inside the radio to keep away from YOU! Sorry. Sorry. You should go outside, Mrs, instead of watching it from the window. Mum says I am not allowed to come anymore.

Mrs And she starts to cry and she starts to pee and she shuffles away, across the estate. What about your school project? Mary! Maryam! Your book! (*Waving the stars school project book which has been left behind.*)
She didn't look back.
I watched out from my window after school but I couldn't see her for days. So I done like she said. I go outside (*acting out the memory*), knock on their door. (*Pause.*) Nothing. Look through the letter box and . . . a black hole . . . Like they were never there. And ever since that night, I been having this recurring dream . . .

DJ Son '3am' . . . from Bearcubs . . .

Scene – Eclipse

Animation of the dream, with music and **DJ Son***'s voice in voice-over, captions.*

DJ Son *(voice-over)* The cold moon passes in front of the sun.
We all stand in the playground with cardboard glasses on.
All the neighbours look up at the sky,
But you are looking at the neighbours,
Searching the crowd, for her.
Some cry, some cheer, some shiver with fear.
The birds fall silent,
And we all feel bitterly cold.
It starts to rain
And when we go back up to the flat,

The door is open,
The radio is white noise,
And the fish is floating in the bowl...
And you know...
You *know*...

Quoting the film Blade Runner:

'All those moments will be lost in time.
Like tears in rain.
Time to die...'

End animation/voice-over.

Mary   Gravity is a grave,

Mrs   she'd say...

Mary   It can only go one way... No matter how hard we pray...

Scene – Call Michael

Mrs   I couldn't go back to mass after that. I had no stomach for praying to a virgin. I had no stomach for tradition, religion. I had no stomach for any of it. I want to leave this flat, this planet. (**Mrs** *gets her phone, music shifts to 'Elegant and Never Tiring' by Lorenzo Senny*.) I phone my Mikey in the middle of the night, crying, 'I've had enough, "beam me up", I wanna go to the stars, with Mary'. He thought I meant that euthanasia clinic in Switzerland. (*Crying, distraught.*) 'No, no you don't understand, Mary came to me, Mary revealed it all, and she made me think about everything I've denied in my life and then she just disappeared as if she was never there, as if she was just a story in the *Mirror* and then last night I had a dream about an eclipse and I heard your voice and now I think she might be dead and she was my sun, my son, she was my reason for getting up in the morning. Michael, Michael, *listen*: at the centre of the whole constellation, there's a bright little girl, there's no future without her but no one can stand to face her... We close our eyes. This is your mother, 'signing off, signing off...' (*Beat.*) That brought him home for Christmas (**DJ Son** *comes down from his studio to sit with his mum.*) Got cover for his radio show and bought me (**Mrs** *unwraps the gift from* **DJ Son**, *delighted*) an iPad! Spends Boxing Day teaching me how to use it.

DJ Son   You can look up your stars. Even does crosswords.

Mrs   Ohhh... And do you think I can send one of them 'emails' on this?

DJ Son   It's a whole universe in there, Mum.

Mrs   Our first Mr-less Christmas. Watched old clips from *Star Trek*! Now I can apply for that Spexit. (*Quoting her horoscope.*) 'The start of a personal adventure'. That's what my stars said.

DJ Son   Live long and prosper, Mum.

DJ Son *returns to his radio studio.*

Mrs Mary will be up there! Betcha!

DJ Son That was 'Elegant and Never Tiring' by Lorenzo Senni . . . Time to 'Chase the Devil'. (*After lyrics 'Lucifer, son of the morning, I'm gonna chase you out of Earth!'* **DJ Son** *says* . . .) The Upsetters . . . and Max Romeo.

Scene – Mrs' Biography

Mrs *speaks during the opening dub section of the track. She searches on her iPad.*

Mrs Project Spexit/Virgin Space Travel Programme. Application. (*Like Richard Branson.*) 'So, first off, tell us a bit about yourself . . .'

Listens to music, rocking, smoking her vape, thinking about what to write on the application. She speaks after the lyrics, 'I'm gonna put on a iron shirt and chase Satan out of earth, I'm gonna put on an iron shirt and chase the devil out of earth, I'm gonna send him to outer space, to find another race, I'm gonna send him to outer space, to find another race . . ." Track switches to dub version from here.

Mrs During the war I was born, 1944
Throwaway baby of a runaway English wife and a Black American GI
But a Jamaican mum and Irish dad rescue me
From a children's home.
Black and White Catholics doing the Lambeth Walk
Mum and Dad were the talk of Southwark.
They always wanted a baby
And didn't mind the controversy.
I was two when they got me
And me mum said I was frozen,
Staring off into space
Whatever they did to me in that place it was no home.

But eventually I learnt to look at adults again
Dreamt of becoming our school's first brown nun,
I could never imagine growing up to marry a man
And that was all that was expected of you back then.
I loved needle-work and I was good at Latin,
Weren't I qualified?
But Mum said –

Mrs' Mum (*Jamaican, gentle*) Why on earth you want to be a nun – be a nurse like me, that's close enough.
But Dad said –

Mrs' Dad (*Irish, soft*) Sure we need money coming in if we we're ever gonna build that house in the Blue Mountains.

Mrs So just before I'm due to start nursing training

Dad gets me a summer job in the sandwich factory
Where he drives deliveries with his drinking buddy,

Mrs' Dad   That joker, Terry.

Mrs   I'm appointed as 'top filling mixer'.
No production line for me
And packaged sandwiches were the future
In 1960.

She gets up, steps into her memory.

Then one hot day, it's egg mayonnaise
So I go into the big fridge
To collect a bucket of eggs
And in comes Terry.
Pulls the big fridge door shut
Says,

Terry (*white, cockney, Jack the Lad*)   Cwor it's hot. Wanna help me cool off?'

Music changes to 'Mourn by' Corbin.

Mrs   I'm frozen to the spot.
Could have been a nurse,
Could have been a nun.
Sixteen years young.
I come out staring into a bucket of eggs
Shivering, bleeding, can't feel me legs
Ashamed.
Two weeks late.
Pregnant.
So Terry asks Dad for me hand
Dad buys a bottle of whiskey
Mum kissed me
I sew a yellow dress
And up we all went down the registry office.
And since that day everybody just called me 'Mrs'
Terry Manners.

Mr   Mind your manners, Mrs!

Mrs   He'd say.
As long as you mind yours, Mr!
I'd reply.
And he gets us this council flat all the way over in Woolwich –
(*An aside.*) Might as well have moved to fucking France.
He carries me across the threshold and I giggle.

Mr   I hope my Mrs ain't frigid.

Mrs   I never laugh at that particular crack.

But I do learn to smile again,
Even learn to like him,
He was happy-go-lucky,
Says:

Mr I could love you, if you let me.

Mrs Gives up deliveries and starts painting and decorating (*Referring to the flat.*)
Getting everything ready for our new baby.
Says he was –

Mr a good man really.
Not a lot of other white blokes would –

Mrs want me.

Mr And we look good together, don't we?
Milk and tea, our baby will be the sugar.
You should take it nice and easy . . .

Mrs But our baby was born as still as a Sunday morning
And from that day
Terry never stops drinking
And I never stop thinking about Gabrielle
My angel,
And what she could have been,
And what she was doing now,
Above the clouds with Jesus . . .

Never did do that nursing training . . .
My dear old mum nursed me until
I went back to work at the sandwich factory
And all the girls gave me fags and made me sweet tea
'So, so, sorry . . .'
I hardly let Terry touch me after that
I only had to look at him and he froze.
I'd stay up late to avoid it
Watch the box (*an aside*) any old shit . . .
Years went by with Terry down the pub
And me sitting on the sofa,
Stroking the cats and staring at the sci-fis on the silver screen . . .
And one day the Evangelicals come knocking at the door

Church Elder One Come to a Sunday Celebration?

Mrs Thought, why not, what am I stuck in here for?
And I finally got pregnant with Michael
And Mr finally left me alone.
Years of affairs but I didn't care.
Got meself a nice desk job at British Telecom –
'Hailing frequencies open, Captain'.

Life was the girls at BT, my son and science fiction.
No worries, no plans, no expectations . . .
But when Michael left home I was stricken with grief again.
Couldn't get up for work anymore and they packed me in
I was due for retiring . . .

Scene – Shahana

DJ Son *plays Jonzon Crew's version of 'Space is the Place'.*

Mrs   I know.
There's something missing.
'Forgive me father for I have sinned
It's been years since my last confession.'
1984:
Before the Evangelicals came to my door, before Michael was born . . .
I never imagined anyone could want me,
Love me,
Make love to me . . .
Until one day
A lady in a launderette offers me fabric softener with
Two drops of her own pressed lavender
And a smile that says –

Shahana *is a British South Asian travelling musician from Lancashire, rich Blackburn or Accrington accent, nomad, free spirit, laid back.*

Shahana   I handle delicates with care.

Mrs   And somewhere between slow soak and fast spin
Everything feels washable and new.

In the laundrette now. Animation of washing machines, soap suds and space . . .

The launderette was my sanctuary,
That's one place Mr would never follow me.
The men who did come in with their black bin bags
Always look a little found-out

Shahana   Huddled over their smalls
Hoping no one sees their white streaks and brown skids,
Ashamed of their own fluids . . .

Mrs   Shahana was as easy as her name and the Lancashire rain.
She saw me watching her and asks

Shahana   Want a bit?

Mrs   Oh, sorry for staring I just . . .

Shahana   Wondered if it makes a difference? It does, it really does.

Mrs   And that's how it starts.

Shahana   Have some lavender for your smalls.

Mrs   Oh no, it's my husband's jumpers and me cat blankets!

Shahana   Aw shame, well let's make them all the fluffier shall we? . . .

Mrs   We'd mostly meet on my morning off, a Monday . . .
Oh hello, Shahana . . . how are you?

Shahana   Shattered.

Mrs   She'd been singing at some world festival or other
While I spent the weekend smiling at spillages on his shirts
Throwing bras in the yellow basket without a care in the world.
She said she finds

Shahana   the launderette relaxing. Watching the washing go round and round.

Mrs   Earth turning around the sun.

Shahana   And the heat in here is better than the leisure centre sauna and you don't have to deal with all the blokes asking about your tattoos.

Mrs   Shahana's got a lot of tattoos and piercings, purple streaks and a couple of teeth missing.
She looks like a pirate, and just as brave
And I only got one invitation.
She wanted to show me her van

Shahana   Correction: classic converted UPS delivery truck. Pine cabin inside – I did it all up meself.

Mrs   And I turned no more than ninety degrees before she kissed me,
Unfolded me
And stretched me out, like a clean sheet.
And I couldn't believe this was happening to me,
'Life begins at forty'.

There was so much water . . .
I never knew there could be so much water . . .
Like she was the force conducting the tides
And not the moon,
Not the moon at all . . .
And she rowed across my belly

Acting out all of this.

Like a pirate on the sea
She smuggled me.
I looked up from the deep
And on and on blindly
She crossed the ocean

Swelling inside me
Until she reached her island in the sun
And arched her back
And threw back her head
And sang out a YESSSSSSSSSS!
And crashed like waves upon my chest
Sshhhhhhhaaaaaaaaannnnaaaaaaahhh . . .
So that is what it is like,
I'd seen it in films but . . .
That is what it's like,
When it's real,
It is *so powerful*.
No wonder they keep trying to stop women from having them.
And me, I was just terrified of what it might do to me,
That if I exploded like her supernova
I'd never be able to put meself back together!

Shahana Come on, Mrs, your turn.

Mrs No. Shahana. Just, hold me.
And she did. Gently. And I wanted nothing more.

Shahana Correction: you don't feel you *deserve* anything more. You need to go home tonight, lock the bathroom door, light some candles and have a hot bath with lavender oil, lay back, let it all go and love yourself first, Mrs. No one else has a chance unless you do.

Mrs I'll give it a try . . .

Shahana (*quoting* Star Wars) 'Try not. Do, or do not.'

Mrs (*finishing the quote, their little joke*) 'There is no try.'
Bye. (*Kisses Shahana goodbye.*)
But I went home to Mr instead
And said:
'It's time we got a washing machine.'
And I weren't being mean.
I just knew it was all over as soon as it began
Because when I looked up, Shahana was closing her eyes and mine were open wide.

'Hail Mary, Full of Grace
The Lord is with thee
Blessed art thee amongst women . . .'

Mondays especially I'd miss her
So instead of the launderette I'd visit the convent and sit with the old nuns

Momentarily sitting with the nuns in the convent.

And wonder if they'd ever had one,
And wonder what my life could have been

If I had a nun's habit instead of a smoking one,
And been married to gentle Jesus instead of Mr Terry Manners.
Who died on the toilet,
Cradling an empty bottle of whiskey,
Like a baby.

Mrs' *action conveys the end of the online application.*

DJ Son   Here's another one of mine, a remix of Jamila Woods, 'Way Up' . . .

Shahana/Maryam's Song

Shahana *sings an a cappella version of 'Way Up' by Jamila Woods, at one of her gigs, strumming a guitar. She sings in her own accent; she is easy with it.*

> I'm an alien from inner space
> They can read my mind all in my face
> No one knows I'd rather spend my days
> Alone on my pillow

> I don't care what they say
> I've been waiting here for so long
> Call me by my name
> They keep telling me I'm wrong
> We are not the same
> I don't belong here
> I don't belong here

Cut to:

> I wanna go
> To my own private planet I've been dreaming of
> Little moon in my head I be moving on
> Up and away, I'm way up
> Up and away,

Now **Maryam/Mary** *is singing, simply, as if for a school assembly, animation is projected of her going into space, inspired by the lyrics below.*

> Just cos I'm born here
> Don't mean I'm from here
> I'm ready to run
> And rocket to sun
> I'm way up
> I'm way up

> I'm an alien from inner space
> They can't read my mind all in my face
> No one knows I'd rather spend my days
> Alone on my pillow

Earth's getting old
So colour me gone
I'm ready to run
And rocket to sun
And it ain't so bad
So don't look so sad
Just cos I'm born here
Don't mean I'm from here

Now **Mrs** *sings, gently to herself, in her kitchen.*

Just cos I'm born here
Don't mean I'm from here
I'm ready to run
And rocket to sun
I'm way up
I'm way up[2]

DJ Son   Going back up with Sun Ra . . .

Scene – Mrs Does the Crossword

Time has passed. **Mrs** *wears her glasses, does the crossword, listening to music, smoking her vape, a cloud of smoke, writing/searching on the iPad.*

Mrs   7 down
'Nerve ending of female pleasure. The Latin for shame.'
P space space E space space space.

Looks on the iPad for the answer, scanning her findings, reflected in the animation.

'As big as a phallus, on the inside:
The clitoris.
Twice as sensitive as the head of a penis
The only organ in the entire human body
Designed purely and only
For pleasure.'
I been Googling.

Mrs *Googles 'cut clitoris' on the iPad. She follows a film on YouTube.*

'200 million women and girls all over the world
Clipped, cut, sliced, sewn up,
Some left only with a hole the width of a matchstick
And on their wedding night, the groom takes a knife and . . .'

YouTube.

2   Lyrics and music by Jamila Woods, https://www.youtube.com/watch?v=fGVW5T7R2U0 accessed 11/06/18.

Overwhelmed.

Resumes crossword.

Seven down
P space space E space space space.
'The nerve ending of female pleasure'
(*Thinks.*) 'Pudenda'
'The Latin for shame'.

Mrs *suddenly thinks she hears* **Mary** *in the toilet. Switches off the radio. No music. Silence for the only moment in the play.*

Mrs   Mary?
Maryam, you in there? . . .
You out there? . . .

Silence. **Mrs**, *a little afraid, turns on the radio again to fill the space.*

Mrs   Eclipse, significance:
'Secrets, omens . . . Hidden emotions . . .'
'Something missing'.
'Turmoil, repressed'.
'Fear of failure,
Fear of success'.
Eclipse, science:
'A cosmic coincidence'.
What are the chances?
That I'd get invited to lunch, by Maxi.

DJ Son   'Sunday Morning' by Seven Davis Junior . . .

Scene – Maxi

Mrs   Maxi was younger than me, we used to work at BT.
We'd have such a laugh back then, but I retired and we drifted apart.
But recently Maxi got married to my butcher, Barry.
He's always decent to me.
Extra chipolatas since Mr died.
Started to feel there was a little bit of hope.
Company and cut-price pork chops,
They live above the shop.
One January Saturday when they were closing up,
Maxi invites me up for Sunday lunch.

Maxi *is in her fifties and young with it, Black, bold, full of life, power and joy.*

Maxi   Barry will be off dangling his maggots in the canal and I can't be bothered to do a roast just for meself. Come up and see me.

Mrs I bought a nice bottle of wine and a box of Quality Street. We chatted for hours.
Maxi said Barry the butcher was good to her: (*The women are tipsy.*)

Maxi I got him trained! Now he's a damn good lover!

Mrs I confided in Maxi on the sofa:
I took no pleasure in Mr what so ever
He might as well have been rubbing sand paper
He paid more attention to cutting in and decorating than he ever did to me.

Maxi Poor you. Me and Barry lift off every Saturday night after *Britain's Got Talent*!

Mrs I knew. Everybody knew. You could hear it half way up the high street.

Maxi It's 'cos of my SUPER-POWER!

Mrs Your what?

Maxi Shall I tell you a story?

Mrs Go on then.

Maxi You sitting comfortable? When I was born, a doctor, named Money, stood at the end my mother's hospital bed and said (**Maxi** *plays* **Dr Money**, *upper-class, cold, arrogant, English surgeon*):

Dr Money I'm afraid your 'daughter' has ambiguous genitalia. But we'll perform simple surgery, a quick cliterodectomy to cosmetically correct the clit –

Maxi's Mum (*who is from Jamaica*)   – but wait!

Dr Money It is far too big to be a normal clitoris.

Maxi's Mum Well, if I had given birth to a son who was hung like a donkey would we still be having this conversation, Dr Money? No, I don't think so.

Maxi And you know what he said?

Dr Money It is deformed! If *that* was hanging off of your face you'd have a job . . .

Maxi You'd have job?!

Maxi, *outraged, goes off on one, fast, rapping along to the music.*

A nose job
A face-lift
A tummy-tuck
A cellulite suck
Botox pump
Breast implant
Buttock enhancement
Wax

Sack back and crack
Bum-hole bleach
Designer vagina
Vagina tightener
Labia reduction
Hymen restoration
Circumcision
Snip-excision
Clitordectomy
Infibulation
Any old genital mutilation
On or off the NHS
What's the difference?!

Beat. Back to the scene with **Maxi's Mum**. **Dr Money** *on the attack.*

Dr Money   Do you want her to have an abnormal life? How will she ever get a husband, be a *normal* wife – this child will grow up confused!

Maxi's Mum   Rewind, rewind, selector, come again. . . (**DJ Son** *rewinds the vinyl.*)
Let me get this straight . . .
You wanna take my baby,
Guess what them would have looked like,
If them didn't look like what them do
Make them look like something that them don't
So it easier for you to know what box to tick on what form?³
I think *you* is the one that's confused, Dr Money!
You can change the boxes on that form in your hand,
But you nah change my baby.
Put your scalpel back in your pocket.
The Lord makes no mistake!
I shall call her: 'Maxi'.
And if she favour a boy, she can call himself Maxi same way. No problem.

Maxi (*as herself*)   They call me 'intersex' and I say too right I am into sex! Heheyyyy!
I'm a Black Panther!
I got a super-power bigger than the King of Wakanda! (*Doing the 'Wakanda' greeting, larger than life now.*)
You can keep your vibranium!
I don't need no vibrator!
My body is natural and my orgasms are out of this wooooooooooooooorld STAR!

DJ *plays 'Cosmic Slop' by Funkadelic. Pause to take it all in.*

Mrs   Wow . . . Inter-sex . . .

---

3   Paraphrased from an interview with Jim Costich, in *Intersexion*, dir. Grant Lahood, 2011: https://www.youtube.com/watch?v=QQdOp3COfSs (accessed 01/06/18).

Maxi There's millions of us all over the planet. It's as common as being a redhead, but it's not connected, otherwise nuff Irish people would be hermaphrodites innit? (*Laughs gently to herself at the though.*) Seriously though, you never really know what's going with people inside, or down below. And I am one of the lucky ones. Cos most intersexys be much worse off than me. I read all about it in *TO THIS DAY!* Magazine. Operating on people with no permission! Doctors lying to us, hiding us, humiliating us, shaming us. Secret surgeries, making out we got cancer, forcing us to be one way or another. Worldwide! It's a (*quoting*) 'Gendercide!'[4] Doctors ain't supposed to play God, doctors ain't supposed to lie! Doctors ain't supposed to decide which bits of my privates look right to their eye! And get this, when I was eleven, yeah, the doctors wanted to operate on me *again*, but my mum says –

Maxi's Mum They been messing with Black women bodies since slavery days! Chain and bit, speculum and whip. Anyone try touch you and we'll sue!

Maxi And I got the balls to do it! Two, still on the inside doing just fine. Yes!

Mrs Bloody hell, Maxi, you never said . . .

Maxi No one talked about it back in the day. But I found this online action group. First off Barry didn't want me to get involved. Didn't want everyone knowing. I said (*to Barry, really going for him*) I'm not exactly going on *Loose Women*, Baz, its only a website! But he says: (**Barry** *is slow, kind, lumbering, cockney*.)

Barry Let's just keep our sex life 'tween you and me, we only just got married, Maxi.

Maxi It ain't about sex, Barry, it's about (*precisely quoting something she has read*) 'bodily integrity'.

Barry Eh?

Maxi Anyway, he's come around now.

Mrs Has he?

Maxi He's much more open-minded since I found him his G.

Mrs His what?

Maxi His G spot. I found it.

Mrs Did you? Where?

Maxi Up there (*simple gesture toward her bum*).

Mrs (*half laugh half scream in horror*) No! No! no!

Maxi (*gleefully*) Yes! Yes, yes, Mrs! Every man's got a G spot up his bum. Just most men are just too proud to let you at it, or too scared it might hurt, but when they

---

4 Intersex activist Hida Viloria and others termed the phrase 'gendercide'. See https://hidaviloria.com/quoted-in-exc-washington-post-intersex-rights-movement-article/ (accessed 22/02/19).

do – wooooooooooooh! (*Singing.*) 'Free your behind and your mind will follow!' It ain't me you can hear screaming down the high street Mrs, it's Barry hahaaaa! He is so happy . . . (**Maxi** *is proud of herself.*)

Mrs Really, Barry, up his bum? I'll never be able to look at his chipolatas the same way again. (*Pause for thought.*) Why the good Lord in his infinite wisdom chose to put a 'G spot' in a man's bum hole I will never know.

Maxi Same reason he blessed us with a clitoris! You should count yourself lucky you got one! Have a holiday!

Mrs (*drifting for a moment*) Yeah . . . (*Snapping back.*) Can't be that much of a sin then can it, Maxi? Enjoying your . . . self.

Maxi What you on about, Mrs? I never understood your thing for religion. Priests, rabbis, urologists, gynaecologists – they're all the same to me. They just wanna control you! They wanna cut off my beautiful big clit! But you wanna see us on a Saturday after *Britain's Got Talent*! (*Beat.*) This chicken's dry. You having that stuffing?

DJ Son That was 'Cosmic Slop' by Funkadelic. And here's Lyman, taking us down 'Joy Road' . . .

Mrs As Maxi tucks into the remains of my plate I contemplate all it means for me . . .

Mrs My mind wanders to all the hours I spent with the Evangelicals . . . Trying not to sneeze . . . Praying for the missionaries smuggling Bibles into Communist China. I wondered if there were any ladies left in Beijing, toddling along on their tiny little feet, stumps, two inches wide. Men found their tangled toes attractive apparently, even under rotting bandages. (*Exhaling in disgust, distress.*) I wondered if anyone in China ever prayed for me.

'Pray for me . . .'

Maxi (*who has been watching* **Mrs**) You all right, old girl?

Mrs Sorry, where's my manners, I am forgetting myself. Whatchusay?

Maxi You're drifting off a lot lately. You OK? . . .

Mrs I don't think so, Maxi. I don't think I am . . .

DJ Son 'Perotation', Floating Points.

Scene – The GP

Mrs Me husband died
And it's taken my whole life
But, doctor,
I've never had one
And I want one
Before I die . . .

My orgasm has got to be out there
Somewhere!
I know you all think I'm losing it
That I'm some kind of a . . . space cadet
And you might just be right about that!

So one last job for you, doctor:
I'll be needing a medical certificate
To prove I am fit for travel.
I'm going away.

Scene – The Plan

Mrs *is hurriedly packing whilst reading from* **Mary***'s stars project book, as if it is an instruction manual.* **Mrs***' speech is directed at Cat. Fragments of animation drawn from the project book are projected as* **Mrs** *is trying to piece together her plan. The animation could be fragments that we have seen throughout the play, running through the scene and then climax at the end.*

Mrs   Cat: there is three things they don't tell you about space travel. One: (**Mary** *reappears to* **Mrs***, spirit like.*)

Mary   It is extremely painful.

Mrs   Up there
Your body is a blissful skin bag of sinews and bones
Floating freeeeeee
But when you land home
The force
Is like a car crash –
I'm not talking whiplash
I mean every part of you feels crushed
And you can spend the rest of your life killing pain.

Mary   Gravity is a grave.
No one is supposed to know.

Mrs   Disabled astronauts ain't the poster NASA wants to sell ya!
But that don't bother me. . . we're only able-bodied *temporarily*
Cos the other thing they don't tell you about travelling to space is . . .
When you're up there, the orgasms are out of this world!
Hahahahahahaha . . .

Mrs *hears Cat in her head, 'What?'*

I know, Cat, that could be an 'alternative fact'
But it is one I am prepared to believe
Cos think about it
Where else do all the orgasms go?

All that energy!
All that power!
Must go somewhere?!
'The Earth moved!'
'I saw stars!' – 'Shooting stars!'
Ain't that what people say?
'Yes! Yes! Yes!'
There's nothing down here for likes of me and
The likes of Mary . . .
(*Remembering* **Shahana**.) 'Love *yourself* first, Mrs . . . There is no try.'
And Maxi's right an' all –
I need a holiday!
One way.
A mission,
To have a '*petite mort*' before I die!
To come and go!
Perhaps sometimes to climax you gotta go that far!
And I ain't bothered about the pain landing back cos I plan to stay in space.
I seen enough saucers flying past my head to last me a lifetime down here
Give me one last pleasure
For all my trauma,
Let me fly!
'Spexit'.
(*Sound of an email pinging in an inbox.* **Mrs** *is so excited!*) THE REPLY!
(*Reading the email optimistically.*) 'Dear Mrs Manners,

We regret to inform you that you are ineligible for the government's 'Spexit': relocation space flight. Priority is given to migrants, refugees from majority-Muslim countries and those still awaiting compensation from the Windrush Generation.
Charming!
And to trump it all:
'We know that this will come as a further disappointment but the Virgin Luxury Space Holiday Travel Programme is only eligible for those aged under twenty-five.'

Pause. Disappointment. Perhaps a puff on her vape.

Mary   You missed number three!

Mrs *looks in* **Mary**'s *stars book again.*

Mrs   The third thing they don't tell you about space travel is. . .

Mary   There is more technology in a modern-day washing machine than the Sputnik that took the rocket dog to heaven all on his own in 1957.

Mrs   HAIL MARY!
I got a washing machine *and* a fridge!

Mrs *ends packing by putting the urn in the fridge. Entering a trance-like state, wide eyes, music gets louder, building to the climax!*

One small step
For a woman.
I'll boldly go
To *inner* space.
I shall
Shut
My
Eyes.
Tight.
I'll take the Gs
Dare
To forget myself
And remember
Who I am![5]
I will be afraid
No more. NO MORE!
My name is NORMA MONAGHAN but you can call me NOMMO!
My name is Norma Monaghan and I am coming HOME OHHHHHH – YES!
MAY THE FORCE BE WITH *ME*!
MAY THE FORCE BE WITH YOU!
MAY THE FORCE BE WITH US AAAAAAAALL!
MY SUN! MY SON! HAIL FREQUENCIES OPEN!

Mrs *shuts her eyes. Dances wildly, as if she is inside a fast washing-machine cycle, until the end of the track which stops suddenly. Blackout. Breathing into the silence for three beats.* **DJ Son** *plays 'Scud Books', the track from the opening. Mirror ball? Club night/star lights.*

DJ Son   Thanks for listening. But remember, this is just the beginning. See you on the dance floor down at (*whichever theatre/venue we are playing in*) 'til 2 a.m. Night's called *STARS* – a celebration of pleasure. Open to all. Entry is free.

A community chorus of women and non-gender-conforming technicians in jump suits burst on stage, transforming the space, collectively constructing the rocket somehow. Alternatively the construction could combine projected animation and or motion capture, with the help of the audience. The women dress **Mrs**/*Norma Monaghan in the Nommo costume and mask from the opening. She takes the goldfish bowl, now a space helmet, and gets into the rocket. During this the concluding credits of the show are projected, animated in* **Maryam**/**Mary**'s *handwriting. The show transforms into a club night – a celebration of pleasure.*

---

5   Thank you to Sue Mayo for this line!

Mojisola Adebayo on *STARS*

Mojisola The tagline for *STARS* is 'the story of a very old woman who goes into space in search of her own orgasm' and the second line could be 'Sometimes you've got to go that far'. I do anything to get some laughter and some humour out of the description of the show, partly because it's dealing with much more difficult and traumatic subject matter than might appear to be the case. *STARS* is very celebratory and very uplifting, and I'm always trying to make something very beautiful out of the brutal. I'm always trying to elevate and transport and take us somewhere else, and that literally happens in *STARS*.

Before I came up with the idea of this old woman who goes into space, what I wanted to talk about really comes from personal experience, and being a survivor – a survivor of many things, including childhood sexual abuse, rape and domestic violence. A lot of that experience is slightly fictionalized in my semi-autobiographical play *Muhammad Ali and Me*, which partly looked at being a survivor, the experience of coming through abuse as a young person and coming out as lesbian. But I also really wanted to look at how difficult it is to live in the same body that has survived trauma, to make love in the same body and so on. I wanted to look at how difficult it can be sometimes to achieve the heights of sexual pleasure in orgasm. I've been thinking about this for many years in secret, kind of in the closet about all of that, and really struggling. I still think it's a taboo, and it's a subject on the edge.

I was thinking about my orgasm, or the lack of it, and also thinking, well actually there are millions of women all over the world who are 'cut off' from sexual pleasure. And the only organ in the body that is designed purely and only for sexual pleasure, the only organ that has no other function but pleasure, is the clitoris. And millions of women all over the world have their clitorises removed without their consent through practices that are known under the broad heading of FGM (female genital mutilation); but a lot of people, including myself, resist the term mutilation, resist the 'M', because it somehow feels a bit accusatory of people who are survivors of that practice. Nobody would like to think of their body as mutilated; and a lot of people who have survived FGM celebrate their bodies and love their bodies and don't consider it mutilation at all. So, it's also called traditional harmful practices. I've been working with an organization called Forward, which is a charity looking at FGM, led by women from communities that know about it, mainly African communities. Although FGM is a practice that happens on every continent, it's often associated with the African continent, and sometimes associated with Islam; but it's not to do with Africa or Islam, it's a practice that happens all over the world. So, I was thinking how do I move beyond myself and think more widely about pleasure and about struggles to achieve full sexual pleasure, orgasm and clitoral pleasure? I was thinking, 'Moj, yes you're a survivor, and yes it's difficult, but there are millions of little girls all over the world that have never had a choice about that'. And a person can, of course, have sexual pleasure and have experienced FGM and you can have orgasms in different parts of the body, not just the clitoris.

There are many different forms of FGM surgery, and it *is* a form of surgery. But in all forms of FGM, the clitoris is removed; that one organ designed for sexual pleasure is removed. I was thinking about how do I not only explore being a survivor of trauma, but also connect with other people who have been affected by the cutting off of pleasure? And then I was thinking, you know what, I've been friends for many years with a very outspoken intersex activist called Del La Grace Volcano, recently becoming friends with a colleague, Valentino Vecchietti, intersex activists who also have been battling to bring the conversation around non-consensual surgery on intersex children – intersex being a term to describe people who have a mixture of biological sex. There are more intersex people in the world than Jewish people in the world. It's about as common as having red hair. Yet the I on the end of LGBTQI often gets left off. Not all intersex people experience surgery as children, but millions do, without their consent. And it's legal in every country in the world apart from Malta. It happens in Britain, and it happens on the NHS. So, I was thinking why is it that there is so much focus on FGM, which, interestingly, is associated with Africa and Islam, but hardly any attention on non-consensual surgery on intersex people? Why is one considered a traditional practice and ritual and the other considered surgery?

So, I was thinking, you know what, I want to make a piece about pleasure and about the cutting off of pleasure and the reclaiming of pleasure and I want to look at all of these subjects in the same play, in the same story, I want to bring it all together. I took a cue from Sue Jennings who wrote *Introduction to Dramatherapy*. Sue Jennings' advice is that when you're looking at traumatic experience, give yourself distance, creative distance through metaphor and through myth. That's why my central character is much older than me. And I also thought how do I make it even more distanced from myself? How about I send this character into space? I'm going to give this character as much physical distance as possible.

So, I thought, I've got this premise, this idea of this old woman who goes into space, but I want to include FGM, and I want to include intersex experience, and I thought how do I bring this together? I'll bring it together in some encounters. So, our old lady, Mrs, has three different encounters. She has an encounter with a child who we discover has been through traditional harmful practice. I wanted to do this play, as all of my plays, and not reproduce stereotypes and old narratives. There's a stereotype and a narrative that Black people, we don't love our children, that we're brutal, that we're violent, that we're savage, primitive and all of those horrendous racist ideas. And so, I wanted to look at this practice through the eyes of this child and this encounter between this child and this adult, Mrs, and look at the subject in a way that would get us questioning and thinking about that. So, this child defends what her parents have done and also points out that they love her and they did it because they love her. I know that can be difficult to get our heads around, but I wanted the child to defend her parents, and it's not that I'm defending FGM. But to look at it through a different kind of lens. This was all worked out with Forward, the FGM charity who really loved the play. I did workshops with them to explore this subject matter in a different way to not reproduce *Daily Mail* headlines about African communities.

Mrs has an encounter with a child, she also remembers an encounter with a would-be lesbian lover in a launderette, and she has an encounter with Maxi who is intersex and also *into sex* and very playful about that. And also, as with FGM, I wanted to find a way to represent an intersex person not in a way that reproduced narratives of victimhood, of pain, of having undergone surgery. It was actually Del La Grace Volcano who said to me, 'Why does your intersex character have to have been through surgery?' And then Valentino Vecchietti really helped me rethink the representation of intersex identity in the play. So, Maxi is a person who is born with what's considered to be a larger than average clitoris. The character of Maxi is partly inspired by Hida Viloria, whose parents refused for her to have her clitoris removed. One of the things that can happen in non-consensual surgeries is that a precise measurement is taken of a girl child's clitoris when she is born and if it looks bigger than average, doctors all over the world, including in Britain, recommend that the clitoris be removed, because it looks too much like a penis. But Hida Viloria's father was a doctor, and said, 'No way, there's nothing wrong with her genitalia, it's just a very large clitoris.' And allowed her to keep her clitoris. So, my character Maxi is partly informed by the life of Hida Viloria, the celebration of having a larger than average clitoris, of being able to enjoy sexual pleasure, challenging this idea that all intersex people will necessarily have undergone surgery and have problems with sex, to get rid of that kind of stereotype and offer a counter narrative. It's very much a celebration of pleasure.

I think probably the closest I get to an orgasm with my clothes on is being on a dance floor surrounded by loads of people in a club. I wanted to bring the feeling of orgasm, of ecstasy and of being out of this world. When you go to a club, it almost doesn't feel like planet earth; the club can feel like an out of this world experience. So that's the reason the play transforms into a club night, and a club night that's a celebration of pleasure in a space-like kind of way. The club night doesn't just pop up at the end, there's a DJ (DJ Debo) who plays music all the way through the show and has been my collaborator on *STARS* from the start. And also, through the club night the idea is that there'll be workshops all the way through the process with people who are coming from communities that experience FGM with intersex people, with youngers and elders, intergenerational workshops; and out of those workshops will be pop-up performances, poetry, singing, which will appear in the club space.

One of the things that felt really important to me, especially in dealing with FGM and questions of trauma, Black pain, and Black bodies and tradition, was that I somehow tried to find a way of imagistically holding all of these things together. One of the ways I did that was to think through the Dogon culture, a very famous culture from Mali, which has massively informed Western art and artists such as Picasso. Unfortunately, in Mali, FGM also takes place, and also, most importantly the Dogon have this incredible history of astronomy, of cosmology. Through animation, the artist that I worked with, Candice Purwin, brings the ideas of Dogon culture and thinking about sexuality all together. There's animation projected all the way through the show, and also creative captioning. So, every word that is spoken through the show is projected for D/deaf and hearing-impaired people to be able to read the text. But it's not just block words like subtitles, it's creatively integrated into the visual animation. Intersex identity, African Dogon art and Dogon tradition intersect and create a style throughout the piece. Most of all, I hope the style and the story brings people pleasure.

On Dreaming of Black Queer/Afriquia Futures

Mojisola   We wondered about the kind of stories, images that you might feel are missing or that you would love to see happen or make, or perhaps you're already writing and creating and filming those stories and missing stories right now. So, it's an opportunity for you to just tell us about what you want to be doing.

Topher   Well, it's funny because, everybody here I don't know how many dreams you have every day, but I think I dream all the time. It's only when I have to go back into those institutional spaces that I get pulled down into this management of life, but most of time I'm just dreaming. I just want to tell stories. Now I'm older, I want to do something on intergenerational love stories, because I'm meditating a lot on my lovers, male and female, and I'm thinking, 'Oh my days, I've been around haven't I.' This would make really interesting stuff. About ten or fifteen years ago I had this film idea called 'Topher's Boys' and it was very much about the idea of what it is to be a Black queer male-identified in the noughties. But now I'm thinking about polyamory and the whole kind of way in which we love. That's something I'd like to see and I think I'm probably going to do at some point. The intergenerational conversation is exciting at the moment. So, I'd love to see that on the screen writ large. And there will be a lot more nakedness and sex and sexuality and joy in our presence. I'm more in that space than I've ever been in a space of love whether that happens on stage on film or both.

One of the last jobs I applied for was to run a well-known middle-scale London theatre and in my application I said that I wanted to turn the place into a centre of Black cultural excellence. This was only in the last five or six years. They turned around and said to me that it's 'too narrow a vision.' So, let us go and do what we need to do where we need to do it, because that's not the space where we can take our energies forward. We need to take our energies forward in this sort of space which has been amazing to share. I'd love to see that; I'd love to see lots of Black centres of excellence everywhere.

Valerie   I had a very lovely conversation with Lady Phyll [Founder of UK Black Pride]. I think that what Lady Phyll has done for Black queerness has just been absolutely amazing. So, dreaming to have more. Lady Phyll hasn't taken on the Western trappings of queerness. When you see Lady Phyll, you see this African woman, that's what you're met with. And I think that to dream, I want to see more of that out there in society. You've heard my dream: it would be great to have a 'Queer Axe.' When I think of *Young Soul Rebels*, which is really important, I think, it's during that time when I think of *Small Axe* and *Lover's Rock*. I grew up in the clubs and as Topher said this was our world. This is our world, what we were doing, and I think it's really important to document that. So, my dream would be to have something like *Small Axe* from a Black queer perspective, that would just be absolutely amazing.

I read Margaret Mead who has done all of this research in Africa about Black queerness. So, even though that's problematic about research, I just knew that it existed. Part of my dreaming would be to get rid of some of these archaic laws in Africa and the Caribbean. We write plays but how is that impacting? So, the dream is,

'How is our theatre impacting and making change in our countries of origin?' That's what we need to be doing. So that would be my dream, that the theatre and the art that we're making is actually having an impact in Africa and the Caribbean so that some of these archaic laws which come from Victorian times are just completely dismantled. So, my dreaming is, it's Sankofa, 'let's go back and fetch what we left behind.' Because when we were taken, we couldn't take anything. And it's time for us to go back and fetch, and remember, in a way, that we have been dismembered, and how can we be remembered? That's our job as artists. That's my dreaming.

Rikki I have all these solid things that I want to achieve and learn and do and share, but it really boils down to wanting to be fierce, and keep getting fiercer and encourage fierceness in others. I want to reclaim the fierceness of those people who got eaten up by the machine – Michael Jackson, Prince, Whitney Houston, James Brown, they just got eaten alive by the machine – and it's even stronger now with all of this Instagramming and constantly monitoring and trying to look artificially amazing instead of how amazing you are. So, I really just want to make work that is as amazing as their work, but survive it, if you know what I mean. And have the audience be able to feel like they can go that deep and burn that brightly. That's really what I want to create, events; my big thing is to get people great experiences. I want to take that up several notches to several levels so that people reclaim this world, that this is their world, this is their sky, this is their sea, this is their world to live in, and to live in unafraid of who they are. So that's what I want all the work to do and I do think that is through our entertainment and music. I do think that we are immensely influential because people will listen to lessons from us where they'd doze off in a classroom.

Tonderai Well, I think you know that the idea that my pronouns are he and him is a lot to do with privacy of actually having been a child that got to be discussed and talked about all the way up to discussing and talking about it myself, that actually one of the things that I hope for myself is that whoever I am, wherever I am, it's private. And then it's sustainable. I support anybody who does the opposite. But I think for me, that's the hope that I am strengthened by my life and that I am brave enough to do the things that I really think are important to do. Because I think if you know better you do better, especially as an artist. So, I'm just curious to see where that would lead me, and I know that what's important for me is to take down the middleman. So, I'm just thinking of different ways of taking down the middleman, and going straight to the audience. That's my dream.

Temi I want to write a lesbian rom-com. I want to write stuff that isn't about queerness, but the characters are queer – some vampires, some ghosts, a musical about a lesbian nun.

Travis I really struggled with diving into visibility as a way to be seen to get work, and now having to navigate the harsh side effects that has had, decide where I can get my consent back, where I made mistakes. So, my goal for my future is to take back control of what that is for me and learn, and not shame myself out of further steps from past choices; and that's what I'm in at the moment which is difficult, and it's alive and I've said no to so many things this year because I haven't quite figured out what that is yet; so I want personally to get to a place where I'm back to saying yes to things and making again, but in a healthy way. I think a lot about Janet Mock, who in the US has created an ecosystem, and a financial system for Black trans and gender-non-conforming people from TV, I think about all the careers that she is able to fund. In a dream sense, I want to get to a space really where I can look at loads of Black trans creators and they are being paid and funded to make their work. If I can make this painfulness of visibility that I'm now regretting, if I can make the choices I made worthwhile, it would be that leverage that has made it possible to fund loads of other people's work, and they can make the choice about whether they need to be visible to do that work or not. So, that's where I want to end up, I hope.

Performance Rights

For *Basin*

All rights whatsoever in this play are strictly reserved and application for performance, etc. should be made before rehearsals to Bloomsbury Permissions Department, Bloomsbury Publishing Plc, 50 Bedford Square, London, WC1B 3DP, UK. No performance may be given unless a licence has been obtained.

For *Boy with Beer*

All rights whatsoever in this play are strictly reserved. Applications for performance, including professional, amateur, recitation, lecturing, public reading, broadcasting, television and the rights of translation into foreign languages, should be addressed to mail@paulboakye.net.

For *Sin Dykes*

All rights whatsoever in this play are strictly reserved and application for performance, etc. should be made before rehearsals to Bloomsbury Permissions Department, Bloomsbury Publishing Plc, 50 Bedford Square, London, WC1B 3DP, UK. No performance may be given unless a licence has been obtained.

For *Bashment*

All rights whatsoever in these works are strictly reserved and application for performance, etc. should be made before commencement of rehearsal to Simon Woods, Burton Woods Solicitors, Wax Chandlers Hall, 6 Gresham Street, London EC2V 7AD (contact@burtonwoods.com). No performance may be given unless a licence has been obtained, and no alterations may be made in any part of these works without the author's prior written consent.

For *BURGERZ*

All rights whatsoever in this play are strictly reserved and application for performance, etc. should be made before rehearsals to Bloomsbury Permissions Department, Bloomsbury Publishing Plc, 50 Bedford Square, London, WC1B 3DP, UK. No performance may be given unless a licence has been obtained.

For *Nine Lives*

All rights whatsoever in this play are strictly reserved and application for performance, etc. should be made before rehearsals by professionals to The Agency (London) Ltd, 24 Pottery Lane, London, W11 4LZ. No performance may be given unless a licence has been obtained.

For *The High Table*

All rights whatsoever in this play are strictly reserved and application for performance, etc. should be made before rehearsals by professionals and by amateurs to Curtis Brown Group Ltd, Haymarket House, 28–29 Haymarket, London, SW1Y 4SP, email info@curtisbrown.co.uk. No performance may be given unless a licence has been obtained.

For *STARS*

All rights whatsoever in this play are strictly reserved and application for performance, etc. should be made before rehearsals to Bloomsbury Permissions Department, Bloomsbury Publishing Plc, 50 Bedford Square, London, WC1B 3DP, UK. No performance may be given unless a licence has been obtained.

www.ingramcontent.com/pod-product-compliance
Lightning Source LLC
Chambersburg PA
CBHW051802230426
43672CB00012B/2607